Volume Graphics

Springer

London
Berlin
Heidelberg
New York
Barcelona
Hong Kong
Milan
Paris
Singapore
Tokyo

Min Chen, Arie E. Kaufman, Roni Yagel (Eds)

Volume Graphics

Springer

Min Chen, BSc, PhD
Department of Computer Science, University of Wales Swansea, Singleton Park, Swansea, SA2 8PP, UK

Arie E. Kaufman, BSc, MSc, PhD
Department of Computer Science, State University of New York at Stony Brook, Stony Brook, NY 11794, USA

Roni Yagel, BSc, MSc, PhD
Insight Therapeutics, TOR Systems, Hasivim 7, PO Box 7779, Petach Tikva 49170, Israel

ISBN-13: 978-1-85233-192-4   e-ISBN-13: 978-1-4471-0737-8
DOI: 10.1007/978-1-4471-0737-8

British Library Cataloguing in Publication Data
Volume graphics
  1.Computer graphics
  I.Chen, Min II.Kaufman, Arie E. III. Yagel, Roni
  006.6
  ISBN-13 978-1-85233-192-4

Library of Congress Cataloging-in-Publication Data
Volume graphics / Min Chen, Arie E. Kaufman, Roni Yagel (eds.).
    p. cm.
    Includes bibliographical references and indexes.
    ISBN 978-1-85233-192-4 (alk.)
    1. Computer graphics. 2. Three-dimensional display systems. I. Chen, M. (Min), 1960-
II. Kaufman, Arie. III. Yagel, Roni.
    T385.V66 2000
    006.6'93-dc21   99-056902

Typesetting:: from editor's electronic files

34/3830-543210 Printed on acid-free paper SPIN 10738508

Preface

Min Chen, Arie E. Kaufman and Roni Yagel

Volume graphics is concerned with graphics scenes defined in volume data types, where a model is specified by a mass of points instead of a collection of surfaces. The underlying mathematical definition of such a model is a set of scalar fields, which define the geometrical and physical properties of every point in three-dimensional space. As true 3D representations, volume data types possess more descriptive power than surface data types, and are morphologically closer to many high-level modelling schemes in traditional surface graphics such as parametric surfaces, implicit surfaces and volume sweeping.

The past decade has witnessed significant advances in *volume visualisation*, driven mainly by applications such as medical imaging and scientific computation. The work in this field has produced a number of volume rendering methods that enable 3D information in a volumetric dataset to be selectively rendered into 2D images. With modern computer hardware, such a process can easily be performed on an ordinary workstation. More importantly, volume-based rendering offers a consistent solution to the primary deficiencies of the traditional surface-based rendering, which include its inability to encapsulate the internal description of a model, and the difficulties in rendering amorphous phenomena.

The emergence of volume-based techniques has not only broadened the extent of graphics applications, but also brought computer graphics closer to other scientific and engineering disciplines, including image processing, computer vision, finite element analysis and rapid prototyping.

These developments have led to beliefs that volume-based techniques have the potential to match and overtake surface-based techniques in computer graphics. In 1993, Kaufman, Cohen and Yagel1 first outlined a framework for *volume graphics* as a sub-field of computer graphics. While the primary objective of volume visualisation is to extract meaningful information from volumetric data, volume graphics is a far broader subject: it is a study of the input, storage, construction, analysis, manipulation, rendering and animation of spatial objects in a true three-dimensional form. Since 1993, considerable progress has been made in volume graphics, much of which was highlighted in the first *International Workshop on Volume Graphics* held in March 1999 at Swansea, UK.

---

[1] Kaufman A, Cohen D, Yagel R. Volume graphics. IEEE Computer 1993; 26(7):51-64.

Structure

This book follows on from the successful Swansea Workshop. It contains a collection of works that represent the latest thinking in volume graphics, and cover a wide spectrum of the subject. All chapters were recommended by a panel of reviewers, were presented and discussed in the Swansea Workshop, and revised by the authors for this book.

The book is divided into eight parts:

- *Part I (Perspectives)* consists of two introductory chapters. *Chapter 1* gives an overview of the current state-of-the-art, and introduces readers to a range of concepts that are central to a study of volume graphics. *Chapter 2* presents the scope of volume modelling, which is a major aspect of volume graphics but whose importance was not fully recognised until recently.
- *Part II (Discrete Modelling)* focuses on the discrete modelling methodology. *Chapter 3* presents a study of discretising triangular meshes — the most commonly-used graphical representations — with voxels, and provides a theoretical insight into the fundamentals of discrete modelling. *Chapter 4* discusses different interpolation schemes for binary volume datasets, and examines the use of high-order interpolators in enhancing the smoothness of reconstructed surfaces. *Chapter 5* introduces readers to the concept of isovolume, and demonstrates the importance of discrete modelling through its application in layered manufacturing.
- *Part III (Complex Volumetric Objects)* is concerned with advanced methods for modelling complex graphics objects using volumetric representations. *Chapter 6* outlines the concept of Constructive Volume Geometry (CVG), and describes the implementation of a rendering system for CVG. *Chapter 7* presents, from a software perspective, an object-oriented approach to the voxelisation of complex graphics models. *Chapter 8* further examines the relationships between surface and volume representations, and describes a solution to the conversion from CSG models to offset surfaces through the use of distance volumes. *Chapter 9* discusses the integration of NURBS and volume representations in creating complex volumetric objects.
- *Part IV (Volume Rendering)* contains work on several aspects of volume rendering, and emphasis is given to the speed of rendering algorithms, the quality of synthesised images, and the capability of creating aesthetic displays. *Chapter 10* introduces readers to the two most fundamental methods for volume rendering, namely ray casting and marching cubes, and gives a qualitative and quantitative comparison between the two methods. *Chapter 11* examines one of the important acceleration techniques, shear-warp factorisation, and presents an extension of the technique for multi-resolution datasets. *Chapter 12* addresses two acceleration techniques, the template-based acceleration and seed filling in view lattice, and proposes a combined algorithm that is suitable for synthesising high resolution images. *Chapter 13* introduces solid textures and hypertextures to the volume rendering pipeline

and hence provides volume rendering with a new dimension that facilitates the creative and aesthetic aspect of volume graphics.

- *Part V (Volume Animation)* presents the latest developments in animating volumetric actors and objects. *Chapter 14* examines the modelling of object dynamics, and focuses on the animation of amorphous phenomena, including fire, smoke and cloud. *Chapter 15* addresses a range of issues in building a volumetric human model, and demonstrates the feasibility of volume animation by bringing life back to the Visible Human dataset. *Chapter 16* discusses the kinematic control of volumetric actors through skeleton trees, and presents an algorithm for automated construction of a skeleton from a volume model.

- *Part VI (Parallel and Distributed Environments)* reports the developments of high performance hardware and software for volume graphics. *Chapter 17* considers the problem of isosurface extraction from tetrahedral datasets, and presents a parallel solution to multi-resolutional isosurfacing. *Chapter 18* discusses the design of special purpose hardware for direct volume rendering, and proposes a pipelined architecture based on look-up tables and crossbar switches. *Chapter 19* further examines the problems in the design of volume rendering hardware, and presents an architecture facilitating algorithmic optimisation. *Chapter 20* looks at the acceleration of the voxelisation processes with high performance hardware, and offers support to a range of graphics objects. *Chapter 21* takes volume graphics to the Internet, and discusses the issues in managing collaborative activities in a distributed rendering environment.

- *Part VII (Applications)* illustrates the potentials of volume graphics by giving several example applications of volume techniques. *Chapter 22* describes the use of volume-based techniques in radiotherapy — a typical application area of volume graphics. *Chapter 23* presents a solution to facial reconstruction for forensic identification using volume deformation. *Chapter 24* examines the modelling of weathering effect on a class of volumetric objects (i.e. stones), and provides an example of effective use of volume models in simulating real life phenomena. *Chapter 25* discusses the generation of 3D artistic text using volume-based techniques.

- *Part VIII (Glossary and Indices)* contains a glossary of terms commonly used in volume graphics, an author index and a subject index.

In addition, the book contains a 16 page colour section that illustrates the main features of volume graphics with images synthesised using a variety of volume-based techniques. There is also a world wide web site set up specially for readers of this book by providing additional resources (e.g. images, animations and links to authors' home pages) and up-to-date information on volume graphics (e.g. regularly maintained glossary and bibliography pages). The URL (Uniform Resource Locator) of this web site is **http://vg.swan.ac.uk/**.

Objectives

This book is intended for students who are studying an advanced course on computer graphics, visualisation or medical imaging. It is suitable as a reference book for researchers and software developers who are working or wish to work in areas of volume graphics. The book draws on an extensive range of sources and materials, with the following aims:

- To provide a framework in a structured manner for established concepts and existing knowledge in volume graphics;
- To present up-to-date developments which will likely form a basis for further investigation and exploration.

While this book marks the adolescence of volume graphics, it also presents us with many technical problems for which solutions are yet to be found. Here we reiterate the following nine questions[2], originally proposed by the Programme Committee of the First International Workshop on Volume Graphics, to challenge readers in pursuing further research and development in areas of volume graphics.

1. Is *storage requirement* for volume representations really more expensive than polygonal representations? What would be the merits and demerits of having volume datasets, instead of triangle meshes, as the *primary graphics representation*? Should one consider *curvilinear* and *irregular grids* as the fundamental representation, and develop more general modelling and rendering techniques based on it?
2. How should *reflection*, *refraction* and *shadow* be specified and rendered in volume graphics, especially, when it involves *amorphous* volume objects?
3. Since a raster image is a 2D "volume" dataset, an animation sequence is a volume dataset, and some image-based modelling methods employ higher-dimensional volume datasets, what are the *mathematical concepts* which may unify various volume-based modelling and rendering techniques, and assist in the development of homogeneous graphics hardware and Application Programming Interfaces (APIs)?
4. Is voxel-based *radiosity* computationally feasible? Do volume representations offer any advantages for the calculation of *global illumination*?
5. Can the "Visible Human" walk? Motion capture and computational physics can naturally operate on connected solid/surface objects. How should physical properties be defined and attached to discrete volume representations, and how can *motion* and *deformation* of volume objects be specified and animated? How would one implement "force and touch" feedback with volume data?

---

[2] Some of the questions have been addressed by the contributions included in this book and some pioneering work in the literature. However, substantial research is required to provide adequate or definite answers to these questions. We also recognise that there may be some other important questions which could be included in the list.

6. Many *digitisation* devices generate volume datasets, but not many graphics objects are available in volume representations (e.g. a teapot containing some tea). Is surface-based digitisation technologically or economically superior to volume-based digitisation? What are the obstacles to the extensive use of volume-based digitisation?

7. In volume graphics, what is the role of the techniques developed for *image processing* and *computer vision*? Can the use of frequency-domain representations of volume data be extended to a wider range of volume graphics applications in addition to data processing? Can wavelets or other methods be used to compress large volume datasets and still produce reasonably accurate images efficiently?

8. How will *real-time volume rendering* be made generally available? When will a single CPU be powerful enough to support interactive volume graphics? What is the future of *parallel* volume rendering hardware and software? Would network bandwidth become a bottleneck for Internet-based volume graphics?

9. Is volume graphics ready to exert any impact upon a wider range of *graphics applications*, i.e. CAD, games, films and digital art? What are the necessary technological developments in both volume-based hardware and software in order to raise the impact of volume graphics and its applications, including medical imaging and scientific visualisation?

Acknowledgements

We wish to thank all authors for their contributions, and their collaborative effort in producing an up-to-date book in such a dynamic field. We thank all referees and sub-referees who reviewed the submissions for this book. We are particularly grateful for their highly professional recommendations and helpful comments. They include *Nicholas Ayache, Ken Brodlie, Daniel Cohen-Or, Michael Doggett, David Duce, Jose L. Encarnajao, Henry Fuchs, Issei Fujishiro, Sara Gibson, Michael E. Goss, Andrew Grant, Sven Gürke, Pat Hanrahan, Chuck Hansen, Karl H. Höhne, Roger Hubbold, Nigel John, Mark W. Jones, Gunter Knittel, Adrian Leu, Bill Lorensen, Martin Maidhof, Tom Malzbender, Nelson Max, Michael Meißner, Greg Nielson, Nao Ozawa, Frits Post, Georgios Sakas, Richard Satherley, Hans-Peter Seidel, Norsert Schiffne, Wolfgang Straßer, Jean-Philippe Thirion, Stephen Treavett, Philip J. Willis, Craig M. Wittenbrink* and *Brian Wyvill*. We would like to thank Rona Chen who compiled the author and subject indices of this book.

We also take this opportunity to express our appreciation all those who gave generous support to the Swansea Workshop, and a special thank you to the sponsors and local organisers of the Workshop.

Last, but not least, we thank *Karen Barker* and *Rosie Kemp* at Springer-Verlag who have been a source of enthusiasm, understanding and support in the process of producing this book.

Contents

Part I: Perspectives

Part II: Discrete Modelling

Part III: Complex Volumetric Objects

Part IV: Volume Rendering

Part V: Volume Animation

Part VI: Parallel and Distributed Environments

Part VII: Applications

Part VIII: Glossaries and Indices

∧ **Plate I.** Volume data types can be used to represent geometric models as well as digital samples. In particular, volume representations can effectively and efficiently support the modelling and rendering of the interiors of objects and amorphous phenomena such as fire, clouds and smoke (Chapter 1). This is one of the most important features of volume graphics and it is illustrated in the above image which shows a volume-sampled plane together with a volumetric cloud over a volumetric model of terrain enhanced with satellite images.

∨ **Plate II.** The image below is from a real-time animation of smoke emanating from a locomotive (Chapter 14), demonstrating the descriptive power of volume graphics.

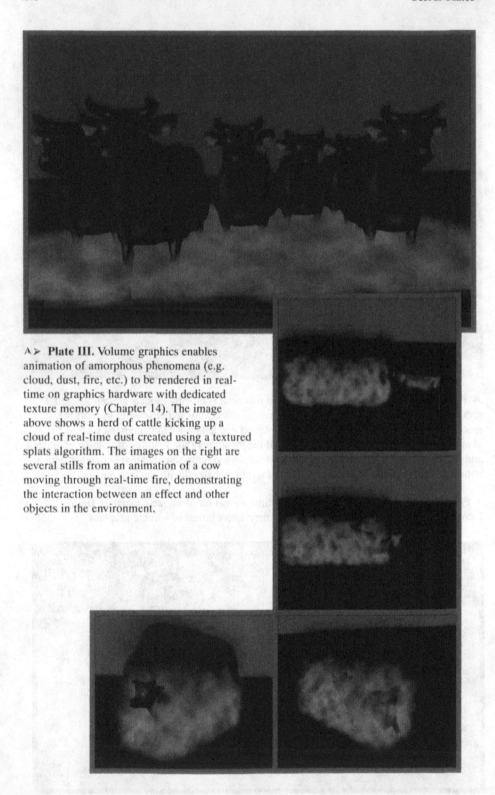

∧➤ **Plate III.** Volume graphics enables animation of amorphous phenomena (e.g. cloud, dust, fire, etc.) to be rendered in real-time on graphics hardware with dedicated texture memory (Chapter 14). The image above shows a herd of cattle kicking up a cloud of real-time dust created using a textured splats algorithm. The images on the right are several stills from an animation of a cow moving through real-time fire, demonstrating the interaction between an effect and other objects in the environment.

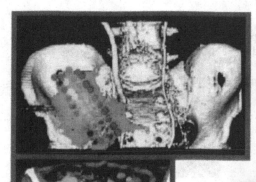

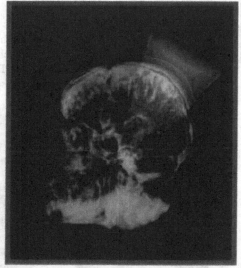

< **Plate IV.** Medical imaging is one of the main applications and driving forces of volume visualisation (Chapter 22). The ability to digitise and visualise internal structures of real-life objects has laid the foundation for volume graphics.

➤ **Plate V.** The most fundamental data structure in volume graphics is a volume buffer where sampled or simulated datasets can be intermixed with geometric objects in a true 3D manner (Chapter 1).

∨ **Plate VI.** The internal structure of a volume object can sometimes be used to control the motion and deformation of the object. This image shows the walking of the Visible Male dataset controlled by a skeleton tree (Chapter 16).

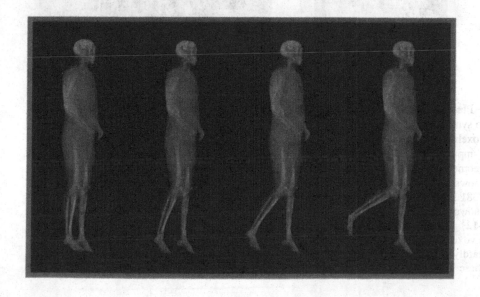

➢ **Plate VII.** Voxelisation is a process that converts surface data types to volume data types. Special purpose hardware has been developed to accelerate such a process (Chapter 20). The image below is a voxelised teapot rendered with a "knot" dataset.

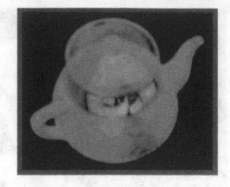

< **Plate VIII.** Complex objects can be constructed through voxelisation. This image shows a voxelised tree trunk that is generated by sweeping a 2D image along a path with both twisting and scaling operations (Chapter 9).

➢ **Plate IX.** Volume graphics can be used to synthesise graphical images with voxelised representations at a quality comparable to surface graphics with geometric representations. The top image shows a 4-level sphereflake composed of 7381 spheres, and the bottom image shows an equivalent volume object with a 512^3 grid, which is obtained using vxt — a voxelisation library (Chapter 7). There is hardly any noticeable difference between these two images.

> **Plate X.** Constructive volume geometry (CVG) facilitates constructive representation of volume objects, including both discrete volume datasets and scalar fields. These operations are normally defined in the real domain, and enable the construction of complex volume objects through the combination of the geometrical and physical properties of simple (solid and amorphous) volume objects (Chapter 6). The top image shows the application of a union operation to a solid cube and an amorphous cube. The bottom image shows a sphere defined by a set of scalar fields, from which an oval object is subtracted to reveal its interior.

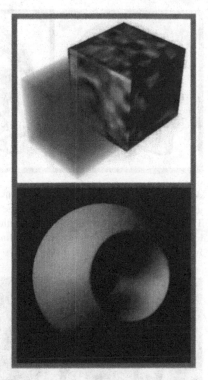

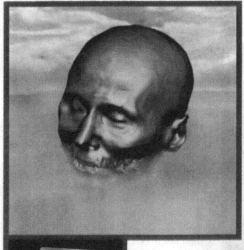

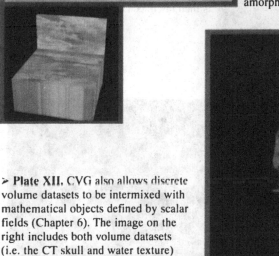

< **Plate XI.** With CVG, images can be integrated naturally into graphics scenes as volume objects. In this scene, an image of a cloud is used to define the solid sky background as well as the amorphous cloud volume (Chapter 6).

> **Plate XII.** CVG also allows discrete volume datasets to be intermixed with mathematical objects defined by scalar fields (Chapter 6). The image on the right includes both volume datasets (i.e. the CT skull and water texture) and mathematical objects (i.e. the sphere and rob).

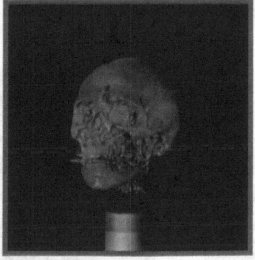

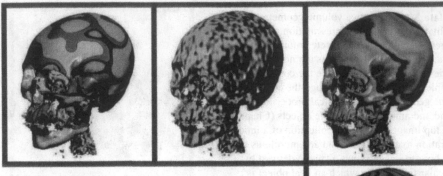

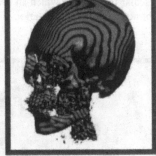

A **Plate XIII.** Texture mapping can be used in volume graphics to add details to objects in a true 3D manner. The images in this plate are rendered with different solid textures constructed from primitive nonlinear basis functions (Chapter 13).

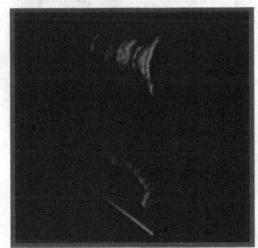

< **Plate XIV.** In volume graphics, textures can be generated during voxelisation as well as rendering. For instance, to synthesise the image on the left, a solid texture is first mapped, during voxelisation, onto the bolt and nut that is defined by a sequence of CSG operations. The volume-sampled dataset is then ray traced (Chapter 1).

➤ **Plate XV.** 3D texture mapping can also be achieved using the real-domain inter-section operation in Constructive Volume Geometry (Chapter 6).

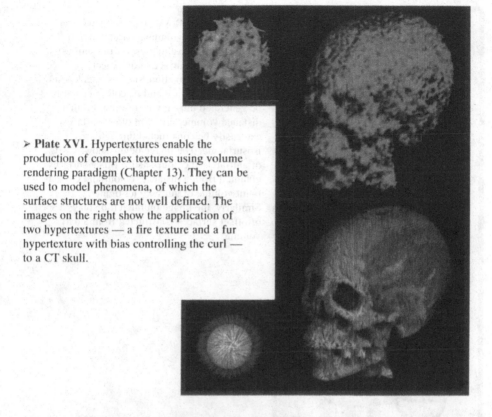

> **Plate XVI.** Hypertextures enable the production of complex textures using volume rendering paradigm (Chapter 13). They can be used to model phenomena, of which the surface structures are not well defined. The images on the right show the application of two hypertextures — a fire texture and a fur hypertexture with bias controlling the curl — to a CT skull.

◁▽ **Plate XVII.** Hypertextures can also be used to simulate the geometrical change of an object. The image on the left shows a melting function applied to a CT skull, while the image below shows a voxelised tank with a hypertextured barrel using a similar melting function (the tank data is courtesy of Arie Kaufman).

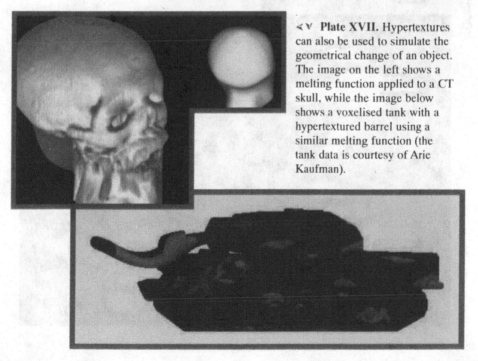

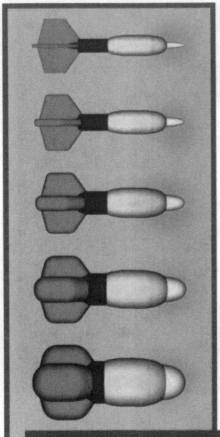

◁ ▽ **Plate XVIII.** A distance volume
(Chapter 8) is a volume dataset where the
value at each voxel represents the shortest
distance to the surface of an object.
Additional information, such as the closest
point on the surface and its colour can also
be generated during voxelisation. From a
distance volume, different offset surfaces
can easily be constructed through
isosurfacing. The image below shows a set
of anti-aliased colour-shaded offset surfaces
obtained from a distance, colour and closest-
point volume of an X-29 jet fighter.
Similarly, the image on the left displays a set
of offset surfaces constructed from a dart
volume.

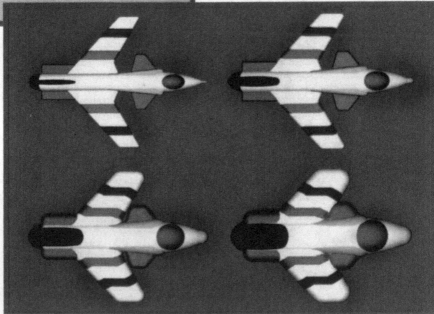

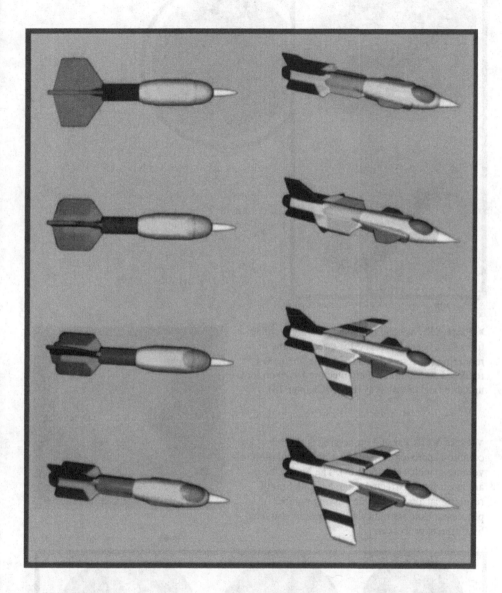

⋀ **Plate XIX.** This is a morphing sequence where a distance volume of a dart (top left) is transformed into a volume model of an X-29 jet fighter (bottom right). The intermediate volumes are generated using level set methods. The intermediate surface colours are obtained by interpolating the information derived from the colours of the dart and jet fighter, and their closest-volumes (Chapter 8).

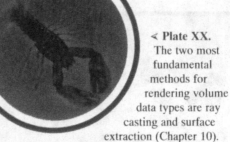

≺ **Plate XX.**
The two most
fundamental
methods for
rendering volume
data types are ray
casting and surface
extraction (Chapter 10).
For instance, consider a volume representation
of a lobster, which was digitised using a
computed tomography scanner, and coloured
according to a classification of resin, shell, and
meat data in the volume (above). We can
synthesis an image by casting rays from the
image plane into the volume (top left), or by
extracting a set of isosurfaces using the
marching cubes algorithm (left).

➢ **Plate XXI.** Special purpose hardware architectures have been developed for direct volume rendering (Chapters 18 and 19). This image was rendered on a simulated architecture based on look-up tables and crossbar switches (Chapter 18).

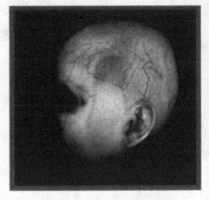

∨ **Plate XXII.** Parallel processing is another common approach for speeding up computation in volume graphics (Chapter 17). The images below are isosurfaces extracted using a parallel multi-resolutional algorithm with varying number of processes. Colours indicate the portions extracted by different processes.

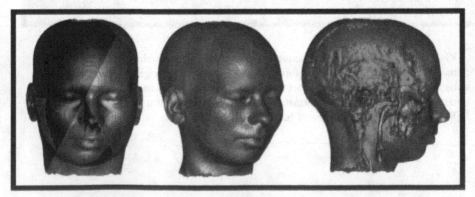

➤ **Plate XXIII.** There are a number of acceleration techniques for direct volume rendering, including template-based ray casting and seed filling in view lattice. The image on the right was rendered using a combination of both acceleration techniques (Chapter 12).

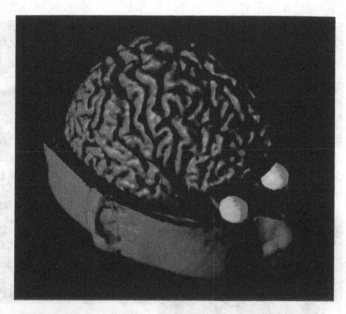

◀▽ **Plate XXIV**. A multi-resolution approach is often used in volume graphics to support interactive activities on computer hardware that is not powerful enough to support real-time rendering. The three images on the left resulted from a multi-resolution algorithm based on shear-warp factorisation which is one of the major acceleration techniques for direct volume rendering by ray casting (Chapter 11). Three different error tolerance values (from a high tolerance value on the left to a zero tolerance value on the bottom-right) were applied to the rendering of the "Engine" dataset.

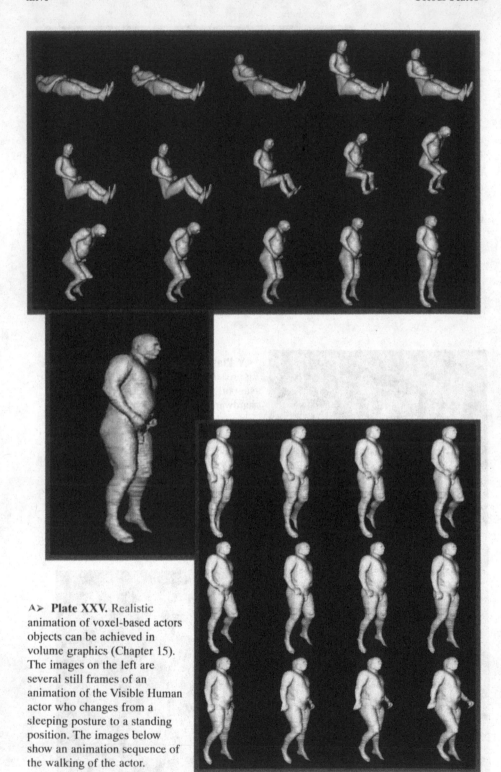

^➤ **Plate XXV.** Realistic animation of voxel-based actors objects can be achieved in volume graphics (Chapter 15). The images on the left are several still frames of an animation of the Visible Human actor who changes from a sleeping posture to a standing position. The images below show an animation sequence of the walking of the actor.

◄ Plate XXVI. Isovolume (also called interval volume) is a volumetric representation of a set of isosurfaces. It is a fundamental data type used in rapid prototyping, and in particular, the layered manufacturing process. An example of such machinery is the Z Corporation Z402 system (Chapter 5).

➤ Plate XXVII. An isovolume is first constructed from a skull dataset (in the Visualization Toolkit), and it is then manufactured into a hardcopy (Chapter 5).

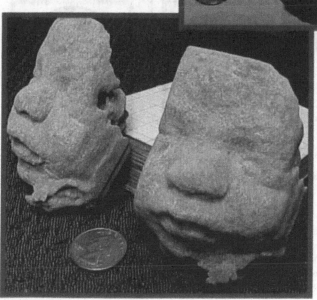

◄ Plate XXVIII. Two manufactured foetal isovolumes (Chapter 5).

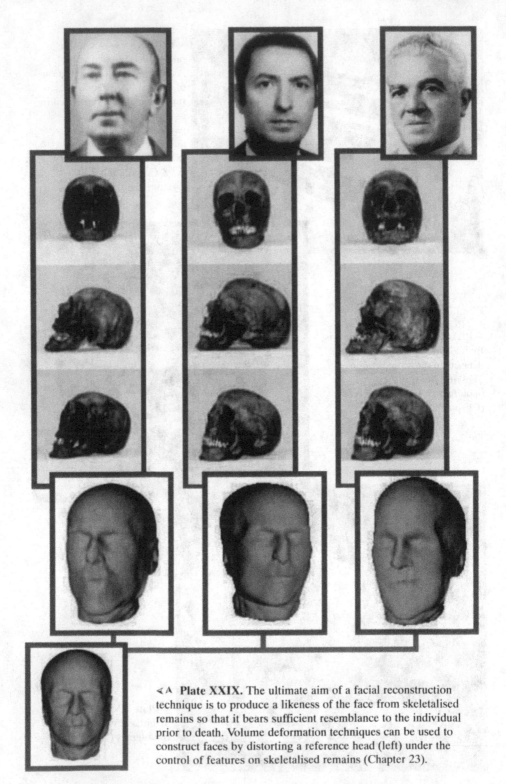

◁△ **Plate XXIX.** The ultimate aim of a facial reconstruction technique is to produce a likeness of the face from skeletalised remains so that it bears sufficient resemblance to the individual prior to death. Volume deformation techniques can be used to construct faces by distorting a reference head (left) under the control of features on skeletalised remains (Chapter 23).

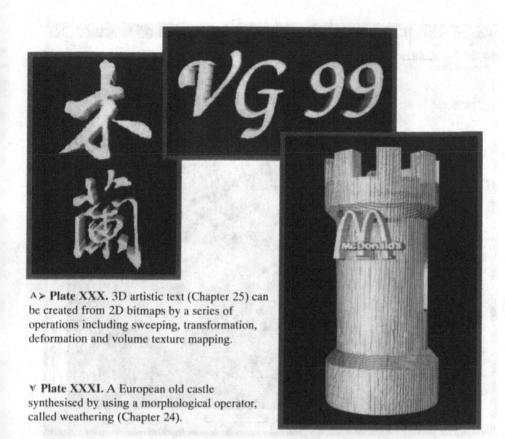

Plate XXX. 3D artistic text (Chapter 25) can be created from 2D bitmaps by a series of operations including sweeping, transformation, deformation and volume texture mapping.

˅ **Plate XXXI.** A European old castle synthesised by using a morphological operator, called weathering (Chapter 24).

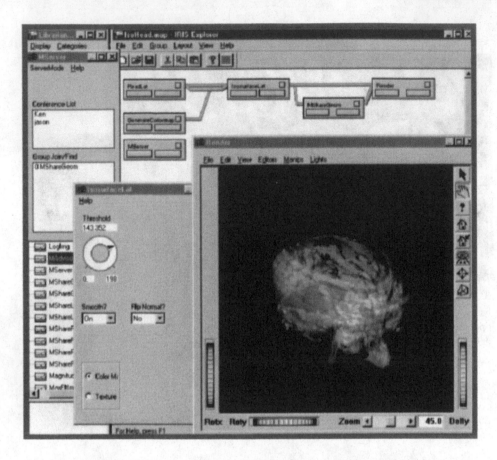

∧∨ **Plate XXXII.** The Internet is becoming a medium for volume graphics (Chapter 21). It offers new opportunities to a range of volume graphics applications, while challenging volume graphics in a number of aspects including its efficiency, data management, and multi-user interaction. The image above shows a user interface where Dr Bone is collaborating with Dr Blood at a remote site to look at CT and SPECT data together. The image below shows Drs. Blood and Bone pointing out features to each other (with different coloured cursors).

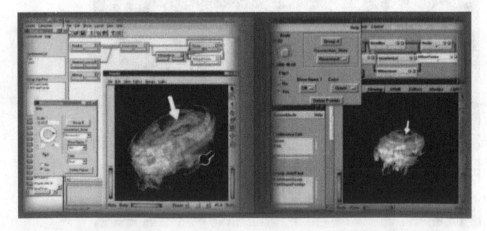

PART I

PERSPECTIVES

1. State-of-the-Art in Volume Graphics

Arie E. Kaufman

1.1 Introduction

Volume data are 3D entities that may have information inside them: they might not consist of surfaces and edges, or they might be too voluminous to be represented geometrically. Volume visualisation is a method of extracting meaningful information from volumetric data using interactive graphics and imaging, and it is concerned with volume data representation, modelling, manipulation, and rendering [1-3]. Volume data are obtained by sampling, simulation, or modelling techniques. For example, a sequence of 2D slices obtained from Magnetic Resonance Imaging (MRI) or Computed Tomography (CT) is 3D reconstructed into a volume model and visualised for diagnostic purposes or for planning treatment or surgery. The same technology is often used with industrial CT for non-destructive inspection of composite materials or mechanical parts. Similarly, confocal microscopes produce datasets which are visualised to study the morphology of biological structures. In many computational fields, such as in computational fluid dynamics, the results of simulation, typically running on a supercomputer, are often visualised as volume data for analysis and verification. Recently, many traditional geometric computer graphics applications, such as CAD and simulation, have exploited the advantages of volume techniques called *volume graphics* for modelling, manipulation, and visualisation.

Volume graphics [4], which is an emerging sub-field of computer graphics, is concerned with the synthesis, modelling, manipulation, and rendering of volumetric geometric objects, stored in a volume buffer of voxels. Unlike volume visualisation which focuses primarily on sampled and computed datasets, volume graphics is concerned primarily with modelled geometric scenes and commonly with those that are represented in a regular volume buffer. As an approach, volume graphics has the potential to greatly advance the field of 3D graphics by offering a comprehensive alternative to traditional surface graphics.

We begin, in Section 1.2, with an introduction to volumetric data. In the following sections we describe the volumetric approach to several common volume graphics modelling techniques. We describe the generation of object primitives by voxelisation (Section 1.3), fundamentals of 3D discrete topology (Section 1.4), binary voxelisation (Section 1.5), 3D antialiasing and multi-valued voxelisation (Section 1.6), texture and photo mapping and solid-texturing (Section 1.7), modelling of amorphous phenomena (Section 1.8), modelling by block operations and constructive solid modelling (Section 1.9), and volume sculpting (Section 1.10). Then, volume graphics is contrasted with surface graphics (Section 1.11), and the corresponding advantages (Section 1.12) and disadvantages (Section 1.13) are discussed. In Section 1.14, we describe special-purpose volume rendering hardware.

1.2 Volumetric Data

Volumetric data is typically a set S of samples (x, y, z, v), representing the value v of some property of the data, at a 3D location (x, y, z). If the value is simply a 0 or 1, with a value of 0 indicating background and a value of 1 indicating the object, then the data is referred to as binary data. The data may instead be multi-valued, with the value v representing a group of measurable properties of the data, including, for example, colour, density, heat or pressure. The value v may even be a vector, representing, for example, velocity at each location.

In general, samples may be taken at purely random locations in space, but, in most cases, the set S is *isotropic* containing samples taken at regularly spaced intervals along three orthogonal axes. When the spacing between samples along each axis is a constant, but there may be three different spacing constants for the three axes, then set S is *anisotropic*. Since the set of samples is defined on a regular grid, a 3D array (also called *volume buffer, cubic frame buffer* and *3D raster*) is typically used to store the values, with the element location indicating the position of the sample on the grid. For this reason, the set S will be referred to as the array of values $S(x, y, z)$, which is defined only at grid locations. Alternatively, either rectilinear, curvilinear (structured), or unstructured grids are employed (e.g. [5]). In a *rectilinear* grid the cells are axis-aligned, but grid spacing along the axes is arbitrary. When such a grid has been nonlinearly transformed while preserving the grid topology, the grid becomes *curvilinear*. Usually, the rectilinear grid defining the logical organisation is called *computational space*, and the curvilinear grid is called *physical space*. Otherwise the grid is called unstructured or *irregular*. An unstructured or irregular volume dataset is a collection of cells whose connectivity has to be specified explicitly. These cells can be of an arbitrary shape such as tetrahedron, hexahedron or prism.

The array S only defines the value of some measured property of the data at discrete locations in space. A function $f(x, y, z)$ may be defined over $\mathbf{R}^3$ in order to describe the value at any continuous location. The function $f(x, y, z)=S(x, y, z)$ if (x, y, z) is a grid location, otherwise $f(x, y, z)$ is defined by applying some interpolation function to S. There are many possible interpolation functions. The simplest interpolation function is known as *zero-order interpolation*, which is actually just a nearest-neighbour function. The value at any location in $\mathbf{R}^3$ is simply the value of the closest sample to that location. With this interpolation method there is a region of constant value around each sample in S. Since the samples in S are regularly spaced, each region is of uniform size and shape. The region of constant value that surrounds each sample is known as a *voxel* with each voxel being a rectangular cuboid having six faces, twelve edges, and eight corners.

Higher-order interpolation functions can also be used to define $f(x, y, z)$ between sample points. One common interpolation function is a piecewise function known as *first-order interpolation*, or *trilinear interpolation*. With this interpolation function, the value is assumed to vary linearly along directions parallel to one of the major axes. Let the point P lie at location (x_p, y_p, z_p) within the regular hexahedron, known as a cell, defined by samples A through H. For simplicity, let the distance between samples in all three directions be 1, with sample A at $(0, 0, 0)$ with a value of v_A and sample H at $(1, 1, 1)$ with a value of v_H. The value v_P, according to trilinear interpolation, is then:

$$v_P = v_A(1-x_p)(1-y_p)(1-z_p) + v_E(1-x_p)(1-y_p)z_p$$
$$+ v_B x_p(1-y_p)(1-z_p) + v_F x_p(1-y_p)z_p + v_C(1-x_p)y_p(1-z_p) \qquad (1.1)$$
$$+ v_G(1-x_p)y_p z_p + v_D x_p y_p(1-z_p) + v_H x_p y_p z_p$$

In general, A is at some location (x_A, y_A, z_A), and H is at (x_H, y_H, z_H). In this case, x_p in Equation 1.1 should be replaced by $(x_p - x_A) / (x_H - x_A)$, with similar substitutions made for y_p and z_p.

Over the years many techniques have been developed to visualise 3D data. Since methods for displaying geometric primitives were already well established, most of the early methods involved approximating a surface contained within the data using geometric primitives [6-7]. When volumetric data are visualised using a surface rendering technique, a dimension of information is essentially lost. In response to this, volume-rendering techniques were developed that attempt to capture the entire 3D data in a single 2D image [1, 8-12]. Volume rendering conveys more information than surface rendering images but at the cost of increased algorithm complexity and, consequently, increased rendering times. To improve interactivity in volume rendering, many optimisation methods as well as several special-purpose volume rendering machines have been developed (see Section 1.14).

The 3D raster representation seems to be more natural for empirical imagery than for geometric objects, due to its ability to represent interiors and digital samples. Nonetheless, the advantages of this representation are also attracting traditional surface-based applications that deal with the modelling and rendering of synthetic scenes made out of geometric models. The geometric model is *voxelised* (*3D scan-converted*) into a set of voxels that "best" approximate the model. Each of these voxels is then stored in the volume buffer together with its precomputed view-independent attributes. The voxelised model can be either binary [13 16] (see also Section 1.5) or volume sampled [17-18] (see also Section 1.6) which generates alias-free density voxelisation of the model. Some surface-based application examples are the rendering of fractals [19], hyper textures [20], fur [21], gases [12], and other complex models [23], including terrain models for flight simulators (Figures 1.1 and 1.2) or volume [4, 24-26] and CAD models (Figure 1.3). Furthermore, in many applications involving sampled data, such as medical imaging, the data need to be visualised along with synthetic objects that may not be available in digital form, such as scalpels, prosthetic devices, injection needles, radiation beams, and isodose surfaces. These geometric objects can be voxelised and intermixed with the sampled organ in the voxel buffer [27].

Figure 1.1. A volume-sampled plane within a volumetric cloud over a volumetric model of terrain enhanced with photo mapping of satellite images.

Figure 1.2. A volumetric model of terrain enhanced with photo mapping of satellite images. The buildings are synthetic voxel models raised on top of the terrain. The voxelised terrain has been mapped with aerial photos during the voxelisation stage.

Figure 1.3. Volume-sampled bolt and nut generated by a sequence of CSG operations on hexagonal, cylindrical, and helix primitives, reflected on a volume-sampled mirror.

1.3 Voxelisation

An indispensable stage in volume graphics is the synthesis of voxel-represented objects from their geometric representation. This stage, which is called *voxelisation*, is concerned with converting geometric objects from their continuous geometric representation into a set of voxels that "best" approximates the continuous object. As this process mimics the scan-conversion process that pixelises (rasterises) 2D geometric objects, it is also referred to as *3D scan-conversion*. In 2D rasterisation the pixels are directly drawn onto the screen to be visualised and filtering is applied to reduce the aliasing artifacts. However, the voxelisation process does not render the voxels but merely generates a database of the discrete digitisation of the continuous object.

Intuitively, one would assume that a proper voxelisation simply "selects" all voxels which are met (if only partially) by the object body. Although this approach could be satisfactory in some cases, the objects it generates are commonly too coarse and include more voxels than are necessary. For example, when a 2D curve is rasterised into a connected sequence of pixels, the discrete curve does not "cover" the entire continuous curve, but is connected, concisely and successfully "separating" both "sides" of the curve [28].

One practical meaning of separation is apparent when a voxelised scene is rendered by casting discrete rays from the image plane to the scene. The penetration of the background voxels (which simulate the discrete ray traversal) through the voxelised surface causes the appearance of a hole in the final image of the rendered surface. Another type of error might occur when a 3D flooding algorithm is employed either to fill an object or to measure its volume, surface area, or other properties. In this case, the non-separability of the surface causes a leakage of the flood through the discrete surface.

Unfortunately, the extension of the 2D definition of separation to the third dimension and voxel surfaces is not straightforward, since voxelised surfaces cannot be defined as an ordered sequence of voxels and a voxel on the surface does not have a specific number of adjacent surface voxels. Furthermore, there are important topological issues, such as the separation of both sides of a surface, which cannot be well-defined by employing 2D terminology. The theory that deals with these topological issues is called *3D discrete topology*. We sketch below some basic notions and informal definitions used in this field.

1.4 Fundamentals of 3D Discrete Topology

The 3D discrete space is a set of integral grid points in 3D Euclidean space defined by their Cartesian coordinates (x, y, z). A voxel is the unit cubic volume centred at the integral grid point. The voxel value is mapped onto $\{0, 1\}$: the voxels assigned "1" are called the "black" voxels representing opaque objects, and those assigned "0" are the "white" voxels representing the transparent background. In Section 1.6, we describe non-binary approaches where the voxel value is mapped onto the interval $[0, 1]$ representing partial coverage, variable densities, or graded opacities. Due to its larger dynamic range of values, this approach supports 3D antialiasing and thus supports higher-quality rendering.

Two voxels are *26-adjacent* if they share a vertex, an edge, or a face (Figure 1.4). Every voxel has 26 such adjacent voxels: eight share a vertex (corner) with the centre voxel, twelve share an edge, and six share a face. Accordingly, face-sharing voxels are defined as *6-adjacent*, and edge-sharing and face-sharing voxels are defined as *18-adjacent*. The prefix N is used to define the adjacency relation, where $N = 6$, 18, or 26. A sequence of voxels having the same value (e.g. "black") is called an *N-path* if all consecutive pairs are N-adjacent. A set of voxels W is *N-connected* if there is an N-path between every pair of voxels in W (Figure 1.4). An *N-connected component* is a maximal N-connected set.

Given a 2D discrete 8-connected black curve, there are sequences of 8-connected white pixels (8-component) that pass from one side of the black component to its other side without intersecting it. This phenomenon is a discrete disagreement with the continuous case where there is no way of penetrating a closed curve without intersecting it. To avoid such a scenario, it has been the convention to define "opposite" types of connectivity for the white and black sets. "Opposite" types in 2D space are 4 and 8, while in 3D space 6 is "opposite" to 26 or to 18.

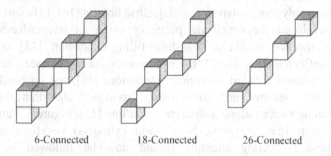

6-Connected   18-Connected   26-Connected

Figure 1.4. 6-, 18-, and 26-connected paths

Assume that a voxel space, denoted by Σ, includes one subset of "black" voxels S. If $\Sigma - S$ is not N-connected, that is, $\Sigma - S$ consists of at least two white N-connected components, then S is said to be N-*separating* in Σ. Loosely speaking, in 2D, an 8-connected black path that divides the white pixels into two groups is 4-separating and a 4-connected black path that divides the white pixels into two groups is 8-separating. There are no analogous results in 3D space.

Let W be an N-separating surface. A voxel p $\in W$ is said to be an N-*simple voxel* if W – p is still N-separating. An N-separating surface is called N-*minimal* if it does not contain any N-simple voxels. A *cover* of a continuous surface is a set of voxels such that every point of the continuous surface lies in a voxel of the cover. A cover is said to be a *minimal cover* if none of its subsets is also a cover. The cover property is essential in applications that employ space subdivision for fast ray tracing [29]. The subspaces (voxels) which contain objects have to be identified along the traced ray. Note that a cover is not necessarily separating, while on the other hand, as mentioned above, it may include simple voxels. In fact, even a minimal cover is not necessarily N-minimal for any N [28].

1.5 Binary Voxelisation

An early technique for the digitisation of solids was spatial enumeration, which employs point or cell classification methods either in an exhaustive fashion or by recursive subdivision [30]. However, subdivision techniques for model decomposition into rectangular subspaces are computationally expensive and thus inappropriate for medium or high-resolution grids. Instead, objects should be directly voxelised, preferably generating an N-separating, N-minimal, and covering set, where N is application dependent. The voxelisation algorithms should follow the same paradigm as the 2D scan-conversion algorithms; they should be incremental, accurate, use simple arithmetic (preferably integer only), and have a complexity that is not more than linear with the number of voxels generated.

The literature of 3D scan-conversion is relatively small. Danielsson [31] and Mokrzycki [32] developed, independently, similar 3D curve algorithms where the curve is defined by the intersection of two implicit surfaces. Voxelisation algorithms have been developed for 3D lines [33], 3D circles, and a variety of surfaces and solids, including polygons, polyhedra, and quadric objects [14]. Efficient algorithms have been developed for voxelising polygons using an integer-based decision mechanism embedded within a scan-line filling algorithm [15] or with an incremental prefiltered algorithm [34], for parametric curves, surfaces, and volumes using an integer-based forward differencing technique [16], and for quadric objects such as cylinders, spheres, and cones using "weaving" algorithms by which a discrete circle/line sweeps along a discrete circle/line [13]. Figure 1.2 consists of a variety of objects (e.g. polygons, boxes, and cylinders) voxelised using these methods. These pioneering attempts should now be followed by enhanced voxelisation algorithms that, in addition to being efficient and accurate, will also adhere to the topological requirements of separation, coverage and minimality.

1.6 3D Antialiasing and Multi-Valued Voxelisation

The previous section discussed binary voxelisation, which generates topologically and geometrically consistent models, but exhibits object space aliasing. These algorithms have used a straightforward method of sampling in space, called point *sampling*. In point sampling, the continuous object is evaluated at the voxel centre, and the value of 0 or 1 is assigned to the voxel. Because of this binary classification of the voxels, the resolution of the 3D raster ultimately determines the precision of the discrete model. Imprecise modelling results in jagged surfaces, known as *object space aliasing* (Figure 1.2). In this section, we first present a 3D object-space antialiasing technique. It performs antialiasing once, on a 3D view-independent representation, as part of the modelling stage. Unlike antialiasing of 2D scan-converted graphics, where the main focus is on generating aesthetically pleasing displays, the emphasis in antialiased 3D voxelisation is on producing alias-free 3D models that are stored in the view-independent volume buffer for various volume graphics manipulations, including, but not limited to, the generation of aesthetically pleasing displays (Figure 1.1).

To reduce object space aliasing, a *volume sampling* technique has been developed [18] which estimates the density contribution of the geometric objects to the voxels. The density of a voxel is attenuated by a filter weight function, which is proportional to the distance between the centre of the voxel and the geometric primitive. To improve performance, precomputed lookup tables of densities for a predefined set of geometric primitives can be used to select the density value of each voxel. For each voxel visited by the binary voxelisation algorithm, the distance to the predefined primitive is used as an index into a lookup table of densities.

Since voxelised geometric objects are represented as volume rasters of density values, they can essentially be treated as sampled or simulated volume datasets, such as 3D medical imaging datasets, and one of many volume rendering techniques for image generation can be employed. One primary advantage of this approach is that volume rendering or volumetric global illumination carries the smoothness of the volume-sampled objects from object space over into its 2D projection in image space [35]. Hence, the silhouette of the objects, reflections, and shadows are smooth. In addition, CSG operations between two volume-sampled geometric models are accomplished at the voxel level after voxelisation, thereby reducing the original problem of evaluating a CSG tree of such operations down to a fuzzy Boolean operation between pairs of non-binary voxels [36] (see Section 1.9). Volume-sampled models are also suitable for intermixing with sampled or simulated datasets, since they can be treated uniformly as one common data representation. Furthermore, volume-sampled models lend themselves to alias-free multi-resolution hierarchy construction [36].

Further study of filtered voxelisation has been conducted by Sramek and Kaufman [17, 37]. The basic idea has been that in voxelisation filter design one needs to consider the visualisation techniques used (i.e. data interpolation and normal estimation). They showed that a combination of first-order filters on voxelisation and visualisation, with proper parameters, results in rendered images with negligible error in estimating object surface position and normal direction. More specifically, when a trilinear interpolation is used for reconstruction of the continuous volume, with subsequent surface detection by thresholding and normal gradient calculation by central differences, best results are obtained if the density of the voxelised object near its surface is linear along the surface normal direction (e.g. [38-39]). This linear profile, which results from convolution of the object with a 1D box filter applied along a direction perpendicular to the surface, is called an oriented box filter [17]. Furthermore, a Gaussian surface density profile combined with tricubic interpolation and Gabor derivative reconstruction outperforms the linear density profile, but for a sharp increase in the computation time.

A C++ library for filtered voxelisation, vxt, has been developed (see Chapter 7). It provides the user with an extensible set of easy-to-use tools and routines for alias-free voxelisation of analytically defined monochromatic and colour objects. Thus, the resulting volumetric data represent a suitable input for both software and hardware volume-rendering systems. The library provides for voxelisation of primitive objects; however, when supplemented by a suitable parser, it represents a basis for voxelisation of complex models defined in various graphics formats.

1.7 Texture Mapping

One type of object complexity involves objects that are enhanced with texture mapping, photo mapping, environment mapping, or solid texturing. Texture mapping is commonly implemented during the last stage of the rendering pipeline, and its complexity is proportional to the object complexity. In volume graphics, however, texture mapping is usually performed during the voxelisation stage, and the texture colour is stored in each voxel in the volume buffer.

In photo mapping, six orthogonal photographs of the real object are projected back onto the voxelised object. Once this mapping is applied, it is stored with the voxels themselves during the voxelisation stage, and therefore does not degrade the rendering performance. Texture and photo mapping are also viewpoint-independent attributes implying that once the texture is stored as part of the voxel value, texture mapping need not be repeated. This important feature is exploited, for example, by voxel-based flight simulators (Figures 1.1 and 1.2) and CAD systems (Figure 1.3).

A central feature of volumetric representation is that, unlike surface representation, it is capable of representing inner structures of objects, which can be revealed and explored with appropriate manipulation and rendering techniques. This capability is essential for the exploration of sampled or computed objects. Synthetic objects are also likely to be solid rather than hollow. One method for modelling various solid types is solid texturing, in which a function or a 3D map models the colour of the objects in 3D (Figure 1.3). During the voxelisation phase each voxel belonging to the objects is assigned a value by the texturing function or the 3D map. This value is then stored as part of the voxel information. Again, since this value is view independent, it does not have to be recomputed for every change in the rendering parameters.

1.8 Amorphous Phenomena

While translucent objects can be represented by surface methods, these methods cannot efficiently support the modelling and rendering of amorphous phenomena (e.g. clouds, fire and smoke) that are volumetric in nature and lack any tangible surfaces. A common modelling and rendering approach is based on a volumetric function that, for any input point in 3D, calculates some object features such as density, reflectivity, or colour (Figure 1.1). These functions can then be rendered by ray casting, which casts a ray from each pixel into the function domain. Along the passage of the ray, at constant intervals, the function is evaluated to yield a sample. All samples along each ray are combined to form the pixel colour. Some examples for the use of this or similar techniques are the rendering of fractals [40], hypertextures [20], fur [21] and gases [22]. The process of function evaluation at each sample point in 3D has to be repeated for each image generated. In contrast, the volumetric approach allows the precomputation of these functions at each grid point of the volume buffer. The resulting volumetric dataset can then be rendered from multiple viewpoints without recomputing the modelling function. As in other volume graphics techniques, accuracy is traded for speed, due to the resolution limit. Instead of accurately computing the function at each sample point, some type of interpolation from the precomputed grid values is employed.

1.9 Block Operations and Constructive Solid Modelling

The presortedness of the volume buffer naturally lends itself to grouping operations that can be exploited in various ways. For example, by generating a multi-resolution volume hierarchy that can support time-critical and space-critical volume graphics applications can be better supported. The basic idea is similar to that of level-of-detail surface rendering which has recently proliferated [41-45], in which the perceptual importance of a given object in the scene determines its appropriate level-of-detail representation. One simple approach is the 3D "mip-map" approach [46-47], where every level of the hierarchy is formed by averaging several voxels from the previous level. A better approach is based on sampling theory, in which an object is modelled with a sequence of alias-free volume buffers at different resolutions using the volume-sampled voxelisation approach [48]. To accomplish this, high frequencies that exceed the Nyquist frequency of the corresponding volume buffer are filtered out by applying an ideal low-pass filter (*sinc*) with infinite support. In practice, the ideal filter is approximated by filters with finite support. Low sampling resolution of the volume buffer corresponds to a lower Nyquist frequency, and therefore requires a low-pass filter with wider support for good approximation. As one moves up the hierarchy, low-pass filters with wider and wider support are applied. Compared to the level-of-detail hierarchy in surface graphics, the multi-resolution volume buffers are easy to generate and to spatially correspond to neighbouring levels, and they are also free of object space aliasing. Furthermore, arbitrary resolutions can be generated, and errors caused by a non-ideal filter do not propagate and accumulate from level to level. Depending on the required speed and accuracy, a variety of low-pass filters (zero order, cubic, Gaussian) can be applied.

An intrinsic characteristic of the volume buffer is that objects in the scene are also represented by neighbouring memory cells. Therefore, rasters lend themselves to various meaningful grouping-based operations, such as *bitblt* in 2D, or *voxblt* in 3D [49]. These include the transfer of rectangular blocks (cuboids) in a volume buffer while supporting voxel-by-voxel operations between source and destination blocks. Block operations add a variety of modelling capabilities that aid in the task of image synthesis and form the basis for the efficient implementation of a 3D "room manager", which is the extension of window management to the third dimension.

Since the volume buffer lends itself to Boolean operations that can be performed on a voxel-by-voxel basis during the voxelisation stage, it is advantageous to use CSG as the modelling paradigm. Subtraction, union, and intersection operations between two voxelised objects are accomplished at the voxel level, thereby reducing the original problem of evaluating a CSG tree during rendering time down to a 1D Boolean operation between pairs of voxels during a preprocessing stage.

For two point-sampled binary objects the Boolean operations of CSG or *voxblt* are trivially defined. However, the Boolean operations applied to volume-sampled models are analogous to those of fuzzy set theory (cf. [50]). The volume-sampled model is a density function $d(x)$ over $\mathbf{R}^3$, where d is 1 inside the object, 0 outside the object, and $0 < d < 1$ within the "soft" region of the filtered surface. Some of the common operations, intersection, complement, difference, and union, between two objects A and B are defined as follows:

$$d_{A \cap B}(x) \equiv \min (d_A(x), d_B(x)) \tag{1.2}$$
$$d_{-A}(x) \equiv 1 - d_A(x) \tag{1.3}$$
$$d_{A-B}(x) \equiv \min (d_A(x), 1 - d_B(x)) \tag{1.4}$$
$$d_{A \cup B}(x) \equiv \max (d_A(x), d_B(x)) \tag{1.5}$$

The only law of set theory that is no longer true is the excluded-middle law (i.e. $A \cap -A \neq \varnothing$ and $A \cup -A \neq Universe$). The use of the min and max functions causes discontinuity at the region where the soft regions of the two objects meet, since the density value at each location in the region is determined solely by one of the two overlapping objects.

Complex geometric models can be generated by performing the CSG operations in Equations 1.2-1.5 between volume-sampled primitives. Volume-sampled models can also function as matte volumes [8] for various matting operations, such as performing cut-aways and merging multiple volumes into a single volume using the union operation. However, in order to preserve continuity on the cut-away boundaries between the material and the empty space, one should use an alternative set of Boolean operators based on algebraic sum and algebraic product [50-51]:

$$d_{A \cap B}(x) \equiv d_A(x) \, d_B(x) \tag{1.6}$$
$$d_{-A}(x) \equiv 1 - d_A(x) \tag{1.7}$$
$$d_{A-B}(x) \equiv d_A(x) - d_A(x) \, d_B(x) \tag{1.8}$$
$$d_{A \cup B}(x) \equiv d_A(x) + d_B(x) - d_A(x) \, d_B(x) \tag{1.9}$$

Unlike the min and max operators, algebraic sum and product operators result in $A \cup A \neq A$, which is undesirable. A consequence, for example, is that when modelling via sweeping, the resulting model is sensitive to the sampling rate of the swept path [36].

Once a CSG model has been constructed in voxel representation, it is rendered in the same way as any other volume buffer. This makes, for example, volumetric ray tracing of constructive solid models straightforward [52] (Figure 1.3).

1.10 Volume Sculpting

Surface-based sculpting has been studied extensively (e.g. [53-54]), while volume sculpting has been recently introduced for clay or wax-like sculptures [55] and for comprehensive detailed sculpting [56]. The latter approach is a free-form interactive modelling technique based on the metaphor of sculpting and painting a voxel-based solid material, such as a block of marble or wood. There are two motivations for this approach. First, modelling topologically complex and highly-detailed objects is still difficult in most CAD systems. Second, sculpting has shown to be useful in volumetric applications. For example, scientists and physicians often need to explore the inner structures of their simulated or sampled datasets by gradually removing material.

Real-time human interaction could be achieved in this approach: since the actions of sculpting (e.g. carving, sawing) and painting are localised in the volume buffer, a localised rendering can be employed to reproject only those pixels that are affected. Carving is the process of taking an existing volume-sampled tool to chip or chisel the object bit by bit. Since both the object and tool are represented as independent volume buffers, the process of sculpting involves positioning the tool with respect to the object and performing a Boolean subtraction between the two volumes. Sawing is the process of removing a whole chunk of material at once, much like a carpenter sawing off a portion of a piece of wood. Unlike carving, sawing requires generating the volume-sampled tool "on-the-fly", through a user interface. To prevent object space aliasing and to achieve interactive speed, 3D splatting is employed.

1.11 Surface Graphics versus Volume Graphics

Contemporary 3D graphics has been employing an object-based approach at the expense of maintaining and manipulating a display list of geometric objects and regenerating the frame-buffer after every change in the scene or viewing parameters. This approach, termed *surface graphics*, is supported by powerful geometry engines which have flourished in the past decade, making surface graphics the state-of-the-art in 3D graphics.

Surface graphics strikingly resembles vector graphics which prevailed in the sixties and seventies, and employed vector drawing devices. Like vector graphics, surface graphics represents the scene as a set of geometric primitives kept in a display list. In surface graphics, these primitives are transformed, mapped to screen coordinates, and converted by scan-conversion algorithms into a discrete set of pixels. Any change to the scene, viewing parameters, or shading parameters requires the image generation system to repeat this process. Like vector graphics, which did not support painting the interior of 2D objects, surface graphics generates merely the surfaces of 3D objects and does not support the rendering of their interior.

Instead of a list of geometric objects maintained by surface graphics, volume graphics employs a 3D volume buffer as a medium for the representation and manipulation of 3D scenes. A 3D scene is discretised earlier in the image generation sequence, and the resulting 3D discrete form is used as a database of the scene for manipulation and rendering purposes, which, in effect, decouples discretisation from rendering. Furthermore, all objects are converted into one uniform meta-object — the voxel. Each voxel is atomic and represents the information about, at most, one object that resides in that voxel.

Volume graphics offers similar benefits to surface graphics, with several advantages that are due to the decoupling, uniformity, and atomicity features. The rendering phase is viewpoint independent and insensitive to scene complexity and object complexity. It supports Boolean and block operations and constructive solid modelling. When 3D sampled or simulated data are used, such as that generated by medical scanners (e.g. CT and MRI) or scientific simulations (e.g. CFD), volume graphics is suitable for their representation too. It is capable of representing amorphous phenomena and both the interior and exterior of 3D objects. These features of volume graphics compared with surface graphics are discussed in detail in 1.12. Several weaknesses of volume graphics are related to the discrete nature of the representation, for instance, transformations and shading are performed in discrete space. In addition, this approach requires substantial amounts of storage space and specialised processing. These weaknesses are discussed in detail in 1.13.

Table 1.1 contrasts vector graphics with raster graphics. A primary appeal of raster graphics is that it decouples image generation from screen refresh, thus making the refresh task insensitive to the scene and object complexities. In addition, the raster representation lends itself to block operations, such as *bitblt* and quadtree. Raster graphics is also suitable for displaying 2D sampled digital images, and thus provides the ideal environment for mixing digital images with synthetic graphics. Unlike vector graphics, raster graphics provides the capability to present shaded and textured surfaces, as well as line drawings. These advantages, coupled with advances in hardware and the development of antialiasing methods, have led raster graphics to supersede vector graphics as the primary technology for computer graphics. The main weaknesses of raster graphics are the large memory and processing power it requires for the frame buffer, as well as the discrete nature of the image. These difficulties delayed the full acceptance of raster graphics until the late seventies when the technology was able to provide cheaper and faster memory and hardware to support the demands of the raster approach. In addition, the discrete nature of rasters makes them less suitable for geometric operations such as transformations and accurate measurements and, once discretised, the notion of objects is lost.

Table 1.1. Comparison between vector graphics and raster graphics and between surface graphics and volume graphics.

2D	Vector Graphics	Raster Graphics
Scene/object complexity	-	+
Block operations	-	+
Sampled data	-	+
Interior	-	+
Memory and processing	+	-
Aliasing	+	-
Transformations	+	-
Objects	+	-
3D	**Surface Graphics**	**Volume Graphics**

The same appeal that drove the evolution of the computer graphics world from vector graphics to raster graphics, once the memory and processing power became available, is driving a variety of applications from a surface-based approach to a volume-based approach. Naturally, this trend first appeared in applications involving sampled or computed 3D data, such as 3D medical imaging and scientific visualisation, in which the datasets are in volumetric form. These diverse empirical applications of volume visualisation still provide a major driving force for advances in volume graphics.

The comparison in Table 1.1 between vector graphics and raster graphics strikingly resembles a comparison between surface graphics and volume graphics. Actually the table is also used to contrast surface graphics and volume graphics.

1.12 Volume Graphics Features

One of the most appealing attributes of volume graphics is its insensitivity to the complexity of the scene, since all objects have been pre-converted into a finite size volume buffer. Although the performance of the preprocessing voxelisation phase is influenced by the scene complexity [13-16], rendering performance depends mainly on the constant resolution of the volume buffer and not on the number of objects in the scene. Insensitivity to the scene complexity makes the volumetric approach especially attractive for scenes consisting of a large number of objects.

In volume graphics, rendering is decoupled from voxelisation and all objects are first converted into one meta object, the voxel, which makes the rendering process insensitive to the complexity of the objects. Thus, volume graphics is particularly attractive for objects that are hard to render using conventional graphics systems. Examples of such objects include curved surfaces of high order and fractals which require expensive computation of an iterative function for each volume unit [19]. Constructive solid models are also hard to render by conventional methods, but are straightforward to render in volumetric representation (see below).

Antialiasing and texture mapping are commonly implemented during the last stage of the conventional rendering pipeline, and their complexity is proportional to object complexity. Solid texturing, which employs a 3D texture image, has also a high complexity proportional to object complexity. In volume graphics, however, antialiasing, texture mapping, and solid texturing are performed only once — during the voxelisation stage — where the colour is calculated and stored in each voxel. The texture can also be stored as a separate volumetric entity which is rendered together with the volumetric object, as in the *VolVis* software system for volume visualisation [57].

The textured objects in Figures 1.1, 1.2 and 1.3 have been assigned texture during the voxelisation stage by mapping each voxel back to the corresponding value on a texture map or solid. Once this mapping is applied, it is stored with the voxels themselves during the voxelisation stage, which does not degrade the rendering performance. In addition, texture mapping and photo mapping are also viewpoint independent attributes, implying that once the texture is stored as part of the voxel value, texture mapping need not be repeated.

In anticipation of repeated access to the volume buffer (such as in animation), all viewpoint independent attributes can be precomputed during the voxelisation stage, stored with the voxel, and can be readily accessible for speeding up the rendering.

The voxelisation algorithm can generate for each object voxel its colour, texture colour, normal vector (for visible voxels), antialiasing information [18], and information concerning the visibility of the light sources from that voxel. Actually, the viewpoint independent parts of the illumination equation can also be precomputed and stored as part of the voxel value.

Once a volume buffer with precomputed view-independent attributes is available, a rendering algorithm, such as a discrete ray tracing or a volumetric ray tracing algorithm, can be engaged. Either ray tracing approach is especially attractive for complex surface scenes and constructive solid models, as well as 3D sampled or computed datasets (see below). Figure 1.3 shows an example of objects that were ray traced in discrete voxel space. In spite of the complexity of these scenes, volumetric ray tracing time was approximately the same as for much simpler scenes and significantly faster than traditional space-subdivision ray tracing methods. Moreover, in spite of the discrete nature of the volume buffer representation, images indistinguishable from the ones produced by conventional surface-based ray tracing can be generated by employing accurate ray tracing, auxiliary object information, or screen super sampling techniques.

Sampled datasets, such as in 3D medical imaging (Figure 1.3), volume microscopy, and geology, and simulated datasets, such as in computational fluid dynamics, chemistry, and materials simulation, are often reconstructed from the acquired sampled or simulated points into a regular grid of voxels and stored in a volume buffer. Such datasets provide for the majority of applications using the volumetric approach. Unlike surface graphics, volume graphics naturally and directly supports the representation, manipulation, and rendering of such datasets, as well as providing the volume buffer medium for intermixing sampled or simulated datasets with geometric objects [27], as can be seen in Figure 1.5. For compatibility between the sampled/computed data and the voxelised geometric object, the object can be volume sampled [18] with the same, but not necessarily the same, density frequency as the acquired or simulated datasets. In volume sampling the continuous object is filtered during the voxelisation stage generating alias-free 3D density primitives. Volume graphics also naturally supports the rendering of translucent volumetric datasets (Figures 1.1 and 1.5).

A central feature of volumetric representation is that unlike surface representation it is capable of representing inner structures of objects, which can be revealed and explored with the appropriate volumetric manipulation and rendering techniques. Natural objects as well as synthetic objects are likely to be solid rather than hollow. The inner structure is easily explored using volume graphics and cannot be supported by surface graphics (Figure 1.5). Moreover, while translucent objects can be represented by surface methods, these methods cannot efficiently support the translucent rendering of volumetric objects, or the modelling and rendering of amorphous phenomena (e.g. clouds, fire, smoke) that are volumetric in nature and do not contain any tangible surfaces (Figure 1.1) [20-22].

An intrinsic characteristic of rasters is that adjacent objects in the scene are also represented by neighbouring voxels. Therefore, rasters lend themselves to various meaningful block-based operations which can be performed during the voxelisation stage. For example, the 3D counterpart of the *bitblt* operations, termed *voxblt* (voxel

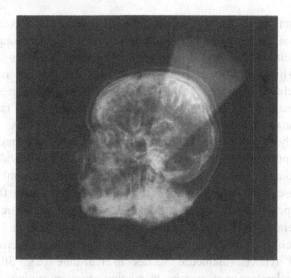

Figure 1.5. Intermixing of a volume-shaped cone with an MRI using a union operation.

block-transfer), can support transfer of cuboidal voxel blocks with a variety of voxel-by-voxel operations between source and destination blocks [49]. This property is very useful for *voxblt* and CSG. Once a CSG model has been constructed in voxel representation, it is rendered like any other volume buffer. This makes rendering of constructive solid models straightforward.

The spatial presortedness of the volume buffer voxels lends itself to other types of grouping or aggregation of neighbouring voxels. For example, the terrain image shown in Figure 1.2 was generated by the voxel-based Hughes Aircraft Co. flight simulator [26]. It simulates a flight over voxel-represented terrain enhanced with satellite or aerial photo mapping with additional synthetic raised objects, such as buildings, trees, vehicles, aircraft, clouds and the like. Since the information below the terrain surface is invisible, terrain voxels can be actually represented as tall cuboids extending from sea level to the terrain height. The raised and moving objects, however, have to be represented in a more conventional voxel-based form.

Similarly, voxels can be aggregated into super-voxels in a pyramid-like hierarchy. For example, in a voxel-based flight simulator, the best resolution can be used for take-off and landing. As the aircraft ascends, fewer and fewer details need to be processed and visualised, and a lower resolution suffices. Furthermore, even in the same view, parts of the terrain close to the observer are rendered at high resolution which decreases towards the horizon. A hierarchical volume buffer can be prepared in advance or on-the-fly by subsampling or averaging the appropriate size neighbourhoods of voxels (see also [48]).

1.13 Weaknesses of Volume Graphics

A typical volume buffer occupies a large amount of memory. For example, for a medium resolution of 512^3, two bytes per voxel, the volume buffer consists of 256M bytes. However, since computer memories are significantly decreasing in price and increasing in their compactness and speed, such large memories are becoming commonplace. This argument echoes a similar discussion when raster graphics emerged as a technology in the mid-seventies. With the rapid progress in memory price and compactness, it is safe to predict that, as in the case of raster graphics, memory will soon cease to be a stumbling block for volume graphics.

The extremely large throughput that has to be handled requires a special architecture and processing attention (see Section 1.14, Chapter 7 and [1]). *Volume engines*, analogous to the currently available geometry (polygon) engines, are emerging. Because of the presortedness of the volume buffer and the fact that only a simple single type of object has to be handled, volume engines are conceptually simpler to implement than current geometry engines (see Section 1.14). Volume engines will materialise in the near future, with capabilities to synthesise, load, store, manipulate, and render volumetric scenes in real-time (e.g. 30 frames/sec), configured as accelerators or co-systems to existing geometry engines.

Unlike surface graphics, in volume graphics the 3D scene is represented in discrete form. This is the source of many of the problems of voxel-based graphics, which are similar to those of 2D rasters [58]. The finite resolution of the raster poses a limit on the accuracy of some operations, such as volume and area measurements, that are based on voxel counting.

Since the discrete data is sampled during rendering, a low resolution volume yields high aliasing artifacts. This becomes especially apparent when zooming in on the 3D raster. When naive rendering algorithms are used, holes may appear "between" voxels. Nevertheless, this can be alleviated in ways similar to those adopted by 2D raster graphics, such as employing either reconstruction techniques, a higher-resolution volume buffer, or volume sampling.

Manipulation and transformation of the discrete volume are difficult to achieve without degrading the image quality or losing some information. Rotation of rasters by angles other than 90 degrees is especially problematic since a sequence of consecutive rotations will distort the image. Again, these can be alleviated in ways similar to the 2D raster techniques. Once an object has been voxelised, the voxels comprising the discrete object do not retain any geometric information regarding the geometric definition of the object. Thus, it is advantageous, when exact measurements are required (e.g. distance, area), to employ conventional modelling where the geometric definition of the object is available. A voxel-based object is only a discrete approximation of the original continuous object where the volume buffer resolution determines the precision of such measurements. On the other hand, several measurement types are more easily computed in voxel space (e.g. mass property, adjacency detection and volume computation).

The lack of geometric information in the voxel may inflict other difficulties, such as surface normal computation. In voxel-based models, a discrete shading method is commonly employed to estimate the normal from a context of voxels. A variety of image-based and object-based methods for normal estimation from volumetric data has been devised [59, 1] (see also Chapter 5) and some have been discussed above. Most methods are based on fitting some type of a surface primitive to a small neighbourhood of voxels.

A partial integration between surface and volume graphics is conceivable as part of an object-based approach in which an auxiliary object table, consisting of the geometric definition and global attributes of each object, is maintained in addition to the volume buffer. Each voxel consists of an index to the object table. This allows exact calculation of normal, exact measurements, and intersection verification for discrete ray tracing [60]. The auxiliary geometric information might also be useful for re-voxelising the scene in case of a change in the scene itself.

1.14 Special-Purpose Volume Rendering Hardware

The high computational cost of direct volume rendering makes it difficult for sequential implementations and general-purpose computers to deliver the targeted level of performance. This situation is aggravated by the continuing trend towards higher and higher resolution datasets. For example, to render a dataset of 1024^3 16-bit voxels at 30 frames per second requires 2 GBytes of storage, a memory transfer rate of 60 GBytes per second and approximately 300 billion instructions per second, assuming only 10 instructions per voxel per projection. To address this challenge, researchers have tried to achieve interactive display rates on supercomputers and massively parallel architectures [61-66].

However, most algorithms require very little repeated computation on each voxel and data movement actually accounts for a significant portion of the overall performance overhead. Today's commercial supercomputer memory systems do not have, nor will they in the near future, adequate latency and memory bandwidth for efficiently transferring the required large amounts of data. Furthermore, supercomputers seldom contain frame buffers and, due to their high cost, are frequently shared by many users.

In the same way as the special requirements of traditional computer graphics lead to high-performance graphics engines, volume visualisation naturally lends itself to special-purpose volume renderers that separate real-time image generation from general-purpose processing. This allows for stand-alone visualisation environments that help users to interactively view their data on a workstation, either augmented by a volume rendering accelerator or connected to a dedicated visualisation server. Furthermore, a volume rendering engine integrated in a graphics workstation is a natural extension of raster-based systems into 3D volume visualisation.

Several researchers have proposed special-purpose volume rendering architectures [1, 67-74] (see also Chapter 7). Most recent research has focused on accelerators for ray-casting of regular datasets. Ray-casting offers room for algorithmic improvements while still allowing for high image quality. Recent architectures [75] include VOGUE, VIRIM, and Cube.

VOGUE [76], a modular add-on accelerator, is estimated to achieve 2.5 frames per second for 256^3 datasets. For each pixel a ray is defined by the host computer and sent to the accelerator. The VOGUE module autonomously processes the complete ray, consisting of evenly spaced resampling locations, and returns the final pixel colour of that ray to the host. Several VOGUE modules can be combined to yield higher performance implementations. For example, to achieve 20 projections per second of 512^3 datasets requires 64 boards and a 5.2 GB per second ring-connected cubic network.

VIRIM [77] is a flexible and programmable ray-casting engine. The hardware consists of two separate units, the first being responsible for 3D resampling of the volume using lookup tables to implement different interpolation schemes. The second unit performs the ray-casting through the resampled dataset according to user programmable lighting and viewing parameters. The underlying ray-casting model allows for arbitrary parallel and perspective projections and shadows. An existing hardware implementation for the visualisation of 256 x 256 x 128 datasets at 10 frames per second requires 16 processing boards.

The Cube project aims at the realisation of high-performance volume rendering systems for large datasets and pioneered several hardware architectures. Cube-1, a first generation hardware prototype, was based on a specially interleaved memory organisation [78], which has also been used in all subsequent generations of the Cube architecture. This interleaving of the n^3 voxel enables conflict-free access to any ray parallel to a main axis of n voxels. A fully operational printed circuit board (PCB) implementation of Cube-1 is capable of generating orthographic projections of 16^3 datasets from a finite number of pre-determined directions in real-time. Cube-2 was a single-chip VLSI implementation of this prototype [79].

To achieve higher performance and to further reduce the critical memory access bottleneck, Cube-3 introduced several new concepts [80-82]. A high-speed global communication network aligns and distributes voxels from the memory to several parallel processing units and a circular cross-linked binary tree of voxel combination units composites all samples into the final pixel colour. Estimated performance for arbitrary parallel and perspective projections is 30 frames per second for 512 sup 3 datasets. Cube-4 [83-85] has only simple and local interconnections, thereby allowing for easy scalability of performance. Instead of processing individual rays, Cube-4 manipulates a group of rays at a time. As a result, the rendering pipeline is directly connected to the memory. Accumulating compositors replace the binary compositing tree. A pixel-bus collects and aligns the pixel output from the compositors. Cube-4 is easily scalable to very high resolution of 1024^3 16-bit voxels and true real-time performance implementations of 30 frames per second.

Enhancing the Cube-4 architecture, Mitsubishi Electric has derived EM-Cube (Enhanced Memory Cube-4). A system based on EM-Cube consists of a PCI card with four volume rendering chips, four 64Mbit SDRAMs to hold the volume data, and four SRAMs to capture the rendered image [53]. The primary innovation of EM-Cube is the block-skewed memory, where the volume memory is organised in subcubes (blocks) in such a way that all the voxels of a block are stored linearly in the same DRAM page. EM-Cube has been further developed into a commercial product where a volume rendering chip, called vg500, has been developed by Mitsubishi. It computes 500 million interpolated, Phong-illuminated, composited samples per second. The vg500 is the heart of a VolumePro PC card consisting of one vg500 and configurable standard SDRAM memory architectures. The first generation, available in 1999, supports rendering of a rectangular dataset up to 256 x 256 x 256 12-bit voxels, in real-time 30 frames/sec [86].

Simultaneously, Japan Radio Co. has enhanced Cube-4 and developed a special-purpose architecture U-Cube. U-Cube is specifically designed for real-time volume rendering of 3D ultrasound data.

The choice of whether one adopts a general-purpose or a special-purpose solution to volume rendering depends upon the circumstances. If maximum flexibility is required, general-purpose appears to be the best way to proceed. However, an important feature of graphics accelerators is that they are integrated into a much larger environment where software can shape the form of input and output data, thereby providing the additional flexibility that is needed. A good example is the relationship between the needs of conventional computer graphics and special-purpose graphics hardware. Nobody would dispute the necessity for polygon graphics acceleration despite its obvious limitations. The same argument can be made for special-purpose volume rendering architectures.

1.15 Conclusions

The important concepts and computational methods of volume graphics have been presented. Although volumetric representations and visualisation techniques seem more natural for sampled or computed datasets, their advantages are also attracting traditional geometric-based applications. This trend implies an expanding role for volume visualisation, and it has thus the potential to revolutionise the field of computer graphics by providing an alternative to surface graphics, called volume graphics. We have introduced recent trends in volume visualisation that brought about the emergence of volume graphics. Volume graphics has advantages over surface graphics by being viewpoint independent, insensitive to scene and object complexity, and lending itself to the realisation of block operations, CSG modelling, and hierarchical representation. It is suitable for the representation of sampled or simulated datasets and their intermixing with geometric objects, and it supports the visualisation of internal structures. The problems associated with the volume buffer representation, such as memory size, processing time, aliasing, and lack of geometric representation, echo problems encountered when raster graphics emerged as an alternative technology to vector graphics and can be alleviated in similar ways. The progress so far in volume graphics, in computer hardware, and memory systems, coupled with the desire to reveal the inner structures of volumetric objects, suggests that volume visualisation and volume graphics may develop into major trends in computer graphics. Just as raster graphics in the seventies superseded vector graphics for visualising surfaces, volume graphics has the potential to supersede surface graphics for handling and visualising volumes as well as for modelling and rendering synthetic scenes composed of surfaces.

Acknowledgements

Special thanks are due to Lisa Sobierajski, Rick Avila, Roni Yagel, Dany Cohen, Sid Wang, Taosong He, Hanspeter Pfister, and Lichan Hong who contributed to this paper, co-authored with me related papers [4, 87, 89-90], and helped with the *VolVis* software. (*VolVis* can be obtained by sending email to: volvis@cs.sunysb.edu.) This work has been supported by the National Science Foundation under grant MIP-9527694 and a grant from the Office of Naval Research N000149710402. The MRI head data in Figure 1.5 is courtesy of Siemens Medical Systems, Inc., Iselin, NJ. Figure 1.2 is courtesy of Hughes Aircraft Company, Long Beach, CA. This image has been voxelised using voxelisation algorithms, a voxel-based modeller, and a photo-mapper developed at Stony Brook Visualization Lab.

References

1. Kaufman A. Volume Visualization. IEEE Computer Society Press Tutorial, Los Alamitos, CA, 1991.
2. Kaufman A. Volume visualization. ACM Computing Surveys, 1996; 28(1):165-167.
4. Kaufman A, Cohen D, Yagel R. Volume graphics. IEEE Computer, 1993; 26(7): 51-64. Also in Japanese, Nikkei Computer Graphics, 1994; 1(88):148-155 and 2(89):130-137.
3. Kaufman A. Volume visualization. In: Tucker A (ed), Handbook of Computer Science and Engineering, CRC Press, 1996.
5. Speray D, Kennon S. Volume probes: Interactive data exploration on arbitrary grids. ACM/SIGGRAPH Computer Graphics, 1990; 24(5):5-12.
6. Cline HE, Lorensen WE, Ludke S, Crawford CR, Teeter BC. Two algorithms for the three dimensional reconstruction of tomograms. Medical Physics, 1988; 15(3):320-327.
7. Lorensen WE, Cline HE. Marching cubes: A high resolution 3D surface construction algorithm. ACM/SIGGRAPH Computer Graphics, 1987; 21(4):163-170.
8. Drebin RA, Carpenter L, Hanrahan P. Volume rendering. ACM/SIGGRAPH Computer Graphics, 1988; 22(4):65-74.
9. Levoy M. Display of surfaces from volume data. IEEE Computer Graphics and Applications, 1988; 8(5): 29-37.
10. Sabella P. A rendering algorithm for visualizing 3D scalar fields. ACM/SIGGRAPH Computer Graphics, 1988; 22(4):160-165.
11. Upson C, Keeler M. V-BUFFER: Visible volume rendering. ACM/SIGGRAPH Computer Graphics, 1988; 22(4):59-64.
12. Westover L. Footprint evaluation for volume rendering. ACM/SIGGRAPH Computer Graphics, 1990; 24(4):144-153.
13. Cohen D, Kaufman A. Scan conversion algorithms for linear and quadratic objects in volume visualization, In: Kaufman A (ed), IEEE Computer Society

Press, Los Alamitos, CA, 1991; 280-301.

14. Kaufman A, Shimony E. 3D scan-conversion algorithms for voxel-based graphics. In: Proc. ACM Workshop on Interactive 3D Graphics, Chapel Hill, NC, October 1986; 45-76.

15. Kaufman A. An algorithm for 3D scan-conversion of polygons. In: Proc. Eurographics '87, Amsterdam, Netherlands, August 1987; 197-208.

16. Kaufman A. Efficient algorithms for 3D scan-conversion of parametric curves, surfaces, and volumes. ACM/SIGGRAPH Computer Graphics, 1987; 21(4):171-179.

17. Sramek M, Kaufman A. Object voxelization by filtering. In: Proc. ACM/IEEE Volume Visualization '98 Symposium, October 1998; 111-118.

18. Wang S, Kaufman A. Volume sampled voxelization of geometric primitives. In Proc. IEEE Visualization '93, San Jose, CA, October 1993; 78-84.

19. Norton VA. Generation and rendering of geometric fractals in 3-D. ACM/SIGGRAPH Computer Graphics, 1982; 16(3):61-67.

20. Perlin K, Hoffert EM. Hypertexture. ACM/SIGGRAPH Computer Graphics, 1989; 23(3):253-262.

21. Kajiya JT, Kay TL. Rendering fur with three dimensional textures. ACM/SIGGRAPH Computer Graphics, 1989; 23(3):271-280.

22. Ebert DS, Parent RE. Rendering and animation of gaseous phenomena by combining fast volume and scanline A-buffer techniques. ACM/SIGGRAPH Computer Graphics, 1995; 24(4):173-182.

23. Snyder JM, Barr AH. Ray tracing complex models containing surface tessellations. ACM/SIGGRAPH Computer Graphics, 1987; 21(4):119-128.

24. Cohen D, Shaked A. Photo-realistic imaging of digital terrain. Computer Graphics Forum 1993; 12(3):363-374.

25. Wan M, Qu H, Kaufman A. Virtual flythrough over a voxel-based terrain. In: Proc. IEEE Virtual Reality Conference, March 1999; 53-60.

26. Wright J, Hsieh J. A voxel-based, forward projection algorithm for rendering surface and volumetric data. In: Proc. IEEE Visualization '92, Boston, MA, October 1992; 340-348.

27. Kaufman A, Yagel R, Cohen D. Intermixing surface and volume rendering. In: Hoehne KH, Fuchs H, Pizer SM (eds), 3D Imaging in Medicine: Algorithms, Systems, Applications, June 1990; 217-227.

28. Cohen-Or D, Kaufman A. Fundamentals of surface voxelization. CVGIP Graphics Models and Imaging Processing, 1995; 56(6):453-461.

29. Glassner AS. Space subdivision for fast ray tracing. IEEE Computer Graphics and Applications, 1984; 4(10):15-22.

30. Lee YT, Requicha AAG. Algorithms for computing the volume and other integral properties of solids: (I) known methods and open issues; (II) a family of algorithms based on representation conversion and cellular approximation. Communications of the ACM, 1982; 25(9):635-650.

31. Danielsson PE. Incremental curve generation. IEEE Transactions on Computers, 1970; C-19:783-793.

32. Mokrzycki W. Algorithms of discretization of algebraic spatial curves on homogeneous cubical grids. ACM/SIGGRAPH Computers and Graphics, 1988;

12(3/4):477-487.

33. Cohen-Or D, Kaufman A. 3D line voxelization and connectivity control. IEEE Computer Graphics and Applications, 1997; 17(6):80-87.

34. Dachille F, Kaufman A. Incremental Triangle Voxelization. Technical Report 99.xx.xx, Computer Science, SUNY Stony Brook, 1999.

35. Wang S, Kaufman A. 3D Antialiasing. Technical Report 94.01.03, Computer Science, SUNY Stony Brook, January 1994.

36. Wang S, Kaufman A. Volume-sampled 3D modelling. IEEE Computer Graphics and Applications, 1994; 14(5):26-32.

37. Sramek M, Kaufman A. Alias-free voxelization of geometric Objects. IEEE Transactions on Visualization and Computer Graphics, 1999.

38. Jones MW. The production of volume data from triangular meshes using voxelisation. Computer Graphics Forum, 1996; 14(5):311-318.

39. Sramek M. Visualization of volumetric data by ray tracing. In: Proc. Symposium on Volume Visualization, Austria, 1998.

40. Hart JC, Sandin DJ, Kauffman LH. Ray tracing deterministic 3-D fractals. ACM/SIGGRAPH Computer Graphics, 1989; 23(3):289-296.

41. Eck M, DeRose T, Duchamp T, Hoppe H, Lounsbery M, Stuetzle W. Multiresolution analysis of arbitrary meshes. In: Proc. SIGGRAPH '95 Conference, August 1995; 173-182.

42. Hoppe H, DeRose T, Duchamp T, McDonald J, Stuetzle W. Mesh optimization. ACM/SIGGRAPH Computer Graphics, 1993; 27(4):19-26.

43. Rossignac J, Borrel P. Multi-resolution 3D approximations for rendering complex scenes. In: Falcidieno B, Kunni TL, (eds), Modeling in Computer Graphics, Springer-Verlag, 1993; 455-465.

44. Schroeder WJ, Zarge JA, Lorensen WE. Decimation of triangle meshes. ACM/SIGGRAPH Computer Graphics, 1992; 26(2):65-70.

45. Turk G. Re-tiling polygonal surfaces. ACM/SIGGRAPH Computer Graphics, 1992; 26(2):55-64.

46. Levoy M, Whitaker R. Gaze-directed volume rendering. ACM/SIGGRAPH Computer Graphics, 1990; 24(2):217-223.

47. Osborne R, Pfister H, Lauer H, McKenzie N, Gibson S, Hiatt W, Ohkami H. EM-Cube: An architecture for low-cost real-time volume rendering. In: Proc. the SIGGRAPH/Eurographics Hardware Workshop, 1997; 131-138.

48. He T, Hong L, Kaufman A, Varshney A, Wang S. Voxel-based object simplification. In: Proc. IEEE Visualization '95, Los Alamitos, CA, October 1995; 296-303.

49. Kaufman A. The voxblt engine: A voxel frame buffer processor. In: Kuijk AAM (ed), Advances in Graphics Hardware III, Springer-Verlag, Berlin, 1992; 85-102.

50. Dubois D, Prade H. Fuzzy Sets and Systems: Theory and Applications. Academic Press, 1980.

51. Goodman JR, Sequin CH. Hypertree: A multiprocessor interconnection topology. IEEE Transactions on Computers, 1981; C-30(12):923-933.

52. Sobierajski L, Kaufman A. Volumetric ray tracing. In: Proc. Volume Visualization Symposium, Washington, DC, October 1994; 11-18.

53. Coquillart S. Extended free-form deformation: Sculpturing tool for 3D geometric

modeling. ACM/SIGGRAPH Computer Graphics, 1990; 24(4):187-196.

54. Sederberg TW, Parry SR. Free-form deformation of solid geometry models. ACM/SIGGRAPH Computer Graphics, 1986; 20(4):151-160.

55. Galyean TA, Hughes JF. Sculpting: An interactive volumetric modeling technique. ACM/SIGGRAPH Computer Graphics, 1991; 25(4):267-274.

56. Wang S, Kaufman A. Volume sculpting. In: Proc. ACM Symposium on Interactive 3D Graphics, Monterey, CA, April 1995; 151-156.

57. Avila R, Sobierajski L, Kaufman A. Towards a comprehensive volume visualization system. In: Proc. IEEE Visualization '92, October 1992; 13-20.

58. Eastman CM. Vector versus raster: A functional comparison of drawing technologies. IEEE Computer Graphics and Applications, 1990; 10(5):68-80.

59. Yagel R, Cohen D, Kaufman A. Normal estimation in 3D discrete space. The Visual Computer, 1992; 278-291.

60. Yagel R, Cohen D, Kaufman A. Discrete ray tracing. IEEE Computer Graphics and Applications, 1992; 12:19-28.

61. Molnar S, Eyles J, Poulton J. PixelFlow: High-speed rendering using image composition. ACM/SIGGRAPH Computer Graphics, 1992; 26(2):231-240.

62. Schroder P, Stoll G. Data parallel volume rendering as line drawing. In: Proc. Workshop on Volume Visualization, Boston, MA, October 1992; 25-32.

63. Silva CT, Kaufman A. Parallel performance measure for volume ray casting. In: Proc. IEEE Visualization '94, Washington, DC, October 1994; 196-203.

64. Silva CT, Kaufman A, Pavlakos C. PVR: High-performance volume rendering. IEEE Computational Science and Engineering, 1996 3(4):16-28.

65. Vezina G, Fletcher PA, Robertson PK. Volume rendering on the MasPar MP-1. In: Proc. Workshop on Volume Visualization, Boston, MA, October 1992; 3-8.

66. Yoo TS, Neumann U, Fuchs H, Pizer SM, Cullip T, Rhoades J, Whitaker R. Direct visualization of volume data. IEEE Computer Graphics and Applications, 1992; 12(4):63-71.

67. Goldwasser SM, Reynolds RA, Bapty T, Baraff D, Summers J, Talton DA, Walsh E. Physician's workstation with real-time performance. IEEE Computer Graphics and Applications, 1985; 5(12):44-57.

68. Jackel D. The graphics PARCUM system: A 3D memory based computer architecture for processing and display of solid models. Computer Graphics Forum, 1995, 4:21-32.

69. Kaufman A, Bakalash R. Cube — An architecture based on a 3-D voxel map. In: Earnshaw RA (ed), Theoretical Foundations of Computer Graphics and CAD, Springer-Verlag, 1988; 689-701.

70. Meagher DJ. Applying solids processing methods to medical planning. In: Proc. NCGA'85, Dallas, TX, April 1985; 101-109.

71. Ohashi T, Uchiki T, Tokoro MA. Three-dimensional shaded display method for voxel-based representation. In: Proc. Eurographics '85, Nice, France, September 1985; 221-232.

72. Stytz MR, Frieder G, Frieder O. Three-dimensional medical imaging: Algorithms and computer systems. ACM Computing Surveys, 1991; 421-499.

73. Stytz MR, Frieder O. Computer systems for three-dimensional diagnostic imaging: An examination of the state of the art. Critical Reviews in Biomedical

Engineering, 1991; 1-46.

74. Yagel R, Kaufman A. The Flipping Cube Architecture. Technical Report 91.07.26, Computer Science, SUNY at Stony Brook, July 1991.

75. Hesser J, Maenner R, Knittel G, Strasser W, Pfister H, Kaufman A. Three architectures for volume rendering. Computer Graphics Forum, 1995; 14(3):111-122.

76. Knittel G, Strasser W. A compact volume rendering accelerator. In: Proc. Volume Visualization Symposium, Washington, DC, October 1994; 67-74.

77. Guenther T, Poliwoda C, Reinhard C, Hesser J, Maenner R, Meinzer H, Baur H. VIRIM: A massively parallel processor for real-time volume visualization in medicine. In: Proc. the 9th Eurographics Hardware Workshop, Oslo, Norway, September 1994; 103-108.

78. Kaufman A, Bakalash R. Memory and processing architecture for 3-D voxel-based imagery. IEEE Computer Graphics and Applications, 1988; 8(6):10-23. Also in Japanese, Nikkei Computer Graphics, 1989; 3(30):148-160.

79. Bakalash R, Kaufman A, Pacheco R, Pfister H. An extended volume visualization system for arbitrary parallel projection. In: Proc. the 1992 Eurographics Workshop on Graphics Hardware, Cambridge, UK, September 1992.

80. Pfister H, Wessels F, Kaufman A. Sheared interpolation and gradient estimation for real-time volume rendering. In: Proc. the 9th Eurographics Workshop on Graphics Hardware, Oslo, Norway, September 1994.

81. Pfister H, Kaufman A, Chiueh T. Cube-3: A real-time architecture for high-resolution volume visualization. In: Proc. Volume Visualization Symposium, Washington, DC, October 1994; 75-82.

82. Pfister H, Wessels F, Kaufman A. Sheared interpolation and gradient estimation for real-time volume rendering. ACM/SIGGRAPH Computers and Graphics, 1995; 19(5):667-677.

83. Kanus U, Meissner M, Strasser W, Pfister H, Kaufman A, Amerson R, Carter RJ, Culbertson B, Kuekes P, Snider G. Implementations of Cube-4 on the teramac custom computing machine. Computers and Graphics, 1997; 21(2).

84. Pfister H, Kaufman A, Wessels F. Towards a scalable architecture for real-time volume rendering. In: Proc. the 10th Eurographics Workshop on Graphics Hardware, Maastricht, The Netherlands, August 1995.

85. Pfister H, Kaufman A. Cube-4: A scalable architecture for real-time volume rendering. In: Volume Visualization Symposium, San Francisco, CA, October 1996; 47-54.

86. Pfister H, Hardenbergh J, Knittel J, Lauer H, Seiler L. The VolumePro real-time ray-casting system, In: Proc. SIGGRAPH'99, August 1999.

87. Avila R, He T, Hong L, Kaufman A, Pfister H, Silva C, Sobierajski L, Wang S. VolVis: A diversified volume visualization system. In: Proc. IEEE Visualization '94, Washington, DC October 1994; 31-38.

88. Kaufman A, Yagel R, Cohen D. Modelling in volume graphics. In: Falcidieno B, Kunii TL (eds), Modeling in Computer Graphics, Springer Verlag, June 1993; 441-454.

89. Kaufman A, Sobierajski L. Continuum volume display. In: Gallagher RS (ed), Computer Visualization, CRC Press, Boca Raton, FL, 1994; 171-202.

2. Volume Modelling

Gregory M. Nielson

2.1 Introduction

This chapter will present an overview of the emerging research area of *volume modelling*. To date, there has been considerable research on the development of techniques for visualising volume data, but very little on modelling volume data. This is somewhat surprising since the potential benefits of volume models are tremendous. This situation is explained by the fact that volume data is relatively new and researchers have spent their efforts in figuring out ways to "look" at the data and have not been able to afford the resources needed to develop methods for modelling volume data. In addition to providing a means for visualising volume data, some of the benefits of a volume model are the generation of hierarchical and multi-resolution models which are extremely useful for the efficient analysis, visualisation, transmission, and archiving of volume data. In addition, the volume model can serve as the mathematical foundation for subsequent engineering simulations and analysis required for design and fabrication.

While interest is steadily growing, the area of volume modelling is still in its infancy and currently there are few techniques and little expertise available. In the next section, we give some precise definitions and describe the scope of our vision of volume modelling and generally make an appeal for its development. It is important to realise that practically all visualisation tools require some type of volume model for their application. Sometimes the model is so obvious that we may fail to notice it. (For example, the linear interpolation into voxels used by the standard marching cubes algorithm.) Many of the relatively simple modelling techniques used for the more popular visualisation tools of today do not apply or scale up to the datasets currently of interest. These datasets require much more sophisticated modelling techniques. Another barrier to analysing volume datasets is the fact that they are often large and, because of this, they are normally associated with complex and complicated phenomena. Multi-resolution models can be helpful in this regard. Wavelet models (and the concepts related to wavelet models) have traditionally been targeted at compression, but they can also form the basis for analysis tools that allow for removal of clutter and detail and assist in efficient browsing and zooming. In the third section of this chapter, we will discuss some research issues in representing volume models.

We think that it would benefit our readers if we were to be clear about some commonly-used terminology in this area:

- *Volume Visualisation.* We use this as the umbrella term. It encompasses all aspects of analysing and visualising volume data and models.
- *Volume Graphics.* This topic deals with the issues of producing the images associated with volume visualisation. It is analogous to the traditional polygon graphics. It includes viewing models, illumination models, and scan-conversion algorithms and related issues required for the creation of images. A more comprehensive definition can be found in [1].
- *Volume Rendering.* While this term appears somewhat generic, over the years it has become associated with that particular method of rendering a volume model which is based upon a certain model of transparency (called the volume rendering integral). We use it in this context.
- *Volume Modelling.* This is the topic of this chapter. Our purpose is to define this topic more precisely and to make a general appeal for its development and growth.

2.2 Definition and Scope of Volume Modelling

In this section, we take three possible approaches to a definition of volume modelling: (1) a volume model can be viewed as the process of modelling volume data; (2) it can be thought of as a generalisation in dimension to surface modelling; (3) it can be viewed as the means to provide the input to the volume rendering integral. In the following subsections, we expand on each of these approaches.

2.2.1 Definition by Modelling of Volume Data

Volume scanning devices produce a value of a dependent quantity at various locations in space. Examples are widespread, and include:

1. The results of MRI and CAT scanners in the medical field;
2. Measurements of mineral concentration from core samples scattered over some typography;
3. Results of a 3D, CFD simulation; and
4. Free-hand ultrasound where a 3D position/orientation sensor is attached to an ultrasound probe.

What is common here is that each sample of the data consists of a position in space and the measurement or computation of an associated dependent variable. Invoking mathematical means of modelling and representing this type of data is one definition of volume modelling. Volume data does not need to have just a single scalar dependent variable. In fact, some volume data has a dependent variable in the form of a vector. This is the case for CFD simulations., where the dependent data may consist of a single scalar (pressure) and a vector (velocity of the flow).

In this subsection, we describe four examples of volume datasets. Each requires some type of volume model before a visualisation tool can be applied. For some of the datasets, adequate volume models are not currently available.

Rectilinear, Cartesian Grids from Medical Scanners

This is an example of the most conventional type of data we see in volume visualisation. It represents the results of some scanning device (such as MRI or CAT) and can be viewed as measurements on a Cartesian grid. Because of this, the domain is implied and so a simple three-dimensional array of dependent values, $d_{ijk}, i = 1, \cdots, N_x, j = 1, \cdots, N_y, k = 1, \cdots, N_z$, can be used to represent the data. The images of Figure 2.1 show isosurfaces which have been extracted from a type of wavelet model applied to this type of data.

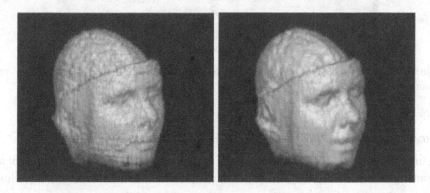

Figure 2.1. Examples of isosurfaces extracted from a volume model called Blend of Linear and Constant (BLaC) wavelets. The left image is based upon $\Delta = 0.0$ and the right, $\Delta = 0.43$.

Seismic Data Samples in Geophysical Studies

This data is typical of measured data extracted from core samples which are taken at scattered locations, as shown in Figure 2.2. The measurements within core samples are not necessarily at uniform depths and can vary from one core sample to the next. Mathematically, we can represent this data as:

$$(X_i, Y_i, Z_{i_j}; M_{i_j}), i = 1, \cdots, N; i_j = 1, \cdots, N_i.$$

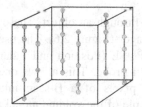

Location (X, Y, Z)			Mineral
5.50	1.00	0.00	11.0
5.50	1.00	10.00	10.0
...	...	...	...
...	...	...	...
...	...	...	...

Figure 2.2. Diagram depicting core samples.

In Figure 2.3, we show a snapshot of an interactive tool for interrogating this type of data. Colour contours are shown at a user specified height. Any number of these can exist and they can be moved up and down. It is clear that this type of visualisation or any other would not be possible without a volume model.

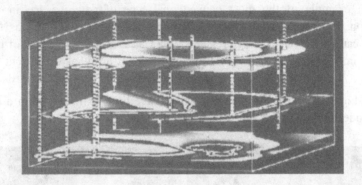

Figure 2.3. Screen snapshot of an interactive tool for visualising model of core sample data. (Courtesy of David Kao).

Curvilinear Grids from Computational Fluid Dynamics Simulations

A time-dependent, 3D curvilinear grid is described by three, four-dimensional geometry arrays, $(X_{ijk\ell}, Y_{ijk\ell}, Z_{ijk\ell})$ which provide the vertices for a cellular decomposition of the domain of interest for each time step, t_ℓ (Figures 2.4 and 2.5). The numerical simulation provides the solution to the Navier/Stokes equations at these vertices. This information is provided by four additional arrays $(P_{ijk\ell}, U_{ijk\ell}, V_{ijk\ell}, W_{ijk\ell})$, where $P_{ijk\ell}$ is a scalar representing pressure and $(U_{ijk\ell}, V_{ijk\ell}, W_{ijk\ell})$ is the velocity at vertex $(X_{ijk\ell}, Y_{ijk\ell}, Z_{ijk\ell})$ at time step t_ℓ. Typical spatial resolutions of interest and value today range from 10^2 to 10^3. For efficiency, time-dependent grids are often partitioned into blocks with vertices of some blocks moving over time and others being stationary. For example, the V-22 Tiltrotor dataset [2] consists of 26 blocks, of which 9 are time dependent and the remaining ones are steady. For this dataset there are 1,400 time steps each consisting of about 100 MB of data.

Free-Hand Ultrasound Data

A typical ultrasound probe produces a "slice" of data through an object. These are called B-scans and are viewed and manipulated as images (Figure 2.6). The use of the phrase "free-hand" means the addition of a 3D POSE (Position and Eularian angles) sensor attached to the conventional ultrasound probe. This allows one to associate a position in 3D space for each of the pixels of a B-scan image. Mathematically, we can then view each pixel as a sample of the volume model and represent it as $(x_i, y_i, z_i; d_i)$, $i = 1, \cdots, N$.

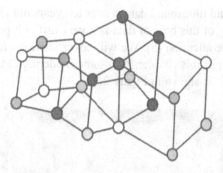

Figure 2.4. A diagram illustrating a 3D curvilinear grid.

Figure 2.5. Curvilinear grid on the left and resampled rectilinear grid on the right.

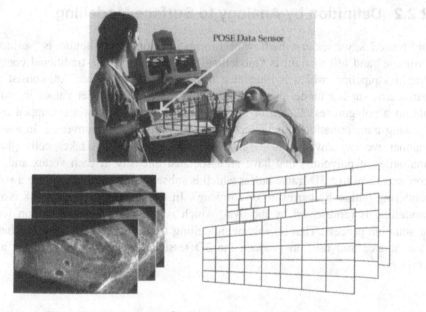

POSE Data Sensor

Figure 2.6. The process of collecting free-hand ultrasound data.

The idea of free-hand ultrasound data is over ten years old [3-4], but the effective and efficient modelling of this type of data is a very difficult problem which is only recently receiving some attention [5]. We will cover some exciting new work in this area in the next section of this chapter. A volume rendering (MIP) based upon these new progressive models is shown in Figure 2.7.

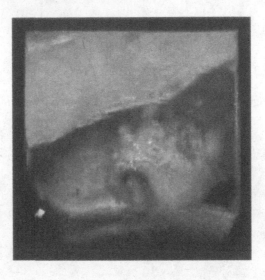

Figure 2.7. A snapshot from an interactive viewing of a progressive volume model (discussed in the next section) of ultrasound data. (Data is courtesy of Bill Lorensen.)

2.2.2 Definition by Analogy to Surface Modelling

In Figure 2.8, we see that the flow of information from top to bottom is "surface" to "volume" and left to right is "modelling" to "graphics". The traditional computer graphics pipeline, which is illustrated in the top half of Figure 2.8, consists of a parametric surface model that is evaluated at a set of parameter values in order to obtain a polygon tessellation or approximation. The polygons are mapped by the viewing transformation to device coordinates and then scan-converted. In a similar manner we can envision a "volume graphics" system that takes cells (the 3D analogues of polygons) that have an associated intensity at each vertex and scan-converts them to a 3D frame buffer which is subsequently used to produce a volume rendering (either by hardware or software). In the diagram of Figure 2.8, volume modelling is represented by the oval, which is providing the information for the tessellation process. That is, volume modelling from this point of view is whatever is evaluated and used to produce the 3D tessellation with density values at the vertices.

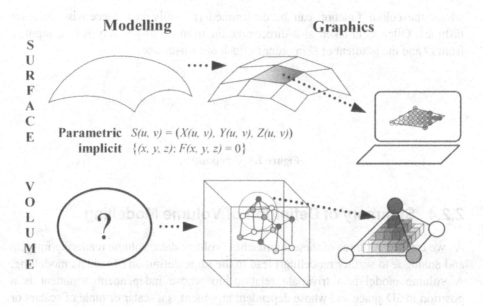

Figure 2.8. Diagram depicting the analogy between surface modelling and volume modelling.

2.2.3 Definition by Input to the Volume Rendering Equation

Ray cast volume rendering images are based upon a compositing process. Given a sorted collection of objects, which emit C_i and have transparency τ_i, we compute the observed intensity by applying a very simple model of transparency and successively computing: $F_i = (1 - \tau_i)C_i + \tau_i F_{i-1}$ (Figure 2.9). A standard limiting process on this discrete compositing leads to the volume rendering integral:

$$F(x) = \int_{x_0}^{x} \delta(s)C(s)e^{-\int_{s}^{x}\delta(t)dt}\,ds$$

where the density and the transparency are related as $\tau(x_0, x) = e^{-\int_{x_0}^{x}\delta(u)de}$. From this point of view, in order to produce a volume rendering we need a trivariate density function, δ, and a trivariate colour function C. The mathematical model from which these two trivariate functions are obtained is called a volume model. In many applications, one data function D leads to both of these. A transfer operator (function) is applied to D to yield δ. One can use the choice of this transfer function to make certain values opaque and visible and other ranges transparent. If additional attributes are known, or if information is known about the location of objects, then it may also be possible to define the colour function C. This is related to the very difficult problem of segmenting the data into different classes of materials from which the colour function can be determined (possibly in a piece-wise constant fashion). Often C is taken as a direct relation from D, or possibly it is computed from D and the gradient of D in order to flush out isosurfaces.

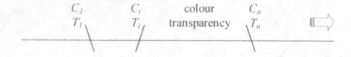

$$C_1 \qquad C_i \qquad \text{colour} \qquad C_n$$
$$T_1 \qquad T_i \qquad \text{transparency} \qquad T_n$$

Figure 2.9. Compositing.

2.2.4 Summary of Definition of Volume Modelling

As we can see, all three of these approaches (volume data, volume rendering integral and analogue to surface modelling) lead to the same definition of volume modelling. A volume model is a trivariate relationship whose independent argument is a position in 3D space and whose dependent argument is a scalar or tuple of scalars or even a vector. The volume model might also have the aspect of varying over time.

Before we leave this section, we should mention some concepts with similar terminology, which are not volume models. Even though it is an important part of certain algorithms in volume graphics, the problem of scan-converting lines, curves, surfaces or solids into discrete voxels [6-7] is not the process of volume modelling. Nor is a model of a volume (Figure 2.10), as, for example, described by the methods of CSG (constructive solid geometry). It is a region of space. For the same reasons

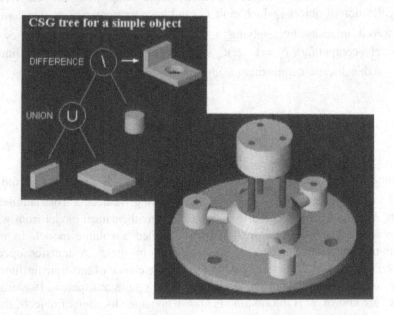

Figure 2.10. A model of a volume is not a volume model

that a collection of pixels is not a curve (Figure 2.11) and a cloud of points is not a surface (Figure 2.12), a collection of voxels or tetrahedra (Figure 2.13) is not a volume model. It is a spatial enumeration and is missing the important component of a relationship possessed by a volume model. On the other hand, we can make the following observation: just as it is possible (though not necessarily easy) to parameterise and fit a collection of points to a curve and just as it possible (but even more difficult) to parameterise a cloud of unorganised points to a surface, it is possible to construct a volume model based upon discrete voxels and points.

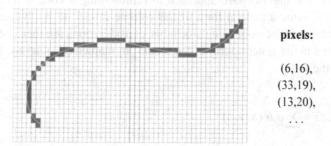

pixels:

(6,16),
(33,19),
(13,20),
...

Figure 2.11. A collection of pixels is not a curve, but it may lead to one when an ordering and other implications are added.

Figure 2.12. A collection of points is not a surface, but it may lead to one when the topology of a triangulation is added. (Images courtesy of UNI-KL.)

Figure 2.13. A collection of voxels is not a volume model. It is a voxelised volume that serves as a means to describe a region of 3D space (see also Sections 1.3 and 1.5). (The left image is courtesy of Arie Kaufman and the right image shows a Lego© model.)

2.3 Research Issues in Representing Volume Models

In this section, we cover a sampling of methods for representing volume models along with some research issues for each of these methods.

Basis Functions

This is the most straightforward approach to representing a volume model. In this approach, we assume a general form of the volume model. It involves coefficients and basis functions. The volume data or other considerations are then used to select the coefficients in the generic form of the model. In mathematical terms, the volume model takes the form:

$$VM(x,y,z) = \sum_{i=1}^{N} a_i b_i(x,y,z) \qquad (2.1)$$

where $b_i(x,y,z)$, $i = 1, \cdots, N$ denote the basis functions and the unknown coefficients are a_i, $i = 1, \cdots, N$. This type of volume model is often used in a visualisation tool even though the form of volume model may not be completely apparent. For example, with the marching cubes algorithm piece-wise linear interpolation into voxels is used. This is equivalent to using a volume model of the form given in Equation 2.1 where the basis functions are the 3D versions of the "hat" functions based upon a Cartesian grid. Viewing the modelling process this way opens up the possibility of using many other, possibly more efficient, basis functions.

Research Issues: The research question for a particular application then becomes how to select the basis functions and then how to select the method of computing the coefficients of the volume model. Ideas about choices for basis functions come from generalising useful and successful basis functions for lower dimension problems. For example, splines have served the surface modelling community very well. So then the question arises as to what are the proper basis functions for a spline volume model. Some suggestions and comparisons are discussed in [8]. Issues as to whether interpolation or approximation is most appropriate must be addressed. Also, should the basis functions have local or global support? Are there numerical condition problems in the computation of the coefficients? What type of basis functions will allow interactive speeds?   □

Mathematical Modelling

Prior to describing this method of representing volume models, let us first establish a context by mentioning a few simple things about mathematical/physical modelling. One of the first uses of mathematical modelling, that we all see, are the equations for a pendulum introduced in a beginners physics course. If $\Theta(t)$ represents the angle of deflection at time t, then Newton's second law takes the form $\dfrac{d^2\Theta}{dt^2} = \dfrac{-g}{L}\sin(\Theta)$

where g is the gravitational constant and L is the length of the pendulum. To completely determine the solution, the initial conditions $\Theta(0) = \Theta_0$ and $\dfrac{d\Theta}{dt}(0) = \Theta_0'$ must be provided. Even though these equations uniquely determine the solution, there is not a simple formula for $\Theta(t)$. A solution usually requires infinite expansions or numerical techniques.

For CFD (computational fluid dynamics) studies, the Navier/Stokes equations characterise the volume model as the solution of a second-order PDE:

$$r\left(\frac{\partial V}{\partial t} + (V * \nabla)V\right) = \nabla p + m\nabla^2 V + F \tag{2.2}$$

where $V = (u, v, w) = (u(x, y, z), v(x, y, z), w(x, y, z))$ represents the velocity vector and $p = p(x,y,z)$ is a scalar valued function representing pressure. The scalar constant r is fluid density, and m is the dynamic viscosity. The external forces are $F = (X, Y, Z)$. As with the pendulum problem, a solution of Equation 2.2 for V and p requires some type of approximation or numerical technique. This is where curvilinear grids come into play. They are often used for the numerical solutions of the PDE's that characterise a volume model. Either they serve as a cellular decomposition for a finite element approach to a solution or they are used in the finite difference approach where partial derivatives are replaced with discrete approximations. In either case, a solution to the volume model is computed at each of the nodes of the curvilinear grid. Later, this data is passed along for post visualisation and analysis. What is often not passed along is the method of solution. Most data visualisation/analysis tools require that the discrete data be modelled or interpolated in some manner. Quite often, the simplest or most readily available method is used for this purpose whether or not it has anything to do with the underlying volume model. This is an unfortunate situation which is likely to change as the scientists themselves are getting more and more involved in the analysis and visualisation of their data and as the general level of knowledge and mathematical sophistication is increasing in the area of volume visualisation.

Research Issues: Can the mathematical model be "attached" to the simulated data? Can the mathematical model be applied locally? In a multi-resolution manner? How much error is associated with each approach?   □

Deformations

In a nutshell, the basic idea here is described as follows: we start with a generic model which has an associated classification function and morph this generic model to a particular model inferred by the collected data. This is done with the use of function norms and a minimisation strategy. The classification function for the particular data is now obtained by composing the morphing function and the generic classification function.

A 3D morph can be accomplished with a trivariate map:

$$
\begin{pmatrix} X_p \\ Y_p \\ Z_p \end{pmatrix} = \begin{pmatrix} F_x(X_g,Y_g,Z_g) \\ F_y(X_g,Y_g,Z_g) \\ F_z(X_g,Y_g,Z_g) \end{pmatrix} = \sum \begin{pmatrix} a_i \\ b_i \\ c_i \end{pmatrix} M_i(X_g,Y_g,Z_g)
$$

which maps a portion of 3D space onto itself. It deforms the space. These types of maps have been used for designing objects [9] and animations [10]. The basis functions $M_i(X_g, Y_g, Z_g)$ would usually be polynomial or piece-wise polynomial. The coefficients of the morph $(a_i, b_i, c_i)^t$ may be thought of as control points and the idea is to manipulate these values so as to accomplish the desired end.

And now more details: suppose the generic model has been segmented so that we have a trivariate function $C(x, y, z)$ which represents the colour or classification function. This function tells us what material is located at position (x, y, z). It might be that $C(x, y, z)$ is piece-wise defined (say, over voxels) but its precise type of function is not important in this context. Also associated with this generic model is a data function $d(x, y, z)$. This is to represent, for example, a model obtained from applying our scanning device to the generic model and then fitting this data with a volume model. This function may possibly be obtained by a simulation of a mathematical model of the generic model using $C(x, y, z)$ and the physical properties of the materials that are classified or even scanning a physical phantom model. Both C and d are based upon some type of basis functions and therefore we can represent them as follows:

$$
C(x,y,z) = \sum a_i C_i(x,y,z), \quad d(x,y,z) = \sum a_i d_i(x,y,z).
$$

Next we obtain the scanned data which we represent as $d_p(x, y, z)$ where p is for "particular". What we want is the colour or classification function for this particular data. Let us call it $C_p(x, y, z)$. We first find a morphing function M which maps the generic model into the particular model. This is done on the basis of the scanned data. We choose M so that the function $d(M(x, y, z))$ is close to function $d_p(x, y, z)$. This will require a representation of M in terms of some unknown coefficients and a norm or method of discretely measuring the error between these two functions. This leads to a minimisation problem where the parameters of M are manipulated until the optimal or best-fitting morphing function is obtained. We then take as the classification function for the particular model to be:

$$
C_p(x,y,z) = C(M(x,y,z))
$$

Research Issues: What is the form of the morphing map? Trivariate Bezier? Catmull/Clark solid? Piece-wise linear over tetrahedra? How to incorporate particular data into the computation of the morphing map coefficients? Least squares with cost function? Simulated annealing?   □

Wavelet-Type Multi-Resolution Models

The ideas and concepts of wavelets have their origins in the univariate world of time varying signals [11-12]. Many of the more useful techniques have been extended to certain types of surface models in the past several years [13]. The first use of wavelet techniques for volume data was by Muraki who used tensor product techniques to obtain wavelet models for MRI data. In [14] he discussed the application of Batelle-Lamarie wavelets and later [15] he compared these results to those of the DOG wavelets (difference of Gaussian). While tensor product methods afford a relatively easy way to extend the original univariate wavelet models to 3D data, they are often not suitable for certain applications and types of volume data. This includes the volumetric curvilinear grids of CFD data, as we will explain later in this section.

Wavelet expansions are often based upon basis functions with different resolutions and within each of these resolutions there are basis functions with different regions of support. This yields two views of the wavelet expansion and allows for two very useful types of reconstructions. We can pick out the resolution of interest and approximate with only these basis functions. This would allow, for example, the elimination of noise or clutter in order to visualise an overview or trend in some data. We can pick a region of interest and only use the basis functions that have support (non-zero values) in this region. This allows for efficient means to zoom in and out for browsing.

$$F(x) = \sum a_i L_i(x) + \sum b_i M_i(x) + \sum c_i H_i(x) = \sum_{regn\,1} \alpha_{1i} R_{1i}(x) + \cdots + \sum_{regn\,N} \alpha_{Ni} R_{Ni}(x)$$

     low   medium   high

Both of the properties of compact support and orthogonality are important to the successful application of wavelets. Unfortunately if we also impose symmetry then we are frustrated in our attempts to define piece-wise linear (polynomial in general) wavelets. A recently developed wavelet [16] overcomes this obstacle with a technique for blending the piece-wise constant and piece-wise linear wavelets. There is a parameter, Δ, which allows the user to emphasise the compact support properties of the Haar wavelet or to emphasise the higher-order approximations possible with a piece-wise linear wavelet.

We now turn our attention to wavelets for curvilinear grids. Recently, we published some results on the development of wavelets for 2D curvilinear grids in [17]. We are currently working on extending these techniques to 3D. In this work, the nested wavelet spaces are defined in a piece-wise manner over nested cellular decompositions. One important constraint that we imposed on this cellular decomposition was that the original inner boundary must persist at all levels. This constraint added considerable complexity to the models and subsequent algorithms but, without it, we felt that the application of the wavelets would suffer. One of the reasons for this is the fact that much of the activity of the flow takes place near the inner boundary and a degradation of this representation at low resolutions would deter the possibility to analyse the flow. We opted for a knot removal approach for building the nested cellular decomposition. We will report on this work in the near future.

Research Issues: How to define wavelet volume models for the types of grids and datasets of interest in volume visualisation today? For example, 3D, time-dependent curvilinear grids, tetrahedral decompositions, spherical curvilinear grids, free-hand ultrasound data and, in general, scattered volume data. How important is the trade-off between orthogonality and local support for this general application? Are nested spaces critical? Is it better to build multi-resolution models for isosurfaces or the volumes from which they are extracted. Can both be done at the same time?   □

Progressive Volume Models

The basic idea of progressive models can be quickly gleaned from the univariate data example illustrated in Figure 2.14. On the left, the raw data is modelled by a piece-wise linear function in the bottom left graph. Successive local, piece-wise approximations are replaced with more global models leading to the final model in the top left graph. (See [18] for a model of this type applicable to Cartesian grids and [19] for a more general algorithm which was applied to curvilinear grids.) On the right, we start with a global model (linear least squares for example) and examine if it is acceptable or not. If not, then the domain is split, a new piece-wise model is computed and the same acceptability criterion is repeated for the submodels. These are simple, yet powerful, ideas for obtaining models whose complexity and ability to fit conform to the complexity and variability of the data. We feel there is great promise for these ideas in volume models, but it is not a trivial matter to extend these ideas to 3D.

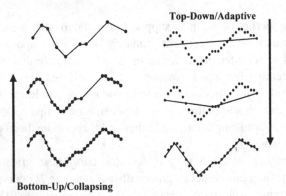

Figure 2.14. The univariate example illustrates the basic ideas of two approaches to progressive models. Volume modelling is interested in these concepts extended to 3D.

In addition to the oracle (the general collapsing or subdivision decision-making process) there is the requirement of an effective and useful means of actually doing the subdivision and collapsing. A general approach to solving the problem is to think up something for 2D and then try to generalise it to 3D. The simplest and most robust cells are triangles in 2D and tetrahedra in 3D. (See [20] for basic algorithms and data structures for triangles and tetrahedra.) The basic problem with building meshes that are coarse in one region and fine in another is the avoidance of the so-called "cracking problem". We mention three approaches (Figure 2.15). The method of Maubach [21] performs a local subdivision and repairs the crack by propagating this split out through the mesh. The method of Bey [22] has been used in FEM [23] and a variation has been discussed and used for volume models by Grosso et al. [24]. It uses a combination of two types of subdivisions to avoid cracks and poorly-shaped tetrahedra. A new approach is based upon not worrying about the crack, but rather using a Coons patch local model that covers it over [25-26]. Each of these approaches has it own set of research issues that must be worked out before the methods become viable, but each shows promise.

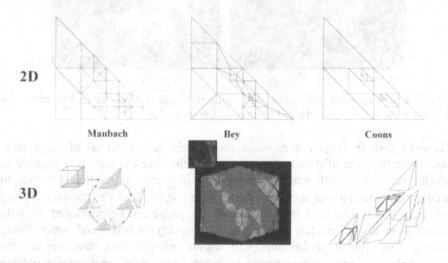

Figure 2.15. Three different approaches to the cellular decomposition for progressive models which avoid the cracking problem. (The 2D is shown only for illustration purposes. Volume modelling is concerned with the 3D case.)

We now describe some current research results in this area. They are rather exciting. In Figure 2.16, samples of some free-hand ultrasound data are shown. This data was collected in the neck region and includes portions of the carotid artery and the thyroid gland. The complete set of data consists of approximately a million data points. It is noisy (due to the ultrasound sensors) and it is redundant due to the overlaps caused by the free-hand method of collection. A typical tetrahedral mesh resulting from the adaptive method of fitting is shown in the right-hand image of Figure 2.16. Note that the tetrahedra are much smaller and denser in the regions where the data is more dense and exhibit greater variation. This shows the ability of the model to conform to the complexity of the data. In Figure 2.17, we show the results of a very low resolution model. The left image of Figure 2.17 shows 5 B-scans of the original data and a "floating window" reconstructed from the volume model. On the right the same five data B-scans are shown alongside their corresponding approximations. Also the reconstruction of the "floating window" is shown on the right. Figure 2.18 shows a higher resolution model. The results are impressive in light of the number of vertices and the detail that is present in the approximations. A different and quite interesting way to compare the approximation is shown in Figure 2.19 and due to the existence of the volume model, tools such as that shown in Figure 2.20 are possible. Figure 2.7 is also based upon the volume modelling techniques we have just described.

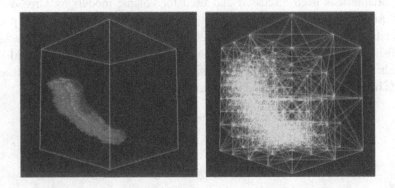

Figure 2.16. Free-hand ultrasound data collection and typical tetrahedral mesh for progressive model. (Data courtesy of Cambridge University.)

Research Issues: These results show the promise and potential of progressive models for this type of data and for this reason they are exciting. Is it possible to develop very fast and efficient algorithms that will operate in real-time? Imagine an environment where a user sees the results of the volume model as the data is being collected. If a region is of special concern, the probe can be positioned so as to collect more and more data in this region resulting in better and better fitting models. This type of performance will require efficient data structures for the tetrahedralisation and efficient means to compute the coefficients of the volume model. What is the best subdivision strategy? The results we just described (Figures 2.7, 2.17-2.21) are based upon a particular 3D version of the Maubach algorithm [21]. We previously mentioned two other possibilities: (1) the red/green strategy of Bey [22] and Banks [23]; and (2) the idea of using triangular Coons patches. Are there others, and what special properties do they have? What is the best oracle or fitting strategy? Top-Down/Adaptive or Bottom-Up/Collapsing? Within either general strategy there are choices to be made. For example, how do you decide which cells to split or collapse? For some splitting strategies and applications, it may be advantageous to go very deep and for others there are reasons for keeping the overall meshing more uniform and shallow. The results reported here use a piecewise linear model. Is it worth it to use higher-order functions? Second order, for example? We suspect that the savings in the total number of tetrahedra will indicate that this is a wise decision for some applications.   □

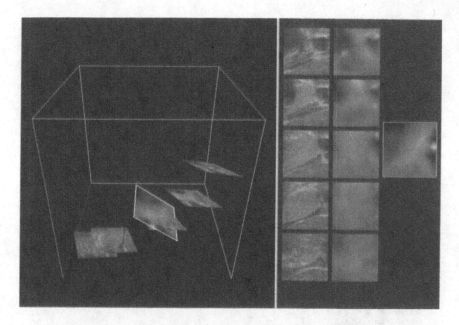

Figure 2.17. Results from progressive fit with a fairly large RMS error of 17.3 with only 909 vertices (approximately 1000 to 1 reduction).

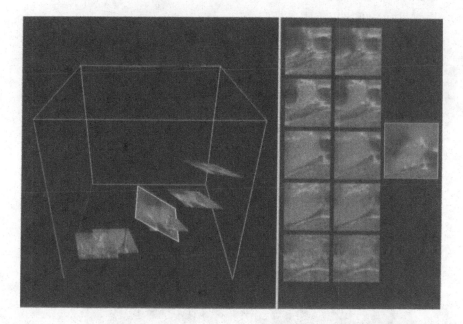

Figure 2.18. The same information as in the previous figure, but the RMS is 9.94 and the number of vertices is 53,995 (approximately a 20 to 1 reduction). The quality of the reconstructed images is excellent.

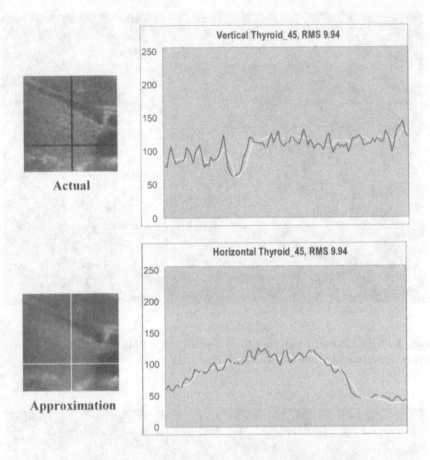

Figure 2.19. Comparison of actual B-scan and approximation.

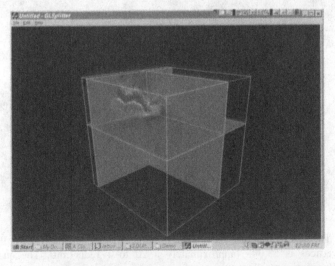

Figure 2.20. Using a slice tool to interactively view a volume model of ultrasound data.

2.4 Conclusions

In this chapter, we have presented a definition of volume modelling, made an appeal for its general development and covered some basic methods of representing volume models. The methods covered are only a sampling. Many techniques have not been covered. For example there have been a number of procedural techniques developed where the primary goal is to generate an image or animation which is acceptable to the viewer. In these applications the picture is the main goal and the volume model is not so important. Fire, gases, clouds, fluids and many other phenomena have been considered. Discussion of these procedural techniques can be found in [27] and the references therein. Also, we did not cover the very interesting, and potentially very useful, topic of layered manufacturing (see Chapter 5). Volume models are needed to drive these new and interesting methods of fabrication, for instance, the use of transfinite deformation maps for describing volume models [28].

References

1. Kaufman K, Cohen D, Yagel R. Volume graphics. IEEE Computer, 1993; 26(7):51-64.
2. Kenwright D, Kao D. Optimization of time-dependent particle tracing using tetrahedral decomposition. In: Proc. IEEE Visualization '95, Atlanta, GA, October 1995; 321-328.
3. Nelson TR. Ultrasound visualization. Advances in Computers, 1998; 47:185-253.
4. Fenster A, Downey DB. 3-D ultrasound imaging — A review. IEEE Engineering in Medicine and Biology Magazine, 1996; 15(6):41-51.
5. Rohling RN, Gee AH, Berman L. Radial Basis Function Interpolation for 3-D Ultrasound. TR 327, Engineering Department, Cambridge University, UK, 1998.
6. Wang SM, Kaufman A. Volume sampled voxelization of geometric primitives. In: Proc. IEEE Symposium on Volume Visualization, Los Alamos, CA, October 1993; 78-84.
7. Wang S, Kaufman A. Volume sculpting. In: Proc. Symposium on Interactive 3D Graphics, April 1995; 151-156.
8. Nielson GM. Scattered data modeling. IEEE Computer Graphics and Applications, 1993; 13(1):60-70.
9. Sederberg T, Parry S. Free-form deformation of solid geometric models. ACM/SIGGRAPH Computer Graphics, 1986, 20(4): 151-160.
10. MacCracken R, Joy K. Free-form deformations with lattices of arbitrary topology. ACM/SIGGRAPH Computer Graphics, 1996; 30(4):181-188.
11. Chui CK. An Introduction to Wavelets. Academic Press, San Diego, CA, 1992.
12. Daubechies I. Ten Lectures on Wavelets. CBMS-NSF Regional Conference Series in Applied Mathematics, 1992; vol. 61, SIAM, Philadelphia, PA, 1992.
13. Stollnitz E, DeRose A, Salesin D. Wavelets for Computer Graphics, Morgan Kaufman, San Francisco, 1996.

14. Muraki S. Volume data and wavelet transforms. IEEE Computer Graphics and Applications, 1993; 13(4): 50-56.

15. Muraki S. Multiscale volume representation by a DoG wavelet. Transactions on Visualization and Computer Graphics, 1995; 1(2):109-116.

16. Bonneau GP, Hahmann S, Nielson GM. BlaC wavelets: A multiresolution analysis with non-nested spaces. In: Proc. IEEE Visualization '96, San Francisco, CA, October 1996; 43-48.

17. Nielson GM, Jung I, Sung J. Wavelets over curvilinear grids. In: Proc. of IEEE Visualization '98, Research Triangle Park, NC, October 1998; 313-317.

18. Zhou Y, Chen B, Kaufman A. Multiresolution Tetrahedral Framework for Visualising Regular Volume Data. In: Proc. IEEE Visualization '97, Phoenix, AZ, October 1997; 135-142.

19. Trotts I, Hamann B, Joy K, Wiley D. Simplification of tetrahedral meshes with error bounds. To appear in IEEE Transactions of Visualization and Computer Graphics, 1999.

20. Nielson GM. Tools for triangulations and tetrahedrizations, In: Nielson, Hagen, Mueller (eds). Scientific Visualization: Surveys, Techniques and Methodologies. IEEE CS Press, 1997; 429-525.

21. Maubach JM. Local bisection refinement for N-simplicial grids generated by reflection. SIAM Journal of Scientific Computing; 16(1):210-227.

22. Bey J. Tetrahedral mesh refinement. Computing, 1995; 55(13):355-378.

23. Bank RE, Sherman AH, Weiser A. Refinement algorithms and data structures for regular local mesh refinement. In: Stepleman R (ed), Scientific Computing, North Holland, Amsterdam, 1983; 3-17.

24. Grosso R, Luerig C, Ertl T. The multilevel finite element method for adaptive mesh optimization and visualization of volume data. In: Proc. IEEE Visualization '97, Phoenix, AZ, October 1997; 387-394.

25. Coon SA. Surfaces for Computer-Aided Design of Space Forms. MIT, MAC TR-41, June 1967.

26. Nielson GM, Holliday D, Rox Roxborough T. Cracking the cracking problem with Coons patches. To appear in: Proc. IEEE Visualization '99, San Fancisco, CA, 1999.

27. Ebert D, Musgrave K, Peachy D, Worley S, Perlin K. Texturing and Modeling: A Procedural Approach. Academic Press, San Diego, CA, 1998.

28. Qian X, Dutta D. Features in layered manufacturing of heterogeneous objects. In: Proc. SFFS '98, Austin, Texas, 1998.

PART II

DISCRETE MODELLING

3. Minimally Thin Discrete Triangulation

Valentin E. Brimkov, Reneta P. Barneva and Philippe Nehlig

3.1 Introduction

The "discrete approach" of volume graphics (that is, the one using internal model, which is a set of voxels) has various advantages over surface graphics [1]. In particular, it is helpful for ensuring the use of exact arithmetic and thus avoiding rounding errors. This may also help to raise significantly the computational efficiency of some computer graphics algorithms, in particular, of the ray-tracing algorithm [2]. Based on a detailed analysis of the matter, Kaufman et al. prognosticated that "... volume graphics will develop into a major trend in computer graphics" [1]. For additional arguments and experience supporting the above thesis, the reader is referred to Chapters 4, 6 and 10.

In recent years, volume graphics has been developed by many authors. One of the main objectives is designing efficient algorithms for discretisation (scan-conversion) of the basic Euclidean primitives (lines, segments, triangles, circles, planes, spheres, etc.) and, on this basis, creating tools for efficient modelling of more sophisticated objects composed by such primitives. In this framework, linear objects, such as lines, planes, or their portions, play a central role. They are of significant practical importance since for various applications it suffices to obtain good polyhedral (usually triangular) approximation to a given real object. Thus, an important task is studying the properties of the above mentioned linear primitives and developing methods for modelling through such primitives. A number of efficient algorithms for discretisation of lines and planar polygons have been designed (e.g. [3–7]). One interesting theoretical issue is to reveal the possibilities for obtaining tunnel-free lines, polygons, or polyhedral surfaces, which are as thin as possible. This may also be interesting from a practical point of view, since the "thin" voxelisation contains less voxels, and the shape of the image is usually good.

A promising approach in volume modelling is one based on *arithmetic discrete geometry*[1]. The main objective here is to obtain a simple analytical description of Euclidean primitives and to develop algorithms for modelling using such primitives. The analytical description of an object allows a very fast (constant time) verification of the membership of a voxel to the object. It also provides a very compact way for encoding an object, which may be useful with regard to image transfer purposes.

---

[1] Sometimes the terms "digital geometry" or "analytic discrete geometry" are used instead.

In recent years, arithmetic geometry has been intensively developed by several authors (see, for example, the bibliography of [8]). This approach is very successful especially when dealing with linear objects. Analytical description and algorithms have been obtained to discretise 2D and 3D straight lines or their segments, as well as Euclidean planes and 3D triangles.

As already mentioned, a challenging task is to obtain tunnel-free triangular mesh discretisation, which is as thin as possible. It has been observed [7, 9–11] that the optimal basis for this seems to be the so-called "naive" planes, which are the thinnest possible discrete planes without holes. However, this idea was recognised as very hard to implement due to some non-trivial obstacles. For example, the intersection of two naive planes does not correspond with the intuitive idea of a line, as it may be a disconnected set of voxels (Figure 3.1) [12]. Therefore, it is difficult to select appropriate naive planes such that the common edge of two adjacent triangles is always tunnel-free. This requirement is very important when the model is rendered through discrete rays, since the penetration of a ray will cause a false hole in the object. In our previous models [11, 13] the interiors of the triangles in a mesh are portions of naive planes and, therefore, they are minimally thin, but it is possible that at certain points the mesh edges are not minimally thin.

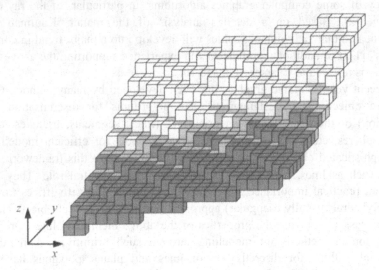

Figure 3.1. The light grey voxels represent the intersection of two naive planes.

Here we cope with the problem by specifying an appropriate subclass of the naive 3D lines, studied in [14]. As a matter of fact, the subclass we use coincides with the generalised (3D) Bresenham lines, which have been algorithmically described in [3]. These lines possess topological properties that let one consider them as the thinnest possible discrete lines. We present an efficient algorithm (with time complexity linear in the number of the voxels generated) to obtain 6-tunnel-free voxelisation of a mesh of triangles. Under this model, a discrete triangle has sides which are naive 3D lines, while the rest of the triangle is a portion of a naive plane, and the obtained voxelisation thus appears to be optimally thin. Both the sides and interiors of the triangles admit an analytical description.

This chapter is organised as follows. In Section 3.2, we formulate some basic notions and facts from discrete geometry. In Section 3.3, we describe an algorithm for discretisation of 3D triangles and triangular meshes. Subsection 3.3.1 offers a description of a triangle's sides, while Subsection 3.3.2 provides a definition of the triangle interior. Algorithm description, discussion on its complexity, comparison to other results, as well as comments about the quality of the obtained image are presented in Subsection 3.3.3. This section also contains a statement of a theorem about the 6-tunnel-freedom of the obtained voxelisation. The proof, which is rather technical, is given separately in Section 3.4. We conclude this chapter with some remarks in Section 3.5.

3.2 Basic Definitions and Facts from Discrete Geometry

In this section, we formulate some basic definitions and facts from discrete geometry, which will be used in the sequel. Most of these notions and properties have been introduced and studied, for instance, in [1, 15–18].

Throughout we use the following standard denotations. $\mathbf{R}$ denotes the set of real numbers, $\mathbf{Z}$ denotes the set of integers, $\mathbf{N}$ denotes the set of natural numbers. $\mathbf{Z}^2 = \{(x, y) \mid x, y \in \mathbf{Z}\}$, $\mathbf{Z}^3 = \{(x, y, z) \mid x, y, z \in \mathbf{Z}\}$. For $a \in \mathbf{R}$, $\lfloor a \rfloor$ denotes the greatest integer not exceeding a. Oxy, Oyz, and Ozx are the coordinate planes in the three-dimensional Cartesian coordinate system. AB denotes the segment with end-points A and B, and $|AB|$ is the length of AB.

A *discrete coordinate plane* consists of unit squares, called *pixels*, centred on the integer points of the two-dimensional Cartesian coordinate system in the plane. *Discrete coordinate space* consists of unit cubes, called *voxels*, centred on the integer points of the three-dimensional Cartesian coordinate system in the space. The position of a pixel (or voxel) is defined by the coordinates of its centre. The edges of a pixel (or voxel) are parallel to the coordinate axes.

Two pixels are *4-adjacent* if they have a common edge. The pixels are *8-adjacent* if they share a vertex or an edge.

A *2D arithmetic line* is a set of pixels $L(a, b, \mu, \omega) = \{(x, y) \in \mathbf{Z}^2 \mid 0 \le ax + by + \mu < \omega\}$, where $a, b, \mu \in \mathbf{Z}$, $\omega \in \mathbf{N}$. ω is called *arithmetical thickness* or *width* of the line, and μ is called *internal translation constant*. An arithmetic line $L(a, b, \mu, \omega)$ is called *8-connected* or *naive* if $\omega = max(|a|, |b|)$.

Any 2D naive line $L = L(a, b, \mu, \omega)$ is *functional* over one of the coordinate axes, i.e., for every fixed x (every fixed y) $\in \mathbf{Z}$ there exists exactly one pixel belonging to L. Clearly, such a property does not hold true for all discrete lines. It is easy to see that the coordinate axis over which an arithmetic line is functional is that one making an angle less than, or equal to, 45 degrees with the slope a/b.

A special case of a naive line, which appears to be the best discrete approximation to the corresponding continuous straight line among the set of all possible naive lines, is the *Bresenham line* [19]. Usually in the literature such lines are described algorithmically, but they also admit an analytical description. Given a Euclidean line $ax + by + c = 0$, the corresponding Bresenham line can be defined as a naive line $L(a, b, c+\lfloor \omega/2 \rfloor, \omega)$, where $\omega = \textit{max}(|a|, |b|)$. We will denote a Bresenham line between two points A and B by $L_B(AB)$. In raster graphics Bresenham lines are widely adopted as a standard tool for line discretisation. They have the following property.

Fact 3.1: The Bresenham line contains only pixels, which are in a "distance", at most 1/2, from the corresponding points of the continuous line. More precisely, let $\mathcal{L}$ be a straight line in the plane, and let L_B be the corresponding Bresenham line. Assume L_B to be functional over the x-axis, and let for some $x \in \mathbf{Z}$, $(x, y) \in L_B$, $(x, y') \in \mathcal{L}$. Then $|y - y'| \le 1/2$.   □

Remark 3.1: While in the continuous case the straight lines $ax + by + c = 0$ and $-ax - by - c = 0$ coincide, in the discrete case there might be an ambiguity: $L(a, b, c+\lfloor \omega/2 \rfloor, \omega)$ coincides with one of the arithmetic lines $L(-a, -b, -c+\lfloor \omega/2 \rfloor, \omega)$ or $L(-a, -b, -c+\lfloor \omega/2 \rfloor -1, \omega)$, which, in general, can be different (e.g. [18]). This means that the line $L_B(AB)$ can differ from $L_B(BA)$. Graphically, if the line is functional over the x-axis, and if for a fixed x two pixels are in a distance 1/2 from the continuous line, then each one of them might belong to the discrete line. For the sake of unambiguity of the definition, we assume throughout that the coefficient a is positive if $|a| > |b|$, otherwise b is positive. Thus, if the line is functional on the x-axis, it contains the pixels with greater y-coordinates.   □

Fact 3.2: Let L_B be a Bresenham line and $\mathcal{L}$ be the corresponding continuous straight line. Let the pixel $p = (x, y) \in L_B$. Then the intersection of $\mathcal{L}$ and p is a segment, and this segment cannot be an edge of p.   □

Similar definitions have been introduced in 3D discrete geometry. Specifically, two voxels are *6-adjacent* if they share a common face. The voxels are *18-adjacent* if they have a common edge or face. They are *26-adjacent* if they have a common vertex, edge, or face. A sequence of voxels is a *k-path* ($k = 6, 18, 26$) if every two consecutive voxels along the sequence are *k*-adjacent. Two voxels are *k*-connected ($k = 6, 18, 26$) if there exists a *k*-path between them. A set of voxels is *connected* if there exists at least a 26-path between every two voxels. Otherwise it is *disconnected*.

An *Arithmetic plane* is a set of voxels $P(a, b, c, \mu, \omega) = \{(x, y, z) \in \mathbf{Z}^3 \mid 0 \le ax + by + cz + \mu < \omega\}$, where $a, b, c, \mu \in \mathbf{Z}$, $\omega \in \mathbf{N}$. ω is the *arithmetical thickness* of the plane and μ is its *internal translation constant*. The vector (a, b, c) is the *normal vector* to the plane.

An arithmetic plane $P(a, b, c, \mu, \omega)$ is called *naive* if $\omega = \textit{max}(|a|, |b|, |c|)$. In this case it is *26-connected*.

An arithmetic plane $P = P(a, b, c, \mu, \omega)$ is *functional* over a coordinate plane, say, Oxy, if for any pixel (x, y) from Oxy there is exactly one voxel belonging to P. The plane Oxy is called a *functional plane* for $P(a, b, c, \mu, \omega)$ and denoted by π_P. Each naive plane is functional over at least one of the coordinate planes Oxy, Oxz, or Oyz. Moreover, if $P(a, b, c, \mu, \omega)$ is a naive plane with $|c| = \boldsymbol{max}(|a|, |b|, |c|)$ then $\pi_P = Oxy$. If $\boldsymbol{max}(|a|, |b|, |c|)$ equals the absolute value of more than one of the coefficients, then the plane P is functional over more than one coordinate plane.

The following plain facts will be used in the proofs of Section 3.4.

Fact 3.3: Given a naive plane P functional over Oxy, the set of all voxels of P for some fixed x (fixed y) is 18-connected. $\square$

Fact 3.4: Given a naive plane P functional over Oxy, and voxels $v_1 = (x_0, y_0, z')$ and $v_2 = (x_0 \pm 1, y_0 \pm 1, z'')$ belonging to P, then $|z' - z''| \in \{0, 1, 2\}$. $\square$

The plane $P(a, b, c, \mu, \omega)$ has k-*tunnel* ($k = 6, 18, 26$) if there exist two k-adjacent voxels $A(x_A, y_A, z_A)$ and $B(x_B, y_B, z_B)$ not belonging to P, such that $ax_A + by_A + cz_A + \mu < 0$ and $ax_B + by_B + cz_B + \mu \geq \omega$. We mention that the naive planes are the thinnest arithmetic planes without 6-tunnels [18].

It is also important to have a more general definition of 6-tunnels, which applies to a finite set of voxels. Such a definition can be given in terms of algebraic topology. Specifically, one can consider a voxel as a closed unit cube centred at a point with integer coordinates in the 3D space. Given a finite set of voxels S, let $\cup S$ denote the polyhedron obtained as a union of the voxels in S. We say that S has 6-*tunnels* if $\cup S$ is not a simply connected set. Otherwise S is 6-*tunnel-free* [11].

3.3 Optimally Thin Triangles and Meshes

In this section we propose a way to obtain voxelisation of Euclidean triangles and, as a consequence, of triangular meshes. Our method applies *mutatis mutandis* to polyhedral surfaces whose faces are arbitrary convex planar polygons. Here we elaborate the case of triangular mesh, since the triangulation of a surface offers some advantages and it is usually employed in practice (for instance, Chapters 4 and 5). We aim to define a discrete triangle possessing good properties. On the one hand, we aspire to obtain a good (possibly the best) approximation to the continuous triangle. On the other hand, we pursue a definition that provides favourable conditions for achieving algorithmical efficiency.

A discrete triangle has sides, which are portions of specific discrete 3D lines defined in the first subsection. The rest of the triangle is a portion of a specific naive plane containing the triangle vertices. It is defined in the second subsection. The third one contains a description of the algorithm, as well as a discussion on its complexity and related topics.

3.3.1 Triangle Sides

In the development of our generation method we will use the class of *naive 3D digital lines* [14]. Such a line is defined as a set of voxels determined by the intersection of two arithmetic planes and satisfying the following two conditions:

a. It is 26-connected;
b. It is minimal in a sense that the removal of any element splits the set into two separate 26-connected components.

It has been shown that if a Euclidean straight line $\mathcal{L}$ in the space is determined by the vector (a, b, c) with $0 \leq a \leq b \leq c$ and passes through the origin of the coordinate system, then the set of voxels (x, y, z) with coordinates:

$$x = \left\lfloor \frac{ai}{c} \right\rfloor, \quad y = \left\lfloor \frac{bi}{c} \right\rfloor, \quad z = i, \quad i \in \mathbf{Z} \tag{3.1}$$

corresponding to the discretisation by truncation of $\mathcal{L}$ is a naive 3D digital line. This set of voxels can be represented as the intersection of two naive planes:

$$\begin{cases} 0 \leq -cx + az + \lambda < c \\ 0 \leq -cy + bz + \mu < c \end{cases}$$

where λ and μ are appropriate translation constants, $0 \leq \lambda, \mu \leq c$.

However, the so defined discrete line may contain voxels not intersected by the corresponding Euclidean line. In our discretisation method we will use a special subclass of naive 3D digital lines, called *regular 3D lines*, and defined as follows:

$$\begin{cases} 0 \leq -cx + az + \left\lfloor \dfrac{c}{2} \right\rfloor < c \\ 0 \leq -cy + bz + \left\lfloor \dfrac{c}{2} \right\rfloor < c \end{cases} \tag{3.2}$$

The regular 3D line relevant to some Euclidean line $\mathcal{L}$ will be denoted by L_R. If $\mathcal{L}$ is determined by two points A and B we will denote the corresponding regular 3D line $L_R(AB)$. An example of a regular 3D line, together with its projections on the coordinate planes, is given in Figure 3.2. This subclass of lines has an important property given by Lemma 3.1, the proof of which is given in Section 3.4.

Lemma 3.1: Let L_R be a regular 3D line corresponding to a Euclidean line $\mathcal{L}$. Then every voxel v of L_R is intersected by $\mathcal{L}$. Furthermore, the intersection $L_R \cap \mathcal{L}$ is a segment which is not contained in a facet of v.   □

We notice that, as a matter of fact, the class of the regular 3D lines is the same as the generalised (3D) Bresenham lines. Kaufman and Shimony presented an efficient algorithm for such lines generation [3], while Formula 3.2 provides a corresponding analytical description.

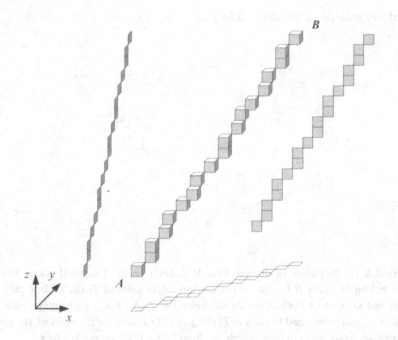

Figure 3.2. A regular 3D line between the points A=(0,0,0) and B=(11,13,18), together with its projections on the coordinate planes.

The simple analytical description of the regular 3D lines, the optimality property given by Axiom (b) in the definition, as well as the property provided by Lemma 3.1, make this class convenient for our purposes. The idea of our method is to approximate the triangle sides by regular 3D lines. The construction of the rest of the triangle is considered in the next subsection.

3.3.2 The Discrete Triangle

Let us first consider a 2D Euclidean triangle $\Delta A'B'C'$ in a coordinate plane, say, *Oxy*. We define the *integer set* $I_{2D}\Delta A'B'C'$ of $\Delta A'B'C'$ as the set of all the integer points which belong to the interior *or* the sides of $\Delta A'B'C'$. Thus, in particular, the vertices A', B', and C' belong to $I_{2D}\Delta A'B'C'$ [2] (Figure 3.3a).

The integer set of a 3D triangle is a portion of a special kind of naive plane, called regular, and defined as follows. Let $P: ax + by + cz + d = 0$ be a plane in the 3D space, and the largest by absolute value of the coefficients a, b, and c be positive. (If this maximum is reached for more than one coefficient, let the first one with this property be positive.) The naive plane $P(a, b, c, d+\lfloor \omega/2 \rfloor, \omega)$, $\omega = \boldsymbol{max}(|a|, |b|, |c|)$ is

---

[2] We notice that in [11] a 2D discrete triangle is defined as consisting of sides which are the Bresenham lines between the corresponding vertices, and *interior*, as containing all the voxels inside $\Delta A'B'C'$ which *do not belong* to the sides. In the present construction we, in fact, do not need a definition of a 2D discrete triangle and restrict ourselves to the given definition of an integer set.

called a *regular plane* and denoted by P_R.

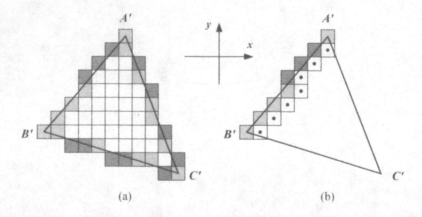

Figure 3.3. (a) Projection of discrete triangle $T(ABC)$ on the functional plane. The white pixels belong to $I_{2D}\Delta A'B'C'$ but do not correspond to sides of $T(ABC)$. Dark grey pixels correspond to sides of $T(ABC)$ but do not belong to $I_{2D}\Delta A'B'C'$. Light grey pixels are in $I_{2D}\Delta A'B'C'$ *and* correspond to sides of $T(ABC)$. (b) Illustration for the proof of Theorem 3.1. The pixels corresponding to their neighbours from $I_{2D}\Delta A'B'C'$ are marked by •.

If the plane P is determined by three points $A(x_A, y_A, z_A)$, $B(x_B, y_B, z_B)$, and $C(x_C, y_C, z_C)$, then its coefficients are given by the formula:

$$
\begin{aligned}
a &= (y_B - y_A)(z_C - z_A) - (y_C - y_A)(z_B - z_A) \\
b &= (z_B - z_A)(x_C - x_A) - (z_C - z_A)(x_B - x_A) \\
c &= (x_B - x_A)(y_C - y_A) - (x_C - x_A)(y_B - y_A) \\
d &= -(a x_A + b y_A + c z_A).
\end{aligned}
\tag{3.3}
$$

We assign $\omega := \boldsymbol{max}(|a|, |b|, |c|)$. Since the coordinates of A, B, and C have integer values, a, b, c, and μ are integers, and $\omega \in \mathbf{N}$. Obviously, the regular plane contains all the voxels whose centres are integers and belong to P. The following lemma shows that the regular plane appears to be a 3D analogue of the Bresenham line.

Lemma 3.2: Let $P: ax + by + cz + d = 0$ be a continuous plane and $P_R = P(a, b, c, d + \lfloor \omega/2 \rfloor, \omega)$ be the corresponding regular plane. Let $0 \le a \le b \le c$ and $c \ne 0$. Let $(x, y) \in Oxy$, $x, y \in \mathbf{Z}$. Then from $(x, y, z') \in P$ and $(x, y, z) \in P_R$ it follows that $|z' - z| \le 1/2$ [11]. $\qquad\square$

Remark 3.2: In the continuous case the planes $ax + by + cz + d = 0$ and $-ax - by - cz - d = 0$ coincide, while in the discrete case there might be an ambiguity. To avoid such an ambiguity, we imposed in our definition of a regular plane the conditions:

- If $|a| = \textbf{\textit{max}}(|a|, |b|, |c|)$, then $a > 0$;
- Else if $|b| = \textbf{\textit{max}}(|a|, |b|, |c|)$, then $b > 0$;
- Else if $|c| = \textbf{\textit{max}}(|a|, |b|, |c|)$, then $c > 0$.   □

Remark 3.3: Let A, B, and C be an arbitrary triple of non-collinear voxels, such that the regular plane P_R^{ABC} through the voxels A, B, and C is functional over Oxy. Let α be the angle between the Euclidean plane P^{ABC} through A, B, and C and the coordinate plane Oxy. Then, from Lemma 3.2, one can easily obtain that:

$$\alpha \leq \arctan \sqrt{2}\ .$$

Note that α can be larger than 45 degrees, in particular the above bound is reached in the case $|a| = |b| = |c|$.   □

We determine an *integer set* of a 3D triangle $\triangle ABC$ as follows. Let A', B', and C' be the projections of A, B, and C onto the functional plane π_P of P_R^{ABC}, and $I_{2D}\triangle A'B'C'$ – the integer set of $\triangle A'B'C'$. Then the *integer set* $I_{3D}\triangle ABC$ of $\triangle ABC$ is defined as the set of voxels belonging to P_R^{ABC} whose projections on π_P constitute exactly the set $I_{2D}\triangle A'B'C'$. Note that the centres of the voxels of the integer set of $\triangle ABC$ do not necessarily belong to $\triangle ABC$.

Now we can define a *3D discrete triangle* $T(ABC)$ as the union of its sides $L_R(AB)$, $L_R(BC)$, and $L_R(CA)$ (which are regular 3D lines) and the integer set $I_{3D}\triangle ABC$ (which is a portion of a regular plane).

We also notice that the discrete sides of $T(ABC)$ and the integer set of $\triangle ABC$ may contain common voxels (Figure 3.3a).

The above constructive definition of a 3D discrete triangle infers an algorithm for discretisation of triangles and meshes of triangles, which is outlined in the next subsection.

3.3.3 The Algorithm

Let a mesh of a finite number of 3D triangles be given. Each triangle is specified by its three vertices, which are supposed to be integer points. To obtain a voxelisation of the triangular mesh, we approximate every triangle by a discrete triangle, as follows.

Algorithm for Discretisation of 3D Triangle (OptThin Algorithm)

Given a triangle $\triangle ABC$ in the 3D space, perform the following steps:

1. Approximate the sides AB, AC, and BC by the corresponding regular 3D lines $L_R(AB)$, $L_R(BC)$, and $L_R(CA)$;
2. Determine the regular plane P_R^{ABC};
3. Find the functional plane π_P of P_R^{ABC};
4. Find the respective projections A', B', and C' of A, B, and C on π_P;

5. Determine the integer set $I_{2D}\Delta A'B'C'$ of ΔABC;
6. Generate the integer set $I_{3D}\Delta ABC$ of ΔABC from $I_{2D}\Delta A'B'C'$. (By construction, $I_{3D}\Delta ABC$ consists of the voxels from P_R^{ABC} whose projections belong to $I_{2D}\Delta A'B'C'$).

The union of the sides and the integer set constitutes the discrete triangle $T(ABC)$.

Remark 3.4: In the above algorithm the discrete sides are obtained directly, while the rest of the triangle is obtained from the corresponding projection on the functional coordinate plane. In contrast, in our previous algorithms from [11, 13] both the sides and the triangles' interiors were obtained on the basis of the projection approach.   □

We can state the following theorem.

Theorem 3.1: A discrete triangle generated by the described OptThin Algorithm is 6-tunnel-free.   □

The proof of the theorem is presented in the next section. From Theorem 3.1 one can obtain the following corollary.

Corollary 3.1: A triangular mesh voxelisation obtained by approximating every triangle of the mesh using OptThin Algorithm is 6-tunnel-free.   □

The proof follows from the observation that if two Euclidean triangles ΔABC and ΔABD have a common side AB then, by construction, the corresponding discrete triangles $T(ABC)$ and $T(ABD)$ share a common discrete side $L_R(AB)$. By Theorem 3.1, $T(ABC)$ and $T(ABD)$ are 6-tunnel-free, and then clearly the mesh voxelisation will be 6-tunnel-free as well.

Remark 3.5: Let us mention the following facts:

- If the used naive 3D lines and plane are not regular (i.e., if they are not "centred" about the continuous line/plane), then 6-tunnels may exist between the discrete triangle sides and the rest of the triangle.
- If instead of the integer set of the triangle one uses the interior of a discrete triangle as defined in [11], then 6-tunnels may exist.
- If the integer points on the sides of ΔABC are not included in $I_{2D}\Delta A'B'C'$, then 6-tunnels may exist.   □

The sides of $T(ABC)$, as well as the regular 3D plane from which $T(ABC)$ is a portion, admit an analytical description. Thus one can easily verify in constant time a membership of a voxel to some of the sides of $T(ABC)$ or to $I_{3D}\Delta ABC$.

Classes of "analytical" 3D discrete linear objects have been studied in [7, 9], where "supercovers" of 3D lines, planes, and triangles have been considered.

Supercover of a continuous object consists of all the voxels intersected by the object. The supercovers have been introduced and studied in [20]. They possess certain interesting and useful properties. For example, supercovers of polygons or polygonal surfaces are clearly tunnel-free. Supercovers of 3D lines and planes are examples of "thick" discrete lines and planes, in contrast to the regular 3D lines and planes considered here.

Time Complexity, Memory Requirements, and Image Quality

Let us consider the designed algorithm step by step. As mentioned, in Step 1 one can apply the well-known Kaufman-Shimony algorithm for scan-conversion of a generalised 3D Bresenham line [3]. This algorithm has time complexity, which is linear in the number of the generated voxels.

In Step 2, the coefficients of P_R^{ABC} can be obtained in constant time by Formula 3.3. Then set $\omega = max(|a|, |b|, |c|)$ and $\mu = d + \lfloor \omega/2 \rfloor$.

To determine the functional plane π_P in Step 3, one needs to find $max(|a|, |b|, |c|)$. For this, two comparisons of integer numbers have to be performed.

In Step 4, one needs to find the projections of A, B, and C on π_P. This can be done by choosing the two relevant coordinates of each of the points and setting the third one to zero.

A membership of a pixel to $I_{2D}\Delta A'B'C'$ can be verified in constant time using integer operations suggested by elementary analytic geometry. Therefore, the integer set of $\Delta A'B'C'$ can be generated in time proportional to the number of the pixels in the integer set, and thus the complexity of Step 5 is linear in this number.

In order to perform Step 6 efficiently, one can use the following simple and well-known fact. Let, for definiteness, the coefficients of a naive plane $P(a,b,c,\mu,\omega)$ satisfy the condition $0 \le a \le b \le c$, $c \ne 0$, and P be functional over Oxy. Then for each $z \in P$ the equation:

$$z = -\left\lfloor \frac{ax + by + \mu}{c} \right\rfloor$$

holds. This function allows one to associate with every voxel $(x, y, z) \in P$ a unique pixel (x, y), and vice versa. That is, the projection of a naive plane onto the functional plane is a bijection. Thus, a naive (in particular, regular) plane can be traced in the domain $[0, x_{max}] \times [0, y_{max}]$ by the following simple procedure.

```
for x:=0 to x_max do
    for y:=0 to y_max do
        z = -⌊(ax + by + μ)/c⌋;
    end for;
end for;
```

The plane can be represented by the values of its z-coordinate over the plane Oxy, and the used memory for representing the set $I_{2D}\Delta A'B'C'$ can be a 2D array of integer type. An additional Boolean array is used for pointing out the pixels of the domain, which belong to the integer set of $\Delta A'B'C'$.

Thus it becomes clear that Step 6 of the algorithm has linear complexity in the number of the generated voxels, and the overall complexity of the algorithm is linear as well.

The algorithm uses integer arithmetic. The obtained discretisation has the advantage that its components admit a simple analytical description. Thus, one can easily verify a membership of a voxel to the discretised surface.

The designed rendering algorithm can be successfully used for obtaining thin 6-tunnel voxelisation of triangles or meshes of triangles. By construction, all the voxels from the discrete sides are intersected by the corresponding sides of the Euclidean triangles, and all the other voxels are intersected by the triangles themselves. It is also clear that voxels, for which the region contained by them is entirely outside the continuous object, do not belong to the discrete object.

Series of experiments have shown that, in practice, the obtained discrete image has a quite satisfactory shape quality. Furthermore, one can verify that a good approximation to the discrete normal of a discrete triangle is the vector (a, b, c) formed by the coefficients of the implicit equation of the Euclidean plane $ax+by+cz+d=0$ containing the triangle vertices. More details about discrete normal can be found in [21]. An example of a discrete mesh of two triangles, obtained through the proposed algorithm, is outlined in Figure 3.4.

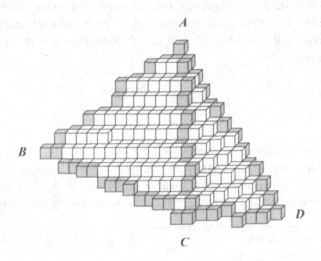

Figure 3.4. The mesh of two 3D discrete triangles $T(ABC)$ and $T(ABD)$, resulting from the described algorithm. The vertices of the mesh are $A(1, 8, 6)$, $B(-8, -2, 0)$, $C(7, -8, -4)$, and $D(14, -4, -5)$.

3.4   Proofs of Lemma 3.1 and Theorem 3.1

Proof of Lemma 3.1: Let $\mathscr{L}$ be determined by the vector (a, b, c). Without loss of generality, we assume that $|a| \leq |b| \leq |c|$, i.e., $\mathscr{L}$ makes maximal angle with the coordinate plane Oxy.

Then, by definition, the projections of L_R on Oyz and Oxy are Bresenham lines. Let $\mathscr{L}_1$ and $\mathscr{L}_2$ be the projections of $\mathscr{L}$ on Oyz and Oxz, respectively, and $v = (x, y, z)$ be an arbitrary voxel from L_R. Let (y', z) and (x', z) be the corresponding points from $\mathscr{L}_1$ and $\mathscr{L}_2$, respectively.

According to Fact 3.1, $|y - y'| \leq 1/2$ and $|z - z'| \leq 1/2$. Provided that $|a| \leq |b| \leq |c|$, this is possible only if $\mathscr{L}$ intersects v. Furthermore, it is not difficult to see that the intersection is always a segment which is not contained in a facet of v. In fact, if we assume that the intersection is a segment which is either an edge of v or a part of its face, then clearly the straight line $\mathscr{L}$ cannot pass through integer points, which contradicts the integrality of A and B. If we assume that the intersection is a single point, then this must be the midpoint of one of the vertical edges of v (Figure 3.5a). In this case, bearing in mind Fact 3.1 and Remark 3.1, it follows that the line $\mathscr{L}$ contains the voxel $w = (x+1, y, z)$ and does not contain v, a contradiction. $\square$

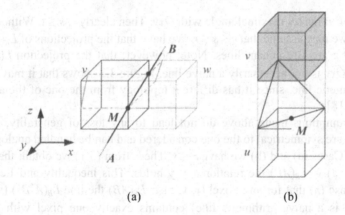

Figure 3.5. (a) Illustration of Lemma 3.1. The straight line AB passes through the midpoint M of a vertical voxel side. (b) Illustration of Lemma 3.3 in the extreme case when the plane of $\triangle ABC$ makes angle **$arctan\sqrt{2}$** with Oxy.

In the proof of Theorem 3.1 we also use the following simple lemma.

Lemma 3.3: Let $v = (x, y, z)$ be a voxel from the side $L_R(AB)$ of $T(ABC)$ and $u = (x, y, z')$ a voxel from $I_{3D}\triangle ABC$. Then $|z - z'| \in \{0,1\}$.

Proof: Assume the opposite, i.e., that $|z - z'|$ may be greater than or equal to 2. We will show that $|z - z'| \neq 2$. For this, we show that $(x, y, z-2) \notin I_{3D}\triangle ABC$.

The plane P_R^{ABC} containing $T(ABC)$ is regular and functional over Oxy.

According to Lemma 3.2, the continuous plane P passes below the point $M = (x, y, z-3/2)$. In view of Remark 3.3, it follows that P does not intersect v. (Figure 3.5b illustrates the extreme case when P makes an angle equal to **$arctan\sqrt{2}$** with Oxy.) Consequently the side AB, which is contained in P, does not intersect the voxel v, which contradicts Lemma 3.1. Similar argument implies that $|z - z'| \neq k$ for any integer $k > 2$. ◻

Proof of Theorem 3.1: Let $A(A_x, A_y, A_z)$, $B(B_x, B_y, B_z)$, and $C(C_x, C_y, C_z)$ be three non-collinear points with integer coordinates – vertices of the Euclidean triangle $\triangle ABC$. Let P_R^{ABC} be the corresponding regular plane, which is supposed to be functional over Oxy.

Consider the side AB of $\triangle ABC$. Let $L_R(AB)$ be the corresponding regular 3D line. Let $n=(r, s, t)=(B_x-A_x, B_y-A_y, B_z-A_z)$ be the vector collinear with this straight line. For definiteness, we will suppose that r, s and t are positive. There are two possibilities, to which we will refer in the rest of the proof as Case (a) and Case (b):

Case (a): n makes maximal angle with Oxz or Oyz. For definiteness, we will always assume that the former is the case. Then clearly r, $t \leq s$. Without loss of generality we may assume that $r \leq t \leq s$.

Then, by definition, the projections of $L_R(AB)$ onto Oxy and Oyz are Bresenham lines.

Case (b): n makes maximal angle with Oxy. Then clearly r, $s \leq t$. Without loss of generality we may assume that $r \leq s \leq t$. We have that the projections of $L_R(AB)$ onto Oxz and Oyz are Bresenham lines. Note, however, that the projection $L(A'B')$ of $L_R(AB)$ on Oxy is not necessarily a naive line. Figure 3.2 shows that it may not even be an arithmetic line, since it has different topology from the one of the arithmetic lines (e.g. [18]).

The assumptions made above do not lead to any loss of generality, since the other cases are symmetrical to the one considered and can be handled analogously.

In both Cases (a) and (b) we have $r \leq s$. Then, from (3.1) we obtain that for any voxel $(x, y, z) \in L_R(AB)$ the relation $x \leq y$ holds. This inequality and Lemma 3.2 imply in Case (a) that for any voxel $(x, y, z) \in L_R(AB)$ the line $L_B(A'B')$ (which, as mentioned, is a naive arithmetic line) contains exactly one pixel with a second coordinate equal to y. In Case (b), the same inequality and Lemma 3.2 imply that $L(A'B')$ (which, as mentioned, is not an arithmetic line, in general) may contain not more than two pixels with second coordinates equal to y.

Let $v = (x, y, z)$ be an arbitrary voxel from $L_R(AB)$. The same arguments as above imply that in both Cases (a) and (b) not more than one of the pixels $(x-1, y)$ or $(x+1, y)$ may belong to $I_{2D}\triangle A'B'C'$ and thus not more than one of the voxels $(x-1, y, z)$ or $(x+1, y, z)$ may belong to $I_{3D}\triangle ABC$.[3] If such a voxel exists, let this for definiteness be

---

[3] Usually any voxel from a discrete side of $T(ABC)$ has a neighbour from the integer set of $\triangle ABC$. Note, however, that if the triangle is very "thin," some part of $T(ABC)$ may consist only of voxels from the side. This may also happen close to the triangle vertices. See, for instance, Figure 3.3. There the voxel corresponding to the pixel A will have no neighbouring voxel from $I_{3D}\triangle ABC$.

the voxel $u = (x+1, y, z)$ (Figure 3.3b).

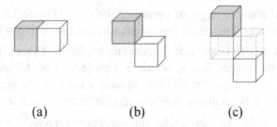

(a) (b) (c)

Figure 3.6. The grey voxels are from $L_R(AB)$, and the white voxels are from $I_{3D}\Delta ABC$. Configurations (a) and (b) are possible, while configuration (c) is not.

We organise the rest of the proof into two phases. In the first phase we will show that v and u always share a common edge or face. This will imply that a side of $T(ABC)$ cannot be disconnected from the integer set $I_{3D}\Delta ABC$. Thus we will exclude possible tunnels due to configurations of the form displayed on Figure 3.6c. In the second phase we will consider two consecutive voxels from the side and their neighbouring voxels from the integer set of ΔABC, and will show that their union is 6-tunnel-free. Thus we will be able to deduce that the discrete triangle too is overall 6-tunnel-free. The two phases are detailed in the next paragraphs.

Phase 1. Consider first the case when the projection (x, y) of the voxel $v = (x, y, z)$ on Oxy belongs to $I_{2D}\Delta A'B'C'$ (Figure 3.7a). Then, according to the algorithm construction, the corresponding voxel $u = (x, y, z')$ from P_R^{ABC} belongs to $I_{3D}\Delta ABC$. From Lemma 3.3 we have that $|z - z'| \in \{0, 1\}$. Now, using Fact 3.3, we can conclude that the possible configurations for v and u are as those shown on Figures 3.6a and 3.6b, and there cannot be a configuration as the one on Figure 3.6c.

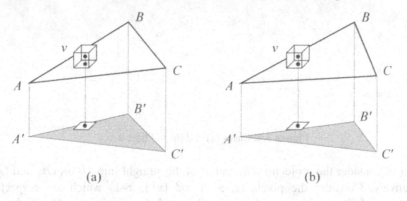

(a) (b)

Figure 3.7. (a) The projection of the voxel v is inside $\Delta A'B'C'$. (b) The projection of v is outside $\Delta A'B'C'$.

We now consider the case when the projection (x, y) of $v(x, y, z)$ does not belong to $I_{2D}\Delta A'B'C'$ (Figure 3.7b).

Consider first Case (a), when $r \leq t \leq s$ and the projections of $L_R(AB)$ on Oxy and Oyz are Bresenham lines. It suffices to consider the extreme case when the plane P forms the maximal possible angle of $\textbf{arctan}\sqrt{2}$ with Oxy (Figure 3.8a). The straight line AB lies in P, makes a maximal angle with Oxz, and is such that the point (x, y) does not belong to ΔABC. Geometrical reasoning implies that these three conditions can hold only if the straight line h, which is a projection of AB onto Oyz, passes below the point $Q = (x-1/2, y, z-1/2)$ but, in such a case, the projection of $L_R(AB)$ onto Oyz cannot be a Bresenham line related to h, a contradiction. Clearly, if the plane P makes with Oxy an angle smaller than $\textbf{arctan}\sqrt{2}$, then the same contradiction holds.

Consider now Case (b), when $r \leq s \leq t$ and the projections of $L_R(AB)$ on Oxz and Oyz are Bresenham lines. Assume that the voxels v and u share neither a face nor an edge. Let $u = (x+1, y, z-2)$. (The case when the difference in the third coordinate of u and v is larger than 2 is rejected analogously.) Since $(x, y) \notin I_{2D}\Delta A'B'C'$, the voxel $w = (x, y, z-1) \notin I_{3D}\Delta ABC$. Since the plane P_R^{ABC} is functional over Oxy and contains the voxel $u = (x+1, y, z-2)$, the voxel $w' = (x+1, y, z-1) \notin I_{3D}\Delta ABC \subset P_R^{ABC}$. From Lemma 3.2 we also have that the continuous plane P passes below the point $N(x, y, z-1/2)$. In view of Remark 3.3, one can see that P makes an angle with Oxy less than or equal to $\textbf{arctan}\sqrt{2}$. The extreme case is illustrated in Figure 3.8b.

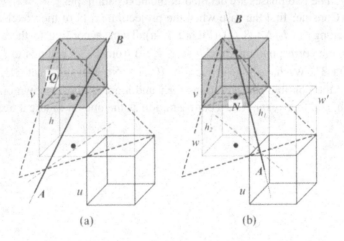

(a)   (b)

Figure 3.8. Cases (a) and (b) in Phase 1.

Let us consider the projections h_1 and h_2 of the straight line AB on Oxz and Oyz, respectively. Consider the pixels $(x, z-1)$ and $(x+1, z-1)$ which are respective projections of the voxels w and w' on Oxz, and the pixel $(y, z-1)$ which is a projection of both w and w' on Oyz. Then, keeping in mind that $r \leq s \leq t$ and $(x, y) \notin I_{2D}\Delta A'B'C'$, one can obtain that for at least one of the voxels w and w' the corresponding projections in Oxz and Oyz belong to the Bresenham lines related to h_1 and h_2, respectively. Hence one of the voxels w or w' belongs to $L_R(AB)$ and thus there is no tunnel between v and u. This completes the proof that a configuration such as the one in Figure 3.6c is impossible. Then the possible configurations are as the ones shown in Figures 3.6a and 3.6b.

Phase 2. We investigate how two consecutive voxels from the side $L_R(AB)$ align with the corresponding neighbouring voxels (if any) from $I_{3D}\Delta ABC$. For the sake of simplifying and shortening the presentation, we consider the case when, for a fixed value y, there is at most one voxel with a second coordinate equal to y, belonging to $L_R(AB)$. The case when there are two such voxels can be considered analogously.

In Figure 3.9a the voxels from $L_R(AB)$ (in grey) share a common face, in Figure 3.9b they share a common edge and, in Figure 3.9c, a common vertex. Keeping in mind Facts 3.3 and 3.4 and Lemma 3.3, one can easily realise that Figures 3.9a and 3.9b represent all the essential possibilities in the first two cases. It can be seen that in these cases there is no tunnel between the voxels from the side and their neighbours from $I_{3D}\Delta ABC$. The configurations in Figure 3.9c are also 6-tunnel-free.

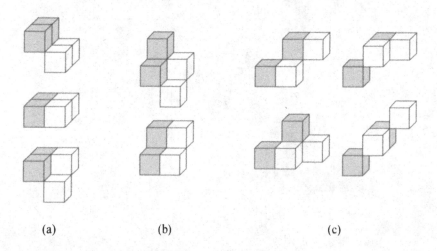

(a)   (b)   (c)

Figure 3.9. Different possible configurations of two voxels from $L_R(AB)$ and their neighbours from $I_{3D}\Delta ABC$.

The only two non-trivial hypothetical cases in which there is a theoretical possibility for tunnels are in the framework of the third case. These two configurations are illustrated in Figure 3.10. We will show that, in fact, they cannot exist.

Let us consider the configurations in Figures $3.10a_1$ and $3.10a_2$. Consider first the case when the projection (x, y) of $v = (x, y, z)$ onto Oxy belongs to $I_{2D}\Delta A'B'C'$. It is easy to show that the voxel $(x, y, z-1) \in I_{3D}\Delta ABC$. Really, if we assume that $v \in I_{3D}\Delta ABC$, then v also belongs to P_R^{ABC}. However, the voxel $u = (x, y-1, z-2)$ belongs to $I_{3D}\Delta ABC$ and thus also to P_R^{ABC}, which contradicts Fact 3.3. It is also clear that $(x, y, z-2) \notin I_{3D}\Delta ABC$, since this would contradict Lemma 3.3. It follows that the voxel $(x, y, z-1) \in I_{3D}\Delta ABC$ and consequently there is no tunnel between v, v' and u, u'.

Consider now the case when the projection of $v = (x, y, z)$ on Oxy does not belong to $I_{3D}\Delta ABC$. Again we distinguish between the Cases (a) and (b). In Case (a)

($r \le t \le s$) one can reach a contradiction in an analogous way as in Case (a) of Phase 1 (Figure 3.10a$_1$).

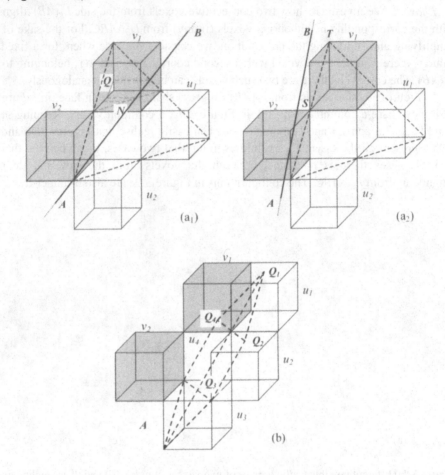

(a$_1$)

(a$_2$)

(b)

Figure 3.10. Two impossible configurations are shown. (a$_1$) and (a$_2$) illustrate the proof of the first configuration. (b) illustrates the proof of the second configuration.

In Case (b) ($r \le s \le t$), it suffices to study the extreme case when the plane P makes the maximal possible angle of **$arctan\sqrt{2}$** with Oxy (Figure 3.10a$_2$). Let us consider the straight line ST determined by the points $S = (x-1/2, y-1/2, z+1/2)$ and $T = (x-1/2, y+1/2, z+1/2)$. ST makes with Oxy an angle equal to 45 degrees. If we assume that the oriented angle $\angle(ST, AB) \le 0$ then, clearly, AB makes with Oxy an angle less than 45 degrees and AB does not make a maximal angle with Oxy. Hence $\angle(ST, AB) > 0$. In view of the fact that AB lies in the plane P, one can see that AB cannot intersect each of the voxels v and v' in a segment, which contradicts Lemma 3.1.

We consider now the configuration in Figure 3.10b. Here the voxels $v_1 = (x, y, z)$ and $v_2 = (x-1, y-1, z-1)$ belong to $L_R(AB)$, while the voxels $u_1 = (x+1, y, z)$, $u_2 = (x+1, y-1, z-1)$, and $u_3 = (x, y, z-2)$ belong to $I_{3D}\triangle ABC \subset P_R^{ABC}$. P_R^{ABC} is a naive plane, which is functional over Oxy. It is easy to realise that if P_R^{ABC} contains voxels whose coordinates are related as ones of u_1 and u_3, then P_R^{ABC} also contains the voxels u_2 (which is assumed to exist in the considered configuration) and $u_4 = (x, y, z-1)$.

If the voxels u_1, u_2, u_3 and u_4 belong to P_R^{ABC} then, according to Lemma 3.2, the plane P must pass below the points $Q_1 = (x+1, y, z+1/2)$, $Q_2 = (x+1, y-1, z-1/2)$, $Q_3 = (x+1, y, z-3/2)$, and $Q_4 = (x, y, z-1/2)$. In such a case, P does not intersect v_2, which contradicts Lemma 3.1.

Thus we have obtained that there are no 6-tunnels between two consecutive voxels from P_R^{ABC} and the corresponding voxels (if any) from the integer set of $\triangle ABC$. Then, clearly, the triangle produced by the OptThin Algorithm will be overall 6-tunnel-free as well. ☐

3.5 Concluding Remarks

In this chapter we have proposed an algorithm for obtaining 6-tunnel-free voxelisation of a mesh of triangles. The discrete triangles admit an analytical description, which may be useful regarding some membership or encoding problems. The algorithm has linear complexity in the number of the generated voxels and uses integer arithmetic. Compared to other algorithms for discretisation of planar polygons (e.g. [4, 6, 7, 9]), our algorithm provides thinner voxelisation. In fact, as already discussed, the obtained voxelisation can be considered as minimally thin, which may be useful regarding certain applications. Some experiments have shown that the suggested method ensures satisfactory quality of the discrete approximation. The method can be applied for solving practical problems arising, for instance, in terrain modelling. For its implementation, one could use the tools and routines for voxelisation of analytically defined objects, introduced in Chapter 7.

It is not difficult to see that the obtained results, in particular the designed algorithm, can be easily adapted for discretisation of polyhedral surfaces whose faces are arbitrary planar polygons.

References

1. Kaufman A, Cohen D, Yagel R. Volume graphics. IEEE Computer, 1993; 26(7):51-64.
2. Yagel R, Cohen D, Kaufman A. Discrete ray tracing. IEEE Computer Graphics and Applications, 1992; 22(5):19-28.
3. Kaufman A, Shimony E. 3D scan-conversion algorithms for voxel-based graphics. In: Proc. 1986 Workshop on Interactive 3D Graphics, Chapel Hill, NC, ACM, New York, 1986; 45-75.
4. Kaufman A. An algorithm for 3D scan-conversion of polygons. In: Proc. Eurographics '87; 197-208.
5. Cohen D, Kaufman A. Scan-conversion algorithms for linear and quadratic

objects. In: Proc. IEEE Symposium on Volume Visualization, Los Alamos, CA, 1991; 280-301.

6. Cohen D, Kaufman A. 3D Line voxelization and connectivity control. IEEE Computer Graphics and Applications, 1997; 17(6).

7. Andrès E, Nehlig P, Françon J. Tunnel-free supercover 3D polygons and polyhedra. In: Proc. Eurographics '97; 16(3): C3-C13.

8. Françon J. On recent trends in discrete geometry in computer imagery. In: Proc. the 6th Workshop on Discrete Geometry for Computer Imagery, Lyon, France, Lecture Notes in Computer Sciences No 1176, Springer-Verlag, November 1996; 141-150.

9. Andrès E, Nehlig P, Françon J. Supercovers of straight lines, planes and triangles. In: Proc. the 7th International Workshop DGCI, Montpelier, France, Lecture Notes in Computer Science No 1347, Springer Verlag, 1997; 243-254.

10. Andres E, Achatya R, Sibata C. The discrete analytical hyperplane. Graphical Models and Image Processing, 1997; 59(5):302-309.

11. Barneva RP, Brimkov VE, Nehlig P. Thin discrete triangular meshes. To appear in Theoretical Computer Science, Elsevier.

12. Debled-Rennesson I, Reveillès J-P. A new approach to digital planes. In: Spie's International Symposium on Photonics for Industrial Applications, Technical Conference Vision Geometry 3, Boston, USA, 1994.

13. Brimkov VE, Barneva RP. Graceful planes and thin tunnel-free meshes. In: Proc. of the 8th Conference on Discrete Geometry for Computer Imagery, March 17-19, 1999, Marne-la-Vallée, France, Lecture Notes in Computer Sciences No 1568, Springer-Verlag, March 1999; 53-64.

14. Figueiredo O, Reveillès J-P. A contribution to 3D digital lines. In: Proc. the 5th International Workshop on Discrete Geometry for Computer Imagery, Clermont-Ferrand, France, September 25-27, 1995; 187-198.

15. Rosenfeld A. Three-dimensional digital topology. Computer Science Center, Univ. of Maryland, Tech. Rep. 963, 1980.

16. Srihari SN. Representation of three-dimensional digital images. Computing Surveys, 1981; 4(13): 399-424.

17. Pavlidis T. Algorithms for Graphics and Image Processing. Computer Science Press, Rockville, MD, 1982.

18. Reveillès J-P. Géométrie Discrète, Calcul en Nombres Entiers et Algorithmique, thèse d'état, Université Louis Pasteur, Strasbourg, 1991.

19. Bresenham JE. Algorithm for computer control of a digital plotter. ACM Transaction on Graphics, 1965; 4(1):25-30.

20. Cohen D, Kaufman A. Fundamentals of surface voxelization. CVGIP-GMIP, 1995; 57(6): 453-461.

21. Kaufman A, Cohen D, Yagel R. Normal estimation in 3D discrete space. The Visual Computer, 1992; 8:278-291.

4. Smooth Boundary Surfaces from Binary 3D Datasets

Daniel Cohen-Or, Arie Kadosh, David Levin and Roni Yagel

4.1 Introduction

Computer graphics relies on several types of internal representations of synthetic worlds. The models so represented are the ones rendered to the screen to create the illusion of reality. Internally, two inherently distinct types of representations exist. The *continuous* representation uses a collection of geometric objects such as polygons or splines to represent the model. The *discrete* representation samples the object and represents it by a discrete collection of points in space. An image is an example of a 2D discrete object while a texture mapped polygon combines elements from both representations. Historically, computer graphics has mainly dealt with the continuous approach and invested most of its efforts in building software and hardware systems for its rapid rendering. In the last decade a growing interest in discrete graphics has emerged, mainly in the applications of texture mapping, volume rendering, and image based rendering. In these applications, a collection of 3D coloured points called *voxels* is commonly employed, and the term *voxel representation* is commonly used to stand for any discrete graphics object.

The pros and cons of these representations have been discussed and debated at length elsewhere [1]. We just mention briefly that one of the advantages of discrete representation is its ability to represent objects' attributes (such as texture, colour, etc.) at every point rather than on an object-wise global basis (such as object colour). The discrete approach has been proven especially effective for photo-mapped high-quality rendering where non-repeated (tiled) textures (photographs) are required. One example is a flight simulator where the terrain is mapped with a huge aerial photograph [2-3]. In another example, various medical scanners produce three-dimensional medical information, in great detail. Continuous representations are incapable of efficiently representing this richness of information, which includes surface detail as well as internal features. Finally, various geometric computations such as Boolean operations [4], distance functions [5] and collision detection [6-7] were shown to be more efficiently computed and rendered from discrete representations than from their continuous counterparts. Some of these applications include the ability to take continuous geometric objects, convert them to discrete representation, in a process called *3D scan-conversion* or *voxelisation*, and then compute, distance to the surface, for example, in discrete space.

One can regard texture mapping as an effort to enhance continuous graphics to benefit from some of the advantages of discrete graphics. Recently, image-based rendering (IBR) has emerged as a method that aims to extend our rendering capabilities by further incorporating discrete objects. An image-based representation includes a depth value at each pixel that, in fact, positions the pixel in space as a 3D coloured point — a classical discrete graphic representation. In IBR, each point sample may be represented by several pixel values. In that respect, a pure voxel-based representation is more compact but, on the other hand, the IBR pixel value is view-dependent and can support view-dependent features like reflections. Like voxel-based representations, image-based representations are discrete and the photographs or textures are mapped onto the continuous object in a preprocessing stage rather than during rendering. However, image-based representation contains only part of the points comprising the object surface — those that are visible from a finite set of viewpoints. As a result, the incomplete synthesised model may exhibit holes when rendered from a different viewpoint. The *layered depth images* representation [8] aims to alleviate this difficulty by including in the model the list of all surface points intersected by a view ray passing through the pixel. This, in fact, is a voxelisation of the scene, similar to previously employed representations in volume rendering [9, 4].

One major disadvantage of discrete representations is their finite resolution. As a result, various artifacts appear when one tries to zoom-in. In continuous graphics this may also happen when a curved surface is approximated by a set of piecewise linear objects — the polymesh. When the viewer approaches the object, even the known tricks of the trade, namely Gouraud and Phong shading, cannot deliver the illusion of smoothness and the linear approximation becomes visible. It is our thesis that the interpolation function used in the generation of close-up images plays a crucial role in their quality. We show that the use of higher-order interpolators greatly enhances one's ability to display discrete objects from up close.

Voxel-based data are at times interpolated by means of the marching cube algorithm, which interprets the surface as a collection of triangles providing, in fact, a piecewise linear approximation of the discrete function. Higher-quality interpolations of the surface use a trilinear interpolation [10]. However, trilinear interpolation is not smooth enough when the voxels are rendered from very close up. Figures 4.1a-c show the results of three interpolation schemes.

Figure 4.1a is a zero-order interpolation where each non-empty voxel is visualised as a unit cube. In this figure the low resolution of the data is noticeable and the figure is used just as a reference to the higher-order interpolations. Figure 4.1b is a trilinear interpolation where the surface is defined by thresholding the trilinear function defined over binary voxels. A higher-order interpolation of the same binary data is shown in Figure 4.1c.

To get a better feeling for the nature of the reconstructed surface, we have generated 2D examples. As shown in Figures 4.2a-d, the level curves (the 2D analogue of a 3D isosurface) are separating the black points from the white points (note that the curve has discontinuities since it has not been computed entirely but for the parts visible from a small number of viewpoints). Clearly, a bilinear interpolation yields a curve that is not C^1 while a higher-order interpolation yields a pleasing smooth curve. Trilinear interpolation is commonly used for volume

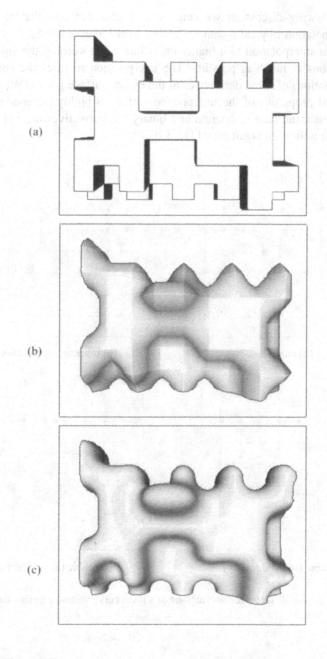

Figure 4.1. Three different reconstructions of a level surface from a simple 3D binary dataset. The scene contains 9×6×3 voxels only.

rendering where there is no explicit definition of the surfaces. The trilinear function is sampled and integrated along the ray-of-sights, and not thresholded. However, when the application requires reconstructing a surface, the smoothness of the surface is a necessary feature [10].

In the following discussion we employ a tricubic function that is based on Hermite interpolation to yield a smooth surface over binary datasets. The goal is to extend trilinear interpolation to a higher order one while keeping the simplicity of the computations as much as possible. The interpolation requires the computation (or precomputation) of some derivatives at the binary surface points. We show that the quality and properties of the interpolated surface is highly dependent of these derivatives. Since the data is discrete and binary the derivatives are not explicitly given and their definition is not trivial [11-12].

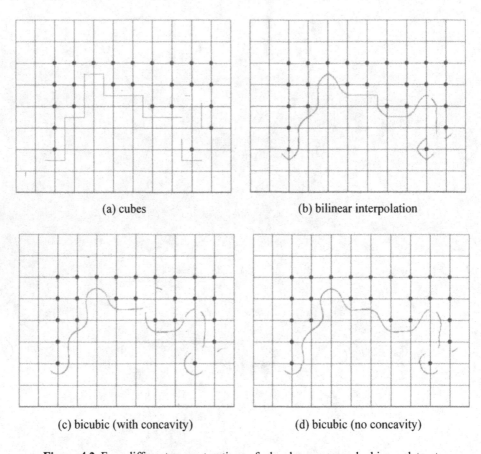

(a) cubes   (b) bilinear interpolation

(c) bicubic (with concavity)   (d) bicubic (no concavity)

Figure 4.2. Four different reconstructions of a level curve around a binary dataset.

4.2 Surface Definition

Given a 3D grid of binary data, a reconstruction algorithm generates a continuous surface S that separates the "black" values from "white" values. The marching cube reconstruction algorithm uses local properties to build the surface that separates the black and white eight vertices of a given cell. The process of simplifying all 256 possible cell combinations into fourteen basic cases leaves some ambiguity that may cause the reconstructed surface not to be a closed surface. In 2D, such ambiguity arises when a cell has two black vertices placed diagonally. It is not clear whether the binary vertices represent an object with a hidden cavity as in Figure 4.2d, or with an open cavity, as in Figure 4.4c. When linearly interpolating the binary data over the continuous space and thresholding at 0.5, we get a surface with a topology of a cavity (Figure 4.2b). Lacking more information any of the topologies may be the correct one. However, it seems, at least intuitively, that the topology of an open cavity is more likely to be the correct one. In other words, if we assume that the discrete samples of the models are 6-connected (4-connected in 2D) then the topology of a reconstructed surface is well defined. Given a discrete 6-connected component we are interested only in reconstructing the outer boundary of the object avoiding the internal boundaries of its possible cavities. The tricubic interpolation method presented in the following section, aims at reconstructing a smooth surface of a given 6-connected component. As mentioned above, the results, and specifically the topology, are dependent on the ability to define appropriate derivatives' values. First, let us define the tricubic function.

4.2.1 The Tricubic Reconstruction

The separating surface is defined as the zero level surface of an approximation to the signed distance function (SDF) [13]. The approximate SDF is obtained as a C^l piecewise tricubic polynomial, $c(x, y, z)$ on the unit cubes $[i, i+1] \times [j, j+1] \times [k, k+1]$, defined as follows:

A: At each vertex v of the lattice $\mathbf{Z}^3$ we assign 8 values, namely, the function value and partial derivatives:

$$c(v), c_x(v), c_y(v), c_z(v), c_{xy}(v), c_{xz}(v), c_{yz}(v), c_{xyz}(v).$$

These values uniquely define a tricubic polynomial on each of the lattice cubes, and the collection of all these local tricubic polynomials defines a C^l function on $\mathbf{R}^3$. $\square$

B: The evaluation of the tricubic polynomial at a general point (x, y, z) in the standard cube $[0, 1]^3$ is as follows:

Let $w(t)$ be the vector of basis functions for the univariate cubic Hermite interpolation:

$$w(t) = (1-3t^2+2t^3, 3t^2 \ 2t^3, t \ 2t^2+t^3, \ t^2 \ t^3).$$

To evaluate the $c(x, y, z)$ we proceed as follows. First we compute:

$$c(x, e) = ((c(0, e), c(1, e), c_x(0, e), c_x(1, e)) \ w(x)^T,$$
$$c_y(x, e) = ((c_y(0, e), c_y(1, e), c_{xy}(0, e), c_{xy}(1, e)) \ w(x)^T,$$
$$c_z(x, e) = ((c_z(0, e), c_z(1, e), c_{xz}(0, e), c_{xz}(1, e)) \ w(x)^T,$$
$$c_{yz}(x, e) = ((c_{yz}(0, e), c_{yz}(1, e), c_{xyz}(0, e), c_{xyz}(1, e)) \ w(x)^T,$$

where e in $\mathbf{E} = \{(0, 0), (0, 1), (1, 0), (1, 1)\}$. Then:

$$c(x, y, 0) = ((c(x, 0, 0), c(x, 1, 0), c_y(x, 0, 0), c_y(x, 1, 0))\, w(y)^T,$$
$$c(x, y, 1) = ((c(x, 0, 1), c(x, 1, 1), c_y(x, 0, 1), c_y(x, 1, 1))\, w(y)^T,$$
$$c_z(x, y, 0) = ((c_z(x, 0, 0), c_z(x, 1, 0), c_{yz}(x, 0, 0), c_{yz}(x, 1, 0))\, w(y)^T,$$
$$c_z(x, y, 1) = ((c_z(x, 0, 1), c_z(x, 1, 1), c_{yz}(x, 0, 1), c_{yz}(x, 1, 1))\, w(y)^T.$$

Finally:

$$c(x, y, z) = ((c(x, y, 0), c(x, y, 1), c_z(x, y, 0), c_z(x, y, 1))\, w(z)^T.$$

The cost of the above evaluation procedure is that of 12 evaluations of univariate cubic polynomials and of 21 inner products of vectors of length 4.   □

4.3 Voxel Data Estimation

Since the voxel-based surface has no parameterisation, the derivatives need to be approximated by a discrete method. The common gray-level computes the gradients of a given voxel based on the gray values of its local neighbouring voxels. However, when the dynamic range of the voxels is low, the method yields poor quality estimation of derivatives. This is especially evident when the voxels are binary. To improve the quality we define a 3D discrete function g, measuring for each voxel how far it is inside the organ. High values of g indicate voxels far inside the organ, while voxels inside the organ which are close to the surface get smaller values. Voxels outside the organ get further smaller values, depending on their distance to the surface. The derivatives' values needed for the evaluation of the tricubic function are approximated by standard differences approximation of g. Further surrounding voxels are considered to make this calculation more robust.

One possible function g which we utilise is defined as follows: for each inside voxel u, set $g(u)$ to be the distance to the nearest outside voxel. Similarly, for an outside voxel v, set $g(v)$ to be the negative distance to the nearest inside voxel. Note that we only need to evaluate g near the surface, where calculating its value is fast. To further improve the quality of the derivatives we calculate another function h which measures the number of surrounding neighbours that agree with the voxel binary value. This function gives low values to voxels, which are relatively isolated, like those on an end of a branch. A weighted value of the g and h functions yields the "gray values" assigned to the voxels for estimating their discrete derivatives. Note that derivatives are computed for the white voxels as well as for the black voxels.

4.4 Reconstruction

The tricubic interpolation described in 4.2.1 together with the discrete derivatives' estimation described in 4.3 defines a smooth surface around 6-connected binary components. To reconstruct the surface we can apply an adaptive space subdivision where each cell whose eight voxels do not agree on their binary value, is subdivided by sampling the tricubic function. Alternatively, the smooth surface can be reconstructed during rendering. In our implementation we have integrated the interpolation into a ray casting mechanism. For each pixel, a ray is cast along the line defined by the viewpoint and the pixel centre. The ray traverses the voxel space by walking along the sequence of grid cells defined by eight voxels. When the ray enters cells whose eight voxels do not agree, the tricubic function is sampled along the ray searching for the surface (a zero distance value).

Note that a cell, in which voxels do not agree, is intersected by the surface, but not necessarily intersected by a given ray. However, the time required for the traversal of the "empty" cell is insignificant, as the voxel space resolution is low. On the other hand, the sampling of the non-empty cell might be expensive and a naive implementation is inefficient. By assuming that the surface does not "fold" within a given cell, the search for intersection can be accelerated by some binary search, or by quasi-Newton iteration. Moreover, in such a case, an adjacent ray can start its search within a given cell from the intersection point of the previous ray.

By applying one level of subdivision with a very simple interpolation rule, the subdivided cells are guaranteed to be simple enough; that is, they do not contain a fold. The rule is that the midpoint between a black and a white value is assigned with a black value. This eliminates the problematic cases that two or more surfaces are defined within one cell, including the ambiguous ones.

4.5 Conclusion and our Current Work

We have presented a surface reconstruction based on an interpolation scheme of a binary dataset. The interpolation scheme yields smooth surfaces that common trilinear interpolation does not achieve. The computation complexity of the proposed reconstruction technique is relatively low. We now intend to investigate our method using "real-life" surfaces of human tissues and other biomedical applications such as virtual colonoscopy. We also plan to explore different methods to accelerate the computation. Such accelerations are needed to be able to integrate the reconstruction algorithm into an interactive rendering system.

References

1. Kaufman A, Cohen D, Yagel R. Volume graphics. IEEE Computer, 1993; 26(7):51-64.
2. Wright J, Hsieh J. A voxel-based, forward projection algorithm for rendering surface and volumetric data. In: Proc. IEEE Visualization '92, Boston, 1992; 340-348.
3. Cohen-Or D, Rich E, Lerner U, Shenkar V. Real-time photo-realistic visual flythrough. IEEE Transactions on Visualization and Computer Graphics, 1996;

2(3).

4. Shareef N, Yagel R. Rapid previewing via volume-based solid modeling. In: Proc. the 3rd Symposium on Solid Modeling and Applications, Solid Modeling '95, Salt Lake City, Utah, May 1995; 281-292.

5. Lu SC, Rebello AB, Miller RA, Kinzel GL, Yagel R. A simple visualization tool to support concurrent engineering design. Computer-Aided Design Journal, 1997; 29(10):727-735.

6. Greene N. Voxel space automata: Modeling with stochastic growth processes in voxel space. ACM/SIGGRAPH Computer Graphics, 1989, 23:175-184.

7. Lengyel J, Reichert M, Donald BR, Greenberg DP. Real-time robot motion planning using rasterizing computer graphics hardware. ACM/SIGGRAPH Computer Graphics, 1990; 24:327-335.

8. Lischinski D, Rappoport A. Image-based rendering for non-diffuse synthetic scenes. In: Proc. the 9th Eurographics Workshop on Rendering, 1998.

9. Yagel R, Ebert DS, Scott J, Kurzion Y. Grouping volume renderers for enhanced visualization in computational fluid dynamics. IEEE Transactions on Visualization and Computer Graphics, 1995; 1(2):117-132.

10. Tiede U, Schiemann T, Hoehne KH. High quality rendering of attributed volume data. In: Proc. IEEE Visualization '98, 1998.

11. Yagel R, Cohen D, Kaufman A. Normal estimation in 3D discrete space. The Visual Computer, 1992, 8(5/6):278-291.

12. Mveller T, Machiraju R, Mueller K, Yagel R, A comparison of normal estimation schemes. In: Proc. IEEE Visualization '97, Phoenix AZ, October 1997; 196-204.

13. Cohen-Or D, Levin D, Solomovici A. Three dimensional distance field metamorphosis. ACM Transactions on Graphics, 1998; 17(2).

5. Manufacturing Isovolumes

Michael Bailey

5.1 Introduction

Displaying a single isosurface provides considerable insight into the distribution of scalar values in a volume. Being able to simultaneously see several isosurfaces provides even more insight. The difference is that a single isosurface displays a point solution. Seeing several isosurfaces also provides "first derivative" information, that is, how fast values are changing in certain regions.

Certainly this insight can be achieved by moving an isovalue slider back and forth very quickly. However, too often, we cannot achieve such dynamics. Either the dataset is too large to be redisplayed at interactive speeds or we are away from our display screens in a presentation environment. The approach described here produces a series of closed isovolumes and then manufactures them, providing a non-volatile display of several isosurfaces. The inspiration for this idea was the common Russian doll set, as in Figure 5.1.

Figure 5.1. Interlocking volumes.

This is essentially an interlocking isovolume situation. It is easy and intuitive to see how the different layers merge into each other. The display is clear and non-volatile. The question then becomes how to best accomplish this for scientific data.

5.2 Previous Work

Most isosurface work focuses on just producing the surfaces themselves because the end goal is usually a computer graphics display. However, some recent work has focused on producing representations that encompass a complete volume. Tetrahedralisation is useful in volume visualisation for display purposes and for determining properties. An excellent overview of triangulation and tetrahedralisation can be found in [1]. An important generalisation of the tetrahedralisation of a volume is known as the *Interval Volume*, and is described in [2]. An Interval Volume tetrahedralises the gap between two isosurfaces to create an isovolume.

However, as will be seen in the next section, tetrahedralisation produces more information than is necessary for prototype manufacturing. Prototype manufacturing only needs the outer "skin" to be defined. The inner volume is then inferred from that. In [3], the outer skin problem is addressed by creating a closed surface that is topologically equivalent to the outer skin of a sphere. This method starts with a spherical grid in the middle of the volume and then spreads the grid points until they meet the isovalue. This produces good results, but it cannot handle an isovolume that contains passages through it or is in multiple pieces, common occurrences within a single dataset.

5.3 The Manufacturing Process and the Information it Requires

To fabricate the isovolumes, we have been using the UCSD/SDSC TeleManufacturing Facility (TMF) [4,5]. The TMF has made solid freeform fabrication into a routinely-used "3D visualisation hardcopy device". This project has connected a Helisys Laminated Object Manufacturing (LOM) [6] and a Z Corporation Z402 [7] system to the Internet. The Z402 and LOM machines are shown in Figure 5.2.

These two technologies are ideally suited for manufacturing isovolumes of arbitrary shape. Like all rapid prototyping or solid freeform fabrication processes, these two are *additive* manufacturing methods [8-10]. The LOM raw material is a roll of paper, 0.11 mm (0.0044 inches) thick, with heat-activated glue on the underside. For each layer, the paper is automatically rolled into place and laminated to the layers underneath it with heat and pressure. A laser then traces the outline of the part at that level. The Z402 raw material is a powder. The 2D cross-section at each layer is hardened with a binder chemical, spread by means of a laserjet printing head.

When the fabrication is completed, both processes require scrap to be removed, revealing the final part. For LOM, this involves plucking out paper scrap cubes. For the Z402, it involves vacuuming excess powder.

Figure 5.2. Z Corporation Z402 and Helisys LOM machines.

Our machines are front-ended by web-based file submission procedures and automated geometry checking. They are back-ended by web-based cameras that monitor the machines' progress. The project has found that physical models can provide considerable visualisation insight in such diverse fields as biochemistry, earth science, fluid dynamics, mathematics, and terrain mapping.

The required input for all solid freeform fabrication machines is the industry-standard STL file. To convert a solid geometry to an STL file requires creating a list of 3D triangles that bound the outer skin of the solid [8]. STL-defined 3D objects must be legal solids, that is, they must be bounded by a complete shell with no holes or cracks. In addition, the triangles of the outer skin must obey the vertex-to-vertex rule: each edge must bound exactly two triangles. Any other edge configuration would result in cracks in the outer surface.

5.4 Forcing the Isovolume to be a Legal Solid

When requesting a graphical isosurface, a single scalar value, S^*, is given. A manufacturable isovolume must be a legal solid, which means that it must be continuously bound on all sides. In requesting an isovolume, two scalar values, S_{min}^* and S_{max}^*, must be specified.[1]

Turning these two isovalues into a legal solid is a two-step process:

1. Compute the corresponding isosurface of each isovalue;
2. At the boundaries of the volume, cap the gap between the isosurfaces.

5.5 Triangle "Incremation"

Much of the current graphics and visualisation literature is concerned with polygon *decimation*. Polygon decimation seeks to eliminate detail that is perceptually unnecessary, in order to achieve better graphics performance. This technique is especially crucial for isosurfaces of large datasets.

This works well for computer graphics. Computer graphics displays can get away with too little detail through techniques such as smooth shading and dynamics. But, physical solids can play no such trickery. Large polygons that look smooth on a graphics display will create a fabricated surface that looks coarse and "chunky". Fortunately, when fabricating isovolumes, display speed is not relevant. Whereas interactive graphics encourages the trading of display quality and accuracy for speed, fabrication encourages the most accuracy and quality regardless of polygon count.

Thus, triangle decimation is not an issue here. In fact, the only such issue is how much we should *increase* the scene detail in pursuit of a quality fabrication. We use the term *triangle incremation* to describe the adding of such scene detail. We have made models composed of over one million 3D triangles, and the count could go quite a bit higher. Thus, in typical volumes, we can apply a considerable amount of polygon incremation before running into manufacturing limits.

5.6 Interpolating within a Marching Cube

The standard isosurface algorithm is Marching Cubes [11-12]. The algorithm looks

---

[1] If just the inside or just the outside is desired, the value of S_{min}^* can be set to $-\infty$ or the value of S_{max}^* can be set to $+\infty$.

at the trilinear behaviour of an isosurface in a single cube and renders it as 1-4 polygons. But, in fact, the isovalues within that cube are a smoothly-varying trilinear function. Thus, the real isosurface within that cube is a smooth surface, not a few flat polygons. This surface can be obtained by solving the trilinear equations. Furthermore, it can be made recursive and adaptive, subdividing the smooth isosurface within the cube as much as necessary to achieve a desired accuracy. Such things are allowed to happen when you do not care about polygon count.

Assume the standard Marching Cube, with eight scalar values, S_{ijk}, at the corners. S_{uvw} is the interpolated scalar value somewhere within the cube, with the values of u, v and w parameterised to lie in the range:

$$0 \leq u, v, w \leq 1.$$

At an arbitrary (u, v, w), the interpolated scalar value is a function of blending equations and the scalar values at the cube's corners:

$$S_{uvw} = \sum_{i,j,k} B_{ijk} S_{ijk} \tag{5.1}$$

where the blending functions are:

$$B_{000} = (1-u) \cdot (1-v) \cdot (1-w) \qquad B_{100} = u \cdot (1-v) \cdot (1-w)$$
$$B_{001} = (1-u) \cdot (1-v) \cdot w \qquad B_{101} = u \cdot (1-v) \cdot w$$
$$B_{010} = (1-u) \cdot v \cdot (1-w) \qquad B_{110} = u \cdot v \cdot (1-w)$$
$$B_{011} = (1-u) \cdot v \cdot w \qquad B_{111} = u \cdot v \cdot w$$

Solving these equations for $S_{uvw} = S^*$ along the edges of each face gives us the vertices of the Marching Cubes triangles. We use these triangles as a first step. The problem then becomes one of turning those triangles into a smoother surface that is closer to the actual isosurface that is passing through the cube. To do this, we will recursively subdivide each triangle until it comes within a specified tolerance of the exact isovalue.

5.7 Recursively Subdividing a Triangle

A legal solid triangulation of an isovolume must not have any cracks where two adjacent surfaces do not meet precisely. (This is often a graphics requirement too, but is sometimes fudged. When the triangles are small, the cracks are less noticeable.) The way to avoid cracks is to be sure that adjacent surfaces share the same edge and vertices. In rapid prototyping terminology, this is called satisfying the "vertex-to-vertex" rule.

Triangles within a single Marching Cube can be made to satisfy the vertex-to-vertex rule by keeping track of common subdivision vertices. However, tracking vertex-to-vertex information between Cubes requires a lot of extra bookkeeping.

Instead our strategy involved subdividing a triangle as a function of what is happening at its bounding vertices. Because adjacent cubes have the same corner vertices, each cube's subdivision decisions will be the same along the shared boundaries.

The vertex data structure records each vertex's u, v and w normalised parametric coordinates. This is a convenience in that all other needed quantities (x, y, z, and S) can be interpolated from these parameters as shown in Equation 5.1.

The first step in the triangle subdivision is to look at the midpoint of each edge. The midpoint is determined in parametric space. From that (u, v, w), a corresponding scalar value, S_{mid}, is computed. S_{mid} is compared against the required isovalue, S^*. If it is outside a specified tolerance ε, it is flagged as needing to be subdivided. As there are three edge midpoints in a triangle, there are $2^3 = 8$ possible subdivision patterns. The eight possibilities are shown in Figure 5.3. Note that there are really only four unique cases, the others being reflections of those four.

- ● edge midpoint is outside
- ○ edge midpoint is within tolerance
- ◯ vertex
- ▦ triangle centroid

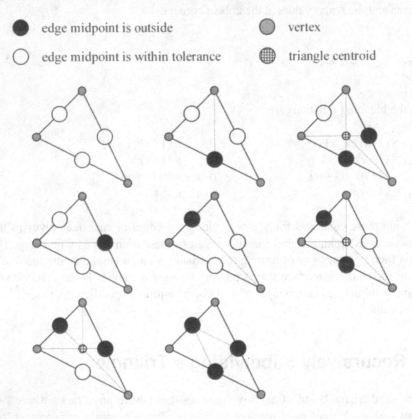

Figure 5.3. Triangle subdivision strategies.

For the case where no interpolated edge midpoint's scalar value is outside the tolerance to S^*, that triangle can be output as is. For all other cases, the errant midpoints are "pushed" so that their scalar value is equal to S^* (see the next section for how this is done), and the triangle is subdivided as shown above. Each of the subdivided triangles is then examined according to the same tests and possibly subdivided. This recursion proceeds until all triangles are within the tolerance of S^*, or until a certain maximum recursion depth is reached.

In the above diagrams, the exact way that the triangles are subdivided is probably not crucial so long as the following rules are obeyed:

1. An edge with a midpoint that is out of tolerance needs to be turned into two edges for two triangles. The rest of this original edge must have the chance to be further subdivided.
2. An edge without a midpoint that is out of tolerance must not be subdivided.

Note that what happens on a particular edge is only dependent on information on its own midpoint, and not on anything that has to do with the other two edges. Thus, adjacent triangles will make the same decision on the shared edge. This is how we can guarantee that no cracks are created in the resulting triangle model.

5.8 Pushing an Arbitrary Point to the Exact Trilinear Isosurface

If we work in parameterised (u, v, w) coordinates, we can slide an arbitrary point within the cube to the isosurface defined by $S = S^*$ by determining how much we need to move in u, v and w. If the isovalue S_{uvw} at (u, v, w) is not within ε of S^*, we need to push the (u, v, w) point enough to change its isovalue by $\Delta S = S^* - S_{uvw}$. From multivariate calculus:

$$\Delta S = S^* - S_{uvw} = \frac{\partial S}{\partial u} \Delta u + \frac{\partial S}{\partial v} \Delta v + \frac{\partial S}{\partial w} \Delta w \qquad (5.2)$$

where $\dfrac{\partial S}{\partial u}$ is found within an individual Cube by differentiating (5.1):

$$\frac{\partial S_{uvw}}{\partial u} = \sum_{i,j,k} \frac{\partial B_{uvw}}{\partial u} S_{ijk} \qquad (5.3)$$

and similarly for $\dfrac{\partial S}{\partial v}$ and $\dfrac{\partial S}{\partial w}$.

Equation 5.2 has three unknowns, Δu, Δv and Δw. Thus, there is no unique $(\Delta u, \Delta v, \Delta w)$ combination that will satisfy Equation 5.2. However, certain combinations will make more sense than others. We chose to push the point (u, v, w) in the direction of the surface normal to the isosurface at that point.

From [11], the surface normal $\vec{N} \equiv (nu, nv, nw)$ is equal to $(\frac{\partial S}{\partial u}, \frac{\partial S}{\partial v}, \frac{\partial S}{\partial w})$.

Letting $(\Delta u, \Delta v, \Delta w) = t \cdot (nu, nv, nw)$ so that the point is pushed along $\vec{N}$, Equation 5.2 becomes:

$$\Delta S = t \cdot (nu^2 + nv^2 + nw^2) \text{ or } t = \frac{\Delta S}{(nu^2 + nv^2 + nw^2)}.$$

Thus:

$$\Delta u = \frac{nu \cdot \Delta S}{(nu^2 + nv^2 + nw^2)} \tag{5.4a}$$

$$\Delta v = \frac{nv \cdot \Delta S}{(nu^2 + nz^2 + nw^2)} \tag{5.4b}$$

$$\Delta w = \frac{nw \cdot \Delta S}{(nu^2 + nv^2 + nw^2)} \tag{5.4c}$$

The general algorithm is:

```
Start with a point (u,v,w) from an edge midpoint;
Compute S_{uvw} from (5.1);
while (|S* - S_{uvw}| > ε) do
   Compute (nx,ny,nz) from (5.3);
   ΔS = S* - S_{uvw};
   Compute Δu, Δv and Δw from (5.4a-c);
   u = u + Δu;
   v = v + Δv;
   w = w + Δw;
   compute S_{uvw} from (5.1);
end while;
```

5.9 Results of a Test Case

An interesting test case is provided in [13]. This paper shows a method of using rational quadric Bezier surfaces as a trilinear interpolant. A single Marching Cube is considered. The scalar data values at the uvw corners are in Table 5.1.

What makes this test case so interesting is that the isosurface contains a saddle point within this one cube. This makes the traditional Marching Cubes algorithm produce a particularly jagged set of polygons.

Figures 5.4-5.6 show the isovolume produced between isovalues of 0.44 and 0.90, using different tolerances. Figures 5.4a-c show the isovolume surfaces. Figures 5.5a-c have shrunk the triangles to show the triangulation decisions made by the algorithm. Figure 5.6 shows a detailed close-up of one region of the triangulation.

Table 5.1. Test Marching Cube

u, v, w	S_{uvw}	u, v, w	S_{uvw}
0, 0, 0	0.2	0, 0, 1	0.9
1, 0, 0	0.9	1, 0, 1	0.2
0, 1, 0	0.7	0, 1, 1	0.1
1, 1, 0	0.0	1, 1, 1	0.9

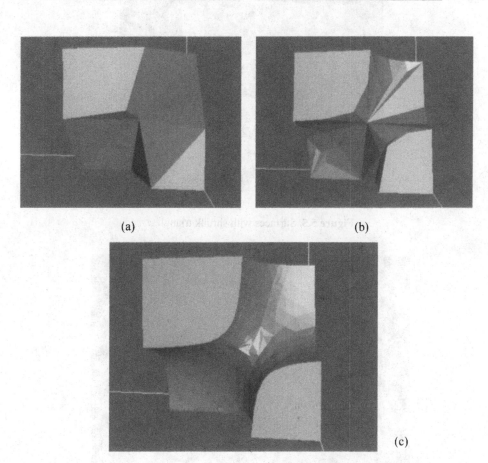

(a)   (b)

(c)

Figure 5.4. Surfaces of an isovolume: (a) $\varepsilon = 0.1$ with 38 triangles, (b) $\varepsilon = 0.01$ with 142 triangles, and (c) $\varepsilon = 0.001$ with 1152 triangles.

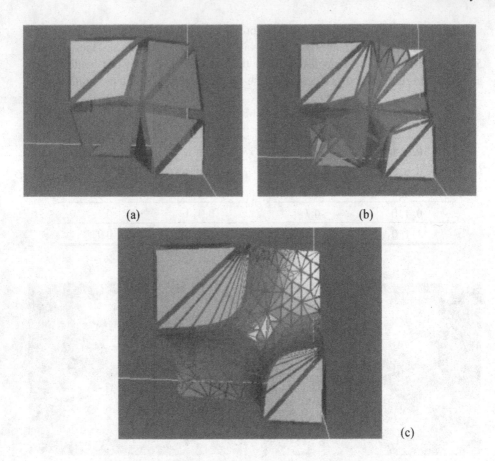

(a)   (b)

(c)

Figure 5.5. Surfaces with shrunk triangles.

Figure 5.6. A close-up view of the $\varepsilon = 0.001$ triangulation.

5.10 An Interlocking Example

One of the strengths of this method lies in producing a series of isovolumes with common S^* values at their boundaries. This makes them fit together like the Russian dolls. This example uses a summation of decaying exponentials to seed the scalar values in a volume. The scalar value was assigned by:

$$S(x, y, z) = \sum_{i=1}^{3} A_i e^{-r_i^2}$$

where:

$$r_i^2 = \left(x - x_i\right)^2 + \left(y - y_i\right)^2 + \left(z - z_i\right)^2.$$

As expected, the isosurface shapes were spherical "waves" emanating from the (x_i, y_i, z_i) points. Several different isovolume ranges were chosen, the STL files were generated, and the parts were fabricated. The results are shown in Figure 5.7.

Figure 5.7. Fabricated interlocking isovolumes.

5.11 Medical Applications

One of the main reasons for this project was to develop better tools for examining medical volume data, as shown in Figures 5.8 and 5.9. Figure 5.8 shows the skull data from the Visualization Toolkit (vtk) [14], turned into a manufactured isovolume. Note in Figure 5.8a how the triangles have been adaptively subdivided, providing more detail in areas of rapid change and less in flatter areas. Figure 5.9 shows a 3D foetal ultrasound isovolume.

5.12 Conclusions

The results from the examples in Figures 5.7-5.9 show that manufacturing isovolumes are a viable way of examining the relationships between different isosurface shapes by looking at both sides of a single isovolume and by examining multiple isovolumes. It is also a way to transport a volume visualisation so it can be seen by multiple viewers without access to a graphics display.

The polygon incremation creates an arbitrarily accurate surface by subdividing only where it is necessary to meet the tolerance. Specifying this tolerance provides a convenient way to trade-off accuracy versus polygon count.

The most obvious benefit of manufacturing isovolumes is that it brings our sense of touch to bear on the task of understanding data that may be too complex to understand by sight alone. Being able to run fingers over and through a physical model conveys extra information that the eye does not even know was missing. We have been surprised how much more is understood about the 3D shape after holding a physical model for even a short amount of time.

There are some less obvious benefits to having a physical model of isovolumes. There appears to be some amount of insight that can be obtained by slightly *twisting* the interlocking pieces as they are fitted together. This imparts a certain sense of spatial derivatives, that is, how much a small physical perturbation changes the isoshape. This is hard to quantify, but everyone who handles these models seems to do this action intuitively. Most likely, we unconsciously do this with items in our everyday life, and have learned to gain insight this way without realising it.

Acknowledgements

This work was supported by ONR grant N00014-97-1-0183 and NSF grant MIP-9420099. The foetal ultrasound data is from Dr. Tom Nelson of the UCSD Medical School.

References

1. Nielson G. Tools for triangulations and tetrahedralizations and constructing functions defined over them. In: Nielson G, Hagen H, Muller H (eds), Scientific Visualization: Overviews, Methodologies, Techniques, IEEE Computer Society, 1997; 429-525.

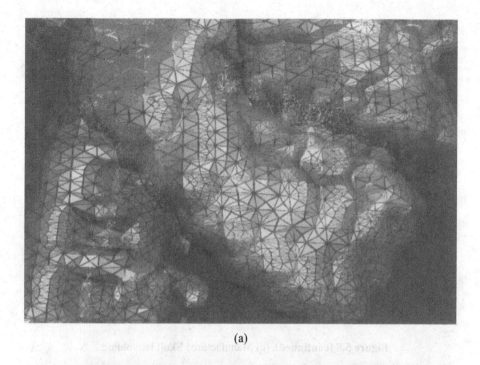

(a)

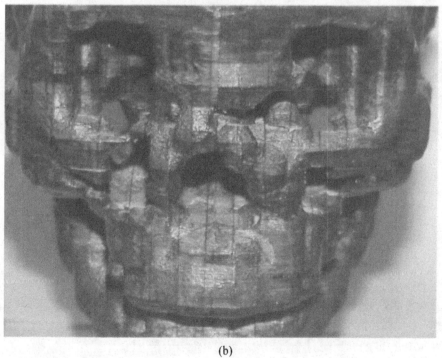

(b)

Figure 5.8. (a) Skull isovolume triangles. (b) Manufactured skull isovolume.

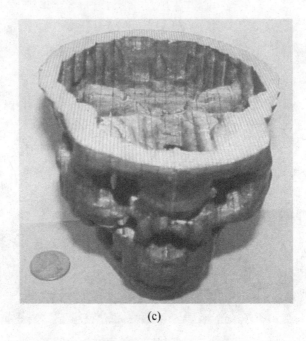

(c)

Figure 5.8 (continued). (c) Manufactured Skull Isovolume

Figure 5.9. Foetal isovolumes.

2. Nielson G, Junwon Sung. Interval volume tetrahedralization. In: IEEE Visualization '97; 221-228.
3. Miller JV, Breen DE, Lorensen WE, O'Bara RM, Wozny MJ. Geometrically deformed models: A method for extracting closed geometric models from volume data, ACM/SIGGRAPH Computer Graphics, 1991; 25:217-226.
4. Bailey M. Tele-manufacturing: Rapid prototyping on the internet with automatic consistency-checking. IEEE Computer Graphics and Applications, 1995; 15(6):20-26.
5. Svitil K. A touch of science, Discover Magazine, June 1998; 80-84.
6. Helisys, Inc. http://www.helisys.com, 1999.
7. Z Corporation. http://www.zcorp.com, 1999.
8. Bailey M. The use of solid rapid prototyping in computer graphics and scientific visualization. In: SIGGRAPH Course Notes: The Use of Touch as an I/O Device for Graphics and Visualization, 1996.
9. Burns M. Automated Fabrication, Prentice Hall, 1993.
10. Johnson JL. A Unified Description of All Free Form Fabrication Technologies Based on Fundamental Principles, Palatino Press, 1994.
11. Lorensen WE, Cline HE. Marching cubes: A high resolution 3D surface construction algorithm. ACM/SIGGRAPH Computer Graphics, 1987; 21(3):163-169.
12. Nielson G, Hamann B. The asymptotic decider: Resolving the ambiguity in marching cubes. In: Proc. IEEE Visualization '91; 83-91.
13. Hamann B, Trotts I, Farin G. On approximating contours of the piecewise trilinear interpolant using triangular rational-quadric Bezier patches. IEEE Transactions on Visualization and Computer Graphics, 1997; 3(3):215-227.
14. Schroeder W, Martin K, Lorensen W. The Visualization Toolkit: An Object-Oriented Approach to 3D Graphics, Second Edition, Prentice Hall PTR, 1998.

PART III

COMPLEX VOLUMETRIC OBJECTS

6. Constructive Representations of Volumetric Environments

Min Chen, John V. Tucker and Adrian Leu

6.1 Introduction

There is a wealth of evidence which demonstrates that for many situations in 3D graphics volume-based techniques are more attractive than traditional surface-based ones. The gradual maturity of volume visualisation, accompanied by the reduction in the cost of computing power and memory, further improves the application of volume-based techniques in mainstream computer graphics, and suggests that volume visualisation can be developed further into volume graphics. Kaufman, Cohen and Yagel first outlined an agenda for volume graphics in 1993 [1]. The 1995 US ONR Volume Visualisation Workshop [2] further highlighted the potential of volume graphics, and some of the technical issues that are yet to be addressed.

Despite the fact that the development of volume rendering techniques has reached its maturity, very limited effort has been made in volume-based modelling methods, in contrast to an extensive range of surface-based modelling methods and tools. In most volume graphics systems, volumetric objects are largely represented in a raw form being identical or close to what was obtained from a digitisation or a simulation process. The most commonly used representation of raw data is a 3D regular grid, often referred to as a 3D raster or volume buffer. Much effort has been concentrated on the *visualisation* of the data — which aims to extract meaningful information from the data. In contrast, little effort has been concentrated on *graphics* which aims to create pictures using the data. For the purpose of graphics, the raw volumetric datasets are often inadequate for the specification of complex objects and scenes. It is thereby desirable to introduce more sophisticated volume data types and combinational operations for modelling complex objects and scenes.

The previous work on volume-based modelling falls into three areas:

a. Object creation through voxelisation. One such example is Wang and Kaufman's voxelisation method which supports CSG operations [3-5] (see also Chapters 1, 7, 8 and 20).

b. Interactive data modification through procedural tools and operators. Examples are Wang and Kaufman's volume sculpting [6], Galyean and Hughes's interactive sculpting [7], and Avila and Sobierajski's haptic interaction model [8].

c. Data reorganisation for effective data interrogation and efficient data storage and visualisation. Examples are Levoy's octree-based volume representation [9], Laur and Hanrahan's hierarchical splatting [10], Nelson's modelling of free-hand ultrasound data [11], and Malzbender's frequency-domain modelling and rendering [12] (see also Chapter 2).

The modelling schemes in both (a) and (b) create and modify volumetric data in its raw form. This inevitably leads to an undesirable re-sampling process in order to create new objects. Particularly in situations where operand objects are of different size and resolutions and where operators involve rotational transformation or deformation, this process may result in space inefficiency and quality degeneration. Re-sampling also prevents operand objects from keeping their own individual properties. Moreover, most of the existing schemes in (a) focus on the modelling of solid objects represented in the form of volume buffers, failing to capitalise on the advantages of volume modelling over traditional solid modelling in handling object interiors and amorphous phenomena. The schemes in (c) have very limited support for combinational operations on volume objects without resorting to another data representation such as an uncompressed volume buffer.

Our recent work on Constructive Volume Geometry (CVG) [13] illustrated many desirable properties of volume data types through an algebraic theory for volume-based modelling and rendering. The theory of CVG provides an algebraic framework for defining a variety of operations appropriate to the geometrical, graphical and physical properties defined in individual computer graphics models.

Our conception of CVG is a major generalisation of Constructive Solid Geometry (CSG). Unlike CSG, CVG does not limit itself to geometrical operations only, and it can also be employed to combine physical properties that are associated with objects. Its combinational operations, mostly defined in the real domain, can be used to model complex interior structures of objects and amorphous phenomena in a constructive manner. Our study [10] has also shown that the CSG model based on union '$\cup$', intersection '$\cap$' and difference '$-$' is embedded in a simple CVG model, that is, the Boolean opacity only model based on volume operations $\cup$, $\cap$ and $-$.

Meanwhile, our other work on TROVE (Two-level Representations Of Volumetric Environments) [14-15], a multi-volume rendering system, also demonstrated the feasibility of rendering complex scenes composed of multiple volumetric datasets on ordinary workstations using a collection of rendering algorithms, including direct surface rendering, volume ray casting and splatting. In the context of modelling, one important feature of TROVE is that it does not require volume objects to be re-sampled into a single volumetric dataset, thus the complexity of a scene depends mainly on the number of objects, and the size of their underlying volumetric datasets, but not so much on how objects are positioned.

This chapter will focus on our effort to combine our work on CVG and TROVE into a more powerful system, called CROVE (Constructive Representations Of Volumetric Environments), for modelling and rendering complex scenes consisting of multiple CVG objects. In particular, CROVE addresses the shortcomings of volumetric CSG through voxelisation [3-5] by equipping itself with a direct rendering engine, though its object and scene representations can also be used as inputs to a voxelisation process. Through this chapter, we will show that the combination of the CVG concepts and the CROVE system has successfully addressed all three scopes of volume modelling proposed by Nielson (see Section 2.2).

In Section 6.2, we will first outline the main concepts of CVG and the algebraic operations for building CVG objects. In Section 6.3, we will present a data representation scheme for specifying graphics scenes with composite volume objects. In particular, we will highlight the main features of CROVE such as object composition, data channels and the use of bounding boxes. In Section 6.4, a sophisticated rendering algorithm will be described which facilitates the direct rendering of solid objects and amorphous phenomena presented in the same scene. This will be followed by our concluding remarks in relation to volume graphics.

6.2 Constructive Volume Geometry

6.2.1 Overview

Simple volume data types are extensively used in medical imaging, scientific computation and many other applications, and have now collectively become one of the most commonly-used modelling schemes in computer graphics and visualisation. These data types offer a true 3D descriptive power to represent an object's interior as well as its surface, and can be used to model solids as well as amorphous phenomena. They require only very simple data structures while facilitating sophisticated direct rendering methods by defining continuous scalar fields upon discrete volumetric datasets. However, the basic volume data types fail to offer adequate inter-operability of volumetric datasets. The previous attempts mostly involved construction of a new volume by re-sampling volumetric datasets [16], resulting in expansion of data size as well as degeneration of data quality.

The discrete and bounded nature of raw volumetric data is the main obstacle to a consistent specification of combinational operations. In order to equip volume data types with such operations, CVG introduces a set of concepts that map volumetric datasets to more inter-operable *volume objects*, which constitute a subset of *spatial objects*, through a series of geometrical generalisations as shown in Figure 6.1.

Intuitively, spatial objects are defined at every point in 3D Euclidean space $\mathbf{E}^3$ and are considered to be mathematically perfect objects in this context, therefore providing the algebra of CVG with a neat basis. The concept of volume object is introduced as a go-between to accommodate both finite object representation (a property of volumetric datasets) and inter-operability (facilitated by spatial objects).

In CVG, volume objects that are defined directly upon volumetric datasets are called *convex volume objects*, and those resulting from combinational operations are called *composite volume objects*. Although it is possible to convert composite volume objects to volumetric datasets prior to rendering through re-sampling, such a process is undesirable in many applications due to the demerits described above. In this work, we decompose each composite volume object into its building blocks (i.e. convex volume objects) during the rendering, and thus the rendering engine needs to

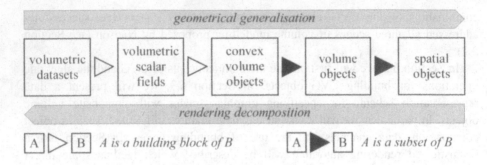

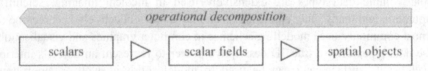

Figure 6.1. The main conceptual entities in constructive volume geometry.

sample only the volumetric datasets which convex volume objects are defined upon. To overcome the difficulty in defining operators directly upon bounded volume objects that may be arbitrarily positioned in $\mathbf{E}^3$, CVG operators are defined upon unbounded spatial objects, and are constructed from simple arithmetic operations on scalars through a series of operational decompositions (Figure 6.2).

Figure 6.2. Operational decomposition of CVG operators.

6.2.2 The Main Concepts of CVG

Spatial Objects and CVG Models

The most fundamental definition in CVG is that of *spatial object*.

Definition: A spatial object is a tuple $\mathbf{o} = (O, A_1, ..., A_k)$ of scalar fields defined in $\mathbf{E}^3$, including an opacity field $O: \mathbf{E}^3 \to [0, 1]$ specifying the visibility of every point in $\mathbf{E}^3$ and possibly other attribute fields $A_1, ..., A_k: \mathbf{E}^3 \to [0, 1]$, $k \geq 0$.   □

Instead of the general real domain $\mathbf{R}$, we restrict scalar fields to the real domain [0, 1], to which all other computer-representable domains can be easily mapped.

The opacity field "implicitly" defines the "visible geometry" of an object. Given an opacity field $O: \mathbf{E}^3 \to [0, 1]$, a point $p \in \mathbf{E}^3$ is said to be *opaque* if $O(p) = 1$, *transparent* if $O(p) = 0$, and *translucent* otherwise. Any point that is not transparent is potentially visible to a rendering algorithm. In other words, the "visible geometry" of the object is $\{p \in \mathbf{E}^3 \mid O(p) > 0\}$.

A *CVG model* is an algebra that defines a set of objects and a set of combinational operations for the objects. A simple CVG model may contain only an opacity field, i.e. an *opacity only model*. This model can be further simplified to a

Boolean opacity only model by restricting opacity values to the Boolean domain {0, 1}. Chen and Tucker's recent work [10] on CVG has shown that the CSG based on union 'U', intersection '∩' and different '−' is isomorphic with the corresponding Boolean opacity only model of CVG based on the U, ∩ and − (Figure 6.3); and hence is embeddable in all CVG models.

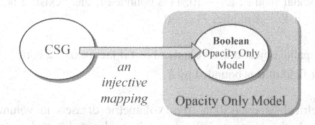

Figure 6.3. The mapping from CSG to the Boolean opacity only model.

In traditional surface-based graphics, the physical properties of an object, such as colour and texture, are defined separately from its geometry. This is largely due to the fact that the physical properties are normally represented in a way very different from that of geometrical properties. On the other hand, in image processing and volume graphics, these two kinds of properties are both defined with the basic primitives, namely pixels and voxels respectively. Such integration has many advantages, including a more uniform data representation and a simpler rendering pipeline (without texture mapping).

CVG facilitates similar integration through the object tuple $\mathbf{o} = (O, A_1, ..., A_k)$, where the set of attributes $A_1, ..., A_k$ is determined by the corresponding CVG model. For instance, a *four-colour channel model* may associate every point in $\mathbf{E}^3$ with an opacity and a colour, and each spatial object in this model is specified by four scalar fields for the opacity, red, green and blue components. In order to simulate correctly the effect of seeing through a coloured medium, it is also possible to construct an algebra for a *seven-colour channel model* [17] which is based on an idealised physical analogy where the colour of an object is separated into the part from pigmented particles, and that from a homogeneous medium. Other models may also include attribute fields for properties such as reflection coefficients and specular reflection exponent. An algebraic concept called *signature* [13] has been introduced to describe the algebraic structure of a graphics model in a consistent manner.

One may also notice that the most fundamental field in any CVG model is the opacity field, and that it is not necessary for a model to have an explicit "geometry" field. This feature is consistent with the principal objective of computer graphics which is to render visible points in a scene. It also suits the volume rendering integral (see Section 2.2.3) better, as such a process samples each point in $\mathbf{E}^3$ for its opacity and colour. The geometry property is considered only when the opacity or colour are not explicitly defined. However, CVG does not prevent the inclusion of a geometry field in a model. Later, in Section 6.3, we will show that our implementation of CVG accommodates models with a geometry field.

Volume Objects and Related Concepts

To bring volumetric representation into the discussion, we introduce the concepts of *volume objects* as spatial objects whose "visible geometry" is contained within a finite region of $\mathbf{E}^3$.

Definition: A scalar field $F: \mathbf{E}^3 \to [0, 1]$ is bounded if there exists a bounded set $X \subset \mathbf{E}^3$ such that $x \in \mathbf{E}^3 - X$ implies $F(x) = 0$.   □

Definition: A spatial object **o** is a volume object if there exists a bounded set X such that each scalar field of **o** is bounded by X.   □

The geometrical generalisation from volumetric datasets to volume object is achieved through the concepts of *volumetric scalar fields* and *convex volume objects*.

Given a finite set $P=\{p_1, p_2, ..., p_n \mid p_i \in \mathbf{E}^3\}$ of distinct points, we call the convex hull $\textit{Vol}(P)$ of the point set P the *volume* of P, and $p_1, p_2, ..., p_n$ *voxels*. When each voxel p_i is associated with a known scalar value $v_i \in [0, 1]$ and there is an interpolation function I that uniquely determines a value at every point within $\textit{Vol}(P)$, a *volumetric scalar field* F can thus be defined in $\mathbf{E}^3$ as:

$$F(p) = \begin{cases} I(p,(p_1,v_1),(p_2,v_2),...,(p_n,v_n)) & p \in \textit{Vol}(P) \\ 0 & p \notin \textit{Vol}(P) \end{cases}$$

In volume graphics, trilinear interpolation is the most typical interpolation function for a volume where voxels are organised in the form of a regular 3D grid. For a non-regular volume with scattered voxels, 3D Delaunay triangulation [18] may be applied to $\textit{Vol}(P)$, and unknown values in each tetrahedron can then be determined by trilinear interpolation or bary-centric interpolation [19]. We can now define the concept of *convex volume object* as:

Definition: A convex volume object based on an interpolation method I is a volume object that consists of a finite set of volumetric scalar fields all of which are defined upon the same $\textit{Vol}(P)$ by the same interpolation method.   □

The above concepts provide a practical method for creating a convex volume object from the scalar values associated to a finite set of points in $\mathbf{E}^3$, a gradual evolution from bounded discrete volumetric datasets to mathematically more desirable spatial objects as illustrated in Figure 6.1.

Decomposition of CVG Operations

With the definition of spatial objects, an operation on two objects, for example, **o**$_1$=(O_1, $A_{1,1}$, ..., $A_{1,k}$) and **o**$_2$=(O_2, $A_{2,1}$, ..., $A_{2,k}$), can be defined by operations on the corresponding scalar fields. The operations on scalar fields can then be defined by operations on scalars (Figure 6.2). For instance, in the four-colour channel model, we build up the definition of the union ∪, intersection ∩ and difference − operations as shown in Table 6.1.

Table 6.1. Three basic CVG operators in the four-colour channel model.

operations on scalars

$$\mathbf{max}(s_1, s_2) = \begin{cases} s_1 & s_1 \geq s_2 \\ s_2 & s_1 < s_2 \end{cases} \qquad \mathbf{min}(s_1, s_2) = \begin{cases} s_1 & s_1 \leq s_2 \\ s_2 & s_1 > s_2 \end{cases}$$

$$\mathbf{sub}(s_1, s_2) = \begin{cases} 0 & s_1 \leq s_2 \\ s_1 - s_2 & s_1 > s_2 \end{cases} \qquad \mathbf{select}(s_1, t_1, s_2, t_2) = \begin{cases} t_1 & s_1 \geq s_2 \\ t_2 & s_1 < s_2 \end{cases}$$

operations on scalar fields

$\forall p \in \mathbf{E}^3 \quad \mathrm{MAX}(S_1, S_2)(p) = \mathbf{max}(S_1(p), S_2(p))$

$\forall p \in \mathbf{E}^3 \quad \mathrm{MIN}(S_1, S_2)(p) = \mathbf{min}(S_1(p), S_2(p))$

$\forall p \in \mathbf{E}^3 \quad \mathrm{SUB}(S_1, S_2)(p) = \mathbf{sub}(S_1(p), S_2(p))$

$\forall p \in \mathbf{E}^3 \quad \mathrm{SELECT}(S_1, T_1, S_2, T_2)(p) = \mathbf{select}(S_1(p), T_1(p), S_2(p), T_2(p))$

operation on spatial objects

$\cup(\mathbf{O}_1, \mathbf{O}_2) = (\mathrm{MAX}(O_1, O_2), \mathrm{SELECT}(O_1, R_1, O_2, R_2), \mathrm{SELECT}(O_1, G_1, O_2, G_2),$
$\qquad \mathrm{SELECT}(O_1, B_1, O_2, B_2)).$

$\cap(\mathbf{O}_1, \mathbf{O}_2) = (\mathrm{MIN}(O_1, O_2), \mathrm{SELECT}(O_1, R_1, O_2, R_2), \mathrm{SELECT}(O_1, G_1, O_2, G_2),$
$\qquad \mathrm{SELECT}(O_1, B_1, O_2, B_2)).$

$-(\mathbf{O}_1, \mathbf{O}_2) = (\mathrm{SUB}(O_1, O_2), R_1, G_1, B_1).$

Figure 6.4 shows the applications of these three operations to two spatial objects, $\mathbf{O}_1 = (O_1, R_1, G_1, B_1)$ and $\mathbf{O}_2 = (O_2, R_2, G_2, B_2)$, which are defined respectively with the following scalar fields:

$$(O_1, R_1, G_1, B_1)(p) = \begin{cases} (0.5, 1, 0, 1) & \text{if } p_x, p_y \in [-2, 1]; p_z \in [-1.5, 1.5], \\ (0, 0, 0, 0) & \text{otherwise.} \end{cases}$$

$$(O_2, R_2, G_2, B_2)(p) = \begin{cases} (1, F_r(p), F_g(p), F_h(p)) & \text{if } p_x, p_y \in [-1, 2]; p_z \in [1, 3], \\ (0, 0, 0, 0) & \text{otherwise.} \end{cases}$$

Object $\mathbf{O}_1$ is associated with a constant colour in a rectangular domain, while the colour fields of $\mathbf{O}_2$, are volumetric scalar fields defined upon some random volumetric datasets. Between the two objects, $\mathbf{O}_2$ is the more "visible" object as it has a stronger opacity field in its visible domain.

In Figure 6.4, composite objects in (a), (b), (c) and (d) are rendered with a direct volume rendering method which gives a better impression of volume density, while the composite object in (e) is rendered with a direct surface rendering method which displays only the interested isosurfaces. We can clearly notice from (a) and (e) that the CVG operations have applied to the entire 3D domain that contains $\mathbf{o}_1$ and $\mathbf{o}_2$. As $\mathbf{o}_2$ has a stronger opacity field than $\mathbf{o}_1$, the resulting objects from these operations are usually not symmetrical. For example, in $\cup(\mathbf{o}_1, \mathbf{o}_2)$, $\mathbf{o}_2$ appears to have penetrated into $\mathbf{o}_1$, but not vice versa. In $-(\mathbf{o}_1, \mathbf{o}_2)$, part of $\mathbf{o}_1$ has been segmented off, while $\mathbf{o}_1$ has only managed to reduce the opacity of part of $\mathbf{o}_2$ in $-(\mathbf{o}_2, \mathbf{o}_1)$.

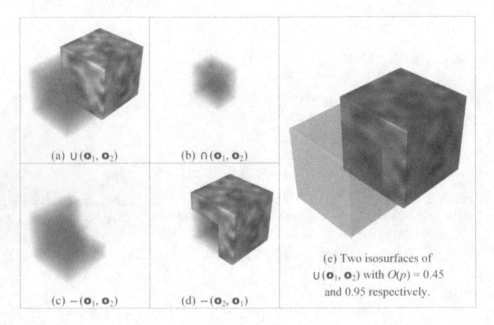

(a) $\cup(\mathbf{o}_1, \mathbf{o}_2)$ (b) $\cap(\mathbf{o}_1, \mathbf{o}_2)$

(e) Two isosurfaces of $\cup(\mathbf{o}_1, \mathbf{o}_2)$ with $O(p) = 0.45$ and 0.95 respectively.

(c) $-(\mathbf{o}_1, \mathbf{o}_2)$ (d) $-(\mathbf{o}_2, \mathbf{o}_1)$

Figure 6.4. Applying basic CVG operations to two cubic spatial objects in the four-colour channel model.

6.2.3 The Merits of CVG

The spatial objects in the four-colour channel model have true 3D "geometry" as well as colour properties. The colour properties can be manipulated in the same way as the opacity property. Figure 6.5 shows a set of spatial objects constructed from volumetric datasets as well as simple primitives such as spheres and cubes.

No texture mapping is necessary during the rendering of the objects in Figure 6.4 since all of them are defined with true 3D colour properties. For example, the object in (a) is described as:

$$-(\cup(\ \cap(\mathbf{sphere}_1, \mathbf{texture}_1), \cap(\mathbf{sphere}_2, \mathbf{texture}_2)\ ), \mathbf{cuboid})$$

where the scalar fields of **sphere**$_1$ and **sphere**$_2$ are defined by two spherical functions that differ slightly in their geometrical position; **texture**$_1$ and **texture**$_2$

are two 3D texture blocks made from 2D images; and **cuboid** is simply a completely opaque rectangular block used to slice off the front of the composite volume object.

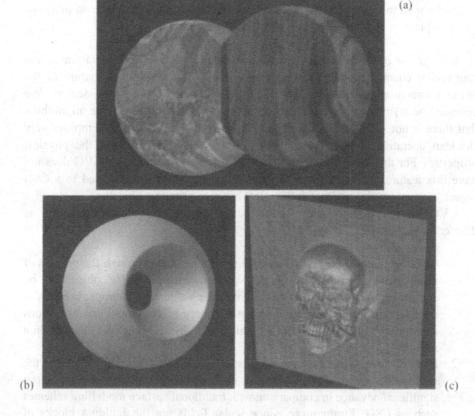

Figure 6.5. Examples of CVG objects in the four-colour channel model.

In comparison with CSG, CVG offers much more descriptive power. Its merits include:

- It operates on the interior as well as the exterior of objects, and therefore preserves the main geometrical properties in volumetric datasets such as volume density and multiple isosurfaces. One could imagine that if CSG were used to model the object in Figure 6.5a, the interior of the spheres would not normally be part of the objects and would have to be texture mapped onto it separately after the CSG operations.
- Physical properties such as colours are defined and manipulated in the same way as geometry. For example, Figure 6.5b shows a sphere, whose scalar fields are all defined in the form of spherical functions that model the changes of opacity and colour from the centre to the outside. We subtract an oval object from the sphere using a − operation to visualise its interior.

- It accommodates objects which are defined mathematically by scalar fields (such as shown in Figure 6.5b) as well as those built from real-life volumetric datasets (such as shown in Figure 6.5c).
- Images can be naturally integrated into a scene as a volumetric object. In addition to their use as texture blocks, as shown in Figure 6.5a, they can also be used to create interesting scenes such as in Figure 6.5c where an image of a piece of textile is used as a semi-transparent screen.

In 6.2.2, we observed the asymmetry associated with the CVG operations in the four-colour channel model. This is largely due to the asymmetric nature of the SELECT operation on colour scalar fields and the real operations on scalars. We consider the asymmetry to be a feature rather than a defect of CVG. One might think that there is not such an issue in CSG. This is simply because CSG employs only Boolean operations which operate only on the geometry and not the physical properties. For the same reason, the Boolean opacity only model of CVG does not have this feature. In fact, when colour or other properties are assigned to a CSG object, asymmetry also appears at the joints between primitive objects.

CVG has successfully addressed all three aspects of volume modelling as defined in Section 2.2.

1. CVG facilitates a process of modelling volume data. Through the process of geometrical generalisation (Figure 6.1), it enables spatial objects to be constructed from regular as well as irregular volumetric datasets. It provides an algebraic framework for defining a variety of combinational operations appropriate to the geometrical, graphical and physical properties defined in a model.
2. CVG is a generalisation in dimension to surface modelling. CVG allows the specification of true 3D properties as discussed above, and hence represents a significant advance in comparison with traditional surface modelling schemes such as CSG. Furthermore, since scalar fields are the building blocks of spatial objects, it is feasible for CVG to operate on more general objects specification in the form of a mathematical scalar field $F(x, y, z)$.
3. CVG provides input to the volume rendering integral. In the following two sections, we will demonstrate that CVG scenes can be directly rendered. An important feature of CVG is that there is hardly any extra costs for rendering a mathematical scalar field when the typical ray casting mechanism is employed [9].

6.3 Representation of Complex Scenes in CROVE

TROVE (Two-level Representations of Volumetric Environments) is a modelling and rendering system for scenes composed of multiple volumetric datasets, designed and developed by Leu and Chen [14-15]. It introduced a number of interesting features in order to maximise the descriptive power of volumetric data, and to enhance the efficiency in storing and rendering complex multi-volume scenes. However, TROVE assumes that volume objects do not intersect with each other. Clearly it is desirable to equip TROVE with CVG capabilities. A new system that integrates CVG and TROVE has been developed and is named as CROVE (Constructive Representations of Volumetric Environments). It currently supports the four-colour channel model and other simpler models of CVG.

6.3.1 Hierarchical Data Environment

As shown in Figure 6.6, the data environment of CROVE is divided into two levels, namely the *voxel level* and the *object level*.

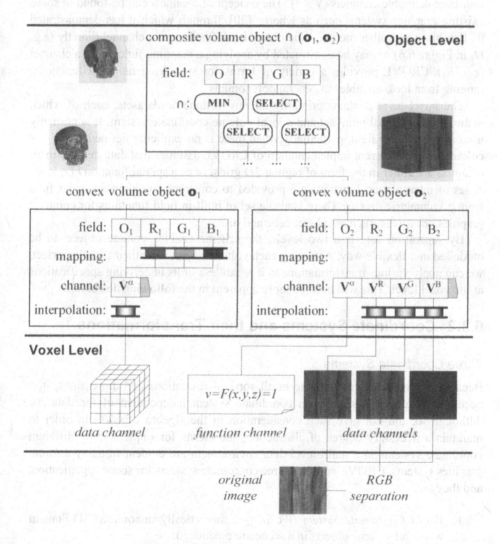

Figure 6.6. The data environment of CROVE.

At the object level, a volume object is represented by a CVG tree that corresponds to a CVG term such as $\mathbf{o} = \cap(\mathbf{o}_1, \mathbf{o}_2)$. Each non-terminal node in the tree represents a CVG operator, and the root represents the final composite volume object. Convex volume objects are represented by terminal nodes, where the specification of each field is given. A convex volume object can be associated with one or more channels — a feature inherited from TROVE — which provide links to the data defined at the voxel level.

In order to provide sufficient flexibility for different graphics models, CROVE allows up to 16 channels and, for easy identification, they are labelled as voxel ($\mathbf{V}$), bit ($\mathbf{V}^1$), grey ($\mathbf{V}^8$), red ($\mathbf{V}^R$), green ($\mathbf{V}^G$), blue ($\mathbf{V}^B$), opacity ($\mathbf{V}^\alpha$), red medium ($\mathbf{V}^r$), green medium ($\mathbf{V}^g$), blue medium ($\mathbf{V}^b$), transparency ($\mathbf{V}^\beta$), interpolation ($\mathbf{V}^I$), and four user-definable channels ($\mathbf{V}^{U1-4}$). The concept of channels can be found in some existing graphics systems such as Khoros [20], through which it has demonstrated its flexibility and other merits. A field may be defined upon a channel directly (e.g. O_1 in Figure 6.6) or may be constructed by applying a mapping function to a channel (e.g. R_1). CROVE provides a variety of forms for specifying mapping functions, ranging from look-up tables to general polynomials.

The voxel level contains primarily all raw volumetric datasets, each of which maintains its original point set and a local volume coordinate system. It is normally used as a geometry field, particularly when there is no explicitly defined opacity or colour data. The current implementation of CROVE assumes that data defined in all channels are either in the form of regular 3D grids, or as a spatial function $F(x, y, z)$. A set of interpolation functions are provided to construct a volumetric scalar field from a volumetric dataset. There is also a set of built-in field functions for common graphics primitives, such as sphere, cube and disc.

By separating data into two levels, the scheme enables volume objects to be modelled in a flexible way. Assuming each volume object is mathematically perfect, we can apply various transformations to it regardless of its underlying specifications at the voxel level. This will become more apparent in the following discussions.

6.3.2 Coordinate Systems and their Transformations

Three Coordinate Systems

Because volumetric datasets come in all sorts of resolutions and dimensions, it is necessary to define a scene in a coordinate system independent of the datasets. Although we did not give such consideration in the algebra of CVG in order to maintain a necessary degree of abstraction, the merits for implementing different coordinate systems in a multi-level data environment are evident in many existing graphics systems. CROVE supports three coordinate systems for scene specification, and they are:

1. *World Coordinate System (WCS)* — a theoretically unbounded 3D domain where all volume objects in a scene are positioned.
2. *Normalised Volume Coordinate System (NVCS)* — a unit cubic domain which is used to standardise the transformation between the world coordinate

system and a local volume coordinate system.

3. *Volume Coordinate System (VCS)* — a 3D domain $[0, N_x-1] \times [0, N_y-1] \times [0, N_z-1]$ that corresponds to a specific volumetric dataset, where N_x, N_y and N_z are the sizes of the dataset.

Figure 6.7 illustrates the three coordinate systems, and various transformations which are detailed in the following sections.

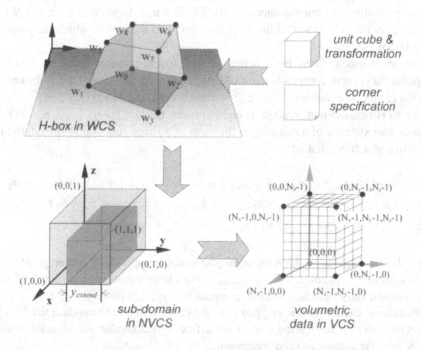

Figure 6.7. Three coordinate systems in CROVE

Hexahedral Box (H-box)

As mentioned in 6.2.2, each convex volume object is associated with a convex hull *Vol(P)*. Since only regular 3D grids are considered in the current implementation of CROVE, each *Vol(P)* is therefore simply a cuboid in its corresponding VCS. Although cuboids would be adequate for most applications, CROVE allows the specification of a *Vol(P)* in WCS by a hexahedral box (called *H-box*) with quadrilateral faces. The position of each H-box therefore defines that of the corresponding object. It is not necessary for any adjacent faces or edges of a H-box to be orthogonal, nor for the size of the H-box to correlate with the dimensions of the corresponding volumetric datasets. In CROVE an H-box can be specified by either giving a series of 4x4 transformation matrices which are to be applied to the unit cube defined by the NVCS, or by specifying the world coordinates of the eight corners of the H-box directly.

The former is more suitable for geometrical transformations that can be easily decomposed into a series of basic transformations such as translation, scaling and rotation. The latter is easier to experiment through trial-and-error, particularly for transformations involving some distortions.

Transformations

One of the operations that is performed most frequently by the CROVE rendering engine is the mapping from a point (x_w, y_w, z_w) in an H-box to a point (x_v, y_v, z_v) in the corresponding volumetric dataset. CROVE first transforms (x_w, y_w, z_w) in WCS to (x_{nv}, y_{nv}, z_{nv}) in NVCS with a function appropriate to the way in which the position of the H-box is specified.

For an H-box defined by a series of 4x4 transformation matrices, CROVE computes the reverse composite matrix $\mathbf{M}$ during a preprocessing stage and stores it with the H-box. We obtain (x_{nv}, y_{nv}, z_{nv}) by simply applying $\mathbf{M}$ to (x_w, y_w, z_w).

For an H-box defined through its eight corners, (x_i, y_i, z_i), $i=1, 2, ..., 8$, CROVE assumes the existence of a mapping in the form of a shape function [19] from the H-box onto a unit cube, that is:

$$x_{nv} = a_1 x_w y_w z_w + a_2 x_w y_w + a_3 y_w z_w + a_4 z_w x_w + a_5 x_w + a_6 y_w + a_7 z_w + a_8$$
$$y_{nv} = b_1 x_w y_w z_w + b_2 x_w y_w + b_3 y_w z_w + b_4 z_w x_w + b_5 x_w + b_6 y_w + b_7 z_w + b_8$$
$$z_{nv} = c_1 x_w y_w z_w + c_2 x_w y_w + c_3 y_w z_w + c_4 z_w x_w + c_5 x_w + c_6 y_w + c_7 z_w + c_8$$

where $0 \leq x_{nv}, y_{nv}, z_{nv} \leq 1$. With eight pairs of corresponding corner points, the coefficients $a_1, ..., a_8, b_1, ..., b_8, c_1, ..., c_8$ in the above equations can be solved in a preprocessing stage, and later used to compute (x_{nv}, y_{nv}, z_{nv}) from (x_w, y_w, z_w).

By default, each H-box is mapped onto the entire unit cube bounding the NVCS. However, CROVE also allows users to define a rectangular sub-domain within NVCS, thus facilitating a "crop" operation.

For each scalar field defined with the object, (x_{nv}, y_{nv}, z_{nv}) in NVCS is then mapped onto a point (x_v, y_v, z_v) in the corresponding VCS, taking the "crop" operation into account wherever necessary. The computation for this transformation is trivial.

6.3.3 Mapping and Interpolation Functions

CROVE has inherited the main concepts of mapping and interpolation from TROVE, except for some improvement in their implementation. When there is a lack of raw data or function to define a scalar field in a CVG model, it is necessary to specify a mapping function for constructing the scalar field from other information at the voxel level. In the four-colour channel model, for instance, if channels $\mathbf{V}^R$, $\mathbf{V}^G$, $\mathbf{V}^B$ are not available (such as the head in Figure 6.8), one may utilise mapping functions or look-up tables to convert data from $\mathbf{V}^\alpha$ (or other available channels) to the colour scalar fields in the same way as it commonly seen in volume visualisation.

In CROVE, mapping functions can be used to specify any of the scalar fields of

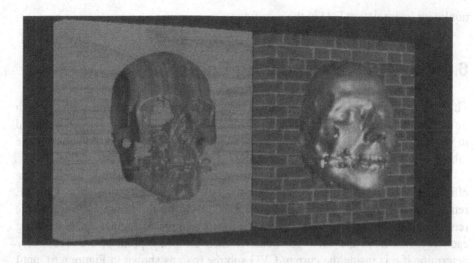

Figure 6.8. A scene is made up of five convex volume objects, "head", "skull", "brick wall", "wooden panel" and "skull texture". The "skull" and the "head" share the same volumetric dataset, and mapping functions are used to colour the "head".

a convex volume object $\mathbf{o}=(O, R, G, B)$. Given a value $v_{in} \in [0, 1]$ from a given input channel, its mapping $v_{out} \in [0, 1]$ can be obtained from one of the following mapping functions:

- *Raw* — it uses the data from a given input channel directly, i.e. $v_{out} = v_{in}$;
- *Index table* — it is a look-up table defined by a sequence of real values, $t_0, t_1, \ldots, t_n \in [0, 1]$, and we have $v_{out} = t_k$, where $k = \textbf{\textit{round}}(v_{in} \cdot n)$;
- *Interpolated index table* — it is similar to an index table except that v_{out} is linearly interpolated between t_k and t_{k+1}, where $k \le v_{in} \cdot n \le k+1$;
- *General polynomial* — it is defined by a sequence of real coefficients, $a_0, a_1, \ldots, a_s$, and we have $v_{out} = a_0 + a_1 \cdot v_{in} + \ldots + a_s \cdot v_{in}^s$;
- *Constant, linear, quadratic and cubic* — they are special forms of polynomial functions, but are given individual type identifiers in CROVE for efficiency purposes;
- *{t_1, t_2}; $t_1, t_2 \in [0, 1]$* — it maps v_{in}'s range $[0, 1]$ to a new range $[a, b]$ as $v_{out} = v_{in} \cdot (t_2 - t_1) + t_1$. Note, it is not necessary to have $t_1 \le t_2$. In many situations, this mapping is more convenient than defining a linear function $a_0 + a_1 \cdot v_{in}$.

In the context of CVG, these mapping functions also allow volume objects at the object level to share volumetric datasets at the voxel level. This is demonstrated by the scene in Figure 6.8, where the skull and the head are defined upon the same volumetric dataset with different opacity mapping functions.

When an input channel is a data channel (Figure 6.6), it is necessary to give an interpolation as discussed in Section 6.2.2. So far only trilinear interpolation and the nearest neighbour function have been implemented in CROVE, although it is intended for CROVE to support some forms of high-order interpolation as well as nonlinear interpolation [21] in the near future.

6.4 The CROVE Rendering Engine

The CROVE rendering engine utilises a ray-casting mechanism, and supports both direct volume rendering [9] and direct surface rendering [22]. The former was used to render objects and scenes in Figure 6.4a-d and Figure 6.5c, and the latter for the others in this paper.

Some volume rendering algorithms utilise a voxel traversal method for rendering efficiency, but it would work only in a single volume situation. The CROVE rendering engine employs the sampling method used by the original direct volume rendering algorithm. The basic mechanism is to sample at regular intervals along each ray cast from the view position. At each sampling point p, we recursively determine if p is inside the current CVG subtree (e.g. as shown in Figure 6.6), until we reach a terminal node (i.e. a convex volume object). If p is inside the H-box of the convex volume object, appropriate opacity and colour values at p are obtained and returned to the parent node. At each internal node, a CVG operation is applied to the values from child nodes, and so on.

A particular rendering method is assigned to the root level of each CVG tree, and is consistently applied to the entire tree. The direct volume rendering method essentially accumulates some opacity and colour at each sampling point along each ray, while the direct surface rendering method follows each ray, seeking an intersection with an interested isosurface. Both may take the advantage of possible early termination of the ray when enough opacity is accumulated.

In single volume rendering, the sampling distance is traditionally determined by the dimensions and resolution of the volumetric dataset. The calculation of the surface normal at each voxel often utilises the neighbouring grid points. Such a simplistic approach is no longer adequate in multi-volume rendering, in particular, in dealing with composite volume objects. CROVE allows the user to control the speed and quality of rendering through a few global parameters defined in WCS, including *sampling domain ε, standard sampling distance Δ* and *actual sampling distance δ*. The sampling domain ε defines a small cubic domain $[x-\varepsilon, x+\varepsilon] \times [y-\varepsilon, y+\varepsilon] \times [z-\varepsilon, z+\varepsilon]$ for each sampling point, and determines the positions of additional samples for computing a normal should there be a "hit". The standard sampling distance Δ specifies a distance such that if samples are taken at regular intervals 1Δ, ..., $k\Delta$, ..., along a ray, the opacity accumulated is considered to be "correct". To achieve a high quality rendering, we normally use a much smaller interval $\delta < \Delta$. In CROVE, a mapping function is used to correct the over-sampled opacity and colours with δ.

6.4.1 Multiple Isosurfaces

To render surfaces, CROVE allows the user to define more than one isosurface, either opaque or translucent, for a CVG tree. Figure 6.9 shows such an example,

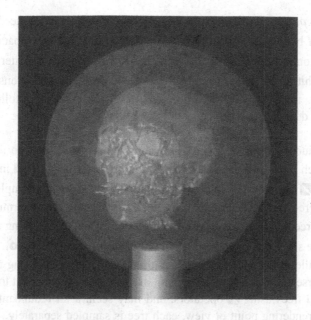

Figure 6.9. Two isosurfaces with different display opacities.

where the CVG term for the composite volume object is:

∪(∩(**sphere**, **water-texture**), ∪(**skull**, **rod**)).

The opacity fields of **sphere** and **rod** are defined using built-in spherical and circular functions respectively, while that of **skull** is through a data channel. The **water-texture** object is made up of a 2D image of water, similar to the texture block in Figure 6.5. Both **water-texture** and **rod** are scaled from a 2D shape using their H-boxes. It is also possible to build a water ball object with a spherical function for its opacity field and an image for its colour fields, and such an object would be more efficient to render. However, it is more flexible to keep them separately as they may often require different transformations for their H-boxes. To facilitate the rendering of two isosurfaces (at $O(p)$=0.1 and 0.78 in the case of Figure 6.9), some opacity mappings are used to ensure that the opacities of **sphere** are within [0, 0.5], and those of **skull** are in [0.5, 1]

6.4.2 Multiple CVG Trees and the ▨ Operator.

Theoretically any graphics scene in CROVE can be modelled by a single CVG tree where disjoint objects are banded together using ∪ operations. Nevertheless, this may lead to a great deal of inefficiency when a scene contains many independent volume objects. Consider a point p and a CSG object A∪B, "p is in A" implies "p is in A∪B". In other words, if sampling A at p has a hit, there is no need to sample B. However, this is not the case in the four-colour channel model of CVG. Given a sampling point p, as defined in Table 6.1, the $\cup(\mathbf{o}_1, \mathbf{o}_2)$ operation needs to obtain the opacities of both $\mathbf{o}_1$ and $\mathbf{o}_2$ at p in order to determine the new opacity with the **max** operation on scalars. In other words, $\mathbf{o}_2$ has to be sampled no matter whether or not there is a hit at $\mathbf{o}_1$. Thus it is not desirable to apply $\cup$ operations to objects which do not intersect. CROVE provides the user with the following two mechanisms to deal with this problem.

- It introduces a "nil" operator ▧ for combining objects that do not intersect with each other. For instance, we can combine **skull** and **rod** in Figure 6.9 using a ▧ operator. Given a volume object ▧($\mathbf{o}_1, \mathbf{o}_2$) and a sampling point p, we first recursively determine if p is inside the H-box of any terminal node of the subtree $\mathbf{o}_1$. If so, we call this a "hit", even when the resulting opacity at p is 0. The subtree $\mathbf{o}_2$ will be sampled only if there is not a hit at $\mathbf{o}_1$.
- It also allows the specification of multiple CVG trees assuming that they do not intersect. From a modelling point of view, this is equivalent to combining all CVG trees using ▧ operators, and may seem a bit redundant. However, from a rendering point of view, each tree is sampled separately. This allows the use of different rendering methods and parameters (such as isovalues) for different CVG trees. For instance, we may render amorphous objects using direct volume rendering, while using direct surface rendering for those objects with more prominent surface features. Despite this advantage, there is a major drawback associated this method, which will be discussed in 6.4.3.

6.4.3 Bounding Box (B-box)

Although it is possible to establish an H-box for every node in a CVG tree, it would be quite costly in terms of computational time. Instead, CROVE preprocesses and stores x, y, z extends of the current subtree as a bounding box (called B-box in CROVE) at each node.

Figure 6.10a shows a 2D illustration of B-boxes at different levels of a CVG tree for ▧($\mathbf{a}$, $\cup(\mathbf{b}, \mathbf{c})$). For each ray, t_{enter} and t_{exit}, which are intersection points between the ray and the B-box at the root, are first computed. Samples are then taken at regular intervals between t_{enter} and t_{exit} until the ray leaves the box or accumulates sufficient opacity. At each sampling point p, we recursively perform a simple inclusion test to see if p is inside the B-box of a subtree. When we reach a terminal node, an inclusion test against the corresponding H-box is carried out through a transformation from WCS to NVCS (as described in Section 6.3.2).

As mentioned in Section 6.4.2, the composite object shown in Figure 6.10a may also be divided into two separate CVG trees, $\cup(\mathbf{b}, \mathbf{c})$ and $\mathbf{a}$ on its own, as shown in Figure 9b. This may allow us to render $\cup(\mathbf{b}, \mathbf{c})$ and $\mathbf{a}$ using different rendering methods. In CROVE, CVG trees are sorted by their t_{enter}'s, and are rendered according to their order. However, from Figure 6.10b, one can easily observe an ambiguity problem in specifying multiple CVG trees. In this example, $\mathbf{a}$ should obviously be rendered before ∪(**b**, **c**). Similar to the depth-sorting algorithm for polygons [23], it is generally difficult to provide a satisfactory sorting solution to all ambiguity problems without further partitioning. With the current implementation of CROVE, multiple CVG trees can be used safely only if their B-boxes do not overlap.

One possible solution is to store all sampled values (opacity and colour) without combining them during the rendering of those CVG trees with intersected B-boxes. The sampled values can then be sorted according to their positions along the ray before being combined together.

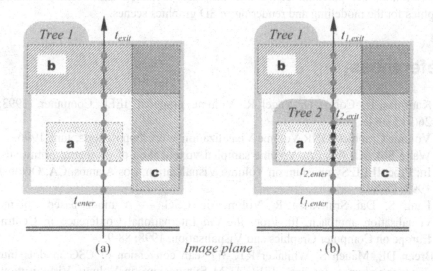

Figure 6.10. Sampling with B-boxes.

6.5 Conclusions

Built on our recent work on CVG, and our experience gained from a multi-volume rendering system (TROVE), we have developed a powerful software system, CROVE, for modelling and rendering scenes composed of composite volume objects. This work has highlighted the influence of the theoretical concepts of CVG upon the design of CROVE, while demonstrating the capability of CROVE in creating "computer graphics". In particular, the geometrical generation facilitated by CVG from volumetric datasets to spatial objects allows combinational operations to be defined consistently in a continuous unbounded domain without being constrained by the discrete and bounded nature of the underlying data. Meanwhile, the rendering decomposition enables a rendering process that handles composite volume objects directly without the need of re-sampling them into a single volumetric dataset. CVG offers a consistent algebraic framework for formulating various constructive volume models for applications in volume graphics and volume visualisation. In addition to direct rendering, CVG also provides a means of input to voxelisation and model-based animation.

From the perspective of volume graphics, the comparison between CVG and CSG has clearly indicated that volume graphics possesses more descriptive power than surface graphics in the context of constructive modelling. The simple integration of images and textures in CROVE has shown the relative merits of using voxels over polygons in their role as graphics primitives. The rendering engine of CROVE has further demonstrated the strength of volume graphics in dealing with both solid and amorphous objects. To a certain degree, this work has given an illustration of the potential of volume graphics to match and overtake surface graphics for the modelling and rendering of 3D graphics scenes.

References

1. Kaufman K, Cohen D, Yagel R. Volume graphics. IEEE Computer, 1993; 26(7):51-64.
2. Volume Graphics. ONR Volume Visualization Workshop Reports, June 1996.
3. Wang SM, Kaufman A. Volume sampled voxelization of geometric primitives. In: Proc. IEEE Symposium on Volume Visualization, Los Alamos, CA, October 1993; 78-84.
4. Fang S, Dai Srinivasan R. Volumetric CSG — A model-based volume visualisation approach. In: Proc. the 6th International Conference in Central Europe on Computer Graphics and Visualisation, 1998; 88-95.
5. Breen DE, Mauch S, Whitaker RT. 3D scan conversion of CSG models into distance volumes. In: Proc. IEEE/ACM Symposium on Volume Visualisation, 1998; 7-14.
6. Wang S, Kaufman A. Volume sculpting. In: Proc. Symposium on Interactive 3D Graphics, April 1995; 151-156.
7. Galyean TA, Hughes JF. Sculpting: An interactive volumetric modeling technique. ACM/SIGGRAPH Computer Graphics, 1991; 25(4):267-274.
8. Avia RS, Sobierajsk LM. A haptic interaction method for volume visualization. In: Proc. IEEE Symposium on Volume Visualization, San Francisco, CA, October 1996; 197-204.
9. Levoy M. Efficient ray tracing of volume data. ACM Transaction on Graphics, 1990, 9(3):245-261.
10. Laur D, Hanrahan P. Hierarchical splatting: A progressive refinement algorithm for volume rendering. ACM/SIGGRAPH Computer Graphics, 1991; 25(4):285-288.
11. Nelson TR. Ultrasound visualization. Advances in Computers, 1998; 47:185-253.
12. Malzbender T. Fourier volume rendering. ACM Transaction on Graphics, 1993; 12(3):233-250.
13. Chen M, Tucker JV. Constructive Volume Geometry. Technical Report, CS-TR-98-19, Department of Computer Science, University of Wales Swansea, July

1998.

14. Leu A, Chen M. Modelling and rendering graphics scenes composed of multiple volumetric datasets. To appear in Computer Graphics Forum, 1999. (Also Technical Report, CS-TR-97-12, Department of Computer Science, University of Wales Swansea, May 1997.)

15. Leu A, Chen M. Direct rendering algorithms for complex volumetric scenes. In: Proc. 16th Eurographics UK Conference, Leeds, March 1998; 1-15.

16. Yagel R, Cohen D, Kaufman A. Discrete ray tracing, IEEE Computer Graphics, and Applications, 1992; 12(5):19-28.

17. Oddy RJ and Willis PJ. A physically based colour model. Computer Graphics Forum, 1991; 10(2):121-127.

18. Preparata FP, Shamos MI. Computational Geometry: An Introduction. Springer-Verlag, New York, 1985.

19. Cuvelier C, Segal A, van Steenhoven AA. Finite Element Methods and Navier-Stokes Equations. D Reidel Publishing Company, Holland, 1986.

20. Rasure J, Kubica. The Khoros application development environment. In: Christensen, Crowley (eds) Experimental Environments for Computer Vision and Image Processing, 1994; World scientific, 1-32.

21. Moller T, Machiraju R, Mueller K, Yagel R. Classification and local error estimation of interpolation and derivative filters for volume rendering. In: Proc. IEEE Symposium on Volume Visualization, San Francisco, CA, October 1996; 71-77.

22. Jones MW. The production of volume data from triangular meshes using voxelisation. Computer Graphics Forum, 1996; 15(5):311-318.

23. Newell ME, Newell RG, Sancha TL. A solution to the hidden surface problem. In: Proc. ACM National Conference, 1972; 443-450.

7. `vxt`: A Class Library for Object Voxelisation

Milos Srámek and Arie E. Kaufman

7.1 Introduction

Volume graphics [1] stands today on a threshold of a new era of its development. For years, two disadvantages of this alternative to the standard computer graphic approach have been cited: its large memory demands and long computational time. However, the first commercially available general purpose volume rendering engine *VolumePro*, manufactured by Mitsubishi and based on the Cube-4 architecture [2] developed at SUNY Stony Brook [3], will dramatically change this situation. Being capable of processing 500Mvoxels/s and comprising a 2×256^3 volume buffer, it will enable fast manipulation and visualisation of volumetric data on a standard PC platform. This step in volume rendering hardware development will give inspiration to software design. New VolumePro interface modules will be added to existing applications and completely new applications will be designed.

One of the greatest advantages of volume graphics is uniformity of representation, which enables not only simultaneous processing of geometric objects of different kinds (say, parametric and implicit surfaces), but also simultaneous processing of synthesised geometric objects with scanned data of real objects [1]. From this point of view one can expect, among others, a demand for basic routines and utilities for voxelisation of geometric objects, converting them from analytical to volumetric representation.

The topic of voxelisation of geometric objects has been the centre of interest for more than 10 years. First, techniques for binary voxelisation were proposed, assigning one value to voxels, either fully or at least partially included in the object of interest, and another value to the remaining voxels (Chapters 1, 3 and 9). From the point of view of rendering, this approach suffered from significant aliasing artifacts due to strict yes/no decisions during the conversion [4]. Later, techniques for antialiased voxelisation were proposed. Their basic idea was to suppress the aliasing artifacts by means of a smooth density transition between inside and outside the object. The *filtering techniques* introduce smoothing into the voxelisation procedure according to sampling theory [5-7]. In this case, a thin transition area is created in the object surface vicinity, comprising a layer of voxels with density gradually varying between some *object* and *non-object* value. This filtering process has many features similar to the scanning of real objects by, for example, tomographic scanners, and therefore their results have many similar properties and appearance. As a consequence, the same techniques can be used for visualisation of the data from both sources. The antialiasing effect of the *distance techniques* in every voxel of the scene is achieved by registering the distance from the object surface to the voxels ([8-10], Chapter 8). An object is thus no more localised as in the filtering case. On one hand, this has some advantages, such as, for example, simple definition of offset surfaces [11], but, on the other hand, it brings some complications in object manipulation.

The goal of this chapter is to introduce the vxt (VoXelization Toolkit) library for filtered voxelisation of objects, being developed at SUNY Stony Brook. It aims to provide the user with an extensible set of easy-to-use tools and routines for voxelisation of a wide set of analytically defined monochromatic and colour objects. Thus, resulting volumetric data would then represent a suitable input for both software and hardware volume rendering systems, including the VolumePro engine. This C++ class library provides for voxelisation of primitive objects; however, when supplemented by a suitable parser, it could represent a basis for voxelisation of complex models such as those represented by Open Inventor or other data formats.

7.2 Filtered Voxelisation of Objects

The vxt voxelisation library is an implementation of a technique advocated in a previous paper [7]. Its basic concept was that in voxelisation filter design it is necessary to remember that voxelisation is often performed for the sake of visualisation and, therefore, it is necessary to design the voxelisation filter with the subsequent visualisation technique (i.e., data interpolation and normal estimation) in mind. We showed that a combination of first-order filters on both stages of the process, if used with proper parameters, results in rendered images with negligible error in estimation of both the object surface position and surface normal direction. More specifically, we have shown that if trilinear interpolation is used for reconstruction of the continuous volume, with subsequent surface detection by thresholding and normal gradient detection by central differences, best results are obtained when the density profile $D_L(x, y, z)$ of the voxelised object near its surface is linear along the surface normal direction (Figure 7.1a):

$$D_L(x, y, z) = \begin{cases} 2T & \text{if } d(x, y, z) < -\delta \\ 0 & \text{if } d(x, y, z) > \delta \\ T\left(1 - \dfrac{d(x, y, z)}{\delta}\right) & \text{otherwise} \end{cases} \tag{7.1}$$

where $d(x, y, z)$ is the distance of the point (x, y, z) from the object surface (negative for points inside the object), 2δ is the thickness of the transient region, and T is the density threshold defining the surface in the volume data. We estimated the optimal value of δ to be 1.8 voxel units (VU) [7]. This linear profile results from convolution of the object with a one-dimensional box filter applied along a direction perpendicular to the surface, which we denoted as an *oriented box filter*.

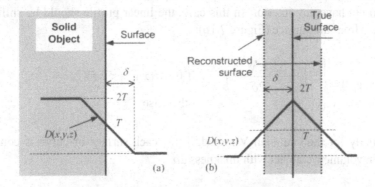

Figure 7.1. Density profile in the vicinity of (a) the boundary of a solid, (b) a surface or a curve. In case (a) the correct boundary is reconstructed; in case (b) a thin solid is reconstructed instead of the zero-thickness surface.

The estimated optimal thickness 2×1.8 VU of the surface transient region is the factor, which defines the minimal dimension of details, representable by a volumetric grid. Objects smaller than this dimension vanish and sharp edges are rounded. One possibility for coping with this drawback is to increase the resolution of the volume buffer.

In a follow-up paper [12] we advocated a different solution, issuing from the spectral analysis of different voxelisation and reconstruction filters. We introduced a theoretical concept of *V-models*, which stands for an object representation in 3D continuous space by a trivariate density function. This function is sampled during the voxelisation process and the resulting samples are then stored in the volume buffer. This approach enabled us to study general issues of sampling and rendering independently of specific object issues. We performed numerous experiments with different combinations of V-models and reconstruction techniques. We found out that the Gaussian V-model with an `erfc` (error function) density profile:

$$D_G(x,y,z) = \frac{1}{2}\text{erfc}\left(\frac{d(x,y,z)}{\sigma}\right) \tag{7.2}$$

where σ is standard deviation which determines sharpness of the transition, combined with tricubic density interpolation and Gabor filter (gradient of a 3D Gaussian) for normal reconstruction, decreased the characteristic dimension of the smallest representable details to about one half in comparison to the linear profile. We experimentally estimated optimal standard deviation of the `erfc` surface profile to be approximately 0.8 VU and standard deviation of the reconstruction Gabor filter to be about 1.0 VU. However, dimensions of these filters, together with the domain dimension of the tricubic filter, lead to higher computational demands in both voxelisation and reconstruction in comparison to the linear filters of the original approach.

Distance $d(x, y, z)$ from the surface in Equations 7.1 and 7.2 is negative at object interior points, and therefore cannot be used for voxelisation of surfaces and curves which do not have any interior. In this case, the linear profile should be shifted by the value δ from the surface (Figure 7.1b):

$$D_L^S(x, y, z) = \begin{cases} 2T\left(1 - \dfrac{d(x, y, z)}{2\delta}\right) & \text{if } 0 < d(x,y,z) < 2\delta \\ 0 & \text{otherwise} \end{cases} \tag{7.3}$$

and similarly for the Gaussian V-model. Thus, each surface or curve is converted into a thin volumetric object with thickness 2δ.

7.3 Object-Dependent Voxelisation Techniques

The *oriented box filter* and *V-model* are abstract concepts describing conversion of an arbitrary analytical object into a discrete volume of densities. Therefore, for each particular object or class of objects, we need a special technique, which would indemnify for the surface density profile according to Equations 7.1-7.3. In the remainder of this section we discuss several such techniques. Usually, there are two or even more possibilities for a given object, which are equivalent from the point of view of quality, but not necessarily equivalent from the point of view of efficiency.

7.3.1 Direct Distance Computation

Distance of each grid voxel to the nearest object point can be computed for any kind of object. However, it might lead to minimisation of systems of nonlinear functions, which is usually costly and may lead to incorrect results (by trapping in local minima). Therefore, we use the direct technique only for simple planar primitives (triangles and polygonal patches) and polyhedra.

7.3.2 Voxelisation of Parametric Surfaces and Curves

The desired linear density profile of the voxelised surface or curve is obtained by a technique based on *splatting* and *non-uniform sampling* of the surface or curve parametric domain. Our version of the splatting technique was described in details elsewhere [7]; therefore, we limit ourselves here to only a brief outline. We sample the object and to each voxel (x, y, z), with distance $d(x, y, z) < 2\delta$ from the current sample, we assign density according to Equation 7.3. If a voxel is influenced by two or more samples, we register the maximum value. The cost of the voxel-to-sample computation is minimised by the introduction of 3D look-up tables. The optimal sampling density was estimated to be approximately 2 samples per voxel unit for $\delta = 1.8$.

In order to avoid unnecessary oversampling, which increases computational time but does not contribute to quality improvement, the voxelised curve or surface has to be sampled as uniformly as possible. Uniform sampling of a curve can be accomplished easily by means of the *unit length* parameterisation, which exists for each regular parametric curve [13]. However, there is no equivalent *unit area* parameterisation of a surface [14]. Thus, we can define only approximately uniform sampling of the surface. One such possibility is based on a binary hierarchical subdivision of the 2D surface domain [7], until dimensions of the corresponding patch in 3D fall below a predefined threshold.

7.3.3 Voxelisation of Implicit Solids

The adopted technique for voxelisation of implicit solids, given by function $f(x, y, z)$, is based on linear approximation of f in the vicinity of the surface $f(x, y, z) = 0$. In such a case the distance of point (x, y, z), lying in the surface vicinity, can be estimated as:

$$d(x, y, z) = \frac{f(x, y, z)}{\|\nabla f(x, y, z)\|} \qquad (7.4)$$

where $\|\nabla f(x, y, z)\|$ is the magnitude of the function gradient. Of course, this estimate works well only for functions for which the linear approximation is reasonable. Violation of this condition usually does not influence the position of the surface, but rather influences the density profile in the vicinity, which may lead to artifacts during rendering due to incorrect estimation of the surface normal direction.

In order to minimise the necessary number of function evaluations, we hierarchically subdivide the grid into octants. If all samples in octant vertices belong either outside or inside the object, the whole octant is filled with the corresponding density value. In order to not skip object details, we start with blocks of 8^3 or even less voxels. The size of the block corresponds to the estimated optimal size of the filter width $\delta = 1.8$ VU (Equation 7.1). Since even the thinnest detail is represented by the transition area of thickness $4\delta \approx 8$ VU, the selected block size ensures that no errors of this kind will occur.

7.3.4 CSG Operations with Voxelised Objects

One of the greatest advantages of volume graphics is the simplicity with which the Constructive Solid Geometry (CSG) operations between objects can be implemented. This simplicity resides in the fact that instead of the original objects, their voxelised counterparts take part in the operation, and thus it can be performed on a voxel-by-voxel basis. Consequently, all we need is a set of primitive binary operations, which assign appropriate density and colour to the pair of voxels (Table 7.1). There are several possibilities how to define the voxel-by-voxel CSG operations [15]. We prefer the version with min and max functions, since it does not affect the linear surface density profile. The weighted average is used to combine

Table 7.1. Voxel-based CSG operations between objects. (d — density of the voxel, c — colour of the voxel, and WA — weighted average of the colours.)

Operation	Symbol	Density	Colour
Intersection	A*B	$d_{A*B} = \min(d_A, d_B)$	$c_{A*B} = WA(A, B)$
Union	A+B	$d_{A+B} = \max(d_A, d_B)$	$c_{A+B} = WA(A, B)$
Difference	A-B	$d_{A-B} = \max(0, d_A - d_B)$	$c_{A-B} = c_A$ if $d_A - d_B > 0$

colours of two voxels:

$$WA(A, B) = \frac{d_A c_A + d_B c_B}{d_A + d_B}, \tag{7.5}$$

where d is the normalised density of the voxel ($0 \le d \le 1$) and c is its RGB colour triple.

7.4 The vxt Class Library

The object oriented approach benefits two aspects of a software system: its usage and its development and extendibility. The *encapsulation* feature directly supports the user by hiding implementation details and by providing an easy-to-use object interface. Both these features enable those parts of the system which are not important for the user to be hidden, so that he/she can easily concentrate on his/her own goals. Encapsulation together with inheritance, polymorphism and operator overloading ensure high clarity of the source code, which is important from the point of view of a designer or team of designers.

The core of the vxt library consists of two basic class hierarchies: vxtObject3D class and its subclasses, representing different kinds of objects and corresponding voxelisation methods, and a vxtGrid3D class hierarchy for representation of volume buffers of different voxel types. An appropriate object voxelisation routine is invoked by calling Voxelize() method of the given object with the target grid as a parameter.

7.4.1 The vxtObject3D Hierarchy

The main goal of a class hierarchy design is to identify object properties from the point of view of their specificity: general properties are encapsulated by the objects on higher levels of the hierarchy, while specific properties are assigned to lower levels or leaf objects (Figure 7.2).

vxtObject3D is an abstract superclass of all object related classes. Its role is twofold:

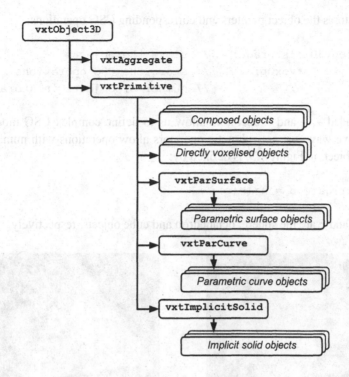

Figure 7.2. A simplified hierarchy of vxt classes for shape representation and voxelisation.

1. To implement object spatial transformations by means of a 4 × 4 homogeneous matrix and corresponding methods;
2. To define class interface by specifying virtual methods Voxelize(), Describe() and Duplicate(), which are implemented on lower levels of the hierarchy.

Implementing the class as abstract enables us to benefit from polymorphism (late binding) for manipulation with objects. Thus, all objects can be represented by a pointer to vxtObject3D, allowing the construction of heterogeneous lists, trees and arrays of objects or the definition of generic methods without an exact specification of the object. This implementation technique has proven itself to be very effective, since it significantly simplifies and clarifies the system architecture. As a consequence, since the late binding technique does not provide all the necessary information for dynamic memory allocation at compile time, it has been necessary to add the Duplicate() method to each object primitive, creating its copy.

The vxtObject3D class has two subclasses. The first is vxtPrimitive, representing *simple* objects treated as one unit. Internally, a simple object can be composed of one or more primitives, but its structure is hidden in the corresponding class and cannot be accessed from outside. The second subclass is vxtAggregate, which permits us to define *composed* objects for the purpose of implementing the CSG operations between objects.

vxtAggregate class, which implements CSG operations between objects, internally stores the object pointers and corresponding CSG operations:

```
vxtObject3D **storage;    // store the objects
csgOp        *voxOp;      // store the CSG operations
int          n;          // number of objects in storage
```

Overloaded +, − and * operators allow us to define complex CSG models in a very intuitive way, just as arithmetic operators allow operations with numbers. For example, object, in Figure 7.3, is defined by:

```
vxtAggregate d = a*(b+c);
```

where a, b and c are the sphere, octahedron and cube objects, respectively.

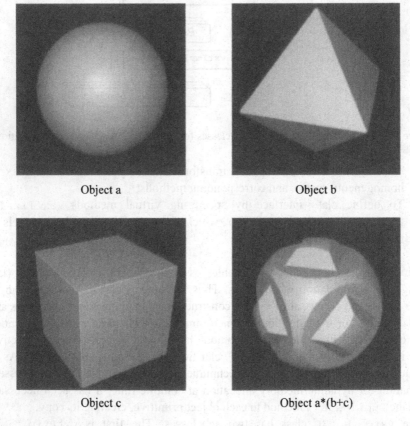

Object a   Object b

Object c   Object a*(b+c)

Figure 7.3. Example of a simple CSG operation between three objects.

vxtAggregate is a regular object and as such can be AND-ed with, OR-ed with and subtracted from other objects, which enables us to build CSG trees of arbitrary complexity. Nodes of such tree are then represented by the vxtAggregate objects, while leaves are occupied by simple objects.

While the internal data structures of the vxtAggregate class, together with the overloaded arithmetic operators, enable us to build the CSG model, method vxtAggregate::Voxelize() provides for a two step voxelisation of this model by means of a temporary grid. At a given level of the CSG hierarchy, objects from the storage list are first voxelised into an empty temporary grid, which is subsequently AND-ed with , OR-ed with or subtracted from the temporary grid at the parent level. Thus, the voxel-by-voxel CSG operations (Table 7.1) have to be implemented at two distinct locations:

1. In the object Voxelize() method. The density computed for the given voxel should be appropriately combined with the density of the corresponding voxel of the grid, into which the object is voxelised and;
2. In the vxtGrid3D::Merge() method, which implements CSG operations between grids.

Multiplication, addition and subtraction are binary operations, which means that only two objects are stored within internal nodes of the CSG hierarchy. In order to avoid extensive memory manipulation overhead, (e.g., in the case of voxelisation of triangular models consisting of thousands of triangles), objects can be directly added to an aggregate by means of the vxtAggregate::addObject() function. In this case, all aggregated objects are voxelised (added, multiplied or subtracted) to the same grid in the order in which they were added to the aggregate.

vxtPrimitive is a superclass of simple objects, which can be either represented by a single entity (e.g., a sphere or a polygon) or composed of several shapes, which, in contrast to aggregates, cannot be manipulated separately (e.g., vxtUtahTeapot object, defined by 32 Bezier patches). The remaining classes, which implement object-dependent voxelisation techniques (Section 7.3), inherit from vxtPrimitive. These are either concrete classes representing objects with direct distance computation, such as vxtPolygon or vxtTriangle, or abstract classes implementing voxelisation of parametric and implicit primitives (vxtImplicitSolid, vxtParCurve and vxtParSurface).

vxtImplicitSolid class implements the algorithm for voxelisation of implicit solids. The object is internally represented by means of a pointer to a function $E^3 \rightarrow E^1$. The user can provide this function either directly (subclass vxtAnyImplicitSolid) or use a predefined implicit object such as vxtSolidSphere or others.

vxtParCurve and **vxtParSurface** classes implement voxelisation of parametric curves and surfaces by sampling their parametric domain and splatting. Similarly, as in the case of implicit objects, a parametric primitive is represented by means of a function returning a triple of point coordinates ($E^2 \rightarrow E^3$ in vxtParSurface and $E^1 \rightarrow E^3$ in vxtParCurve). Again, the user can provide the function directly, or he/she can instantiate predefined primitives.

7.4.2 The vxtVolume Class

The vxtVolume class implements data structures and methods for storing and manipulating with both monochromatic and colour volumetric data. It is a template class, which enables instantiation of 3D grids with various types of voxels (8-, 16- and 32-bit integers and float precision). Usually, due to limited memory resources, 8-bit integers are used for storage of volumetric datasets. However, this resolution has proven to be not fine enough for storage of voxelised models [7]. Different voxel types in the place of the class template parameter thus enable us to balance the requirements of space and quality. In order to simplify the manipulation with vxtVolume<T> variables, an abstract superclass vxtGrid3D (Figure 7.4) was defined. Now, variables of *vxtGrid3D type can be used instead of the parameterised vxtVolume<T> variables, which we find more convenient.

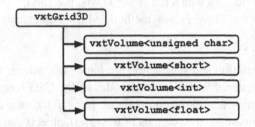

Figure 7.4. Classes for manipulation with volume grids.

vxtVolume is the class which stores voxelisation parameters as, for example, width and type of the surface transition area and the corresponding data structures (look-up tables for splatting). From the point of view of voxelisation itself, it would be possible to use different parameters for different objects, and to store the necessary information in one of the classes of the vxtObject3D hierarchy. However, this freedom of choice could cause trouble during rendering, for then it would be necessary to use different reconstruction filters for different objects. Whereas this object information is no more available after the voxelisation, we have to use the same parameters for all objects of the scene.

The vxtVolume class adopts the basic functionality for 3D data access and storage from the f3dGrid3D<T> class, which is a part of the f3d (Format 3 Dimensional) package, developed at SUNY Stony Brook. f3d constitutes both a C and C++ library of routines for manipulation and file storage of Cartesian, regular and rectilinear grids. The main goal of the f3d project has been to provide the user with an easy-to-use set of tools for efficient storage of the 3D datasets by means of lossless data compression.

7.5 Performance: Ray Tracing of Geometric and Volumetric Models

In this section, we provide a brief performance analysis of both geometric and volumetric approaches to ray tracing by means of a simple experiment using sphereflakes of different complexity as test objects. Our goal is to illustrate one of the advantages of volume graphics over the standard geometric rendering, namely independence of the rendering time on the scene complexity, and to provide the reader with an idea of which artifacts are introduced in the voxelisation/rendering process.

A sphereflake is a recursively defined object composed of spheres: for each sphere of level l there are 9 spheres defined on level $l+1$, with radius ratio 3:1 (Figure 7.5). Thus, a level l sphereflake is composed of $\sum_{i=0}^{l} 9^i$ spheres. Since the number of spheres grows exponentially, sphereflakes are popular test objects for performance assessment of different rendering techniques.

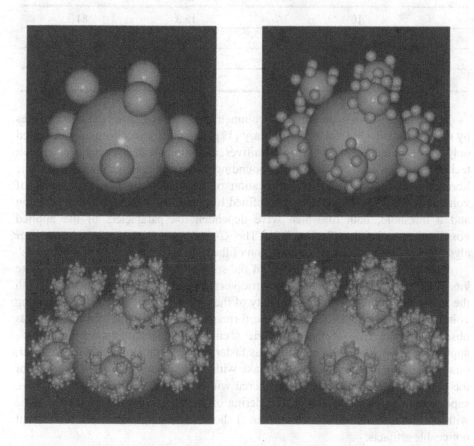

Figure 7.5. Level 1 – 4 sphereflakes.

The level 1 – 4 sphereflakes were voxelised with the linear surface profile with $\delta = 1.8$ VU into cubic grids with resolutions from 128 to 512 voxels along each side. From Table 7.2 we can see that the voxelisation time grows both with the number of objects and resolution of the scene. Due to optimisations involved in the vxtImplicitSolid class (a superclass of the vxtSolidSphere, Section 7.3), this growth is far slower than the linear with respect to the overall volume of the voxelised objects. Specifically, increasing the resolution from 128^3 to 512^3 results in 64 times larger volume, indicating also 64 times larger the number of samples to be evaluated. However, the ratio of real voxelisation times indicates only a 10 to 20 fold increase of the processing time. These, as well as the following tests, were performed on a Silicon Graphics Challenge workstation equipped with 3GB of main memory.

Table 7.2. Voxelisation time for sphereflakes of different complexity and grid resolution.

Sphereflake level	Number of spheres	Voxelisation time [s] at resolution		
		128^3	256^3	512^3
1	10	3.7	15.3	81.3
2	91	4.6	18.5	97.1
3	820	6.0	22.0	110.0
4	7381	10.9	30.3	128.0

We rendered both geometric and volumetric representation of the sphereflakes by means of the OORT ray tracing library [17]. The library was originally designed only for the rendering of geometric primitives, and implemented several acceleration techniques, such as, for example, the bounding volume hierarchy. We extended the library by adding a class for computation of ray intersections with surfaces of volumetric objects. The surface was defined by means of a reconstruction function and a threshold, both of which were dependent on parameters of the applied voxelisation technique (Section 7.2). The *Chessboard Distance voxel traversal* algorithm [18] was used for fast detection of the ray-surface intersection in the grid.

Results obtained by the rendering of the sphereflakes are summarised in Figure 7.6. The measured time for all volumetric versions was nearly independent of both the resolution of the grid and complexity of the object. Yet, in spite of the bounding volume acceleration, a decreasing performance with growing complexity was observed in the case of the geometric scene. For a small number of objects, approximately below 500, rendering was faster for the geometric version. However, rendering of the most complex sphereflake with 7381 spheres took about 8 hours for the 600×600 image in Figure 7.7, rendered with 3 levels of reflection and adaptive supersampling. On the other hand, rendering of the corresponding volumetric scene with a 512^3 resolution took less than 1 hour, including voxelisation, without noticeable artifacts.

As we have concluded in our research papers [7, 12], if correct voxelisation and reconstruction filters are used, no other errors are introduced except for those connected with high frequency details. Obviously, this is a feature of all discrete systems. Figure 7.8, which shows the difference of the rendered images of voxelised and geometric sphereflakes, provides us with a deeper insight. We can see that errors are actually introduced only in areas with small details where spheres touch each other.

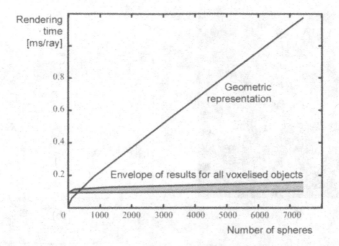

Figure 7.6. Rendering of voxelised and geometric sphereflakes: dependency of rendering time per ray on the scene complexity, measured by number of spheres.

Figure 7.7. The level 4 sphereflake, composed of 7381 spheres: (left) direct rendering of the geometric definition, (right) rendering by means of voxelisation into a 512^3 grid.

7.6 Using the **vxt** Library

The vxt library was developed in the UNIX environment. However, it was designed to be platform independent, and it can be compiled by other C++ compilers.

Figure 7.9a lists the source code of a simple program, defining, manipulating and voxelising objects of the scene shown in Figure 7.10. We wrote a simple lex/yacc parser vxtVox, as an example of the library usage as well as to provide the user with a voxelisation tool, which would not need scene description compilation. The corresponding source code, voxelising the same scene, is given in Figure 7.9b.

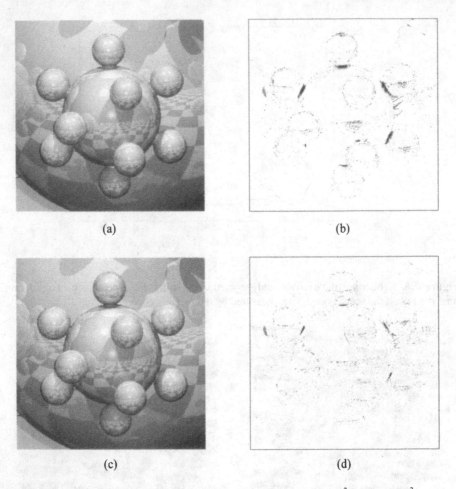

(a)   (b)

(c)   (d)

Figure 7.8. Close-up of a level 2 sphereflake, voxelised into (a) 256^3 and (c) 512^3 volume buffers. (b) and (d) show the difference with respect to a geometrically rendered image.

Currently, the vxt library enables us to define about 20 different object primitives. Except for adding new primitives, in the future, we would like to focus our interest on the development of new effective voxelisation routines, adding new functionality (2D and 3D textures) as well as writing parsers of popular 3D scene description formats. Both vxt and f3d tools and libraries are freely available for non-profit use at www.cs.sunysb.edu/~vislab/vxtools.

Acknowledgements

This work has been supported by grants ONR N0001 49710402, NSF MIP9527694, and VEGA 2/6017/99 (Slovak Republic). Some parts of the vxt library were implemented by students of the CSE 523 course at SUNY Stony Brook. Milos Sramek is currently on leave from the Institute of Measurement Science, Slovak Academy of Sciences, Bratislava, Slovakia.

```
int s(300);                      num s = 300;
float rt(0.4*s);                 num rt = 0.4*s;
float rc = 0.25*s;               num rc = 0.25*s;
vxtVolume<short>
grid(s,s,s);                     grid(s,s,s);
vxtPlatHexa a(rc);               obj a = hexahedron3D(rc);
a.Transform(                     scale(a,1,1,0.5);
  ScaleMatrix(1,1,0.5)
);
vxtPlatHexa b(a);                obj b = a;
b.Transform(                     rotatez(b,PI/4);
  RotationZMatrix(M_PI/4)
);
Aggregate ab(a+b);               obj ab = a+b;
ab.Transform(                    translate(ab,0,0,-rc/2);
  TranslationMatrix(
    Vector3D(0,0,-rc/2)
));
vxtUtahTeapot c(rt);             obj c = utahTeapot(rt);
(ab+c).Voxelize(grid);           add(ab+c);
grid.save("example");            save(example);
```

Figure 7.9. Definition of the scene as shown in Figure 7.10. (a) C++ source code, (b) vxtVox source code.

Figure 7.10. Rendition of the voxelised object defined in Figure 6.9.

References

1. Kaufman K, Cohen D, Yagel R. Volume graphics. IEEE Computer, 1993; 26(7):51-64.
2. Osborne R, Pfister H, Lauer H, McKenzie N, Gibson S, Hiatt W, Ohkami H. EM-Cube: An architecture for low-cost real-time volume rendering. In: Proc. SIGGRAPH/Eurographics Workshop on Graphics Hardware, 1997; 131-138.
3. Pfister H, Kaufman A. Cube-4 — A scalable architecture for real-time volume rendering. In: Proc. ACM/IEEE Symposium on Volume Visualization, 1996; 47-54.
4. Yagel R, Cohen D, Kaufman A. Discrete ray tracing. IEEE Computer Graphics and Applications, 1992; 12(5):19-28.
5. Wang SW, Kaufman A. Volume sampled voxelization of geometric primitives. In: Proc. IEEE Visualization '93, San Jose, CA, October 1993; 78-84.
6. Sramek M. Gray level voxelisation: A tool for simultaneous rendering of scanned and analytical data. In: Proc. the 10th Spring School on Computer Graphics and its Applications, Bratislava, Slovak Republic, 1994; 159-168.
7. Sramek M, Kaufman A. Object voxelisation by filtering. In: Proc. IEEE Symposium on Volume Visualization, Research Triangle Park, NC, October 1998; 111-118.
8. Jones MW. The production of volume data from triangular meshes using voxelisation. Computer Graphics Forum, 1996; 15(5):311-318.
9. Breen DE, Mauch S, Whitaker RT. 3D scan conversion of CSG models into distance volume. In: Proc. IEEE Symposium on Volume Visualization, Research Triangle Park, NC, October 1998; 7-14.
10. Gibson SFF. Using distance maps for accurate surface reconstruction in sampled volumes. In: Proc. IEEE Symposium on Volume Visualization, Research Triangle Park, NC, October 1998; 23-30.
11. Payne BA, Toga AW. Distance field manipulation of surface models. IEEE Computer Graphics and Applications, 1992; 12(1):65-71.
12. Sramek M, Kaufman A. Alias-free voxelisation of geometric objects. IEEE Transactions on Visualisation and Computer Graphics, 1999. To be published.
13. O'Neill B. Elementary Differential Geometry. Academic Press, New York, 1966.
14. Kaufman A. Efficient algorithms for 3D scan-conversion of parametric curves, surfaces, and volumes. ACM/SIGGRAPH Computer Graphics, 1987; 21(4):171-179.
15. Wang SW, Kaufman A. Volume-sampled 3D Modeling. IEEE Computer Graphics and Applications, 1994; 14(5):26-32.
16. Schroeder W, Martin K, Lorensen B. The Visualization Toolkit, An Object-Oriented Approach To 3D Graphics. Prentice Hall, 1996.
17. Wilt N. Object-oriented ray tracing in C++. Wiley, New York, 1994.
18. Sramek M. Fast surface rendering from raster data by voxel traversal using chessboard distance. In: Proc. Visualization, Washington, DC, October 1994; 188-195.

8. 3D Scan-Conversion of CSG Models into Distance, Closest-Point and Colour Volumes

David E. Breen, Sean Mauch and Ross T. Whitaker

8.1 Introduction

Volume graphics is a growing field that generally involves representing three-dimensional objects as a rectilinear 3D grid of scalar values, a volume dataset. Given this kind of representation, numerous algorithms have been developed to process, manipulate and render volumes. Volume datasets may be generated in a variety of ways. Certain scanning devices, e.g. MRI and CT, generate a rectilinear grid of scalar values directly from their scanning process. The scalar values can represent the concentration of water or the density of matter at each grid point (voxel). Additionally, volume datasets can be generated from conventional geometric models, using a process called *3D scan-conversion*.

When 3D scan-converting a geometric model to a volumetric representation, it is not always clear what value should be stored at each voxel of the volume, and what that value should represent. Here, we propose the use of distance volumes. A distance volume is a volume dataset where the value stored at each voxel is the shortest distance to the surface of the object being represented by the volume. If the object is closed, a signed distance may be stored to provide additional inside-outside information. We store negative values inside the object and positive distances outside. In this chapter, we will describe an algorithm for generating a distance volume with subvoxel accuracy from one type of geometric model, a Constructive Solid Geometry (CSG) model, and we will show that this type of volume representation is useful in a number of computer graphics applications, namely CSG surface evaluation, offset surface generation, and 3D model morphing.

CSG modelling is a well-developed technique that combines simple solid primitives using spatial Boolean operations to produce complex three-dimensional objects [1]. Some of the most commonly used primitives in CSG modelling are quadrics, superquadrics [2], and closed polygonal objects. These primitives can be added, subtracted, or intersected with each other to create a variety of solid geometric models. A CSG model is ordinarily stored in a binary tree structure. The leaf nodes of the tree contain solid primitives, superellipsoids in our case. A Boolean operation is associated with each non-leaf node and a transformation matrix is associated with each arc of the tree. The CSG binary tree may also be derived from a directed acyclic graph.

While CSG is a powerful modelling paradigm, unfortunately its modelling representation cannot be directly displayed on today's graphics workstations. Additionally, it is a representation not suitable for many other types of modelling operations. Frequently, the CSG tree or graph must first be evaluated and converted into a polygonal surface before it can be interactively displayed, processed or manipulated. We have found that first scan-converting the CSG model into a distance volume allows us to perform several types of graphics operations on the model. Applying the Marching Cubes algorithm [3] to the distance volume and extracting the isosurface at value zero produces a polygonal surface, which approximates the evaluated CSG model. Extracting an isosurface at a value other than zero produces offset surfaces to the CSG model. The distance volume may also be used to perform 3D model morphing. An active implicit model can utilise the distance information to change from one shape into another [4]. Given a volumetric representation of an initial object and the distance volume representing a second object, the surface of the initial object may be deformed into the surface of the second object.

Most volume datasets contain scalar values at each voxel, but multi-dimensional volumetric models are becoming more prevalent. In these models a vector or tensor is stored at each grid point. This multi-dimensional data can also be obtained from scanning devices, and generated from numerical simulations, similar to their scalar counterparts. Additionally, specific types of vector data can be produced during the 3D scan-conversion process, in our case closest-point and colour data. A closest-point volume stores, at each voxel, the (X, Y, Z) coordinates of the closest point on the scan-converted object's surface from the voxel. A colour volume contains, at each voxel, the $[R, G, B]$ colour of the object at the (X, Y, Z) closest point stored in the same voxel in the closest-point volume. The closest-point and colour volume data may be used to colour shade polygonal surfaces extracted from the associated distance volume. The derived polygonal surface may be colour shaded by conceptually imbedding it within the colour and closest-point volumes. When the polygonal surface is rendered, the colour value at any location (X, Y, Z) on the model's surface may be retrieved as the interpolated value in the colour volume at (X, Y, Z). If the colour is not constant within a small region around (X, Y, Z) in the colour volume, the information in the closest-point volume may be used to supersample the colour in the associated surface region on the original CSG model in order to produce an average colour value for the point (X, Y, Z) on the polygonal model.

Distance, closest-point and colour volumes may be generated in a two-step process. The first step begins by computing a set of points lying on the CSG model's surface, labelled the zero set. The colour of the CSG model at each point is also calculated. The closest point in the zero set and its colour is associated with each grid point in a one-voxel narrow band around the evaluated CSG surface. The shortest distance from each narrow band grid point to the CSG model may now be computed. Once the narrow band and zero set are calculated, a *Fast Marching Method* similar to Sethian's [5] is employed to propagate the shortest-distance, closest-point and colour information out to the remaining voxels in the volume. Sethian's approach has been used to numerically solve partial differential equations, but we have modified it to use a heuristic rule for propagating closest-point and colour information instead of calculating distance with a finite-difference scheme. The accuracy of our method depends on the discretisation of the surface (resolution of the zero set) and is independent of the final volume grid spacing. We therefore are able to calculate shortest distance at resolutions greater than the resolution of the final distance volume.

The zero set points are produced by performing closest-point calculations from a grid of user-specified resolution within the narrow band. We utilise a variation of the Constructive Cubes algorithm [6] and Tilove's CSG classification algorithm [7] to perform this computation. The first step of the CSG closest-point computation involves calculating the closest point to a single superellipsoid primitive, as well as the colour at the closest point. In general, this is accomplished with an iterative minimisation scheme. Given the closest points to separate geometric primitives (and therefore the shortest distances), a set of combinations rules are applied to merge the distance values of the individual primitives to produce the closest point and colour on the evaluated CSG model. Unfortunately, there are small regions near the CSG model surface where this "calculate-and-combine" approach generates invalid results. These cases can be easily detected and discarded.

The remainder of the chapter first presents related work in 3D scan-conversion and colour shading polygonal models. The chapter then details the steps required to produce distance, closest-point and colour volumes: generating the narrow band of points near the CSG model surface and zero set on the surface, followed by the propagation of the closest-point and colour information into the remaining voxels of the volume with the Fast Marching Method. We then describe our colour-shading method, which utilises the closest-point, and colour volumes to calculate surface colours on the polygonal models extracted from the distance volumes. The final section presents the results of our 3-D scan-conversion method within three applications: CSG surface evaluation, offset surface generation, and 3D model morphing.

8.2 Previous Work

3D scan-conversion takes a 3D geometric model, a surface in 3D or a solid model, and converts it into a 3D volume dataset [8-12], where voxels that contain the original surface or solid have a value of one. The remaining voxels have a value of zero. Using the volume-sampling methods of Wang and Kaufman [13] aliasing artifacts may be significantly reduced. These methods produce voxels with values between zero and one, where non-integer values represent voxels partially occupied by the original object. Scan-converted primitives may then be rendered, or combined using CSG operations [14] with other scan-converted primitives or acquired volume datasets. Payne and Toga [15] present a method for calculating distance volumes from a polygonal model. They use distance volumes to perform a variety of surface manipulation tasks. Extensions to discrete distance transforms [16-17], e.g. Chamfer methods, were considered for our work. They were deemed insufficient for our needs, because they do not provide subvoxel accuracy.

Our scan-conversion algorithm differs from previous efforts to 3D scan-convert CSG models because we evaluate the parametric primitives directly and combine the results in object space, before scan-conversion. This avoids the sampling errors produced when performing CSG operations on scan-converted primitives that are seen in other methods. If the primitives are first scan-converted, then combined with CSG operations, errors may occur at the boundaries of the primitives, where exact surface information has been lost [13]. It is also possible to evaluate the CSG model to produce a polygonal approximation to the final object [18]. Payne and Toga's method may be used to then calculate a distance to the polygonal model. We preferred to make our calculations directly on the original model, and avoid the extra step of approximating the CSG model with polygons and the errors associated with calculating distance to a faceted model. Our approach also generates additional closest-point and colour information, which may be used in a variety of graphics applications.

The relevant colour-shading work focuses on determining the colour of surfaces with complex or no parameterisation. Much of this work deals with texture mapping implicit or complex, unparameterised surfaces. Maillot et al. [19] define a deformation process based on energy minimisation that lessens the distortion of texture maps interactively placed on complicated surfaces. Litwinowicz and Miller [20] provide additional improvements to this work. Agrawala et al. [21] present an interactive technique for painting unparameterised 3-D polygonal meshes. Pedersen describes a technique for applying texture maps to implicit surfaces [22], as well as a general framework for texturing other kinds of surfaces [23]. Smets-Solanes [24] places texture maps on animated implicit objects by wrapping them in a virtual skin and deforming the skin with vector fields as the underlying objects change over time. Both Tigges and Wyvill [25], and Zonenschein et al. [26] trace particles through a gradient vector field in order to produce the parameterisation needed for texture mapping implicit surfaces. Shibolet and Cohen-Or [27] extend Bier and Sloan's Two-Part Texture Mapping technique [28] with a discrete dilation process in order to texture map concave voxel-based objects. Our work is similar to many of these techniques, except that we do not just use 2D textures to colour our models. We utilise the original 3D CSG model along with solid colour, 2D image textures and 3D procedural textures defined on the model to calculate the antialiased colour of a polygonal surface derived from the CSG model's distance volume.

8.3 Generating the Distance, Closest-Point and Colour Volumes

This section describes the two major components of our scan-conversion algorithm. The first step generates a set of closest points and associated colours on the surface of the evaluated CSG model. Additionally, it calculates the shortest distance to another set of points in a narrow band near the surface. The second step uses a Fast Marching Method to propagate this information to the remaining voxels of the distance, closest-point and colour volumes.

8.3.1 Calculating Closest Points, Shortest Distances and Colours for the Narrow Band and Zero Set

The narrow band and zero set needed for the Fast Marching Method are generated with a modified version of the Constructive Cubes algorithm [6] and Tilove's CSG classification algorithm [7]. The algorithm involves traversing the CSG model's acyclic graph, calculating each primitive's closest-point and colour value at the voxel location, and combining subcomponent values based on the shortest distance at each non-leaf node of the graph to produce the closest point, shortest distance and colour for the complete model at a particular voxel.

Calculating the Closest Point to a Superellipsoid

The parametric equation for a superellipsoid is:

$$\vec{S}(\eta,\omega) = \begin{bmatrix} a_1 \cos^{e_1}(\eta)\cos^{e_2}(\omega) \\ a_2 \cos^{e_1}(\eta)\sin^{e_2}(\omega) \\ a_3 \sin^{e_1}(\eta) \end{bmatrix} \begin{array}{c} -\pi/2 \le \eta \le \pi/2 \\ -\pi \le \omega \le \pi \end{array} \tag{8.1}$$

where η and ω are the longitudinal and latitudinal parameters of the surface, a_1, a_2, a_3, are the scaling factors in the X, Y, and Z directions, and e_1 and e_2 define the shape in the longitudinal and latitudinal directions [2].

The distance to a point on the surface of a superellipsoid defined at [η, ω] from an arbitrary point $\vec{P}$ is:

$$d_1(\eta,\omega) = \left\| \vec{S}(\eta,\omega) - \vec{P} \right\|. \tag{8.2}$$

Squaring and expanding Equation 8.2 gives:

$$d_2(\eta,\omega) = (a_1 \cos^{e_1}(\eta)\cos^{e_2}(\omega) - \vec{P}_x)^2 + (a_2 \cos^{e_1}(\eta)\sin^{e_2}(\omega) - \vec{P}_y)^2 + (a_3 \sin^{e_1}(\eta) - \vec{P}_z)^2 \tag{8.3}$$

The closest point to the superellipsoid from an arbitrary point $\vec{P}$ can then be calculated by determining the values of [η, ω] which minimise Equation 8.3. In general Equation 8.3 is minimised with a gradient descent technique utilising variable step-sizes. The resulting values of [η, ω] may then be plugged into Equation 8.1 to give the closest point on the surface of the superellipsoid, which in turn may be used to calculate the shortest distance.

Several issues must be addressed when minimising Equation 8.3. First, the special degenerate cases of the superellipsoid must be dealt with separately, because their surface normals are discontinuous. The most common cases are the cuboid ($e_1 = e_2 = 0$), the cylinder ($e_1 = 0$, $e_2 = 1$), the double cone ($e_1 = 2$, $e_2 = 1$), and the double pyramid ($e_1 = e_2 = 2$). The shortest distance to these primitives may be determined with non-iterative, closed-form solutions.

Finding the values of η and ω at the closest point with a gradient descent technique involves calculating the gradient of Equation 8.3:

$$\nabla d_2 = \left[\frac{\partial d_2}{\partial \eta}, \frac{\partial d_2}{\partial \omega} \right]. \tag{8.4}$$

Unfortunately, superellipsoids have a tangent vector singularity near values of η or ω which are multiples of $\pi/2$. To overcome this problem, we re-parameterise $\vec{S}$ by arc-length [29]. That is:

$$\vec{S}(\eta, \omega) = \vec{S}(\eta(\alpha), \omega(\beta)) = \vec{S}(\alpha, \beta), \tag{8.5}$$

where:

$$\left\| \frac{\partial \vec{S}(\alpha, \beta)}{\partial \alpha} \right\| = 1 \text{ and } \left\| \frac{\partial \vec{S}(\alpha, \beta)}{\partial \beta} \right\| = 1. \tag{8.6}$$

Given this we can say:

$$\left\| \frac{\partial \vec{S}(\alpha, \beta)}{\partial \alpha} \right\| = \left\| \frac{\partial \vec{S}(\eta, \omega)}{\partial \eta} \right\| \cdot \left\| \frac{\partial \eta(\alpha)}{\partial \alpha} \right\| \tag{8.7}$$

and:

$$\left\| \frac{\partial \vec{S}(\alpha, \beta)}{\partial \beta} \right\| = \left\| \frac{\partial \vec{S}(\eta, \omega)}{\partial \omega} \right\| \cdot \left\| \frac{\partial \omega(\beta)}{\partial \beta} \right\|. \tag{8.8}$$

If we assume that the arc-length parameterisation is in the same direction as the original parameterisation, we have:

$$\left\| \frac{\partial \eta(\alpha)}{\partial \alpha} \right\| = \left\| \frac{\partial \vec{S}(\eta, \omega)}{\partial \eta} \right\|^{-1} \text{ and } \left\| \frac{\partial \omega(\beta)}{\partial \beta} \right\| = \left\| \frac{\partial \vec{S}(\eta, \omega)}{\partial \omega} \right\|^{-1}. \tag{8.9}$$

Now we re-express our steepest descent (on d_2) so that it is steepest with respect to the normalised parameters:

$$\frac{\partial d_2}{\partial \alpha} = \frac{\partial d_2}{\partial \eta}\frac{\partial \eta}{\partial \alpha} = \frac{\partial d_2}{\partial \eta}\left\|\frac{\partial \vec{S}(\eta,\omega)}{\partial \eta}\right\|^{-1}$$

(8.10)

and:

$$\frac{\partial d_2}{\partial \beta} = \frac{\partial d_2}{\partial \omega}\frac{\partial \omega}{\partial \beta} = \frac{\partial d_2}{\partial \omega}\left\|\frac{\partial \vec{S}(\eta,\omega)}{\partial \omega}\right\|^{-1}.$$

(8.11)

We now can use the gradient of the re-parameterised d2:

$$\nabla d_2' = \left[\frac{\partial d_2}{\partial \alpha}, \frac{\partial d_2}{\partial \beta}\right]$$

(8.12)

to find the closest point with greater stability.

The general formulation of Equation 8.12 significantly simplifies for values of η and ω near multiples of $\pi/2$. Instead of deriving and implementing these simplifications for all regions of the superellipsoid we chose only to perform the calculation in the first octant ($0 \leq \eta \leq \pi/2$, $0 \leq \omega \leq \pi/2$). Since a superellipsoid is 8-way symmetric, point $\vec{P}$ may be reflected into the first octant, the minimisation performed, and the solution point reflected back into $\vec{P}$'s original octant.

Once the closest point is calculated, the colour at that point may be determined by three different methods. The superellipsoid may be assigned a constant colour, which is the colour assigned to all closest points on the primitive. The $[\eta, \omega]$ values may be used to access a 2D texture map or the (X, Y, Z) value of the closest point may be used to calculate a colour from a 3D procedural texture map [30].

Combining Shortest Distance Calculations

The CSG graph is processed in a depth-first manner. The closest point and colour on and shortest distance to individual superellipsoids are calculated at the leaf nodes. The results from the non-leaf nodes' subcomponents (A and B) are then combined based on the shortest-distance values. Since the subcomponents may be combined with a variety of Boolean operations (union, intersection and difference), just choosing the closest point to the subcomponents does not produce the correct result. Similar to CSG classification methods [7], a set of combination rules are utilised at each non-leaf node to evaluate the complete model, and are defined in Tables 8.1, 8.2, and 8.3. The rules are formulated for combining signed-distance values, which have no predefined limits. The values of A and B are negative inside an object and positive outside. Combination decisions are based on the signed distances computed from the non-leaf node's subcomponents. Additionally the closest point and colour are appropriately updated at each non-leaf node, until the complete model has been evaluated.

The entries in the tables have the following meanings. The IN conditions are

Table 8.1. Union combination rules.

			B	
$A \cup B$		IN	OUT	ON
	IN	MIN	A	A
A	OUT	B	MIN	B
	ON	B	A	A

Table 8.2. Intersection combination rules.

			B	
$A \cap B$		IN	OUT	ON
	IN	MAX	B	B
A	OUT	A	MAX	A
	ON	A	B	A

Table 8.3. Signed-distance difference combination rules

			B	
$A - B$		IN	OUT	ON
	IN	$-B$	MAX(A, $-B$)	B
A	OUT	MAX(A, $-B$)	A	A
	ON	$-B$	A	A

Table 8.4. Inside-outside difference combination rules.

			B	
$A - B$		IN	OUT	ON
	IN	$2-B$	MAX(A, 1/B)	B
A	OUT	MIN(A, $2-B$)	A	A
	ON	$2-B$	A	A

used when the point being tested against subcomponent A or B is inside the subcomponent, and the shortest distance to that subcomponent is negative. The OUT conditions are used when the point being tested against subcomponent A or B is outside the subcomponent, and the shortest distance to that subcomponent is positive. The ON conditions are used when the point being tested against subcomponent A or B is on the subcomponent, and the shortest distance to that subcomponent is zero. MAX states that the two values may be combined by taking the maximum of the values returned by evaluating A and B. MIN states that the two values may be combined by taking the minimum of the two. 'A' states that the values of A and B are combined by taking the shortest distance to A. 'B' states that the values of A and B are combined by taking the shortest distance to B. '−B' states that the values of A and B are combined by taking the negative of B. MAX(A, −B) states that the combination is produced by taking the maximum of the value of A and the negative of B.

Even though the range of the superellipsoid's inside-outside function, $[0, \infty]$, is different than the signed distance, $[-\infty, \infty]$, the rules for combining signed distances are the same as the inside-outside combination rules for union and intersection used in the original Constructive Cubes algorithm, and are given in Tables 8.1 and 8.2. A detailed explanation of these rules may be found in [6]. The inside-outside difference combination rules (Table 8.4) are different than the signed-distance combination rules given in Table 8.3.

The Constructive Cubes combination rules for difference (A−B) have been changed to work with signed distances rather than inside-outside values, and may be explained with Figure 8.1.

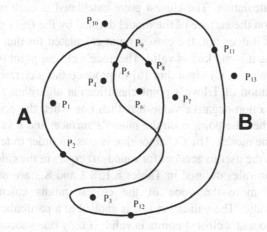

Figure 8.1. Evaluation points for a CSG model.

In Figure 8.1, point P_6 is the IN-IN condition. The shortest distance to the evaluated surface is the shortest distance to B. Since P_6 is inside of B the shortest distance to B is negative. P_6 is outside the evaluated model, and therefore must be negated to produce the correct signed distance. In the IN-OUT case, A is negative and B is positive. Therefore MAX(A, −B) compares two negative numbers, producing the number with the smallest absolute value. The correct answer for P_1 is A, while the correct answer for P_4 is −B. P_5 is in A and on B. B or zero is the correct result for this combination. The OUT-IN combination rule is also MAX(A, −B). In this case A is positive and B is negative, and it compares two positive numbers, producing the distance with the largest absolute value. The correct answer at P_7 is −B, recalling that B is negative, and must be negated to produce the correct signed result. The correct answer at P_3 is A. P_{10} is the OUT-OUT condition, with A providing the closest point to the evaluated model. P_{12} is the OUT-ON condition, with A also being the correct answer. P_8 represents the ON-IN condition. A is zero in this case, and B is negative. B is negated to produce the correct signed distance. P_2 is the ON-OUT condition, which returns A, which is zero. The ON-ON case occurs at the intersection point of the two objects (P_9), and returns A, which is zero.

Detecting Invalid Results

It is possible that at any node in the CSG graph one or both of the closest points to its subcomponents do not lie on the final evaluated surface. For example in Figure 8.1, the closest points to both A and B from point P_6 do not lie on the final evaluated surface of A $\cup$ B. Additionally, the closest points to both A and B from point P_{13} do not lie on the final evaluated surface of A – B. When generating colour information it is crucial to detect these invalid combinations when they first occur, and to flag them so they do not propagate invalid results up through the CSG graph during the closest-point/shortest-distance/colour calculations.

A test for invalid combination results is performed at each non-leaf node of the CSG graph during the depth-first traversal of the "Calculate-and-Combine" step of the closest-point calculation. The closest point calculated at each node is tested to determine if it lies on the surface of the model defined by the CSG subtree rooted at the current node. If it does not, the closest point calculated for that node is marked as invalid; otherwise it is marked as valid. The node's closest point is evaluated with the Constructive Cubes (CC) algorithm [6] to produce this determination. The CC algorithm is a variation of Tilove's point classification algorithm for CSG models [7], which returns a non-negative value less than one when the point is inside the CSG model, one when the point is on the model's surface, and a value greater than one when outside the model. The CC algorithm is used in order to test for a value of $1 \pm \varepsilon$, which allows the user to account for round-off errors in the calculations.

The combination rules defined in Tables 8.1, 8.2 and 8.3 are only applied at a particular node if more than one of the closest points calculated from its subcomponents is valid. The validation test is applied at a particular node if at least one of its subcomponent's closest points is valid. If only one subcomponent closest point is valid the combination rules are not applied, and the valid point and the colour associated with the point are returned to the next higher level of the CSG graph. If none of the subcomponents are valid, no closest-point/colour information is returned, and the node is marked as invalid. Ultimately this process produces a valid closest point to the complete model and the colour at that point, or a notification that no valid closest point can be calculated for the given input point.

The process may be further explained with Figure 8.2. The closest-point calculation is always valid for leaf nodes (superquadrics in our case) of the CSG graph. Given that valid closest points are returned for both nodes C and D to node 5, these results are combined at node 5 using the combination rules in Tables 8.1, 8.2 and 8.3. The closest point result at node 5 is now tested for validity by evaluating the closest point with the Constructive Cubes algorithm against the CSG submodel defined at node 5. Let us assume that node 5's closest point is invalid, i.e. the closest point does not lie on the evaluated surface defined by node 5. Now a closest point from one of node 3's subcomponents is invalid (node 5's) and one is valid (node C's). The combination rules are not applied at node 3, because it only has one valid subcomponent. C's closest point becomes the closest point for node 3. It is now tested for validity against the submodel defined at node 3.

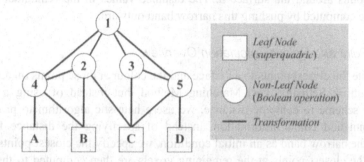

Figure 8.2. A CSG acyclic graph.

8.3.2 Fast Marching Method for Computing Closest Points and Colours

We present a Fast Marching Method for computing the approximate closest point to a surface from the points in a regular grid, as well as the colour at the closest point. Shortest-distance information may then be derived from the closest-point information. The accuracy of the method depends on a discretisation of the surface and is independent of the volume grid spacing, allowing us to calculate distance to subvoxel accuracy.

The Eikonal Equation and the Fast Marching Level Set Method

Let $u(x, y, z)$ denote the signed distance from the closed surface S. u is a weak solution of the Eikonal equation:

$$|\nabla u| \equiv \sqrt{\left(\frac{\partial u}{\partial x}\right)^2 + \left(\frac{\partial u}{\partial y}\right)^2 + \left(\frac{\partial u}{\partial z}\right)^2} = 1, \text{ subject to } u|_S = 0. \tag{8.13}$$

The characteristics of Equation 8.13 are straight lines that are normal to S. For each point (x, y, z) in space, there is a line segment from the surface to the point that is a characteristic of the entropy-satisfying solution of the Eikonal equation. The point (x, y, z) and the closest point on the surface S are the endpoints of this line segment.

Sethian [5,31] has developed a Fast Marching Level Set Method to solve the Eikonal equation:

$$|\nabla u| f(x, y, z) = 1, \text{ subject to } u|_S = g(x, y, z). \tag{8.14}$$

in the case that f is either always positive or negative. The method uses an upwind, viscosity solution, finite-difference scheme to numerically solve this equation. For $f(x, y, z) = 1$ and $g(x, y, z) = 0$, the solution gives the signed distance from the surface S. The initial condition $u|_S = 0$ is specified by giving the value of u on a narrow band of points around the surface S. The distance values in the remainder of the volume are computed by pushing this narrow band outward.

Closest Point and Colour Calculation Overview

To calculate the closest points to a surface and the colour at those points on a regular grid, we utilise Sethian's Fast Marching Method, but instead of using a finite-difference scheme to compute distance, we use a heuristic algorithm to propagate closest-point and colour information. Instead of specifying the distance for the points in the narrow band as an initial condition, we specify the closest points to the surface. The closest points at the remaining voxels are then computed to the point samples on the original surface. In one step of the closest-point and colour method:

1. The point gp with the smallest distance is removed from the narrow band and its shortest-distance, closest-point and colour value are frozen.
2. Points are added to the narrow band to maintain unit thickness.
3. The closest points of the neighbours with larger distances than gp are recomputed using the closest-point information from gp.

The closest-point and colour method is based on the following idea. The closest point on the surface to a point in the grid is usually close to one of the closest points of its neighbours in the grid. Thus, if one knows the closest points of the neighbours of a grid point gp, one can compute an approximate closest point for gp by assuming that it is near one of the closest points of its neighbours. This is only a heuristic, and in Figure 8.3 we see cases in two dimensions for which the heuristic succeeds and fails. In the cases where the heuristic fails to determine the correct closest point, it still gives a reasonable approximation of the distance. The heuristic may fail if the characteristics from several different portions of the surface S intersect near gp. Fortunately, if the heuristic fails at a point, this mistake is usually not propagated outward to increasing distances. This is because "information" in the Eikonal equation and the closest-point method is propagated along characteristics of Equation 8.13. Where characteristics collide, information goes into the shock and is lost.

Terminology

Let the *distance, closest-point* and *colour volumes* be represented by $N \times N \times N$ grids that span the space around the scan-converted object. We will refer to points in these volumes with (i, j, k) coordinates. Let the *zero set grid* be an $M \times M \times M$ uniform grid that spans the same Cartesian domain. We refer to the ratio M/N as the *super-sampling factor* of the zero set grid. In most cases the zero set grid is finer than the volume grid, providing distance calculations with subvoxel accuracy. We will refer to points in the zero set grid with (I, J, K) coordinates. For any grid point, the closest point is defined as the Cartesian coordinates of the zero set point on the CSG model surface that is closest to that grid point.

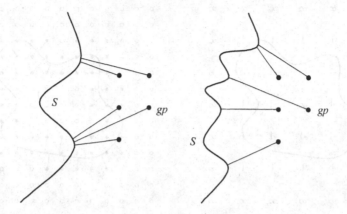

Figure 8.3. The closest-point heuristic.

Initial Data

The fast marching algorithm takes as input: a set of grid points in an initial working volume that forms a *narrow band* around the CSG model surface and a point sampling of the surface. This second set of points will be called the *zero set*, since they are points lying on the isosurface of zero distance. The narrow band contains all the points in the working volume having the property that a neighbour[1] of the point has opposite inside/outside status. We generate the narrow band by evaluating the inside/outside status [7] of all the grid points of the working volume, and note where inside/outside transitions occur. For the points in the narrow band we must supply the (i, j, k) coordinates of the points and their inside/outside status. The narrow band is used as a starting point for propagating the closest-point and colour information outward and inward to the rest of the grid points in the working volume. Note that specifying the inside/outside status of the points in the narrow band determines the inside/outside status of the other points in the grid.

During this stage of our calculations the CSG model surface is represented with a set of points that lie on the surface, the zero set. The zero set is made by first constructing a thin band of points in the zero set grid that surrounds the CSG model surface. This set of grid points will be called the *zero band*. The zero set is the set of closest points on the model surface to the grid points in the zero band. The method used to calculate the zero set has been described in the Section 8.3.1. Given a point p in the zero set that is closest to the grid point (I, J, K) in the zero band, one can determine all the points in the zero set that lie in a neighbourhood of p by determining all the points in the zero band in a neighbourhood of (I, J, K). As input to the algorithm, we must supply the (I, J, K) coordinates of the grid points in the

---

[1] In three dimensions *neighbour* means one of the 26 locations surrounding each grid point.

zero band and the corresponding (X, Y, Z) coordinates of the points in the zero set. In Figure 8.4 the initial data is shown graphically in two dimensions.

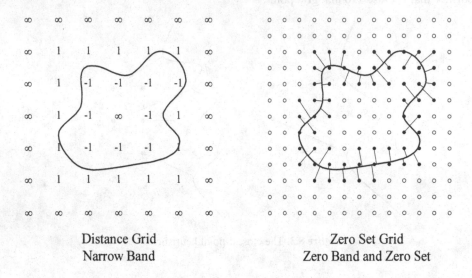

Distance Grid   Zero Set Grid

Narrow Band   Zero Band and Zero Set

Figure 8.4. Initial data for the Fast Marching algorithm.

Propagating the Closest-Point and Colour Data

Initially, we have the closest-point and colour data in the zero band that surrounds the surface. We use the closest-point and colour data in the zero band to determine the closest points and colours in the narrow band of the working volume and then march the narrow band outward and inward to calculate the closest points and colours in the rest of the working volume. Consider a point gp that neighbours the band and whose closest point is unknown. The closest point of gp is probably close to one of the closest points of its neighbours in the band. Thus for each neighbour of gp in the band, we compute the shortest distance at gp by considering zero set points that are near the closest points of that neighbour. First we will present the marching algorithm that moves the band outward and then inward. Next, we will show the algorithm for recomputing the distance at a point gp, given the closest point of one of its neighbours.

Let in_out_{ijk} denote the inside/outside status for a point in the working volume; $+1$ for outside, -1 for inside. Let $dist_{ijk}$ denote the computed distance at a working volume grid point. A value of ∞ indicates that the distance has not yet been computed. Let $source_{ijk}$ denote the point in the zero set Z from which this distance was computed.

Initially, the closest point to each (I, J, K) in the zero band is known. For each (i, j, k) in the narrow band $dist_{ijk} = in\_out_{ijk}$. For each point not in the narrow band $dist_{ijk}$ and in_out_{ijk} are set to be undefined. The closest points of the zero band are used to generate approximate closest points for the narrow band. Below is the fast marching closest-point/colour algorithm.

```
// March forward to find positive distances.
put each point with a non-negative, finite
    dist_ijk in the set U;
while U ≠ ∅ do
    remove the grid point gp with the smallest
        distance from U;
    for each of the 26 neighbours of gp do
        if the source of the neighbour is unknown then
            add that neighbour to U;
        end if;
        if the distance of the neighbour is
            larger than the distance of gp then
            recompute the neighbour's distance
                using gp's source s;
        end if;
    end for;
end while;
```

Next the narrow band is marched backward to compute the closest points and colours with negative distance. Once the closest point, shortest distance and colour have been computed for all the grid points of the working volume, separate closest-point, distance and colour volumes are written to individual files.

Below is the algorithm to recompute the distance $dist_{ijk}$ to the working grid point gp, using a zero set source s. Let (I, J, K) be the coordinates in the zero band for which s is the closest point. The user chooses the search radius parameter R. This is the radius of a cube around the point (I, J, K) in the zero band that defines a neighbourhood on the surface around the point s. The parameter, $\sigma = 2R + 1$ is the diameter of the cube. When recomputing the distance, all the points in the zero set in a neighbourhood around s are considered as possible closest points.

```
for each grid point (l,m,n) in a σ × σ × σ cube
        surrounding (I,J,K) do
    t ∈ Z is the closest point to (l,m,n);
    calculate the distance from gp to t;
end for
dist_ijk = minimum of the σ³ computed distances
source_ijk = the source of this minimum distance
            (an element of Z);
```

From experience we have found that for most surfaces, a search radius R of half the supersampling factor of the zero set grid will provide satisfactory closest-point information to the set Z. Finally, note that since the zero band is of small constant thickness, the number of points in the zero band in the $\sigma \times \sigma \times \sigma$ cube is $O(\sigma^2)$.

8.3.3 Computational Complexity

There are N^3 grid points in the working volume. At any point in the algorithm, there are $O(N^2)$ points in the narrow band. There are 2P nodes in the binary tree representing the CSG model, where P is the number of superellipsoids in the model. Each node of the model must be evaluated (in constant time) to determine if a particular grid point is inside or outside the model. Determining which grid points are in the initial narrow band requires $O(N^3P)$ operations. Determining the closest point on the CSG model from a particular grid point is also an $O(P)$ operation. This is only computed on the points of the zero band. Calculating the zero set requires $O(M^2P)$ operations, recalling that the zero set grid has resolution $M \times M \times M$. Unfortunately it is difficult to characterise the amount of time needed to calculate the closest point to each superellipsoid, since each one is evaluated with an iterative technique. This calculation typically requires approximately 30 iterations in our variable step-size gradient descent routine.

Each working grid point is removed from the narrow band once, giving us a factor of N^3. The cost of adding and deleting elements from the narrow band is proportional to the logarithm of the number of points in the narrow band. This gives us a factor of $O(\log N)$. The computational cost of recomputing the distance for a given grid point is proportional to the number of zero band points in a $\sigma \times \sigma \times \sigma$ cube neighbourhood of a point s in the zero band. This gives us a factor of $O(\sigma^2)$. Thus the computational complexity of propagating the narrow band into the whole volume is $O(N^3\sigma^2\log N)$.

8.4 Colour Shading Polygonal Isosurfaces

A polygonal approximation of an isosurface imbedded in the distance volume may be generated with the Marching Cubes algorithm [3]. The colour and closest-point volumes may then be used to colour shade the isosurface. In this approach the colour at any point on the isosurface is defined as the colour at the closest point on the original CSG model from the isosurface point.

When a colour value at (X, Y, Z) of the polygonal surface is needed during rendering, a user-defined number of trilinearly interpolated samples are taken from the colour volume around the (X, Y, Z) location. The colour value is calculated by:

$$\vec{C} = \vec{C}_{fff}(1-u)(1-v)(1-w) + \vec{C}_{cff}(u)(1-v)(1-w)$$
$$+ \vec{C}_{fcf}(1-u)(v)(1-w) + \vec{C}_{ccf}(u)(v)(1-w) + \vec{C}_{ffc}(1-u)(1-v)(w) \qquad (8.15)$$
$$+ \vec{C}_{cfc}(u)(1-v)(w) + \vec{C}_{fcc}(1-u)(v)(w) + \vec{C}_{ccc}(u)(v)(w),$$

where $u = (X - \text{floor}(X))$, $v = (Y - \text{floor}(Y))$, and $w = (Z - \text{floor}(Z))$. $\vec{C}_{xyz}$ defines the colour value stored at a specific voxel in the colour volume. 'f' and 'c' designate the floor or ceiling of the X, Y or Z value used to reference the colour. The distance between adjacent voxel locations is defined to be 1. For example, if the point on the polygonal surface being shaded is (34.27, 129.78, 56.45) the colour at that point would be computed by:

$$\vec{C} = \vec{C}_{34,129,56}(1-0.27)(1-0.78)(1-0.45)$$

$$+ \vec{C}_{35,129,56}(0.27)(1-0.78)(1-0.45)$$

$$+ \vec{C}_{34,130,56}(1-0.27)(0.78)(1-0.45)$$

$$+ \vec{C}_{35,130,56}(0.27)(0.78)(1-0.45)$$

$$+ \vec{C}_{34,129,57}(1-0.27)(1-0.78)(0.45)$$ (8.16)

$$+ \vec{C}_{35,129,57}(0.27)(1-0.78)(0.45)$$

$$+ \vec{C}_{34,130,57}(1-0.27)(0.78)(0.45)$$

$$+ \vec{C}_{35,130,57}(0.27)(0.78)(0.45),$$

where $\vec{C}_{34,129,56}$ signifies the value stored in the colour volume at (34, 129, 56).

In the examples in this chapter we take samples at the corners of the cube centred around (X, Y, Z), as well as at (X, Y, Z), with the length of the edges of the cube equal to one, the distance between voxels. If all of the colour values are the same, the constant colour value is returned as the colour of the polygonal surface at (X, Y, Z). If any of the sampled colour values are different, a trilinearly-interpolated closest-point value is calculated from the closest-point volume at the same sample locations. Since these interpolated points do not necessarily lie on the surface of the original CSG model, the closest point from each of the interpolated points to the CSG model and the associated colour are calculated using the "calculate-and-combine" step of the method described in Section 8.3.1. The colours calculated at all of the samples are averaged together to produce the final colour for (X, Y, Z).

Our raytracer automatically supersamples and antialiases those regions of the image where large colour changes take place. Therefore, our approach quickly renders those parts of the model where there are constant colour values, and only performs expensive closest-point/colour calculations along edges of differing colours. Since the supersampling of the closest-point volume is driven by the rendering process, only the extra closest-point calculations necessary for proper antialiasing are performed, saving the computation time and storage space that would be needed to supersample the entire volume.

The complete process of colour shading a distance-volume-derived polygonal surface is summarised in Figure 8.5. Distance, colour and closest-point volumes are generated from a CSG model using the 3D scan-conversion algorithm (Step 1). A polygonal surface is generated from the distance volume using the Marching Cubes algorithm (Step 2). The resulting surface is rendered (Step 3). In order to determine the colour at a specific point on the surface, the colour volume is sampled around that location (Step 4). If all of the samples are the same colour, the colour is used to shade the point on the surface. If the colours are different, the closest-point volume is sampled at the same locations as the colour volume (Step 5). The closest points on the original CSG model are calculated for the interpolated sample points, as well as the colour using the "calculate-and-combine" algorithm (Step 6). The colours calculated in Step 6 are combined and the average colour is used when rendering the specific point on the polygonal surface (Step 7).

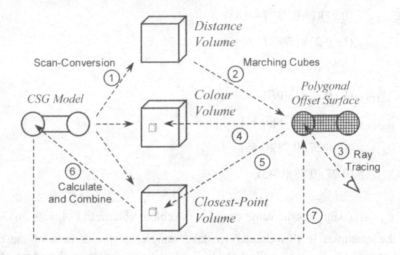

Figure 8.5. Overview of the colour-shading algorithm.

8.5 Results

A number of moderately complex CSG models have been scan-converted into distance, closest-point and colour volumes with our approach. Each of the CSG models consists of superellipsoids, which have been unioned, intersected, and/or differenced to produce the final shapes. The scan-converted volumes have been used to generate an evaluated surface of the model, as well as offset surfaces. Additionally, the volumes have been utilised to morph one model into another [4]. The results contain rendered polygonal surfaces that have been extracted from the distance volumes using the Marching Cubes algorithm. The surfaces have been colour shaded using the algorithms described in Section 8.4.

Figure 8.6 presents an evaluated CSG surface of an X-29 jet fighter, consisting of 38 primitives and generated from a 96 × 192 × 240 distance volume. Additionally three offset surfaces are generated by applying the Marching Cubes algorithm with an isovalue greater than zero. Figure 8.7 presents the same polygonal models with the colour-shading algorithm applied to the surfaces. Figure 8.8 presents five colour-shaded isosurfaces generated from the scan-converted volumes of a dart model, consisting of 21 primitives and sampled at a resolution of 96 × 192 × 240. Figure 8.9 presents four colour-shaded isosurfaces generated from the scan-converted volumes of a CSG part, consisting of 5 primitives and sampled at a resolution of

195×90×120. Figure 8.10 presents a morphing sequence where the dart model transforms into the X-29 model. The morphing process involves manipulating and changing voxel values of the dart distance volume based on the values in the X-29 distance volume [4]. Since the basic model representation of the morphing object is volumetric, the colour and closest-point volumes associated with the initial and final models may be used to colour shade the intermediate shapes. For a given point (X, Y, Z) on the morphing surface, the associated colour is calculated from both the initial and final models' colour and closest-point volumes. These two colours are linearly interpolated based on the time parameter of the morphing sequence to produce an average colour for (X, Y, Z) on the intermediate shape.

The various volume resolutions were chosen because they produced satisfactory results given the cost in time (several hours) and memory (~17 MBtyes) to produce them. The excessive time needed to produce our results is significantly affected by the message-passing overhead imposed by the object-oriented environment used to prototype our algorithms [30]. We believe that the processing times can be improved by at least an order magnitude if the algorithm is custom coded in a conventional programming environment.

8.6 Conclusion

We have described a technique for generating distance, closest-point and colour volumes with subvoxel accuracy from one type of geometric model, a CSG model consisting of superellipsoid primitives. The volumes are generated in a two-step process. The first step calculates the shortest distance to the CSG model at a set of points within a narrow band around the evaluated surface. Additionally, a second set of points, labelled the zero set, which lies on the CSG model's surface and contains colour information is computed. A point in the zero set is associated with each point in the narrow band. Once the narrow band and zero set are calculated, a Fast Marching Method is employed to propagate the shortest-distance, closest-point and colour information out to the remaining voxels in the volume. In addition, we have described a colour-shading technique that utilises the closest-point and colour volumes to calculate the surface colours on polygonal surfaces extracted from the distance volumes. Our techniques have been used to scan-convert a number of CSG models, producing volumes and colour-shaded polygonal surfaces which have been utilised in a variety of computer graphics applications, e.g. CSG surface evaluation, offset surface generation, and 3D model morphing

Acknowledgements

We would like to thank Dr. Alan Barr and the other members of the Caltech Computer Graphics Group for their support and assistance. Timothy Doyle created the dart model used in Figures 8.8 and 8.10. This work was financially supported by

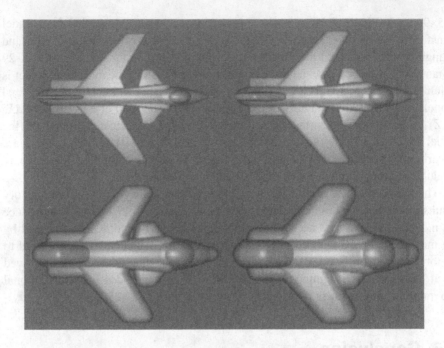

Figure 8.6. Offset surfaces from the X-29 distance volume.

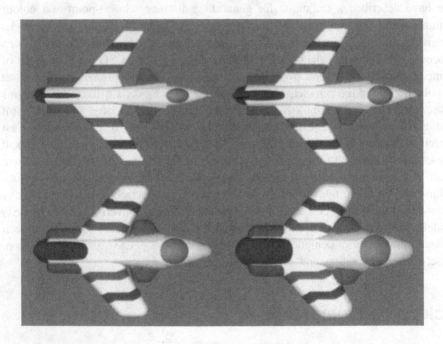

Figure 8.7. Antialiased colour-shaded offset surfaces from the X-29 distance, colour and closest-point volumes.

Figure 8.8. Antialiased colour-shaded offset surfaces from the dart distance, colour and closest-point volumes.

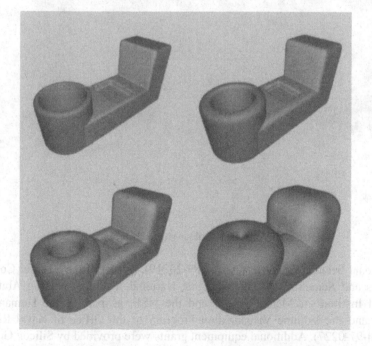

Figure 8.9. Antialiased colour-shaded offset surfaces from the CSG part distance, colour and closest-point volumes.

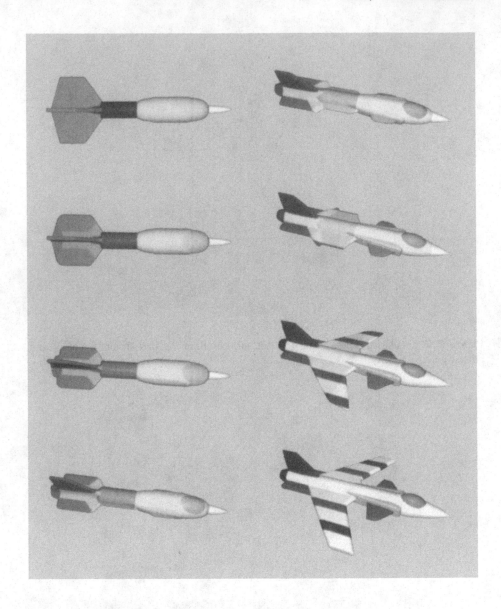

Figure 8.10. Antialiased colour-shaded morphing surfaces.

the National Science Foundation (ASC-89-20219), as part of the STC for Computer Graphics and Scientific Visualization; the National Institute on Drug Abuse, the National Institute of Mental Health and the NSF, as part of the Human Brain Project; and the Volume Visualization Program of the Office of Naval Research (N00014-97-0227). Additional equipment grants were provided by Silicon Graphics, Hewlett-Packard, IBM, and Digital Equipment Corporation. This work was initially funded by the former shareholders of the European Computer-Industry Research Centre: Bull SA, ICL PLC, and Siemens AG.

References

1. Requicha AAG, Voelcker HB. Solid modeling: A historical summary and contemporary assessment. IEEE Computer Graphics and Applications, 1982; 2(2):9-22.
2. Barr A. Superquadrics and angle-preserving transformations. IEEE Computer Graphics and Applications, 1981; 1(1):11-23.
3. Lorensen WE, Cline HE. Marching cubes: A high resolution 3D surface construction algorithm. ACM/SIGGRAPH Computer Graphics, 1987; 21(4):163-169.
4. Whitaker RT, Breen DE. Level-set models for the deformation of solid objects. In: Proc. the 3rd International Workshop on Implicit Surfaces, Seattle, WA, June 1998; 19-35.
5. Sethian JA. Level Set Methods. Cambridge University Press; Cambridge, UK; 1996.
6. Breen DE. Constructive Cubes: CSG evaluation for display using discrete 3D scalar data sets. In: Proc. Eurographics '91, Vienna, September 1991; 127-142.
7. Tilove RB. Set membership classification: A unified approach to geometric intersection problems. IEEE Transactions on Computers, 1980; C-29:874-883.
8. Cohen D, Kaufman A. Scan-conversion algorithms for linear and quadratic objects. In Volume Visualization. IEEE Computer Society Press; 1990; 280-301.
9. Jones MW. The production of volume data from triangular meshes using voxelisation. Computer Graphics Forum, 1996; 15(5):311-318.
10. Kaufman A. An algorithm for 3D scan-conversion of polygons. In: Proc. Eurographics '87, Amsterdam, August 1987; 197-208.
11. Kaufman A. Efficient algorithms for 3D scan conversion of parametric curves, surfaces, and volumes. ACM/SIGGRAPH Computer Graphics, 1987; 21(4):171-179.
12. Shareef N, Yagel R. Rapid previewing via volume-based solid modeling. In: Proc. 3rd Symposium on Solid Modeling and Applications, May 1995; 281-292.
13. Wang SM, Kaufman A. Volume-sampled 3D modeling. IEEE Computer Graphics and Applications, 1994; 14(5):26-32.
14. Fang S, Srinivasan R. Volumetric-CSG — A model-based volume visualization approach. In: Proc. the 6th International Conference in Central Europe on Computer Graphics and Visualization; 1998.
15. Payne B, Toga A. Distance field manipulation of surface models. IEEE Computer Graphics and Applications, 1992; 12(1):65-71.
16. Borgefors G. Distance transformations in digital images. Computer Vision, Graphics, and Image Processing, 1986; 34:344-371.
17. Cohen-Or D, Levin D, Solomivici A. Three-dimensional distance field metamorphosis. ACM Transactions on Graphics, 1998; 17(2):116-141.
18. Requicha AAG, Voelcker HB. Boolean operations in solid modeling: Boundary evaluation and merging algorithms. Proceedings of the IEEE, 1985; 73(1):30-44.
19. Maillot J, Yahia H, Verroust A. Interactive texture mapping. In: Proc. SIGGRAPH '93, Anaheim, CA, August 1993; 27-34.

20. Litwinowicz P, Miller G. Efficient techniques for interactive texture placement. In: Proc. SIGGRAPH '94, Orlando, FL, July 1994; 119-122.

21. Agrawala M, Beers AC, Levoy M. 3D painting on scanned surfaces. In: Proc. Symposium on Interactive 3D Graphics, April 1995; 145-150.

22. Pedersen HK. Decorating implicit surfaces. In: Proc. SIGGRAPH '95, Los Angeles, August 1995; 291-300.

23. Pedersen HK. A framework for interactive texturing operations on curved surfaces. In: Proc. SIGGRAPH'96, New Orleans, August 1996; 295-302.

24. Smets-Solanes JP. Vector field based texture mapping of animated implicit objects. Computer Graphics Forum, 1996; 15(3):289-300.

25. Tigges M, Wyvill B. Texture mapping the blobtree. In: Proc. 3rd Int. Workshop on Implicit Surfaces, Seattle, WA, June 1998; 123-130.

26. Zonenschein R, Gomes J, Velho L, de Figueiredo LH. Controlling texture mapping onto implicit surfaces with particle systems. In: Proc. the 3rd International Workshop on Implicit Surfaces, Seattle, WA, June 1998; 131-138.

27. Shibolet O, Cohen-Or D. Coloring voxel-based objects for virtual endoscopy. In: Proc. IEEE Symposium on Volume Visualization, Raleigh, NC, October 1998; 15-22.

28. Bier EA, Sloan Jr. KR. Two part texture mapping. IEEE Computer Graphics and Applications, 1986; 6(9):40-53.

29. do Carno MP. Differential Geometry of Curves and Surfaces. Prentice Hall, Englewood Cliffs, NJ, 1976.

30. Getto P, Breen DE. An object-oriented architecture for a computer animation system. The Visual Computer, 1990; 6(2):79-92.

31. Sethian JA. A fast marching level set method for monotonically advancing fronts. Proceedings of the National Academy of Science, 1996; 93(4):1591-1595.

9. NURBS Volume for Modelling Complex Objects

Zhongke Wu, Hock Soon Seah and Feng Lin

9.1 Introduction

Geometric modelling of objects is one of the main research issues in computer graphics. 3D solid objects are traditionally represented by their surface boundaries. To construct free-form boundaries, Non-Uniform Rational B-Spline (NURBS) curves and surfaces are widely used in various modelling systems. NURBS has become the *de facto* industry standard for the representation, design and data exchange of geometric information processed by computers. Its excellent mathematical and algorithmic properties, combined with successful industrial applications, have contributed to the enormous popularity of NURBS.

Surface boundaries, however, do not contain information about the interior of 3D objects. Traditional NURBS-based modelling systems only work with objects made of homogeneous materials. Furthermore, due to the difficulty of computation in free-form surface intersections and other operations, these modelling systems are seldom used for modelling objects in complex forms.

We have developed a NURBS representation of volumes, which is a generalisation of NURBS representation of curves and surfaces. It defines not only the surface boundary of an object but also its interior. Much more information can be contained in this model than in the traditional surface model. This representation makes it possible to model 3D objects with inhomogeneous (heterogeneous) scalar fields and vector fields (such as magnetic field). We shall call such a model a *NURBS volume model*. On the other hand, in volume graphics, an object is represented by a set of voxels. We shall call such a model a *voxel-based model* (or *volume model*). By combining voxel-based models with NURBS models, we can take full advantage of both modelling methods in constructing complex objects.

This chapter describes concepts of the NURBS volume modelling method, with a brief discussion on exploiting the ability of NURBS-based free-form modelling in voxel-based modelling processes.

9.2 Concepts and Data Structure

9.2.1 Continuous Model

Definition 9.1: *Topological Manifold.* An n-dimensional topological manifold is defined by a Hausdorff space M in which each point p has a neighbourhood $U(p)$ homeomorphic to an open set of $\mathbf{R}^n$.   □

Definition 9.2: Let M' be a Hausdorff space in which each point p of M' has a neighbourhood $U(p)$ homeomorphic to an open set of H^n, where H^n is the half-space $\{(x_1, x_2, ..., x_n) \in \mathbf{R}^n \mid x_n \geq 0\}$. Let $\partial M'$ denote the set consisting of points p of M' such that p corresponds to a point of:

$$H_0^n = \{\{(x_1, x_2, ..., x_n) \in H^n \mid x_n = 0\} \subset H^n$$

under the homeomorphism from $U(p)$ to an open set of H^n. M' is called an n-dimensional topological manifold with boundary. If $\partial M' \neq \Phi$, $\partial M'$ is called the boundary of M'; otherwise, M defined in 9.1 or M' with $\partial M' = \Phi$ is called topological manifold without boundary. The interior of M' is the complement of the boundary: $M_0 = M' - \partial M'$. The boundary of an n-dimensional topological manifold is an $(n\text{-}1)$-dimensional topological manifold.   □

In geometric modelling, there are three types of objects: curve, surface and volume in $\mathbf{R}^3$. A curve (or a path) in $\mathbf{R}^3$ is a continuous function $\alpha\colon I \to \mathbf{R}^3$, where I is some open interval in real number field $\mathbf{R}$. A surface in $\mathbf{R}^3$ is a closed subset of $\mathbf{R}^3$, that is, a 2-manifold or a 2-manifold with boundary. A volume in $\mathbf{R}^3$ is a closed subset of $\mathbf{R}^3$, that is, a 3-manifold or a 3-manifold with boundary.

Parametrically, a curve is represented as a single-parameter vector function $r(u)\colon [0, 1] \to \mathbf{R}^3$. A surface is represented as a two-parameter vector function $r(u, v)\colon [0, 1]\times[0, 1] \to \mathbf{R}^3$. And a volume is represented as a three-parameter vector function $r(u, v, w)\colon [0, 1]\times[0, 1]\times[0, 1] \to \mathbf{R}^3$.

9.2.2 NURBS Representation of a Volume

NURBS curves and surfaces are widely used in various modelling systems. Details of NURBS curves and surfaces can be found in many books (e.g. [1]). We define a NURBS volume in homogeneous coordinate form as:

$$V(u,v,t) = \sum_{i=0}^{m}\sum_{j=0}^{n}\sum_{k=0}^{l} N_{i,p}(u)N_{j,q}(v)N_{k,r}(t)P_{i,j,k}$$

where $P_{i,j,k} = (x_{i,j,k}, y_{i,j,k}, z_{i,j,k}, w_{i,j,k})$ are the homogeneous coordinates of the volume control points, p, q, r are the order of the volume in the parameter u-

direction, v-direction and t-direction respectively, and:

$$U = \{u_0, u_1, ..., u_f\}, \quad V = \{v_0, v_1, ..., v_g\} \text{ and } T = \{t_0, t_1, ..., t_h\}$$

are knot vectors in the respective directions:

$$f = m + p, \quad g = n + q, \quad h = l + r.$$

$N_{i,p}(u), N_{j,q}(v), N_{k,r}(t)$ are pth-order, qth-order and rth-order B-spline basis functions defined on the knot vectors U, V and T respectively.

A NURBS volume in the Cartesian coordinate form is thereby defined as:

$$V(u,v,t) = \frac{\sum_{i=0}^{m}\sum_{j=0}^{n}\sum_{k=0}^{l} N_{i,p}(u)N_{j,q}(v)N_{k,r}(t)w_{i,j,k}\hat{P}_{i,j,k}}{\sum_{i=0}^{m}\sum_{j=0}^{n}\sum_{k=0}^{l} N_{i,p}(u)N_{j,q}(v)N_{k,r}(t)w_{i,j,k}} \tag{9.1}$$

where $\hat{P}_{i,j,k} = (x_{i,j,k}, y_{i,j,k}, z_{i,j,k})$ are the Cartesian coordinates of the volume control points, and $w_{i,j,k}$ is the weight on the control point $\hat{P}_{i,j,k}$. The definition of other parameters is defined in the same way as the NURBS volume in homogeneous coordinates.

A function that is defined on a NURBS volume object can thus be defined as:

$$f(u,v,t) = \frac{\sum_{i=0}^{m}\sum_{j=0}^{n}\sum_{k=0}^{l} N_{i,p}(u)N_{j,q}(v)N_{k,r}(t)w_{i,j,k}f_{i,j,k}}{\sum_{i=0}^{m}\sum_{j=0}^{n}\sum_{k=0}^{l} N_{i,p}(u)N_{j,q}(v)N_{k,r}(t)w_{i,j,k}} \tag{9.2}$$

where $f_{i,j,k}$ are the control points of the continuous function. Other coefficients are defined in the same way as Equation 9.1. The function $f(u, v, t)$ can be used to describe the physical properties of an object. If $f(u, v, t)$ is scalar function, it represents a scalar field on the object, such as 3D texture, temperature field, density field, etc. If $f(u, v, t)$ is a vector function, it represents a vector field on the object, such as pressure field, gravitational field and electromagnetic field, etc.

Almost all the properties of, and algorithms for, NURBS curve and surfaces [1] can be generalised for NURBS volume, and these include de lastejau algorithm, interpolation, elevation, knot insertion and modification, division, combination, etc.

9.2.3 Voxelisation of a Continuous Model

Definition 9.3: A *voxel* (x, y, z) in a 3D discrete space is defined by a unit cube centred at (x, y, z). Two voxels are said to be 6-adjacent if they share a face, 18-adjacent if they share a face or an edge, and 26-adjacent if they share a face, an edge, or a vertex. The 6-neighborhood (18-neighborhood, 26-neighborhood) of a voxel is the set of all voxels that are 6-adjacent (18-adjacent, 26-adjacent) to it. A sequence of voxels becomes a 6-path (18-path, 26-path) if every two consecutive voxels along the sequence are 6-adjacent (18-adjacent, 26-adjacent). Two voxels are said to be 6-connected (18-connected, 26-connected) if there exists a 6-path (18-path, 26-path) between them. (See also [2-3], Section 1.4 and Chapter 3.)   □

Definition 9.4: A *voxel object* is defined by a set of voxels. In particular, we have a *voxel curve*, a *voxel surface* and a *voxel volume* generated by voxelising a curve, a surface and a volume model respectively.

The model, which we call a voxel-based model, abides 3D discrete topology [4-6]. A *slice* in 3D space is a special case of voxel surface.   □

We use a hybrid model including the continuous NURBS representation and the voxel-based model. A voxel object can be generated through voxelisation of its NURBS volume. The key is therefore to exploit the flexibility of NURBS in free-form model generation and use the voxelised models as components to construct complex objects.

9.3 Modelling Processes

9.3.1 NURBS Volume Modelling

NURBS volume modelling is a process that constructs objects with heterogeneous scalar and vector fields in $\mathbf{R}^3$. Such a process can be in one of the following three forms:

- *Primitive modelling* — using NURBS volumes to generate commonly-used primitives such as sphere, torus, cylinder, cube, cone, etc.;
- *Generative sculpture shaping* — using NURBS curves and surfaces to produce sculpture NURBS volumes, such as ruled shape, revolution shape, sweeping, skinning, driving methods, etc.;
- *Deformation* — based on the NURBS primitives, complex NURBS shapes can be generated by deformation. The types of deformation include regular deformation, freedom deformation and physically-based deformation.

Figure 9.1 shows examples of NURBS volume models which have been voxelised prior to the rendering process.

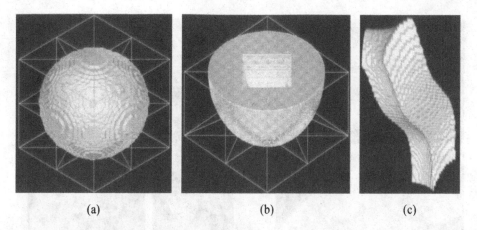

(a)   (b)   (c)

Figure 9.1. NURBS volumes: (a) a sphere defined by a NURBS volume (the lines connect the NURBS volume control points); (b) a ruled shape generated by NURBS-represented polygons and a half-sphere surface; (c) arbitrary deformation of a NURBS volume.

9.3.2 Voxel-Based Modelling

Voxel-based modelling is a process of constructing and manipulating objects represented by voxels. (A more comprehensive discussion on volume modelling can be found in Chapter 2.) We have considered the following operations in voxel-based modelling:

- *Sweeping a slice* — moving a slice or a voxel surface along some path to generate a voxel-based object. It includes translational sweeping, rotational sweeping, helix sweeping and general sweeping, whose paths are defined by line, circle, helix curve and free-form curve respectively. During sweeping, some transforms (such as scaling and twisting) on the slice position, orientation and size may be applied. Figure 9.2 shows several examples resulting from some sweeping operations.

- *Deformation* — this operation, which is built on voxel-based models, differs from the deformation based on continuous models discussed in 9.3.1. The voxel-based deformation includes regular deformation, freedom deformation and physically based deformation. It is an important method for generating free-form objects.

- *Voxel-based Boolean operations* (see also Section 1.9 and Chapters 6-8) — as the values associated to each voxel in a voxel-based model may represent different physical properties other than "geometry", there are more meanings to the Union, Intersection and Difference in voxel-based Boolean operations. Under certain conditions, Boolean operations in voxel-based modelling can be easily implemented without some of the difficulties experienced in traditional solid modelling. Figure 9.3a shows an object constructed using voxel-based Boolean operations.

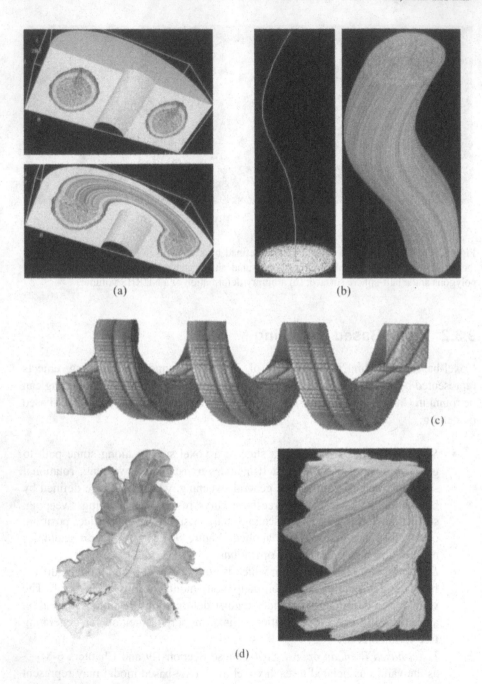

Figure 9.2. Sweeping operations: a rotational sweeping, (b) helix sweeping, (c) translational sweeping a slice with twisting and scaling, (d) general sweeping — sweeping a slice along a picked NURBS.

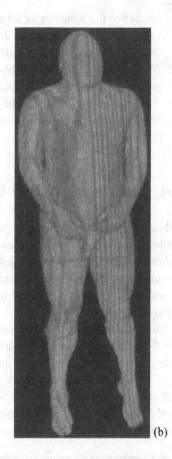

(a)   (b)

Figure 9.3. (a) A complex model generated by Boolean operations and voxel texture mapping. (b) Mapping a 3D wood texture to the Visible Man dataset to get a wooden human model.

- *Voxel texture mapping* — this operation generates a voxelised volume with an internal structure by mapping 3D texture into a closed domain, which is defined by a group of voxel surfaces or a voxel-based object (Figure 9.3b). This operation is different from texture mapping in surface modelling which is normally performed during rendering.

9.3.3 Combined Modelling

By combining NURBS volume modelling and voxel-based modelling, we have facilitated the following modelling operations:

- *Sweeping along a NURBS curve* — a voxel-based object can be generated by moving a slice or a voxel surface along a NURBS curve. During sweeping some geometric transformations, such as translation, rotation and scaling, may be applied to the image or voxel surface (Figure 9.2b).

- *Project sweep* — a voxelised volume can be generated by projecting an image or a voxel surface onto a NURBS surface.
- *Drive shape* — by driving one or more images as moving cross-sections along one or more trajectory curves, a voxelised volume can generated.
- *Boolean operations* — a complex structure is generated by union, intersection and difference operations between NURBS volumes and other voxel objects (Figure 9.3a).

9.4 Discussion and Conclusion

Volume graphics is an emerging area of computer graphics. It is concerned with the synthesis, manipulation, and rendering of volumetric objects in a grid of voxels. Volume modelling, or voxel-based modelling, is one of the most important aspects of volume graphics. Voxel-based modelling systems are useful for synthesising natural and artificial objects, and integrating them into a hybrid scene represented by a grid of voxels.

Fundamentally, all geometrical models represented in a computer are discrete. Voxel-based modelling may be used to unify all the representations. However, due to its discrete nature, the control and manipulation of the voxel-based models are not easy. To overcome this drawback, we have proposed a new approach by combining NURBS representations and the voxelisation process. The modelling system based on this new approach is capable of modelling both artificial objects, such as, mechanical components, and natural objects, such as tree trunks (Figure 9.4).

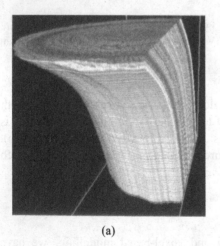 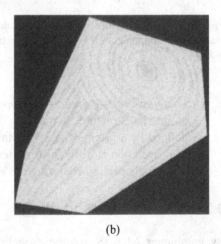

(a)   (b)

Figure 9.4. Modelling of the tree trunk: (a) cutting of a voxel volume (a trunk), (b) annual ring of the tree trunk.

References

1. Piegl L, Tiller W. The NURBS book, Springer-Verlag, New York, 1997.
2. Feng L, Soon SH. An efficient 3D seed fill algorithm. Computers and Graphics, 1998; 22(5): 641-644.
3. Kaufman A, Cohen D, Yagel R. Volume graphics. IEEE Computer, 1993; 16(7):51-64.
4. Cohen-or D, Kaufman A, Kong TY. On the soundness of surface voxelizations. In: Kong TY, Rosenfeld A (eds), Topological Algorithms for Digital Image Processing, Elsevier Science B.V., 1996; 181-204.
5. Cohen-or D, Kaufman A. 3D line voxelization and connectivity control. IEEE Computer Graphics and Applications, 1997; 17(6):80-87.
6. Cohen-or D, Kaufman A. Fundamentals of surface voxelization. Graphical Models and Image Processing, 1995; 57(6):453-461.

References

1. ...
2. ...
3. ...

PART IV

VOLUME RENDERING

10. Voxels versus Polygons: A Comparative Approach for Volume Graphics

Dirk Bartz and Michael Meißner

10.1 Introduction

Different Direct Volume Rendering techniques (DVR) are introduced in the literature. The most important is the Ray Casting (RC) approach [1-2], the forward projection approach [3-4], the splatting algorithm [5], and the 3D texture mapping based projection technique [6]. In this chapter, we focus on the RC approach, since it is so far the only approach which enables adjustable sampling in all dimensions, perspective projections, and gray-level gradients. Although there are several improvements for splatting [7-8] and for texture mapping-based volume rendering [9], the overall quality and generality is not yet comparable to RC.

So far, the implementations of the RC approach are mostly software based. In the near future, ray casting hardware architectures like Mitsubishi's VolumePro [10] or Vizard [11] will be available publicly, thus decreasing the reconstruction and rendering time.

Generally, a volume dataset is viewed from a viewpoint through a viewplane. Starting from the viewpoint, the RC algorithm casts a ray through each pixel of the viewplane into the volume. Within the volume, samples are taken by trilinear interpolation from the voxel values of the volume. Each sample is classified using transfer functions for R, G, B, and *alpha*. Thereafter, the samples are shaded and composited. This is done by accumulating samples along the ray corresponding to the line integral. Reconstruction and rendering is performed in one single pass. Hence, any change of the view, or of the transfer functions, requires a complete re-computation. Furthermore, increasing the size of the viewplane results in a similar increase in the number of rays cast through the viewplane.

In contrast to the DVR paradigm, there is one dominating technique for Indirect Volume Rendering (IVR), the Marching Cubes (MC) algorithm [12]. Using this algorithm, each cell of eight neighbouring voxels is visited. The voxels of the cell are classified as *inside*, *outside*, or *intersecting* (also called *contributing*) with the isosurface. All contributing cells are further examined for the reconstruction of the isosurface. There are 254 cases of combination where a contributing cell consists of at least one voxel below (outside), and at least one above (inside), the isovalue (isosurface). Using a table of these cases, up to five triangles per cell can be generated and shaded by using linear interpolation and central difference gradients for the approximation of the vertex normal. Finally, the reconstructed polygonal isosurface can be rendered using common polygon-based graphics hardware. In contrast to the RC approach, the reconstruction is considered as a preprocess of the actual rendering. The re-computation of the isosurface is only required after a change of the isovalue. Furthermore, the polygonal rendering is usually not fill-limited; thus the rendering time is not significantly increased if the viewplane is enlarged.

The scope of this chapter covers the evaluation of RC as a DVR technique and MC as an IVR technique. We consider aspects of visual quality, such as volumetric representation and isosurface extraction (Section 10.3.1), and resource consumption, such as memory and time in terms of theoretical complexity and actual usage (Section 10.3.2). The basis of this evaluation is the two volume datasets, which are to be introduced in Section 10.2.

10.2 Experiments

In this section, we outline the performed experiments. Specifically, we describe the setup (datasets and viewing parameter) and the algorithms used. Measurements were performed on an R10000 at 250 MHz SGI Octane with MXE graphics.

10.2.1 Setup

We performed our experiments on two different volume datasets, each with eight-bit voxel data. The first dataset is a CT scan of a lobster of resolution 301×324×38 — with an anisotropic spacing of [1:0, 1:0, 1:5] — immersed in a cylinder of resin. Three different materials can be classified, namely resin, meat and shell of the lobster. An image of the dataset is given in Figure 10.1a.

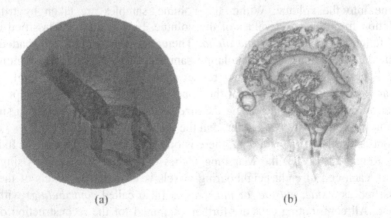

(a)   (b)

Figure 10.1. Datasets: (a) CT scan of a lobster (enhanced for b/w printing), (b) MRI scan of a human head.

The second dataset is a CISS-reconstruction of a T2-weight MRI scan of a human head of resolution 258×258×126 — with an isotropic spacing of [0.9, 0.9, 0.9]. Head tissue and brain cerebrospinal fluid in the ventricular system[i] of the MRI head are easy to classify, due to the good contrast of the CISS/T2-MRI-reconstruction. An image of the dataset is given in Figure 10.1b.

Both datasets have been visualised using RC and MC. For both rendering algorithms, we used a unified environment including one directional light source, similar material properties, and parallel projection for visualisation. We chose a viewplane of size 324×324 for the CT lobster dataset, and a viewplane of size 258×258 for the MRI head.

The lobster dataset contains three different materials, as shown in Figure 10.2a. We have chosen red for meat, white for shell, green for resin, and the opacity function selected for RC is shown in Figure 10.2b. Correspondingly, isovalues, colour values, and opacity for the materials have been selected for the MC algorithm as depicted in Table 10.1.

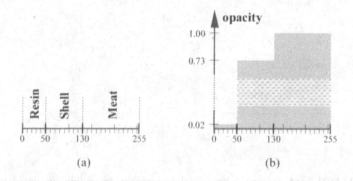

(a)   (b)

Figure 10.2. CT lobster dataset: (a) material assignment depending on voxel values; (b) opacity function for voxels used in ray casting.

Table 10.1. Overview of dataset material properties for Marching Cubes.

Materials	Isovalue	Colour (RGB)	Opacity
CT Lobster Dataset			
Resin (R)	2	0.0, 1.0, 0.0	0.13
Shell (S)	50	0.8, 0.8, 0.8	0.27
Meat (M)	130	1.0, 0.1, 0.1	1.0
MRI Head Dataset			
Tissue (T)	30	1.0, 1.0, 1.0	0.02
Cerebrosoinal Fluid (F)	70	1.0, 1.0, 1.0	1.0

---

[i] The ventricular system of the human brain is responsible for the production and resorption of brain cerebrospinal fluid.

We assign different opacities for resin using MC and RC (Figure 10.2 and Table 10.1). This is necessary to achieve somewhat similar visual results because the MC algorithm only extracts one layer of triangles (with some exceptions at the centre of the cylinder). Therefore, the contribution of the resin is much smaller than the multiple samples taken within the resin using the RC approach. We improve the visual impact of the resin for MC by using a larger opacity for the reconstructed isosurface of the resin.

For the MRI head dataset, the assignment of voxels to materials is shown in Figure 10.3a.

White has been selected as the colour for all voxels in the dataset and the opacity function selected for RC is depicted in Figure 10.3b. Likewise, the isosurface values, the corresponding material properties, and the opacity function for the MC algorithm are shown in Table 10.1.

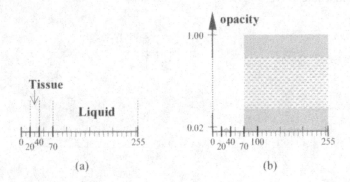

(a)   (b)

Figure 10.3. MRI head dataset: (a) material assignment depending on voxel values (b) opacity function of the voxels for ray casting.

10.2.2 Two Algorithms for Volume Graphics

Indirect Volume Rendering

For the reconstruction of the isosurfaces, we use an adapted version of the MC algorithms implemented in VTK [13]. All cells of the dataset are visited and classified if they are contributing cells. The gradients are only computed for these contributing cells. In order to prevent ambiguities, a full 256 case set is used. The generated vertices are checked for multiple generation and stored in a bucketsort-like data structure. This reduces the consumed memory significantly below the upper bound estimated in Section 10.3.2. Finally, triangle strips or triangle fans were not generated. Rendering time of polygonal isosurfaces depends very much on the used graphics subsystem. Therefore, we only consider the reconstruction time of the MC algorithm.

The rendering is performed using OpenInventor on a SGI Octane with MXE graphics. Depending on the rendering complexity of the extracted isosurfaces (number of polygons and opacity), the actual rendering ranged from approximately

0.5 seconds to approximately 5 seconds for the MRI head dataset (similar for the CT lobster dataset).

Direct Volume Rendering

There are several techniques to accelerate RC or MC. These are mostly methods which require some preprocessing such as hierarchical data representations and rough object approximations. For the Ray Casting algorithm, we only exploit early ray termination as the basic acceleration technique, where a ray is not processed any further, once the accumulated pixel opacity has reached 98%, which means that practically not much further contribution could be made to this pixel. Furthermore, only the gradients of the contributing samples (opacity is greater than zero) are computed and shaded. In contrast to the rendering of MC-generated isosurfaces, RC depends only on the processing performance of the used computer. Since RC is a single pass algorithm, reconstruction and rendering cannot be distinguished. Therefore, these timings are inherently included in the measurements.

10.3 Triangles versus Samples

10.3.1 Visual Quality

The RC approach is commonly considered as a technique for directly visualising volumetric data, while the MC algorithm extracts isosurfaces from volumetric data which can then be displayed using commonly available polygon-based graphics hardware. The properties of both algorithms seem to be obvious but as can be seen in Section 10.3.2, the impact to resource consumption can be quite severe. To enable a proper understanding of the differences, it is necessary to have a closer look at the features of both techniques with respect to volume graphics. In the following discussions, we will contrast the two approaches, and highlight their features in order to describe their strengths and weaknesses. Hereby we will try to answer the following questions:

1. How accurately can smallest structures be displayed?
2. How good is the 3D understanding from generated images?
3. How well can depth be understood from generated images?

Display of Volumetric Information

As mentioned earlier, the MC algorithm extracts isosurfaces from volumetric data. Hence, real thickness, or the volumetric dimension of an object, cannot be represented. This is inherent to the isosurface paradigm which is designed to extract infinitely thin isosurfaces from volumetric data. As an example, images generated by looking at an object with different thickness will always look alike. Therefore, the depth of highly transparent objects and the position of objects within highly transparent materials cannot be determined without rotating the object (Figure

10.4b).

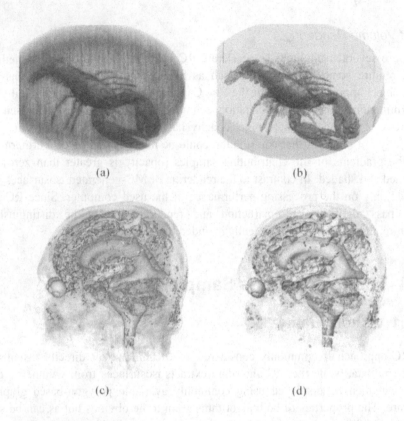

(a)   (b)

(c)   (d)

Figure 10.4. (a) Lobster dataset rendered using RC, classifying resin, shell, and meat. (b) Same as (a) except using MC. (c) Head dataset rendered using RC, classifying tissue and cerebrospinal fluid. (d) Same as (c) except using MC.

In contrast, RC samples volumetric data along rays and accumulates the obtained information. Therefore, the thickness of a material is represented, since absorption and emission of light are calculated along the ray. The thickness of the material is therefore noticeable by the accumulated colour of the individual pixels. Hence, cloudy objects such as fog, which do not necessarily have a surface, can be displayed in a very realistic way. However this is not possible using MC. Such an effect can be seen in Figure 10.4a, where the resin is rendered as a cloudy (transparent) object but, still, the position of the lobster within the resin can be conceived.

Display of Isosurfaces

When it comes to displaying real surfaces within volumetric data, the MC algorithm is capable of precisely extracting a surface that is defined by a certain isovalue. As long as a dataset does contain a surface, specifiable by an isovalue, MC extracts the accurate isosurface. However, the surface of an object might not be specifiable by a single isovalue. This very much depends on the volume dataset. For example, in the CT lobster data, the overall surface of the object resin, including the surface between lobster and resin, can only be captured applying two isovalues. For MC in general, the number of isosurfaces which can be displayed, mainly depends on the memory limitations and on the polygonal rendering performance of the graphics subsystem. Hence, MC is capable of extracting smallest structures, preserving their nature, as long as the structures can be specified by isovalue(s).

Using RC, volumetric data is sampled along rays and the samples are interpreted using transfer functions. These are used to assign a quadruple [R, G, B, alpha] which is used to colour the sample and blend it according to the volume rendering line integral. In contrast to MC, RC does not deal with specific isovalue(s), but the classification of all generated samples using the transfer functions. The sampling rate is therefore very important to achieve sufficient image quality and to prevent aliasing artifacts[2]. As a result of the RC approach, structures can appear smaller since the samples generated at the border of a structure might be classified as outside. Only the rays which sample the inside of a structure will detect the structure. This can be seen in Figure 10.5a where the legs and antennae of the lobster are not as well defined as in Figure 10.5b.

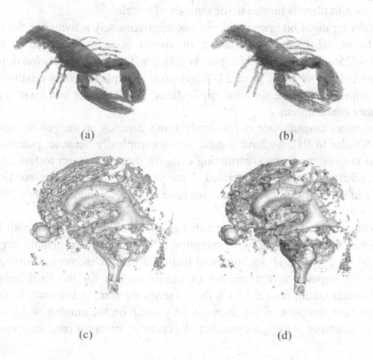

(a)   (b)

(c)   (d)

Figure 10.5. (a) Lobster dataset rendered using RC, classifying shell and meat. (b) Same as (a) except using MC. (c) Head dataset rendered using RC, classifying cerebrospinal fluid only. (d) Same as (c) except using MC.

---

[2] Techniques to adapt RC for accurately computing isosurfaces are available. However, we only examine the "standard" approach of RC.

Furthermore, it is obvious that due to this effect very small structures which are just one voxel wide might be missed depending on sampling and classification. Therefore, classification is the most crucial part of any DVR. Better results can be achieved using already segmented data or applying higher sampling rates, whereas the images in this chapter were generated by rendering the original dataset without any over-sampling.

10.3.2 Quantitative Comparison

In this section, we describe our measurements and complexity considerations of the two different methods, RC as a DVR technique, and MC as an IVR technique. In particular, we examine memory and time consumption (Tables 10.2 and 10.3).

Memory Consumption

Memory consumption of DVR applications is limited to the actual representation of the volume. Some acceleration structures like octrees or BSP-trees do need significant additional memory. However, our implementation of the RC algorithm uses only the standard representation, i.e. a 3D array of voxel values. Therefore, the memory consumption is limited to the number of voxels.

Considering eight bits per voxel, we use approximately n bytes for the volume representation, where n is the number of voxels in each dimension in a cubic volume; 4×256 bytes (eight bits per voxel) for the [R, G, B, $alpha$] transfer functions; and $x \times y \times 4$ bytes for a 24+8 bits/pixel viewplane. For a relatively large volume, which is the case for most applications, the 3D voxel array will dominate the memory consumption.

The memory consumption of MC applications depends on the volume resolution as well. Similar to RC, we have a cubic space complexity because, potentially, all cells in a volume might be contributing cells. In those cases, up to five triangles[3] with three vertices each are generated. Each vertex is described by six floats for position and normal vector. Therefore, we have an upper bound of 360 (= 5×3×6×4) bytes per cell[4].

Our complexity sketch shows that although the space complexity of both RC and MC is cubic, the actual memory consumption of MC can be significantly larger than RC (Tables 10.2 and 10.3). An important feature is that the memory consumption of RC does not depend on the number of samples taken for the final image; the memory consumption, considering a fixed viewplane size, is constant. In contrast, the memory consumption of MC depends very much on the number of contributing cells. If this number is high, the number of generated triangles (and their respective

---

[3] On average, two triangles per contributing cell of the examined datasets were generated.
[4] As mentioned earlier, VTK eliminates vertices which are generated more than once. Therefore, the actual number of vertices is only a fraction of the estimated upper bound. Tables 10.2 and 10.3 shows only the memory used by the volume itself, the pointers of the generated triangles to the actual stored vertices, and these vertices themselves.

vertices) is high as well. Therefore, the size of the memory needed is directly related to the number of contributing cells.

Table 10.2. Resource consumption of RC: **R** denotes resin, **M** denotes the meat of the lobster, **S** denotes the shell of the lobster, **T** denotes the tissue of the MRI head, and **L** denotes the cerebrospinal fluid of the MRI head. Memory consumption is constant for all classifications of the same datasets.

Material	Time/[s]	Number of Visited Samples	Number of Contributing Samples
CT Lobster Dataset: 4,126,840 bytes used			
M	10.9	4,803,006	6,965
S	11.9	4,868,610	109,091
R	31.9	5,064,276	3,431,673
M, S	10.5	4,739,096	87,622
M, S, R	30.4	4,682,680	3,318,655
MRI Head Dataset: 8,654,344 bytes used			
T	24.1	8,453,628	1,193,236
L	11.4	6,890,357	18,480
T, L	17.5	6,890,357	841,856

Table 10.3. Resource consumption of MC: **R** denotes resin, **M** denotes the meat of the lobster, **S** denotes the shell of the lobster, **T** denotes the tissue of the MRI head, and **L** denotes the cerebrospinal fluid of the MRI head. Memory consumption represents the actual used memory.

Material	Time /[s]	Memory /[bytes]	No. Vertices	No. Triangles	No. Contributing Cells
CT Lobster Dataset: 3,585,300 visited cells, 3,705,912 voxels					
M	5.2	7,044,496	71,207	139,968	72,478
S	9.6	10,800,408	147,470	296,268	144,102
R	18.3	15,617,640	248,297	496,050	252,855
M, S	14.8	10,483,080	218,677	436,236	216,580
M, S, R	57.2	22,294,808	466,974	932,286	479,435
MRI Head Dataset: 8,256,125 visited cells, 8,387,064 voxels					
T	120.2	70,978,920	1,318,170	2,579,648	1,374,041
L	23.8	21,899,520	285,513	555,012	293,528
T, L	165.3	84,491,376	1,603,683	3,134,660	1,667,569

Time Consumption

In the previous paragraphs, we showed that memory consumption of RC applications is dependent on the resolution of the volume dataset, but not on the number of samples taken. However, the number of samples determines reconstruction and rendering time of these applications. In order to provide some operation quantification, we estimated the number of operations for both approaches (Table 10.4). In addition to the mentioned operations there are numerous branching (if) and loop (for) constructs which are not considered in this time complexity sketch.

Generally, sampling along the rays first calculates the sample (one trilinear interpolation). Thereafter, this sample is classified (one access to the opacity function table). If the sample has a contribution to the final image (its opacity is not equal to zero), its classification is completed (three accesses in the transfer function tables) and it is gradient shaded, which requires a gradient approximation using central differences (including 48 accesses to voxels that surround the sample[5]), and one trilinear interpolation of a vector. Finally, the sample is combined with the already accumulated samples in the compositing process.

Table 10.4. Number of multiplications and additions for each high-level operation, and for the respective cell/sample types. For the number of operations for MC contributing cells, we consider the worst case of five triangles per contributing cells (first value) and the measured average case of two triangles per contributing cell (second value).

High-Level Operation	Multiplications	Additions	Others
Trilinear Interpolation	7	14	
Linear Vertex Interpolation	7	14	
Gradient Approximation	18	12	
Transfer/Voxel Access	1	1	
Cell Access (eight voxels)	8	20	
Normalisation (per vertex)	6	2	1 sqrt
Compositing	7	4	
Summary			
MC Contributing Cell	362/236	386/224	15/6 sqrt's 8 bit op's
MC Non-Contributing Cell	8	20	8 bit op's
RC Contributing Sample	169	132	
RC Non-Contributing Sample	8	15	

The number of rays cast through the volume depends on the pixel resolution of the viewplane. However, from the perspective of the sampling theory, this pixel resolution is closely related to the volumetric resolution of the dataset. According to

---

[5] Although all voxel accesses are only in a 32-voxel neighbourhood, no optimisation is used.

the sampling theorem, at least four rays (four pixels of the viewplane) should be cast through each voxel. Assuming a volume of n^3 voxels, this gives a quadratic complexity of the number of rays ($O(n^2)$). Furthermore, we sample through the volume. Again, taking the sampling theorem into account, we should sample with a step size of at least half the smallest spacing of the volume. Overall, we have a viewplane resolution that depends on the volume resolution, and we have a sampling distance that depends on the volume resolution. Therefore, we can describe the time complexity as cubic.

For the reconstruction and rendering times using RC (Table 10.2), the time costs do not simply depend on the numbers of "visited samples", which are more or less equal. More important are the samples which do contribute to the final image, that is, the samples with a non-zero opacity. These samples cause most of the computational costs (gradient-shading and compositing) of RC. If the opacity of a large area of the volume is low (i.e. resin in the lobster dataset), there will be a good chance that a substantial portion of the area will contain contributing samples. Therefore, the total number of these samples will be high, resulting in not an early but a late ray termination and, consequently, many shading operations (e.g. experiments **R** and **M, S, R** in Table 10.2).

The time consumption of the reconstruction process using the MC algorithm depends on the number of cells. As mentioned earlier, each cell is visited and classified, as inside, outside, or intersecting with the isosurface, which requires a cell lookup and eight bit operations. For each contributing cell, we need one multiplication to calculate the positions with respects to the grid spacing[6]. The cell gradients for shading are determined similar to RC by using eight vector central differences (no optimisations used), which includes 48 voxel accesses. Finally, up to five triangles — depending on the classification case — are generated. Each vertex of these triangles involves a linear vertex interpolation of position and normal, and one vector normalisation. Note that especially the final estimate is only an upper bound that is usually never met in practice. In our measurements, on average two triangles per contributing cell were generated (Table 10.3).

The complexity is determined by the number of cells of the volume dataset, because all cells are visited by the VTK implementation of the MC algorithm (thus the similarity between voxels and the number of visited cells). Consequently, the complexity is cubic, similar to the space complexity of RC. For each cell, we can give a constant upper bound of 5 triangles (and 15 vertices) for the costs of gradient, position and normal computation.

Table 10.3 shows the timing of the reconstruction process using the MC algorithm. The VTK implementation of MC checks if a vertex was already generated by a previous triangle of the current or a neighbouring cell. This checking overhead consumes a significant share of the overall time costs. For the extraction of the isosurface of the MRI head dataset, the overhead accounts for approximately 50% (isosurface of **L**) up to 68% (isosurfaces **T** and **L**) of the total extraction time.

---

[6] One multiplication is needed for each slice, for each scan-line within a slice, and for each cell of a scan-line. This results on average and approximately one multiplication for each cell.

Furthermore, this overhead grows faster than the actual number of vertices. Therefore, the time spent on the generation of multiple isosurfaces is higher than the sum of each individual isosurface. The reconstruction time of the different isosurfaces does vary a lot, due to the significantly larger number of contributing cells, hence the larger number of generated triangles (Table 10.3).

Marching Cubes versus Ray Casting

Generally, the memory costs of MC, which is dominated by the triangles and vertices, are significantly larger than the constant memory costs for RC, which is dominated by the volume itself. For the time costs, RC was faster than MC on the MRI head dataset, while MC was faster on the smaller CT lobster dataset. The isotropic MRI head dataset has a similar number of contributing cells and contributing samples.

Consequently, the number of operations of MC is larger than that of RC. Furthermore, the data structure overhead of MC accounts for more than 50% of the time costs for this dataset.

The anisotropic CT lobster dataset has a significantly smaller number of contributing cells or samples for opaque isosurfaces (i.e. **M** or **S**) than the MRI head dataset. Hence the data structure overhead of MC in this case is not as severe as for the MRI head, resulting in lower time costs. Additionally, the number of visited cells is smaller than the number of visited samples, which increases the time costs for RC more than MC. Furthermore, the semi-transparent samples classified as resin cause the rays of RC to travel throughout most of the dataset (see experiments **R** and **M, S, R** in Table 10.2), thus increasing the costs for RC. Once opaque samples are added (experiments **M, S** and **M, S, R**), the rays are attenuated faster, which results in lower time costs. Transparent visualisation of MC generated isosurfaces is done during the rendering stage. Therefore, it does not affect the reconstruction stage.

Overall, MC is very efficient for individual isosurfaces with a low number of contributing cells (and triangles), while RC is faster for large volume datasets. This is especially true for opaque structures, which can be exploited for early ray termination. However, it is important to note that rendering of MC generated polygonal isosurfaces is much faster and the reconstruction can be viewed as a preprocessing step. Furthermore, the polygonal isosurface is a continuous representation, and its rendering is not usually fill-rate limited. Therefore, a larger viewplane can be used at almost no additional rendering costs. This is different using RC. If a larger viewplane is used, more rays are cast through the volume. These additional rays significantly increase the reconstruction and rendering time.

10.4 Conclusion and Future Work

We presented a comparison of the RC approach (DVR) and the MC approach (IVR) for volume graphics. Not surprisingly, neither of the methods is preferable in all situations. Furthermore, this is a multi-dimensional problem and only a few aspects are presented in this chapter. However, our results show that DVR techniques can have significant resource consumption advantages compared to IVR techniques. The presented RC images often give better insights and depth perception than the MC generated images. However, to display accurate surfaces, the latter algorithm can preserve very small details, while they can get lost in the standard RC approach. Applying over-sampling can solve this problem but is very cost intensive. In contrast, the MC algorithm cannot correctly represent volumetric features, such as cloud-like semi-transparent objects like the resin in our example. This is inherent to the infinitely thin polygonal representation of volumetric aspects of the dataset.

Finally, the presented performance measures need to be interpreted carefully. Whereas the storage requirements of RC are constant while using the same dataset, the memory consumption of MC can become very costly, depending on the number of contributing cells.

The time costs for the reconstruction using the IVR technique need to be spent only once per isosurface, while the rendering time will, later on, depend only on the rendering performance of the graphics subsystem used. This is different when using DVR, because reconstruction and rendering is performed as a single pass, and it is currently not possible to achieve interactive frame rates. However, once DVR accelerators become available [10-11] near real-time performance will be possible for DVR as well.

Future work will focus on the evaluation of other DVR approaches. Furthermore, we are interested in the evaluation of acceleration techniques and special features, such as cut planes and their impact on complexity.

Acknowledgments

This work has been supported by the MedWis program of the German Federal Ministry for Education, Science, Research and Technology, and by project 382 of the German Research Council (DFG).

The MRI head dataset was provided by the Department of Neuroradiology of the University Hospital Tübingen. Finally, we would like to thank Michael Doggett for proof-reading and Edelhard Becker for help using LaTeX.

References

1. Tuy H, Tuy L. Direct 2D display of 3D objects. IEEE Computer Graphics and Applications, 1984; 4(10):29-33.
2. Levoy M. Display of surfaces from volume data. IEEE Computer Graphics and Applications, 1988; 8(3):29-37.
3. Frieder G, Gordon D, Reynolds R. Back-to-front display of voxel-based objects. IEEE Computer Graphics and Applications, 1985; 5(1):52-59.
4. Wilhelms J, van Geldern A. A coherent projection approach for direct volume rendering. In: Proc. ACM SIGGRAPH Conference, 1991; 275-284.
5. Westover L. Footprint evaluation for volume rendering. In: Proc. ACM

SIGGRAPH Conference, 1990; 367-376.

6. Cabral B, Cam N, Foran J. Accelerated volume rendering and tomographic reconstruction using texture mapping hardware. In: Proc. Symposium on Volume Visualization, 1994; 91-98.

7. Mueller K, Yagel R. Fast perspective volume rendering with splatting by utilizing a ray-driven approach. In: Proc. IEEE Visualization '96; 65-72.

8. Mueller K, Crawfis R. Elminating popping artifacts in sheet buffer-based splatting. In: Proc. IEEE Visualization '98; 239-246.

9. Westermann R, Ertl T. Efficiently using graphics hardware in volume rendering applications. In: Proc. ACM SIGGRAPH Conference, 1998; 169-177.

10. Osborne R, Pfister H, Lauer H, McKenzie N, Gibson S, Hiatt W, Ohkami T. EM-Cube: an architecture for low-cost real-time volume rendering. In: Proc. Eurographics/SIGGRAPH Workshop on Graphics Hardware, 1997; 131-138.

11. Meißner M, Kanus U, Straßer W. VIZARD II, A PCI-Card for real-time volume rendering. In: Proc. Eurographics/SIGGRAPH Workshop on Graphics Hardware, 1998; 61-68.

12. Lorensen W, Cline H. Marching cubes: A high resolution 3D surface construction algorithm. In: Proc. ACM SIGGRAPH Conference, 1987; 21(4):163-169.

13. Schroeder W, Martin K, Lorensen B. The Visualization Toolkit, 2nd Edition, Prentice Hall, Upper Saddle River, NJ., 1998.

11. Fast Multi-Resolution Volume Rendering

Yuting Yang, Feng Lin and Hock Soon Seah

11.1 Introduction

A fast volume rendering process is of primary importance for interactive manipulation of volumetric datasets. This chapter studies acceleration methods of volume rendering.

In previous research, a multi-resolution method has been proposed to accelerate volume rendering by reorganising an original dataset at the cost of controlled degradation in image quality. Attention has been paid to the reorganisation of the original datasets, but only ordinary rendering algorithms have been applied to these approximated models, e.g. splatting [1], ray tracing [2], tetrahedral projection [3] and ray casting [4]. Meanwhile, the shear-warp method has been utilised to accelerate rendering of full datasets (e.g. [5] and [6]). It is proven efficient in simplifying the addressing arithmetic in projection. Combined with run-length data structure, shear-warp factorisation of view transformation makes it simple and efficient to explore early ray termination and object-space leap simultaneously [6].

In this chapter, we propose a volume rendering algorithm exerting shear-warp factorisation of viewing transformation on the multi-resolution model of the original volumetric dataset. Our method will encode a homogeneous region in the approximated model as a run-length. We shall show that the number of elements processed in projection can be further reduced. Combining multi-resolution with shear-warp, our algorithm will advance further towards the real-time and interactive volume rendering.

11.2 Algorithm

11.2.1 Pipeline of the Algorithm

Figure 11.1 shows an overview of the proposed algorithm pipeline. The algorithm is based on a feedback loop, which supports the adjustment of parameters at all levels. The result of data reorganisation can be used repeatedly for different opacity transfer functions, viewpoints and shading conditions. The result of classification and run-length encoding can be repeatedly used for different viewpoints and shading conditions. Our strategy is to use high error-tolerance to try various opacity mappings, viewing directions and shading conditions when exploring a new volume dataset. Once an appropriate set of parameters is obtained, zero error-tolerance can be used to obtain a final image.

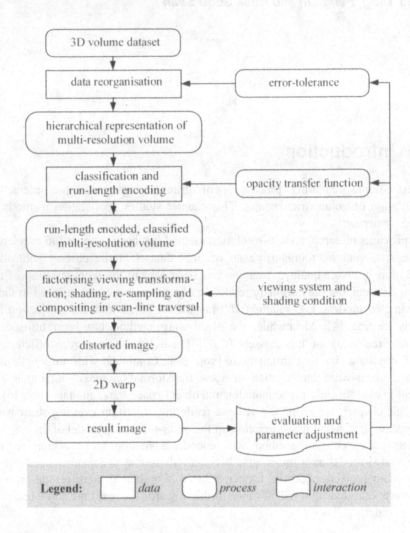

Figure 11.1. Algorithm pipeline.

11.2.2 Data Reorganisation

The principle of data reorganisation in our algorithm is to use high resolution for high frequency regions and low resolution for low frequency regions. Such data reorganisation will result in limited loss to image quality. Furthermore, any loss can be controlled by user's interactive adjustment of error-tolerance. Hierarchical decomposition of the volume is appropriate to realise this idea. We use *pyramid* to represent the succession of volumes of various resolutions, and use *octree* to represent the subset of the pyramid that completely spans the volume (Figure 11.2). These two data structures are the same as those used in the hierarchical splatting algorithm [1].

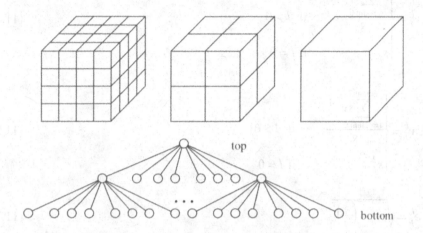

(a)   Pyramid is a succession of volumes. Volume resolution decreases
      from the bottom of the pyramid to the top.

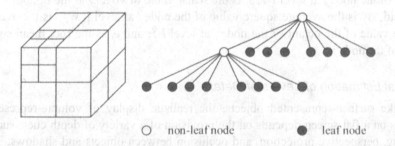

(b) Octree is a subset of the pyramid that completely spans the volume.

Figure 11.2. Pyramid and octree.

Construction of Pyramid

The pyramid is constructed from the voxels in the original volume, and then grows upwards by iteratively condensing the scalar values of eight octants into their parent using the average value. Such iteration ends when reaching the root node. Every non-leaf node in the pyramid contains a variable indicating the average error associated with that node. This error term is to measure the average cost of approximating the subvolume represented by the node with the average of the voxel values contained in the subvolume, rather than with those voxels values themselves. The root mean square error [7] is a good choice.

The average values and the error measures of all nodes in the pyramid can be calculated efficiently using a single traversal of the pyramid from bottom to top according to Equations 11.1 - 11.3:

$$
v_j^l = \begin{cases} \dfrac{\displaystyle\sum_{i=\text{octant }0}^{\text{octant }7} v_i^{l-1}}{8} & \text{if } l > 0 \\[4mm] s_j & \text{if } l = 0 \end{cases}
\tag{11.1}
$$

$$
sv_j^l = \begin{cases} \dfrac{\displaystyle\sum_{i=\text{octant }0}^{\text{octant }7} sv_i^{l-1}}{8} & \text{if } l > 0 \\[4mm] s_j^2 & \text{if } l = 0 \end{cases}
\tag{11.2}
$$

$$
e_j^l = \sqrt{sv_j^l - \left(v_j^l\right)^2}
\tag{11.3}
$$

where v_j^l is the average value of the node j at level l; v_i^{l-1} is the average value of the octant of the node j at level l-1; s_j is the scalar value of voxel j at the bottom of the pyramid; sv_j^l is the average square value of the node j at level l; sv_i^{l-1} is the average square value of the octant of the node j at level l-1; and e_j^l is the root mean square error of the node j.

Normal Estimation of Levels-of-Details

Just like surface-represented objects, the realistic display of volume-represented objects on a flat screen depends on the provision of a variety of depth cues, such as shading, perspective projection, and occlusion between objects and shadows. They are used to convey to observers the illusion of the third dimension. These depth cues are computer simulations of the physical behaviour of light, and are functionally bound to the inclination of the surface of real objects. Volume-represented objects do not contain the notion of surface. To implement the depth cues mentioned above, we can imagine that at each voxel (i, j, k), whose scalar value $f(i, j, k)$ is C, there exists an isosurface where f remains at the constant value C. On one side of this surface f is greater than C and on the other side f is less than C. The gradient of f at (i, j, k) is proven to be perpendicular to this virtual surface [8]. Therefore, it can act as the normal vector of the virtual surface.

The gradient can be calculated using several different methods in discrete space. The central difference gradient estimator [9] is a commonly-used operator. It is not the best operator in terms of quality, but it is fast and easy to implement.

In the pyramid constructed in the last step, each level represents the volume with a fixed resolution. The resolution increases by factor 2 along each axis per level from top to bottom. We can imagine that the virtual isosurfaces pass through nodes in different levels. By calculating central difference for all nodes in each level (Equation 11.4), we estimate normals in levels of details.

$$\nabla v_{i,j,k}^{l} = \begin{bmatrix} v_{i+1,j,k}^{l} - v_{i-1,j,k}^{l} \\ v_{i,j+1,k}^{l} - v_{i,j-1,k}^{l} \\ v_{i,j,k+1}^{l} - v_{i,j,k-1}^{l} \end{bmatrix} \tag{11.4}$$

Octree Extraction

An octree is a subset of the pyramid that spans the whole volume. Once the user selects an error-tolerance, the octree can be extracted from the pyramid by a single traversal of the pyramid from top to bottom. At each level in the pyramid, the user-defined error-tolerance is compared to the error measure for the given node. If the error measure is less than the error tolerance, the traversal is terminated at that level; otherwise it proceeds downward. The result of the traversal is an octree, where each of the leaf-nodes represents a homogeneous (within the user-defined error tolerance) region. The whole octree represents a multi-resolution volume. Different regions in the volume have different levels-of-details. Moreover, the lowest resolution in the pyramid that falls within the error-tolerance is used. The error caused by this reorganisation is uniformly distributed throughout the volume.

11.2.3 Classification

By classification, we mean to assign an opacity to each homogeneous region represented by the leaf-node of the octree. The opacity transfer function comes from the one for voxel classification in [10]. It is expressed as:

$$\alpha = O(v, |\nabla v|) \tag{11.5}$$

where α is the opacity, O is the mapping function, v is the average value of the leaf-node of the octree, and $|\nabla v|$ is its gradient magnitude.

11.2.4 Run Length Encoding

Run-length code is a natural choice for representing the sheared volume. Furthermore, like octree, run-length code is also a data structure appropriate for representing the homogeneous region. It is easy to convert from octree to run-length code.

The conversion is done by scan-line ordered traversal of all the leaf nodes of the octree. Each scan-line will pierce some leaf nodes. The scan-line is divided into some segments by the octree nodes. Each segment is a voxel-run with unique scalar value v, normal vector N and opacity α. Users can define the minimum voxel opacity, under which the run is treated as transparent voxel-run. Every two adjacent transparent voxel-runs will merge into one run.

Moreover, adjacent scan-lines often intersect the same set of leaf nodes of octree. If the size of the smallest leaf node penetrated by one scan-line is of n^3 voxels, then the runs resulting from this scan-line can be reused for n adjacent scan-lines in one slice (Figure 11.3a).

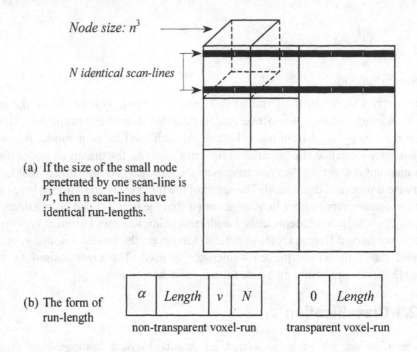

Node size: n^3

N identical scan-lines

(a) If the size of the small node penetrated by one scan-line is n^3, then n scan-lines have identical run-lengths.

(b) The form of run-length

α	Length	v	N

non-transparent voxel-run

0	Length

transparent voxel-run

Figure 11.3. The reuse of scan-line and the form of run-length

The form of the run-length is illustrated in Figure 11.3b. The scalar values and normal vectors of non-transparent voxel-runs are reserved for shading. Transparent voxel-runs can be simply skipped because they have no contribution to the result image. There is no need to reserve scalar values and normal vectors for them.

11.2.5 Rendering of the Run-Length Encoded Volume

In the rendering of run-length encoded and classified multi-resolution volume in parallel projection, our algorithm firstly exerts the shearing factor of user-defined viewing transformation on all voxel-runs. Secondly the sheared slices are projected along the direction perpendicular to the slices. This manipulation produces a distorted image as an intermediate result. Finally the distorted image is warped into the correct image.

Shear-Warp Factorisation of Viewing Transformation

The principle of shear-warp factorisation is to decompose the viewing transformation (from object space to image space) into two parts: shearing and warp. Shearing transforms the volume from object space into sheared object space, where all viewing rays are perpendicular to the slices of the volume. Therefore, in the sheared object space, the projection is simple and efficient. The result of the projection is a distorted image that can be corrected by warp.

Lacroute and Levoy [6] summarised, and dexterously used in the projection, the three geometric properties of sheared object space:

- *Property* : Scan-lines of pixels in the distorted image are parallel to scan-lines of voxels in the volume array.
- *Property 2*: All voxels in a given voxel slice are scaled by the same factor.
- *Property 3 (parallel projection only)*: Every voxel slice has the same scale factor when projected into the image, and this factor can be chosen arbitrarily. In particular a unity scale factor is selected so that for a given scan-line there is a one-to-one mapping between voxels and pixels.

These properties accelerate the projection in the following aspects:

- The reusability of one set of resampling weights for all voxels in one slice.
- The simultaneous traversal of run-length encoded volume and image. Run-length data structure is used to encode and skip both the full transparent voxels in the volume (object-space leap) and full opaque pixels in the image (early ray termination). Simultaneous traversal makes both object-space leap and early ray termination simple and efficient.

In our algorithm, shearing factor is exerted on the run-length encoded and classified multi-resolution volume

Slice-by-Slice Projection

The projection is done slice-by-slice. Each slice and the distorted image are traversed simultaneously line-by-line. The process of the traversal is illustrated in Figure 11.4. When streaming through the voxel scan-line and image scan-line at the same time, the algorithm checks whether the current voxel-run is transparent. If it is transparent, the algorithm simply skips this run and the corresponding number of pixels. Such skipping may span more than one pixel-run. Otherwise, the algorithm performs shading, resampling and compositing.

In the implementation, due to the resampling filter, two scan-lines of voxels are required to produce one scan-line of pixels (Figure 11.5a). Therefore, the pixels can be skipped only when corresponding voxel-runs in both scan-lines are transparent. The shading, resampling and compositing are also performed in both scan-lines in a synchronous manner. If a transparent voxel-run in one input scan-line aligns with a non-transparent run in other input scan-line, it is skipped and only that non-transparent run is shaded, resampled and composited into pixels.

Scan-line of voxels in sheared volume

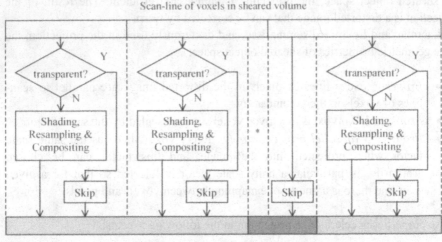

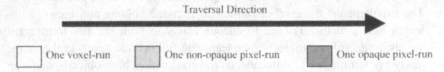

Scan-line of voxels in distorted volume

Traversal Direction

☐ One voxel-run   ▨ One non-opaque pixel-run   ▨ One opaque pixel-run

* *This run-length is also skipped. If the voxel-run that it belongs to is transparent, then this run-length is skipped as a part of the voxel-run. Otherwise, the voxel-run is truncated. This run-length it skipped as a part of the opaque pixel-run.*

Figure 11.4. Simultaneous traversal of the scan-line of the sheared volume and the image scan-line.

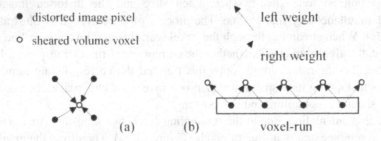

● distorted image pixel   left weight

○ sheared volume voxel   right weight

                    (a)   (b)   voxel-run

Figure 11.5. Resampling weights and the weighting operations: (a) resampling weights of the voxels. (b) For one voxel-run, at most three weighting operations are needed: one for left, one for right and one for both left and right.

The shading is done run-by-run due to the homogeneity of voxels in each run. We use the Phong illumination model to compute colour for non-transparent runs according to the given shading conditions.

The resampling and compositing of non-transparent voxel-runs should be done voxel-by-voxel. However, the geometric properties of sheared object space make the resampling weights the same for every voxel in a slice, therefore, for every voxel in a non-transparent run. Moreover, each voxel in a non-transparent run has the same shading colour. So for each run, at most three weighting operations are needed: the first for left, the second for right, and the third for both left and right. The last operation is the sum of the first two (Figure 11.5b).

In voxel-by-voxel compositing, when an opaque pixel-run is encountered with the accumulated opacity of each pixel exceeds the user-defined maximum pixel opacity, the corresponding voxels can be efficiently skipped. Such skipping may span more than one voxel-run.

11.3 Experimental Results

Figures 11.6-11.8 show the images of three datasets rendered on a Pentium II in the Compaq Deskpro EP/SB Series at 266Mhz with 256 MB RAM without any hardware graphic accelerator.

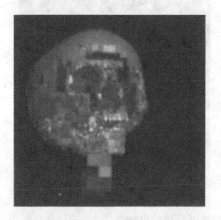
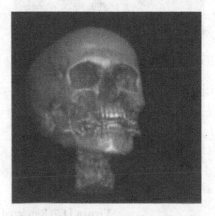

(a) our algorithm, error-tolerance=35   (b) our algorithm, error-tolerance=15

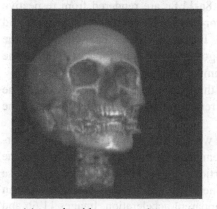
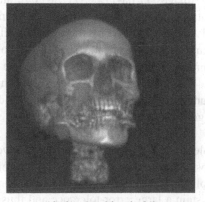

(c) our algorithm, error-tolerance=0   (d) the algorithm in [6]

Figure 11.6. Rendered images of "Head" dataset.

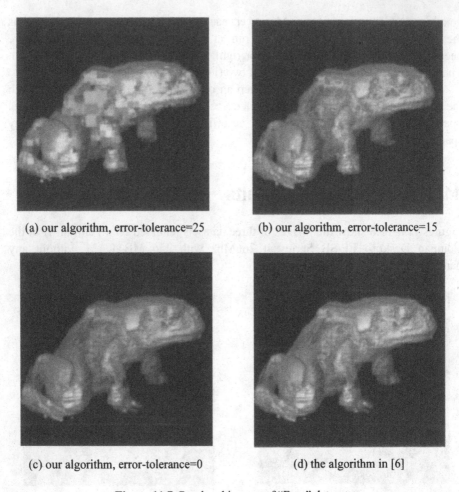

(a) our algorithm, error-tolerance=25   (b) our algorithm, error-tolerance=15

(c) our algorithm, error-tolerance=0   (d) the algorithm in [6]

Figure 11.7. Rendered images of "Frog" dataset.

Images 11.6a-11.6c, 11.7a-11.7c and 11.8a-11.8c are rendered from respective datasets by our algorithm with different error-tolerances. Images 11.6d, 11.7d and 11.8d are rendered by the algorithm in [6]. For each volume dataset, we use the same classification and shading in both algorithms. In rendering, we define the minimum voxel opacity as 0.05 and the maximum pixel opacity as 0.95.

Table 11.1 lists the information on the three volumes, the error-tolerance, the number of the non-transparent runs, and the rendering time of our algorithm and the algorithm in [6].

From Figures 11.6-11.8 and Table 11.1 we can see that with increasing error-tolerance, our algorithm processes fewer elements and thus spends less time at the cost of degradation in image quality proportional to the error-tolerance. For those volume datasets of high regional homogeneity, a little quality degradation can sustain a large error-tolerance and thus an apparent acceleration. Images 11.6b and 11.7b are such examples. When error-tolerance is zero, our algorithm has the same result as that of the algorithm in [6] and the rendering time is almost the same as that of the algorithm in [6].

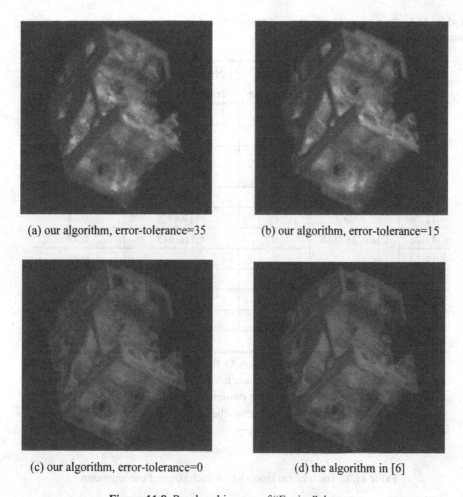

(a) our algorithm, error-tolerance=35   (b) our algorithm, error-tolerance=15

(c) our algorithm, error-tolerance=0   (d) the algorithm in [6]

Figure 11.8. Rendered images of "Engine" dataset.

From Table 11.2 we can see that the time for data reorganisation of a 256^3 volume, including pyramid construction, normal estimation and octree extraction, is less than one minute, which is affordable. Furthermore, the time for octree extraction, classification, run-length encoding, and rendering depends heavily on the user-defined error-tolerance. With increasing error-tolerance, all these three entries decrease.

11.4 Conclusions

In conclusion, by exerting shear-warp factorisation of viewing transformation on run-length encoded multi-resolution volumes, our algorithm accelerates projection in the following aspects:

Table 11.1. Properties of the three datasets used for our experiments, some rendering parameters and the timing of the rendering.

Image No.	Volume & Resolution	Error-Tolerance	Number of Non-transparent runs	Rendering Time* (Sec.)
11.6a		35	138,613	0.31
11.6b	Head	15	618,933	0.5
11.6c	256×256×225	0	771,119	0.61
11.6d				0.59
11.7a		25	327,356	0.28
11.7b	Frog	15	719,882	0.44
11.7c	256×256×138	0	1,116,617	0.77
11.7d				0.78
11.8a		35	300,377	0.66
11.8b	Engine	25	439,378	0.83
11.8c	256×256×110	0	525,860	0.97
11.8d				0.98

*   For images (a)-(c) this entry refers to the time for rendering the run-length encoded, classified multi-resolution volume from a new viewing direction. For image (d), it refers to the time for rendering the run-length encoded, classified volume. Both of them include the time for computing the shear-warp factorisation, shearing, shading, resampling, compositing and warp.

Table 11.2. The time (in seconds) for each stage of our algorithm.

Image No.	Pyramid Construction	Normal Estimation In LOD	Octree Extraction	Classification & Run-Length Encoding	Rendering Time
11.6a			0.01	1.21	0.31
11.6b	7.03	32.84	0.71	7.42	0.5
11.6c			11.26	29.41	0.61
11.7a			0.11	3.02	0.28
11.7b	6.75	17.96	0.38	6.48	0.44
11.7c			11.48	22.79	0.77
11.8a			0.11	2.63	0.66
11.8-b	6.59	24.5	0.28	4.17	0.83
11.8-c			12.41	15.32	0.97

- Both object space leap and early ray termination are performed efficiently.
- Homogeneity of voxels in a run makes it possible to perform shading only once for each run.
- The property that every voxel in a slice has the same resampling weights makes it possible to compute resampling weights only once for each slice and reuse them for all voxels in the slice.
- Homogeneity of voxels in a run and reusage of resampling weights make it possible to perform weighting operations no more than three times for each run in resampling.

Some experimental results verify these acceleration designs. Furthermore, the proposed algorithm supports full interactions including changes of viewpoints, shading conditions, opacity transfer functions and the levels of data reorganisation. It is especially suitable for interactive activities for discovering information in new volume datasets.

References

1. Laur D, Hanrahan P. Hierarchical splatting: A progressive refinement algorithm for volume rendering. ACM/SIGGRAPH Computer Graphics, 1991; 25(4):285-288.
2. Muraki S. Volume data and wavelet transforms. IEEE Computer Graphics and Applications, 1993; 13(4):50-56.
3. Guo BN. A multiscale model for structure-based volume rendering. IEEE Transaction on Visualization and Computer Graphics, 1995; 1(4):291-301.
4. Westermann R, Ertl T. A multiscale approach to integrated volume segmentation and rendering, In: Proc. Eurographics '97; 16(3):C-117-127.
5. Yagel R, Kaufman A. Template-based volume viewing. In: Proc. Eurographics '92; C153-167.
6. Lacroute P, Levoy M. Fast volume rendering using a shear-warp factorization of the viewing transformation. ACM/SIGGRAPH Computer Graphics, 1994; 451-458.
7. DeGroot MH. Probability and Statistics, Second Edition, Chapter 4, Addison-Wesley Publishing Company, 1986.
8. Davis HF, Snider AD. Introduction to Vector Analysis, Fifth Edition, Chapter 3, Allyn and Bacon, Inc., 1987
9. Fröberg CE. Numerical Mathematics, Theory and Computer Applications, Chapter 5, The Benjamin/Cummings Publishing Company, 1985.
10. Levoy M. Display of surfaces from volume data. IEEE Computer Graphics and Applications, 1988; 8(3):29-37.

12. High-Quality Volume Rendering Using Seed Filling in View Lattice

Jarkko Oikarinen, Rami Hietala and Lasse Jyrkinen

12.1 Introduction

Immense amounts of computer power are involved in volumetric rendering. New algorithms and acceleration techniques have been developed during the last ten years with faster computer hardware. The two main paths that have been taken to visualise volumetric data are surface rendering and volume rendering.

The surface rendering approach creates a surface, usually a triangular mesh, and then renders the polygons using graphics accelerator boards. The best known triangulation algorithm is the Marching Cubes algorithm proposed by Lorensen and Cline in 1987 [1]. The main advantage of this approach is that a multitude of hardware manufacturers provide powerful graphics accelerators that can render millions of polygons per second.

Our research belongs to the volume rendering approach, which renders the volumetric data directly; hence it is often called direct volume rendering. The main advantages of this approach include the possibility to do some modifications to the displayed objects without time-consuming recreation of the triangular mesh as is usually the case with surface rendering. These modifications include varying the threshold when rendering isosurfaces and having cut planes to cut the volumetric object to be displayed.

Direct volume rendering can be divided into object-driven and image-driven direct volume rendering. Object-driven methods process the dataset voxel by voxel while building up the final image. Our research concentrates more on image-driven algorithms, which process the resulting image pixel by pixel.

Image-driven algorithms usually operate by tracing a ray from each pixel on the screen through the volume. This process is called ray casting if the ray is terminated when it hits an opaque object or accumulates an opaque value. Ray tracing is the term used when reflections, shadows and refractions are taken into account. The path of voxels traversed by a ray may be 6-connected or 26-connected. Fast traversal algorithms are studied in depth in [2].

The template method uses a pre-calculated template or look-up table, which contains the steps taken by each ray [3]. These identical steps are then taken by all rays to traverse the dataset. The template algorithm produces a warped image that has to be post-processed to create the final image.

The time spent in interpolation starts to dominate the total rendering time, if the sample points are taken evenly and the sample value is trilinearly interpolated [4]. Therefore acceleration techniques that aim to reduce the number of interpolations have been developed.

One image-driven acceleration technique that reduces the processing of empty voxels is to use seed filling in view lattice to calculate the rendered image [5-7]. The method presented in [6] uses template traversal [3] to create the view lattice. However, using only one template for each voxel in the dataset limits the effective view size to the size of the dataset. Hence, high-resolution views do not come with improved image quality.

In this study we improve the image quality of the seed filling acceleration technique. We reach this goal by improving the preprocessing algorithms and using multiple templates. The use of multiple templates has been previously proposed for ray casting in [8], but in this research we use it for the first time together with the seed filling technique.

The rest of this chapter is structured into five parts. First we present the seed filling acceleration technique. Then we explain the modifications that we have made to improve the quality and size of the rendered views. Next we present the experiments and results of the experiments. Finally we discuss the results and present conclusions.

12.2 Seed Filling

We will first define some terms before describing the seed filling algorithm.

The dataset from which the rendered views are calculated consists of a three-dimensional regular grid of voxels, where the voxels are located at integer-valued coordinates in three-dimensional space. *Sample points* are points that are placed within the same space and defined by three coordinates, x, y and z. Sample points may reside in the space between voxels, and therefore different interpolation techniques are needed to approximate the value of a sample point that does not exactly coincide with a voxel point. The interpolation techniques used in this chapter are nearest-neighbour and trilinear interpolation.

In this chapter we are concentrating on parallel projection, as opposed to perspective projection. In parallel projection parallel rays are cast through the dataset and sampled at regular intervals. Under these circumstances, the sample points also form a regular grid. Figure 12.1 illustrates a volumetric dataset, rays cast through it and sampled at regular intervals.

In our situation the volumetric dataset has been preprocessed into empty and non-empty voxels, having zero and non-zero opacity, respectively.

3-dimensional seed filling algorithm is an algorithm which, given a seed point, fills a 6-connected region starting from the seed point and including only points satisfying given criteria, such as non-zero opacity. Seed filling algorithms may be used in view lattice to accelerate direct volume rendering, because the algorithm accesses only those points in the region that may contribute to the final image and their direct 6-neighbors [5]. An example of a dataset consisting of empty and non-empty voxels is presented in Figure 12.2. Two seed voxels are also shown, one for each 6-connected non-empty object within the dataset.

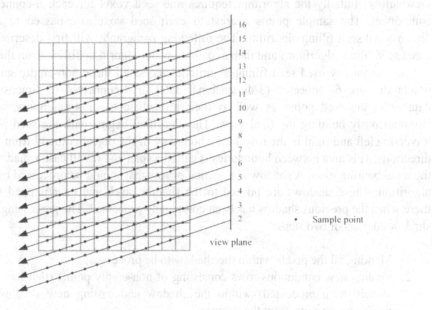

Figure 12.1. Parallel rays cast through the dataset and sampled at regular intervals.

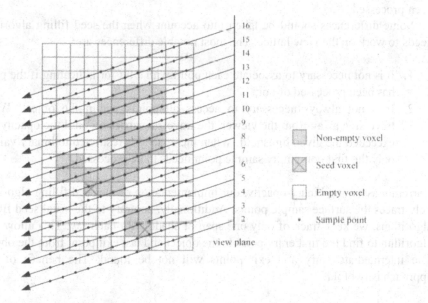

Figure 12.2. The non-empty voxels in the volume lattice can be divided into 6-connected components, each indicated by a seed voxel.

The seed filling acceleration technique is applicable when the view lattice is dense enough and samples the volume lattice at such a high resolution that the connectivity of the 6-connected components is maintained from volume lattice to view lattice. Initially the algorithm requires one seed voxel for each 6-connected component. The sample points nearest to each seed voxel are passed to a 3-dimensional seed filling algorithm. The following paragraphs will first describe the usual seed filling algorithms and then explain how our algorithm differs from them.

The commonly used seed filling algorithms access all those non-empty sample points that are 6-connected (3-dimensional data) or 4-connected (2-dimensional data) with the seed point, as well as their immediate 6- or 4-neighbors, while simultaneously building the final view. The algorithm begins with the seed point, traversing left and right in the row until a boundary of the object is found from both directions. This area between boundaries is called a span and it will cast a shadow to the neighbouring rows. A shadow is a section of row that should be processed by the algorithm. These shadows are pushed to the shadow stack and later popped from there when the previous shadow has been completely processed. The processing of a shadow consists of two steps:

1. Marking all the pixels within the shadow to be processed;
2. Finding new continuous rows consisting of non-empty points (that have not already been processed) within the shadow and casting new shadows to neighbouring rows from those areas.

The algorithm terminates when the shadow stack is empty, i.e. all shadows have been processed.

Some differences should be taken into account when the seed filling algorithm needs to work on the view lattice. The most notable differences are:

1. It is not necessary to associate each point with a bit for indicating if the point has been processed or not;
2. It is not always necessary to access all points within the object. When traversing away from the viewer, the traversal carries on until the opacity has exceeded the given threshold. When the opacity is restricted to binary values, only the first non-empty sample point needs to be processed.

Currently assuming binary opacity, our implementation of the seed filling algorithm only traces the surface sample points. Additionally, contrary to the usual seed filling algorithms, we keep track of only one span or shadow for each ray. This allows the algorithm to find the first entry point to the object and last exit point from the object. The intermediate entry and exit points will not be found. The benefit of this approach is twofold:

1. Less memory is required during the algorithm execution. Only one span (points that have already been processed) and one shadow (points that should be processed) need to be stored for each ray. Our algorithm currently keeps track of these in the z-buffer.

2. The processing of shadows will add new information only to the beginning or end of existing spans; that is, with only one span it is not possible to add new spans in the middle of that. This facilitates accumulation of opacity using common techniques including both front-to-back and back-to-front algorithms. However, it may increase references to sample points e.g. in case of hollow objects.

We refer to the algorithm described above as the 3-dimensional seed filling algorithm and it has been described in detail in [5]. Left side of Figure 12.3 shows the sample points accessed by the 3-dimensional seed filling algorithm as hollow spheres.

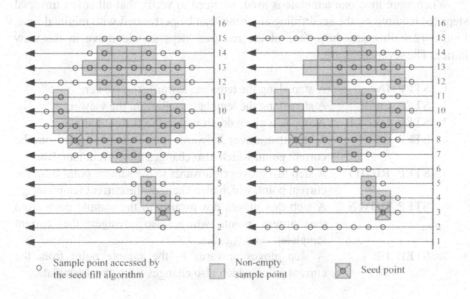

| ○ | Sample point accessed by the seed fill algorithm | | Non-empty sample point | | Seed point |

Figure 12.3. Volume rendering using 3-dimensional seed filling (left) and 2½-dimensional seed filling (right) in view lattice as an acceleration technique.

A better performance for rendering binary opacity objects is obtained with the 2½-dimensional seed filling algorithm presented in [7]. It follows only the front surface of the object. Conceptually the far ends of the spans and shadows are moved to infinite distance from the viewer (or at least outside the dataset). This removes the need to track the far end of the spans and shadows, thus almost halving the number of sample point accesses for simple convex objects [7]. This algorithm is illustrated on the right-hand side of Figure 12.3, where the sample points accessed by the 2½-dimensional seed filling algorithm are shown as hollow spheres. The accesses to the other sample points are completely avoided.

12.3 Image Resolution and Quality

The use of one template limits the effective rendering resolution to the volume resolution. With four templates and trilinear interpolation, it is possible to increase the resolution and quality of the rendered view. The mere use of trilinear interpolation with one template will not significantly improve the image quality, as the effective image resolution does not increase.

The seed filling algorithm presented in [6] introduced seven primitives for traversal of the template lattice [3]. In this work we show how these seven primitives need to be modified when multiple templates are used to reach denser view lattice and thereafter higher quality images.

When more than one template is used, we need to verify that all seven traversal steps [6] required by the seed filling algorithm can be performed with minimal time. Figure 12.4 illustrates how four of the required steps should move in the view lattice. The seven steps are:

1. **STEP_IN**   A step along the template towards the viewer;
2. **STEP_OUT**   A step along the template away from the viewer;
3. **STEP_DEPTH**   A step to a given depth within the current template;
4. **STEP_LEFT**   A step that moves leftwards to the sample point from the current point, which also changes the current template;
5. **STEP_RIGHT**   A step that moves rightwards to the sample point from the current point, which also changes the current template;
6. **STEP_DOWN**   A step that moves downwards to the sample point from the current point, which also changes the current template;
7. **STEP_UP**   A step moves upwards to the sample point from the current point, which also changes the current template.

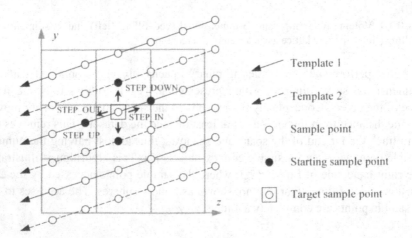

Figure 12.4. Traversal primitives move from starting sample point to target sample point in view lattice (STEP_DOWN is towards the positive y-axis, as it points downward on a screen).

Modifications of the first three primitives (which are sufficient for plain ray casting) for multiple templates have been described in [8].

The last four primitives were re-implemented in order to support multiple templates. The modification we made was that the header section for each template is appended to contain four links, one for each neighbouring template. When stepping to a neighbouring template, the value of the respective link is assigned as the current template. In addition to this, the current data pointer needs to be adjusted when the step will cross voxel boundaries. To facilitate this each entry in the template array contains four bits, one for each of the four directions. If the bit is set, then the data pointer needs to be adjusted when stepping into the given direction.

In addition to the support for multiple templates, we took several steps to ensure the quality and rendering speed. These steps are described next.

The number of acquired slices is usually rather small in routine imaging procedures, typically ranging from 20 to 60 slices. Therefore the voxels of the original datasets are often non-isotropic. If the distance between individual slices is more than two times the distance between neighbouring pixels, the image quality starts to suffer. This effect is apparent in Figure 12.5.

New slices have to be interpolated between old slices to maintain good quality images when with non-isotropic voxels; in our case the preprocessing algorithm interpolated new slices until the voxel size in z-direction is less than twice the voxel size in x- and y-directions.

The data to be interpolated consists of the segmented data, which is given by a bit for each segment in each voxel. If the bit is one, the voxel belongs to the segment, and if the bit is zero, the voxel does not belong to the segment. Shape-based interpolation [9] was used. It calculates a distance transform separately for each image slice. When the pixel value is negative, it indicates that the pixel is outside the object and the value indicates the distance to the nearest pixel that is inside the object. Positive pixel values indicate pixels that are inside the object and the value gives the distance to the nearest pixel that is outside the object. When new slices are interpolated in-between original slices, the distance transform values are interpolated and the sign of the new value is used to determine if the pixel in the new slice is inside or outside the object.

We created a new dataset during the preprocessing step. This dataset contains 16 bits for each voxel. Four of these bits were allocated for the segment information, giving a total of 15 different segment combinations and one value for a voxel which does not belong to any segment. The remaining 12 bits were used to store the gradient direction information. Our earlier implementations stored the shade for each voxel into the dataset. This solution had the limitation that changes in lighting conditions required a recalculation of the dataset. Now the 4096 gradient values are used to access a look-up table that can easily be recreated for each image frame, thus allowing interactive adjustment of lights while simultaneously rotating the object. The look-up table was recreated for each frame using Phong shading model with all three components, diffuse, ambient and specular.

12.4 Experiments

In our experiments we have used two MR datasets obtained from a GE Signa MR scanner. The datasets had 22 and 124 slices, each slice with 256×256 resolution. New slices were interpolated using the shape-based interpolation into the 22 slice dataset to create new datasets of 43, 64 and 85 slices. Only the skin was segmented from the smaller dataset. Brain, eyes and skin were segmented from the larger dataset by setting a threshold, planting seeds into the dataset and then performing threshold-bounded region growing. We used the skin segment for timing measurements in all but one case where a block was applied to cut the skin away to reveal the brain surface. This was done to illustrate the ability to handle multiple segments.

We rendered the datasets into a 1024×1024 true colour RGB view using the 2½-dimensional seed filling rendering method. We used both one-template and four-template methods for all datasets. The sampling rate along the ray in the four-template method was twice as that of the one-template method, i.e. the size of the view lattice in the 4-template method is eight (2^3) times the size of the view lattice in the one-template method. The one-template method directly used the shade obtained by applying the gradient direction to the shade look-up table, while the four-template method took the shade value from the 8 neighbouring voxels of the sample point and then trilinearly interpolated them using the weights in the template. The warping step that is done after projection used only nearest-neighbour interpolation. The warping step was implemented using the algorithm from the "Generic Convex Polygon Scan Conversion and Clipping" article in [10]. We measured the rendering times on a 266 MHz Intel Pentium II system with 192MB RAM under Linux 2.1.89 operating system. The shared memory extension in X Window System Release 6 was used to speed up the copying of the data into the frame buffer. The display board used was Matrox Millenium II with 8 M memory and 32-bits per pixel.

12.5 Results

The timing results are given in Tables 12.1 and 12.2. The column "Voxels accessed" lists the number of references made to the view lattice sample points by the seed filling algorithm (excluding the interpolations needed to calculate the pixel shade). The column "Interpolations done" lists the number of interpolations (nearest-neighbour for one template and trilinear for four templates) done to calculate the shade value. The column "Render time" includes the time spent on projecting the dataset. The warping step of the template algorithm is not included in this measurement, but listed separately in the column "Warp time". The column "Total display time/frame" includes all the time it took to render and display one image to screen, i.e. the user-observed rendering time. Example images are shown in Figures. 12.5, 12.6, 12.7 and 12.8.

Table 12.1. Timing measurements, rendering with one template.

Dataset	Voxels accessed	Interpolations done	Render time (ms)	Warp time (ms)	Total display time/frame (ms)
256×256×22	172,000	12,300	18.1	27.1	210
256×256×43	220,000	20,300	26.2	27.6	220
256×256×64	267,000	27,800	34.1	27.2	227
256×256×85	310,000	34,500	41.3	26.7	234
256×256×124	407,000	40,600	59.3	26.1	256
256×256×124 (cut)	448,000	40,500	61.1	30.5	259

Table 12.2. Timing measurements, rendering with four templates.

Dataset	Voxels accessed	Interpolations done	Render time (ms)	Warp time (ms)	Total display time/frame (ms)
256×256×22	627,000	49,700	89.6	31.6	283
256×256×43	780,000	83,400	141.8	31.7	335
256×256×64	936,000	112,000	189.3	33.0	384
256×256×85	1,085,000	136,900	232.9	34.8	428
256×256×124	1,419,000	156,700	297.3	36.0	505
256×256×124 (cut)	1,617,000	158,300	305.1	40.3	507

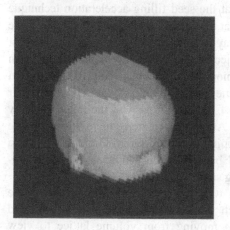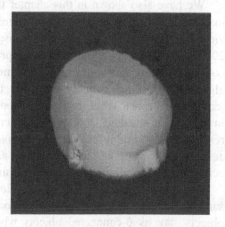

Figure 12.5. The 256×256×22 dataset rendered by the seed filling algorithm with one template (left) and four templates (right). The distance between individual slices is 5 mm and the pixel size is 0.9mm×0.9mm.

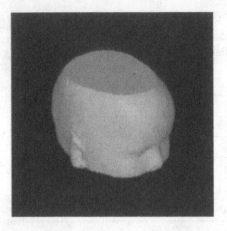 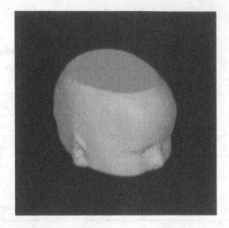

Figure 12.6. The 256×256×22 dataset interpolated into 256×256×85 size and rendered by the seed filling algorithm with one template (left) and four templates (right).

12.6 Discussion

The measurements show that the number of interpolations grows roughly fourfold with the four-template algorithm as compared to the one-template approach. This is as expected, because the number of rendered pixels grows by a factor of four. Fourfold increases are also seen in the number of voxels accessed by the seed fill algorithm (excluding the increase caused by using trilinear interpolation instead of nearest-neighbour interpolation), which indicates that the complexity of the seed filling algorithm is much closer to $O(N^2)$ than to, for instance, $O(N^3)$, where N^3 is the total number of voxels in the dataset.

We have also shown in this chapter that the seed filling acceleration technique may be used to render high-quality images at reasonably interactive frame rates. The view size 1024×1024 on a true colour display is quite challenging, as it takes almost 200 ms to warp (i.e. texture map) the projected data into a 24-bit image and then copy the 24-bit image using shared memory to the screen. The 3D projection algorithm consumes roughly the same time with the largest datasets using four templates. We reached a rendering speed of roughly 2 fps with the highest quality images on a standard desktop computer. An obvious extension to speed up the rendering would be to use the texture mapping hardware on a 3D graphics card to accelerate the warping step. An additional benefit of this would be the hardware-accelerated interpolation during the warping step.

One issue that needs special attention with the one template approach is the sampling rate. The one-template approach does not guarantee that 6-connected objects stay as 6-connected objects when moving from volume lattice to view lattice. This can be avoided by additional preprocessing as described in [7]. The four-template approach avoids these problems, because the sampling rate is sufficient to maintain the 6-connectivity also in view lattice.

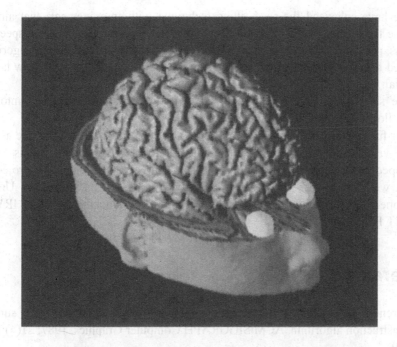

Figure 12.7. The 256×256×124 dataset cut and rendered by the seed filling algorithm with one template.

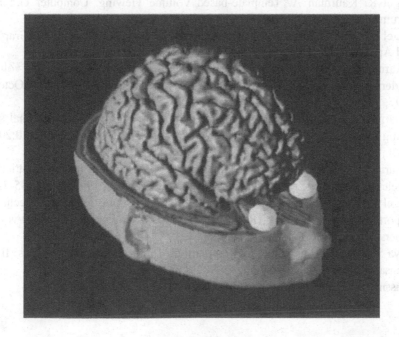

Figure 12.8. The 256×256×124 dataset cut and rendered by the seed filling algorithm with four templates.

We have enhanced the seed filling technique with improvements that aim to increase the quality of the rendered view while maintaining the rendering speed as high as possible. The use of multiple templates with the seed filling algorithm required the re-implementation of four of the seven basic primitives for view lattice traversal.

The shape-based interpolation and coding of the gradient directions into the voxel allow more realistic light interaction.

Our future plans include the use of the seed filling acceleration technique as one of the visualisation techniques for the interventional MRI system that is being developed in the Oulu University Hospital and University of Oulu. The project in which we plan to use the results is partly funded by the European Union; "Intraoperative Real-time Visualisation and Instrument Tracking in MRI", IRVIT-ESPRIT P27230.

References

1. Lorensen W, Cline H. Marching cubes: A high resolution 3D surface construction algorithm. ACM/SIGGRAPH Computer Graphics, 1987; 21(4):163-169.
2. Cohen-Or D, Kaufman A. 3D line voxelization and connectivity control. IEEE Computer Graphics and Applications, 1997; 11(6):80-87.
3. Yagel R, Kaufman A. Template-based volume viewing. Computer Graphics Forum (Eurographics '92); 11(3):153-167.
4. Yagel R, Cohen D, Kaufman A. Discrete ray tracing. IEEE Computer Graphics and Applications, 1992; 12(5):19-28.
5. Oikarinen J. Using 3-dimensional seed filling in view space to accelerate volume rendering. In: Proc. IEEE Visualization '97, Late Breaking Hot Topics, October 1997; 17-20.
6. Oikarinen J, Jyrkinen L. Maximum intensity projection by 3-dimensional seed filling in view lattice. Computer Networks and ISDN Systems, 1998; 30:2003-2014.
7. Oikarinen J. Using 2- and 2.5-dimensional seed filling in view lattice to accelerate volumetric rendering. Computers and Graphics, 1999; 22(6):745-757.
8. Yagel R, Ciula K. High quality template-based volume rendering. Technical Report OSU-CICRC-3/94-TR17, 1994; http://www.cis.ohio-state.edu/volviz/Papers/1994/TR17.ps.gz.
9. Raya S, Udupa J. Shape-based interpolation of multidimensional objects. IEEE Transactions on Medical Imaging, 1990; 9(1):32-42.
10. Glassner A (Ed). Graphics Gems I. Academic Press, 1990.

13. Extending Hypertextures to Non-Geometrically Definable Volume Data

Richard Satherley and Mark W. Jones

13.1 Introduction

The increasing use of computer-generated graphical representations of everyday objects, in both entertainment and industry (including such areas as medical imaging), has led to the development of powerful rendering tools such as *ray tracing*, *radiosity* and *volume rendering* (see [1, 2] for a description). However, the images produced by such applications are somewhat bland when compared to their real-life counterparts. The surfaces of the objects appear smooth and plastic (Figure 13.1), not textured and natural. Therefore, increased realism in computer imagery is needed.

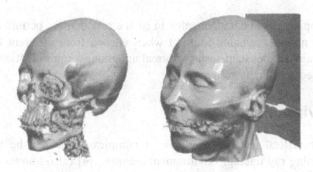

Figure 13.1. Computer-generated images.

13.2 Surface Detail Algorithms

Such realism can be incorporated into a computer-generated image with the application of *surface detail* algorithms, including:

- *Bump mapping*;
- *Environment mapping*; and
- *Texture mapping* in one, two and three dimensions.

13.2.1 Bump Mapping

The majority of surface detail algorithms add a *texture* to the surface of an object via the manipulation of surface colours. Bump mapping [3], however, fools the illumination model into believing the surface has an actual texture, by perturbing the surface normals. Thus creating the effect of a wrinkled or dimpled surface (Figure 13.2) without geometrically altering the underlying object.

A problem arises when (part of) the bump mapped image appears in silhouette. As the bump map is not part of the surface model, the silhouetted section of the image will not be given a texture, thus creating a different effect to that expected.

Figure 13.2. A bump mapped skull viewed with different light sources.

Bump mapping must be implemented in such a way that the perturbation applied to the surface normals remains constant when viewed from different locations. In order to maintain this constant surface normal agitation, the perturbation is based on a locally defined coordinate system.

13.2.2 Environment Mapping

Rendering the reflections encountered in a complex scene can be prohibitively costly when using ray tracing. Environment mapping [4] (also known as *reflection mapping*) reduces the cost of rendering these reflections, although with reduced accuracy.

In [4] Blinn and Newell position the object in question inside a large sphere, onto which the surrounding environment is projected. Next, using a simplified ray tracer (only reflection rays are considered, with one surface intersection as shown in Figure 13.3), the reflected rays, R, are used to index a latitude-longitude map of the *environment sphere*.

The main problem with this approach, aside from the difficulty in projecting a scene onto the interior of a sphere (where singularities are created at the z-axis poles), is the dependence on the object being positioned at the centre of the environment sphere, furthermore the environment is considered to be at a distance from the reflective object. Therefore as the object moves away from the central axes, or becomes large in relation to the environment sphere, the geometric distortion due to the spherical nature of the environment increases.

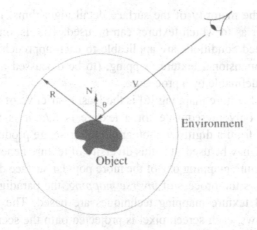

Figure 13.3. Blinn Newell environment mapping.

Greene [5] introduces an improvement to Blinn and Newell's approach with the use of a cubic environment map created with six mutually orthogonal images, reducing the distortion effects and removing the singularities. These images can be pictures taken by camera, although there can be discontinuities at the picture seams, or generated by a scene rendering tool.

Environment mapping differs from the majority of surface texturing algorithms by the fact the texture remains stationary during animation. That is, the texture moves across the surface of an object when it is moved within the environment.

13.2.3 One-Dimensional Texture Mapping

One-dimensional texture mapping models the natural phenomenon of film interference; the colour changes seen in a thin film lying on top of a surface, for example, the effect seen when a film of oil lies on the surface of water. These effects are seen due to the light waves reflected from the surface interfering with those reflected from the film (Figure 13.4), causing components of the white light to be cancelled.

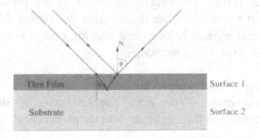

Figure 13.4. Example of a one-dimensional texture map.

13.2.4 Two-Dimensional Texture Mapping

The problem with the majority of the surface detail algorithms, is the restrictions enforced on the user as to which textures can be used. That is, only those textures that satisfy predefined conditions are applicable to each approach, for example (in the case of three-dimensional texture mapping, (to be discussed in Section 13.2.5) the texture must be definable by a procedure.

Two-dimensional texture mapping [6] is the least restrictive of the surface detail approaches, as the only prerequisite for a texture is that it is two-dimensional. Therefore, anything from a digitised photograph to an image produced on a general purpose art package may be used. It is this diversity of texture generation that makes two-dimensional texture mapping one of the more popular surface detail algorithms.

Figure 13.5 shows the process of *inverse mapping*, the paradigm around which all two-dimensional texture mapping techniques are based. The inverse mapping paradigm is as follows, each screen pixel is projected onto the scene. If a projected pixel lies on the surface of an object, to which a texture is to be added, the area covered is mapped onto the desired texture. The portion of the texture covered by the mapping is averaged, and a pixel colour gained.

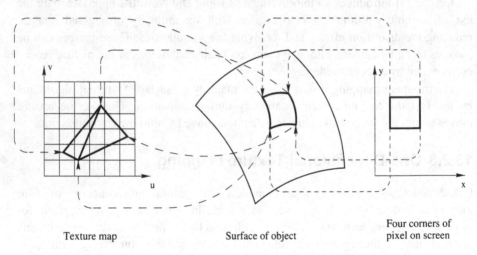

Texture map   Surface of object   Four corners of
                                                            pixel on screen

Figure 13.5. Inverse texture mapping.

Two-dimensional texture mapping is let down by its proneness to aliasing effects, which distort textures that are distant from the viewer. However there are several techniques that try and reduce these aliasing effects with the use of extra calculations for each pixel. These include:

- *Supersampling* — extra samples are taken for each pixel.
- *Gaussian integration* — the extra samples taken by supersampling are weighted according to their distance from the pixel centre[1].

---

[1] Supersampling and Gaussian integration can take the extra samples at random locations in an attempt to reduce noise.

- *MIP mapping* [7] — extra copies of the texture are made at reduced resolutions. The lower resolution textures are used as the distance from the viewer increases, resulting in the blurring of the image.
- *Summed-area tables* [8] — the texture is converted so each texture point holds the sum of the texture pixels in the rectangle from the origin to itself. The rectangle that best approximates the projected pixel is used to give the pixel colour.
- *Adaptive precision* [9] — the rectangle given by summed-area tables is adapted by removing sections to give a better approximation of the projected pixel.

13.2.5 Three-Dimensional Texture Mapping

Three-dimensional texture mapping techniques are more resistant to such aliasing effects, as the need for image warping is removed by the fact that the texture map is mathematically defined throughout $\mathbf{R}^3$, thus any point on the surface of the rendered object has a predefined texture value. Therefore, the 3D texture mapping approach is analogous to carving a statue from a block of material as shown in Figure 13.6.

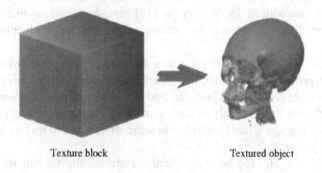

Texture block   Textured object

Figure 13.6. Three-dimensional texture mapping.

Perlin and Hoffert [10] extended the three-dimensional texture mapping paradigm to produce *hypertextures*, allowing a computer to model such phenomena as fur, fire and smoke. This chapter shows how hypertextures can be extended for use with non-geometrical datasets. In Section 13.3, we introduce the area of three-dimensional texture mapping through solid textures, followed by a description of hypertextures in Section 13.4 Finally, in Section 13.5.1, we show how a volume dataset is modified with the use of distance transforms, thus allowing the application of the hypertexture model. Section 13.5.2 shows images produced with extended hypertextures, and Section 13.5.3 shows how the extended hypertextures produce images that are consistent, allowing the production of animations.

13.3 Solid Texturing

13.3.1 Related Work

Recent trends in research into the addition of detail to the surface of an object have turned towards the field of three-dimensional texture mapping. Early work in this field, such as that by Schachter [11], used summations of long crested narrow-band noise waveforms to produce textures, that vary in two dimensions, by Fourier synthesis.

Peachey [12] shows how popular two-dimensional texturing techniques, such as Fourier synthesis and stochastic texture models, can be extended to produce three-dimensional textures. Combinations of these extended techniques, along with 3D projections of 2D images, make up what Peachey coined *solid textures*. Perlin also used the term "solid textures" to describe the work in [13]. Here complex three-dimensional textures, such as marble, are created from primitive, nonlinear, *basis functions*, the most fundamental of which is *noise*, a function that returns a random value at each point in space. In [14], Lewis reviews several existing algorithms for noise generation, resulting in two new algorithms that are more efficient, have improved control over the noise power spectrum, and have no artifacts. A further basis function, introduced by Worley in [15], creates flagstone-like textures by calculating the distance between the surface points and randomly placed *feature points*.

As mentioned above, Peachey projects a digitised 2D image in order to create a 3D texture. A problem arises when the object is larger than the texture, resulting in the need for texture repetition, which can lead to visible artifacts between the texture tiles. Research into texture analysis aims to remove such effects by synthesising a new texture (of any size), that looks like (in terms of colour and texture properties) a given sample image.

Heeger and Bergen [16] base their analysis around the way in which the eye perceives texture, utilising the fact that it is difficult to discriminate between textures that produce similar responses in a bank of linear filters. Therefore, with the application of simple image processing operations (e.g. histograms, convolution, etc.), in a pyramidal format, white noise can be modified to take on the appearance of a sample image.

Solid textures produced by Heeger and Bergen's method can be imagined as a stack of "*photocopies*", with each layer being an exact copy of the one below. Ghazanfarpour and Dischler [17] use some of the spectral information, gained during the analysis of the sample image, to apply a selective filter to white noise. The filtered noise is next used to perturb the layers of the synthesised texture, thus removing the monotony of Heeger and Bergen's method and creating far more realistic solid textures. In a second paper [18], Ghazanfarpour and Dischler show that solid textures synthesised from a single 2D sample are only controllable in two dimensions. They continue to show that with the use of three samples, taken in the directions of the orthogonal axes, it is possible to control the texture synthesis in all three dimensions.

13.3.2 Perlin's Solid Textures

It has already been pointed out (Section 13.2.5) that three-dimensional texture mapping is equivalent to computer sculpture, a fact that inspired Perlin to create *solid textures*; complex three-dimensional textures constructed from primitive, nonlinear, *basis functions*, namely *noise*, *turbulence* and n^{th} *closest*.

Noise. The most fundamental of the basis functions is *noise* (Figure 13.7), which returns a pseudo-random value, in the range $(-1, 1)$, by interpolating gradient vectors between predefined lattice points. There are numerous implementations of the noise algorithms [14], which all exhibit the following properties:

- Statistical invariance under rotation;
- A narrow bandpass limit in frequency;
- Statistical invariance under translation.

These properties make noise an ideal texturing tool, due to its ability to create desired stochastic effects, without affecting the execution of general graphical tools (*rotation, scaling and translation*).

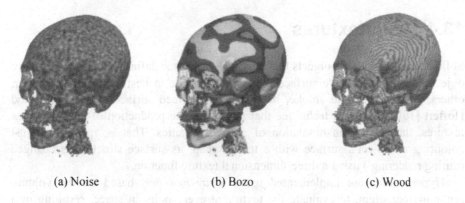

(a) Noise   (b) Bozo   (c) Wood

Figure 13.7. Solid textures created using the *noise* basis function.

Turbulence. The *turbulence* basis function (Figure 13.8) gives the impression of Brownian motion (or turbulent flow) by summing noise values at increasing frequencies (Equation 13.1), introducing a self-similar $1/f$ pattern[2]. The discontinuities of turbulent flow are introduced into the model with the use of the mathematical function *abs*, which reflects the gradient vectors used by noise.

$$Turbulence = \sum abs\left(\frac{1}{2^i} noise\left(2^i \mathbf{x}\right)\right) \qquad (13.1)$$

---

[2] Where f is the frequency of the noise.

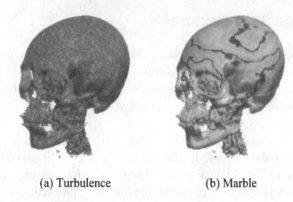

(a) Turbulence   (b) Marble

Figure 13.8. Solid textures created using the *turbulence* basis function.

nth Closest. A third basis function, introduced by Worley [15], places *feature points* at random locations in $\mathbf{R}^3$. The nth *closest* basis function calculates the distance from a surface point to each of the n closest feature points. Combinations of these distances can then be used to index a colour spline, adding a flagstone style texture to the surface of the object.

13.4 Hypertextures

Solid texturing produces objects that have *simple* surface definitions. However many objects, such as fur, have surface definitions that are at best complex. Moreover, others, such as fire and smoke, have no well defined surface at all. Perlin and Hoffert [10] introduce a technique that allows for the production of such complex textures, through the manipulation of surface densities. That is, rather than just colouring an object's surface with a texture map, its surface structure is changed (during rendering[3]) using a three-dimensional texture function.

Hypertextures are implemented using a *ray marcher*, based on the volume rendering paradigm, to evaluate the texture at every point in space, resulting in a complexity of $O(n^3)$. Worley and Hart [19] improve the efficiency of this implementation by replacing the ray marcher with *sphere tracing*. Execution enhancements are also introduced by Worley and Hart, found from inspection of the basis functions.

13.4.1 Implementation

Hypertextures introduce the idea of *soft objects*; objects with a large boundary region, modelled using an *object density function*, D(**x**), thus giving three possible states to a point:

---

[3] As with other non-view dependent operations the hypertexture may be added as a preprocessing step prior to rendering.

- *Inside* — the point is inside the object;
- *Outside* — the point is outside of the object;
- *Boundary* — the point is in the boundary, *soft*, region of the object.

As with solid textures, combinations of *noise* and *turbulence* (Section 13.2*)* together with two new *density modulation functions (DMF)*, namely *bias*, which controls the density variation across the soft region, and *gain*, which controls the rate at which density changes across the midrange of the soft region, are used to manipulate $D(x)$ to create hypertextured objects. Figure 13.9 shows examples of hypertextured objects.

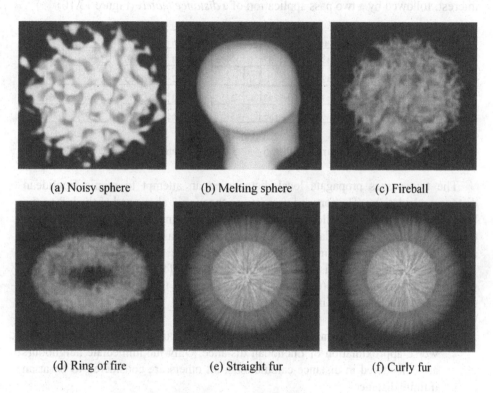

| (a) Noisy sphere | (b) Melting sphere | (c) Fireball |
| (d) Ring of fire | (e) Straight fur | (f) Curly fur |

Figure 13.9. Examples of hypertextures.

13.5 Extending Hypertextures

Figure 13.9 shows the pleasing effects that can be produced when the hypertexture approach is applied to geometrically definable datasets. The major setback with this approach is the inability to apply the method to irregular (or non-geometrically definable) datasets, such as CT scans.

13.5.1 Distance Transforms

Examination of datasets, generated by solving geometric formulae, shows that the data points give the *distance* to some point (or surface) within the dataset. The datasets used to create the hypertextures shown in Figure 13.9 were produced in this manner. Therefore, if the dataset of a non-geometric object can be converted to such a *distance volume*, the hypertexture paradigm will become applicable to the non-geometric object.

Such a conversion can be accomplished with the use of *distance transforms* [20-30]. A distance transform involves *segmenting* the dataset, to extract the surface of interest, followed by a two pass application of a *distance matrix* (Figure 13.10).

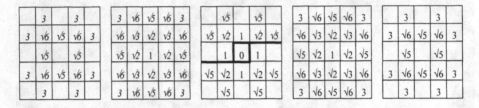

Figure 13.10. A 5×5×5 distance matrix.

The two passes propagate local distance in an attempt to mimic Euclidean distance calculations. The forward pass (using the matrix above and to the left of the bold line in *italic font*) calculates the distances moving away from the surface towards the bottom of the dataset, with the backward pass (using the matrix below and to the right of the bold line) calculating the remaining distances.

There are numerous distance matrices available for the distance transform process, each giving a different result (Figure 13.11) at the cost of execution time[4] (Table 13.1). Such matrices include[5]:

- *City block* — the simplest and fastest of all distance transforms, giving the worse approximation of Euclidean distance. Only the immediate neighbours are considered in distance calculations, all others are considered to be at an infinite distance.

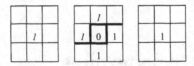

- *Chess board* — neighbours that are diagonal in only two of the orthogonal axes are also considered in distance calculations.

---

[4] Execution timings where taken on a DEC Alpha 2100 4/275.
[5] See [21] for a detailed introduction to distance transform matrices.

	1	
1	1	1
	1	

1	1	1
1	**0**	1
1	1	1

	1	
1	1	1
	1	

- *Quasi-Euclidean (√2)* — diagonal neighbours are given more realistic distance values.

	√2	
√2	1	√2
	√2	

√2	1	√2
1	**0**	1
√2	1	√2

	√2	
√2	1	√2
	√2	

- *5×5×5* — distances to matrix positions are calculated using Pythagoras' theorem (Figure 13.10).

	3		3	
3	√6	√5	√6	3
	√5		√5	
3	√6	√5	√6	3
	3		3	

3	√6	√5	√6	3
√6	√3	√2	√3	√6
√5	√2	1	√2	√5
√6	√3	√2	√3	√6
3	√6	√5	√6	3

	√5		√5	
√5	√2	1	√2	√5
	1	**0**	1	
√5	√2	1	√2	√5
	√5		√5	

3	√6	√5	√6	3
√6	√3	√2	√3	√6
√5	√2	1	√2	√5
√6	√3	√2	√3	√6
3	√6	√5	√6	3

	3		3	
3	√6	√5	√6	3
	√5		√5	
3	√6	√5	√6	3
	3		3	

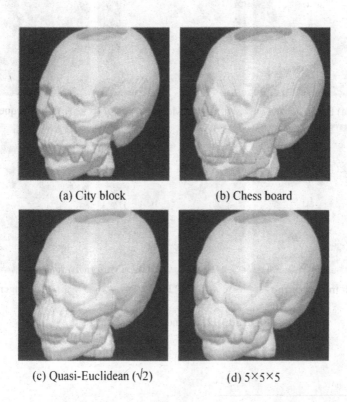

(a) City block (b) Chess board

(c) Quasi-Euclidean (√2) (d) 5×5×5

Figure 13.11. Results of distance matrix application.

Table 13.1. Comparison of distance transform execution times.

Distance matrix	Average execution time (sec.)	Average time to render a 300x300 image (sec.)
City Block	10.016	141.211
Chess Board	26.266	163.493
Quasi-Euclidean ($\sqrt{2}$)	28.166	161.577
5×5×5	226.408	142.244

13.5.2 Results

Figure 13.12 shows the results gained from the application of the hypertextures of Figure 13.9 to a 256×256×113 CT dataset[6], modified with the 5×5×5 distance matrix.

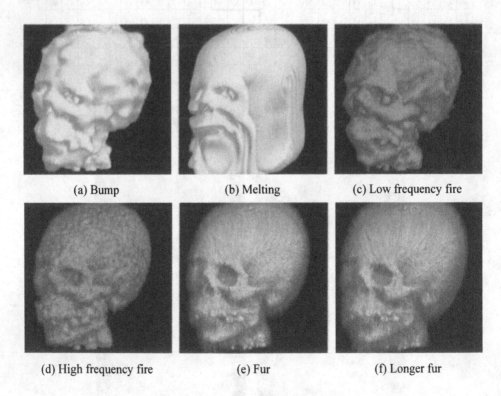

(a) Bump   (b) Melting   (c) Low frequency fire

(d) High frequency fire   (e) Fur   (f) Longer fur

Figure 13.12. Extended hypertextures.

---

[6] Obtained from the University of North Carolina, Chapel Hill.

13.5.3 Animation

As mentioned in Section 13.4, a hypertexture is created by manipulating the surface densities of an object with a three-dimensional texture function. The use of a three-dimensional texture function allows a hypertextured object to be rendered, from different view points, without any inconsistencies in the texture thus introducing frame coherency for animation. Figure 13.13 shows a series of frames from such an animation.

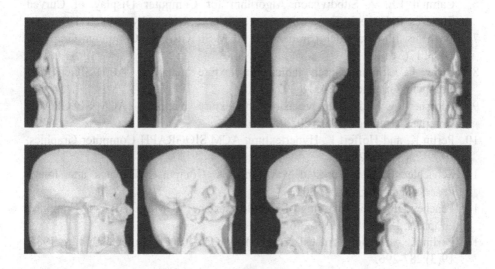

Figure 13.13. Selected frames from an animation of a hypertextured (melting) skull.

13.6 Conclusion

It has been shown that Perlin and Hoffert's hypertexture paradigm [10] can be easily applied to volume datasets created by invoking a geometric formula at each voxel. It has also been shown that, with the use of distance transforms, the datasets of a non-geometric object (for example CT scans) can be altered to appear geometric, allowing the application of hypertexture functions. Figure 13.12 shows the application of the hypertexture functions to a CT dataset which has been altered using the distance transform approach, therefore it has been shown that the hypertexture paradigm can be applied to non-geometrically definable datasets.

References

1. Foley JD, van Dam A, Feiner SK, Hughes JF. Computer Graphics Principles and Practice. Addison-Wesley, Second Edition, 1990.

2. Watt A, Watt M. Advanced Animation and Rendering Techniques Theory and Practice. Addison-Wesley, 1992.
3. Blinn JF. Simulation of wrinkled surfaces. ACM/SIGGRAPH Computer Graphics, 1978; 12(3):286-292.
4. Blinn JF, Newell ME. Texture and reflection in computer generated images. Communication of the ACM, 1976; 19:542-546.
5. Greene N. Environment mapping and other applications of world projections. IEEE Computer Graphics and Applications, 1986; 6(11):21-29.
6. Catmull EE. A Subdivision Algorithm for Computer Display of Curved Surfaces. PhD thesis, Dept. of Computer Science, University of Utah, 1974.
7. Williams L. Pyramidal parametrics. ACM/SIGGRAPH Computer Graphics, 1983; 17(3):1-11.
8. Crow FC. Summed-area tables for texture mapping. ACM/SIGGRAPH Computer Graphics 1984; 18:207-212.
9. Glassner A. Adaptive precision in texture mapping. ACM/SIGGRAPH Computer Graphics, 1986; 20:297-306.
10. Perlin K, and Hoffert E. Hypertexture. ACM/SIGGRAPH Computer Graphics, 1989; 23(3):253-262.
11. Schachter B. Long crested wave models. Computer Graphics and Image Processing, 1980; 12:187-201.
12. Peachey DR. Solid texturing of complex surface. ACM/SIGGRAPH Computer Graphics, 1985; 19(3):279-286.
13. Perlin K. An image synthesizer. ACM/SIGGRAPH Computer Graphics, 1985; 19(3):287-296.
14. Lewis JP. Algorithms for solid noise synthesis. ACM/SIGGRAPH, 1989; 23(3):263-270.
15. Worley S. A cellular texture basis function. ACM/SIGGRAPH, 1996; 30: 291-294.
16. Heeger DJ, Bergen JR. Pyramid-based texture analysis/synthesis. ACM/SIGGRAPH, 1995; 29(2):229-238.
17. Ghazanfarpour D, Dischler JM. Spectral analysis for automatic 3-D texture generation. Computer and Graphics, 1995; 19(3):413-422.
18. Ghazanfarpour D, Dischler JM. Generation of 3D texture using multiple 2D models analysis. In: Proc. EUROGRAPHICS, 1996; 15(3):C331-C323.
19. Worley SP, Hart JC. Hyper-rendering of hyper-textured surfaces. In: Proc. Implicit Surfaces, 1996: 99-104.
20. Danielsson PE. Euclidean distance mapping. Computer Graphics and Image Processing, 1980; 14:227-248.
21. Borgefors G. Distance transformations in digital images. Computer Vision, Graphics, and Image Processing, 1986; 34(3):344-371.
22. Paglieroni DW. Distance transforms: Properties and machine vision applications. CVGIP: Graphical models and Image Processing, 1992; 54(1):56-74.
23. Payne BA, Toga AW. Distance field manipulation of surface models. IEEE Computer Graphics and Applications, 1992; 12(1):65-71.
24. Herman GT, Zheng J, Bucholtz CA. Shape-based interpolation. IEEE Computer

Graphics and Applications, 1992; 12(3):69-79.
25. Ragnemalm I. Neighbourhoods for distance transformations using ordered propagation. CVGIP: Image Understanding, 1992; 53(3):399-409.
26. Yagel R, Shi Z. Accelerating volume animation by space-leaping. In: Proc. IEEE Visualization, 1993; 62-69.
27. Cohen D, Sheffer Z. Proximity clouds – An acceleration technique for 3D grid traversal. The Visual Computer, 1994; 11:27-38.
28. Breu H, Gill J, Kirkpatrick D, Werman M. Linear time Euclidean distance transform algorithms. IEEE Transactions on Pattern Analysis and Machine Intelligence, 1995; 17(5):529-533.
29. Semwal SK, Kvarnstrom H. Directed safe zones and the dual extent algorithms for efficient grid traversal during ray tracing. Graphics Interface, 1997; 76-87.
30. Cohen-Or D, Levin S, Solomovici A. Three-dimensional distance field metamorphosis. ACM Transactions on Graphics, 1998; 17(2):116-141.

PART V

VOLUME ANIMATION

14. Fast Volume Rendering and Animation of Amorphous Phenomena

Scott A. King, Roger A. Crawfis and Wayland Reid

14.1 Introduction

Virtual environment technology, such as flight simulators, medical simulators and games, is making vast steps in realism and speed. For convincing interactive environments, gaseous effects, such as fire, dust and smoke, are needed. To achieve this realism, we have several design goals we wish to meet:

- Animation must support real-time applications;
- The method should be able to represent a variety of phenomena;
- The effect must occupy three-dimensional space;
- Other objects in the environment must be able to interact with the effect;
- A variety of shapes should be supported;
- The basic shape should allow for easy deformations or propagation.

Rendering gaseous phenomena has been an active area of research since the visualisation of the rings of Saturn [1] and the Genesis effect in the film *Star Trek II: The Wrath of Khan* [2]. Blinn creates new illumination methods to handle the scattering of light [1]. Reeves uses particle systems to simulate fire, grass and trees [2, 3]. Kajiya ray traces volume densities [4]. Perlin procedurally generates realistic 2D fire based on a noise function [5], which is extended to generate 3D fire using hypertextures [6]. Gardner uses 3D textures with transparency to represent clouds [7]. Ebert and Parent combine volume ray casting with a scan-line A-buffer to render scenes containing both volume and geometry models [8].

Recent research has focused on physically-based modelling. Stam and Fiume reformulate the advection-diffusion equations for densities composed of "warped blobs", which more accurately model the distortions that gases undergo when advected by wind fields, using a model for the flame and its spread [9]. Stam and Fiume formulate global illumination in the presence of gases and fire. Sakas uses spectral turbulence theory using Kolmogorov's exponential law with a phase-shift in the frequency domain [10]. Sakas develops a spectral synthesis model to generate a voxel grid containing densities which stochastically places and migrates eddies and other turbulent features. Chiba et al. model vortices in a turbulent field, with particles acting as tracers within this field, giving both vortices and particles behaviour which allow them to appear, disappear, and interact with each other and the environment [11]. Foster and Metaxes use specialised forms of the equations of motion for a hot gas, solving the differential equations at low resolutions for speed, to develop an algorithm useful for rendering rolling, billowing gases [12].

The performance of the above systems is dependent on the resolution of the volume grid. Increasing the resolution slows down the generation and rendering process substantially, especially in 3D. For example, Sakas achieves near real-time performance with a medium-resolution (64×64) 2D field [10]. Sakas reports that when the method is extended to 3D the computation time increases exponentially, achieving near real-time speeds only for 8×8×8 fields, while high-resolution grids require minutes to calculate. For a medium resolution grid (60×60×45), Foster requires 49 seconds to calculate and 23 minutes to render (ray-tracing) [12]. These physically-based methods [10-12] create volumetric models of fire, which then need to be rendered, making them candidates to be combined with our rendering method. This combination will be discussed further in Section 14.6.

The above methods focus either on rendering [1, 3, 8, 9] or on modelling [2, 4, 7, 9-12] the desired effect. All of these techniques require a high number of primitives to generate realistic detail for any volume consuming a substantial portion of the scene or view. This chapter focuses on very fast, visually realistic animation of three-dimensional amorphous materials, which allows objects, the camera or both within the effect. By incorporating detail into the rendering primitive (splats) and cycling through coherent primitives, only a coarse voxel grid is required allowing real-time rendering speeds.

Several different volume rendering techniques have been developed for regular grids: ray casting [13, 14], shear-warp [15], Fourier-domain rendering [16], cell projection [17, 18], and splatting [19]. Our approach capitalises on the efficient voxel-based projection paradigm of the splatting algorithm.

In splatting, the volume is thought of as a field of overlapping interpolation kernels h. One such kernel is placed at each voxel location j and weighted by the voxel's value v_j. The overlapping voxel kernels then reconstruct a continuous representation of the volume. The task of volume rendering can be interpreted as the process of casting viewing rays into the volume and integrating the volume along these rays. Ray casting calculates this integral by sampling the volume along the ray and compositing the samples in front-to-back order. This sampling operation is an expensive one, and furthermore, a voxel may be involved in many such sampling operations, depending on the sampling distance. Splatting provides a more efficient way to generate the ray integral. It works by simplifying the volume integral and separating a single voxel, v_j's, contribution to a ray as:

$$V_j \cdot \int h(s)ds$$

where s follows the integration of the interpolation kernel in the direction of the viewing ray. If the viewing direction is constant for all voxels or if the interpolation kernel is radially symmetric, then we may pre-integrate:

$$\int h(s)ds$$

into a lookup-table, termed a kernel *footprint*, and use this table for all voxels. For volume projection, we map the voxel footprints, scaled by the voxel values, to the screen where they accumulate into the projection image [20]. We use the splatting algorithm in its first incarnation, i.e., in the *composite-every-sample* mode [19], where each footprint is considered an atomic entity and is immediately composited on the image plane, in back-to-front order. We see that, in contrast to ray casting, splatting considers each voxel only once (for a 2D interpolation on the screen), and not several times (for a 3D interpolation in world space). Also, in contrast to ray casting, line integrals across a voxel are now continuous or approximated with good quadrature, and do not require normalisation of α to compensate for sample distance. We also only need to project those voxels with relevant values, which reduces the projection task tremendously. Finally, the efficient pre-integrated kernel representation allows splatting to use qualitatively better kernels (with larger extents) than the trilinear filter typically employed by ray casting. Possible kernels are the Gaussian function or the Crawfis-Max kernel [21, 22], which is a kernel optimised for splatting, and designed to yield a low-variance volume reconstruction by the field of interpolation kernels.

Laur and Hanrahan [20] extended this technique for octree data structures. They also approximated the Gaussian with a triangular mesh of varying opacities. Crawfis and Max support octree data structures and employ texture mapping to render the splats [21]. Crawfis and Max develop an optimal splat with a small footprint extent to render smoothly varying functions. Crawfis and Max added anisotropic icons within the textures to represent vector fields by using a simple phase-shift through the overlapping textures. This provides the illusion of coherent motion. Mueller et al. have extended splatting to account for antialiasing of the projected voxel grid [23]. Muller et al., separately, have improved the volume integration by using an image-aligned splatting approach [24]. In this chapter, we provide a framework for texture synthesis and animation of gaseous volumes that is closely related to the textured splats in [21].

The rest of the chapter will discuss our technique. Section 14.2 describes our algorithm in detail and compares it to more general volume rendering. Section 14.3 explains the three types of motion possible with our method. Section 14.4 discusses the creation of textures, which add the detail to the splat, using various techniques. Section 14.5 presents some results from our method applied to various types of gaseous effects, with some performance measurements. In Section 14.6 we give our conclusions and discuss future work.

14.2 Our Approach

We model an effect with a small regular grid, assigning colours and opacities at each voxel. Using an optimal splat footprint function [21] rather than a Gaussian, the splatting algorithm [19] has been used to render the volume shown in Figure 14.1a.

The resulting image resembles more of a semi-transparent blob than a raging fire. In comparison, using the same grid, our new technique achieves the rendering shown in Figure 14.1b. For distant views, the traditional volume rendering may be sufficient, as would a single texture mapped facade. Neither volume rendering nor 2D facades are effective when the viewpoint is near or inside the fire. 2D facades are also not effective when additional objects or surfaces need to be embedded into the fire.

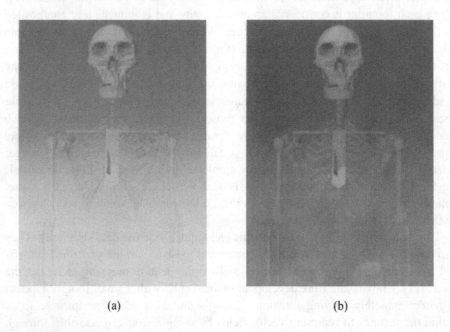

(a)   (b)

Figure 14.1. Modelling fire with a 7×20×5 voxel grid. (a) Using traditional splatting results in a fuzzy semi-transparent blob. (b) Using our method of incorporating detail into the splats results in a fast turbulent fire.

The cornerstone of our algorithm is the realisation that the detail within an amorphous volume is ill-defined, with edges and shapes (other than the overall gross shape) that are not only difficult to perceive visually, but are also constantly changing. We model an effect with a coarse, regular voxel grid of opacity values. Each voxel or point is then rendered independently in a back-to-front order, with respect to the viewpoint, using the splatting technique. To model fine details, we use anisotropic footprints which provide interpolation kernels that are neither monotonic nor smooth, but rather exhibit a more fractal-like nature. As will be shown in Section 14.5, our technique is applicable to a wide variety of volumetric effects. For purposes of discussion, and without loss of generality, we primarily focus on the techniques to model and render fire in this and the next two sections.

Our basic algorithm consists of the following steps:

1. Select a set of textures to represent the volume and create the footprint table;
2. Create a volume out of regularly spaced voxels;
3. Assign an initial texture to each voxel;

4. Render the current frame by drawing the volume in back-to-front order;
5. Assign new textures to each voxel.

Steps 4 and 5 are done for every frame and by varying the implementation of Steps 3 and 5 and the choice of textures in Step 1, different visual effects are achieved.

The first step is to create a small set of textures that contain the frequencies we wish to model. These textures can be created in a variety of ways including procedurally, from measured data, from photos, manually, or by subsampling other textures in various ways. The set of textures is converted to grayscale and windowed with an optimal splat footprint function [21], creating a splat that contains high frequency detail while preserving the overall characteristics of a footprint function. Figure 14.2 illustrates how a textured splat is constructed from a texture and a footprint. The texture selection process is discussed in Section 14.4.

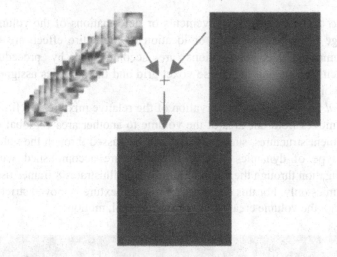

Figure 14.2. A texture is weighted with the splat footprint function to produce a textured splat containing embedded detail.

Step two is to represent the overall shape of the effect as a regular grid. A regular grid allows for quick geometric modelling. We allow for sparse grids by describing the volume as a set of grid points. Opacities represent how much of the gaseous material is present within each voxel.

In Step three, the voxels are given an initial textured splat, currently chosen randomly. The dynamic updates, discussed below, quickly change the initial value in most situations, however, the choice should be consistent with the criteria employed in Step five.

In Step four, drawing each voxel's weighted footprint in a back-to-front manner, with respect to the viewpoint, renders the volume. The textured splat is used as the opacity, and the colour is generated from a colour look-up table; or the colour and opacity can be combined directly into the textured splat. For fire, we developed an inexpensive method to approximate temperature by using the voxel height as the index into the colour look-up table. Mixing effects, such as smoke and fire, can be achieved with multiple colour tables and differing texture sets.

Finally, in Step five, a new texture for each voxel is determined for the next frame. This cycling of textures creates the illusion of motion. The possible dynamics are discussed in Section 14.3.

14.3 Dynamics

Our method allows for the control of motion in three complementary ways. These can be viewed as three different scales or frequencies of motion. For fire, these are the spread of the fire, the material density mixture propagation, and the local turbulent mixing. For general applicability, we label these as:

- *Object Dynamics.* Large movements or deformations of the volume, which change the perceived shape or location of the entire effect, are the object dynamics. These deformations are accomplished by procedurally (or explicitly) changing the coarse voxel grid and the opacities assigned to each grid point.
- *Global Dynamics.* The preservation of the relative mixture of a finite volume as it moves from one area of the volume to another area is global dynamics. Turbulent structures, such as eddies can be passed through the volume using this type of dynamics. Global dynamics are accomplished with texture propagation through the volume. Figure 14.3 illustrates 8 frames using global dynamics only. For this demonstration, each texture is moved strictly upward through the volume creating an upward, global, motion.

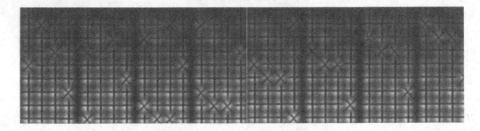

Figure 14.3. These frames show global dynamics in action. Each texture rises through the volume giving the illusion of upward global motion.

- *Local Dynamics.* Movements within or through a local neighbourhood of the volume, the turbulent structures themselves, are local dynamics. For a fire, these movements would be the twirling vortex or licking flames. These are accomplished by phase-shifting through coherent textures to provide the illusion of movement [21]. Figure 14.4 shows local dynamics in action. A set of textures, representing rotation, is cycled at differing rates for each voxel creating local, rotational motion at each voxel.

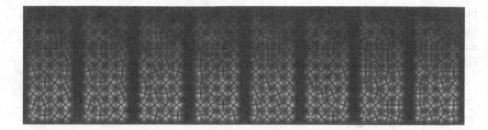

Figure 14.4. These frames show local dynamics in action. Here, the set of coherent textures (in this case forming a rotating pattern) is cycled for each voxel at differing rates

This chapter primarily addresses the latter two scales of movement, relying on traditional object animation for object dynamics, for which effective solutions exist. A physically-based fire modelling technique [10-12] can be used for this purpose. The next three subsections will discuss each of these dynamics in turn.

14.3.1 Object Dynamics

By shifting the detail to the textured splats, we can use very coarse voxel grids for the overall or gross shape of the fire. Many of the images presented in this chapter use grid sizes containing less than three hundred voxels (10×5×6). This allows a simple Eulerian or fluid flow calculation to be performed across the grid, propagating substructures and properties through the mesh. More flexible tools and procedural algorithms are areas of future interest and are discussed in the conclusions. The focus of this chapter is on the local and global dynamics.

14.3.2 Global Dynamics

Many phenomena exhibit dynamics even if the gross shape of the volume remains static. A pillar of smoke, for instance, has the appearance of upward motion with many complex interactions and details within the rather static plume. These movements must occasionally be handled across voxel cells, such as when a feature migrates through the volume. For the upward motion of fire we match the texture characteristics used from one frame to the next, while propagating those characteristics upward through the volume. This motion is accomplished by advecting the texture indices through the coarse voxel grid. This texture index is then offset slightly before a final texture is selected and used in the splat. The resulting animations provide a smooth propagation of material through the volume.

14.3.3 Local Dynamics

For local motion, we can employ texture animation techniques to cycle through a set of textures [21, 22]. If these textures have a cyclical pattern to them, a continuous and smooth animation results. A surprising result is the apparent motion perceived when textures were selected randomly. Using texture cycling by itself can also produce the illusion of global motion due to overlapping coherency in the textures, but when it is used in conjunction with the above technique, better results are achieved. By careful selection of the textures, we can produce different motion, such as licking flames, rolling clouds, or billowing smoke.

14.4 Creating Textures

Creating textures for computer graphics imagery is a difficult process that takes talent, practice and patience. We developed a system that allowed quick texture creation from existing images, to aid the animator.

For the images in Figures 14.1b, 14.2 and 14.5-14.7, we used textures generated from a version of Perlin's [5] turbulence function. These textures, in general, provide adequate results for many of the effects we are after. We have experimented with several dozen different textures and while not all were suitable for fire, many provided other interesting effects, which may be useful for rendering water, clouds or other phenomena.

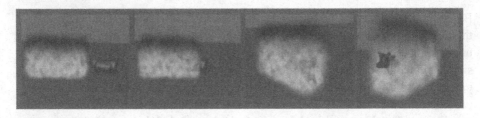

Figure 14.5. Several stills from an animation of a cow moving through fire demonstrating that since the method is 3D, objects in the environment can interact with the effects.

Figure 14.6. A herd kicking up a cloud of real-time dust using our algorithm.

Figure 14.7. A Utah teapot with real-time steam produced with our method.

We also examined the use of textures selected from stock photography. Here, the user can specify a set of positions within a much larger image. For each position, a texture is extracted from the image and added to the set of textures. This allows us to easily experiment with real images of fire. Figure 14.8 shows an image of an actual bonfire from which a set of textures is selected, shown in Figure 14.9. The set of textures is then used to render the fire in Figure 14.10.

 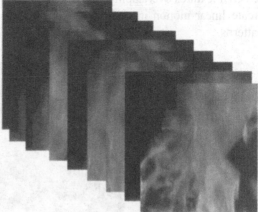

Figure 14.8. A bonfire cut from a photograph of real fire.

Figure 14.9. Resulting set of textures generated by randomly sampling Figure 14.8.

Figure 14.10. Fire image generated with our method using the textures from Figure 14.9.

The texture locations can also be selected automatically. Spectral analysis can be used to select only those portions of the image with certain frequency components, or to maximise a variation in frequencies across the set of textures. Generating textures along certain curves within the image is useful for local dynamics. Checking existing images for interesting motion can be done quickly by randomly selecting textures from the images. Random selection was used in Figures 14.10-14.13 with surprisingly good results for extremely simple and regular textures.

Sampling along a specified path through the image can create desired local and global dynamics. For instance, selecting textures along a linear path, with the selected textures overlapping, will create linear motion. A piecewise linear path will create linear motion in multiple directions, possibly causing intricate interference patterns.

Figure 14.11. Image from real-time animation of smoke emanating from a locomotive. Here, a voxelised cone and cylinder represent the volume of the effect demonstrating that non-rectangular effects are possible.

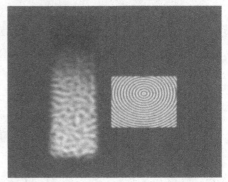

Figure 14.12. As an example of an artistic application, a low-resolution volume textured with human faces gives a ghostly effect.

Figure 14.13. The volume effect on the left was created by randomly sampling the texture on the right.

14.5 Applications/Results

14.5.1 Fire

As previously mentioned, Figures 14.1 and 14.10 show images of fire created with our method. Since our method produces a three-dimensional volume effect, objects can easily interact with that effect. For example, Figure 14.5 shows several stills from an animation in which a cow walks through a wall of fire. So far we have only concentrated on the local and global dynamics. By adding a method that physically models fire [10-12], other fire effects, such as cross wind motion, fuel simulation, and conversion to smoke, can be created.

14.5.2 Smoke/Steam

Figure 14.11 shows a still from an animation of a steam engine moving along a track. The smoke is fully three-dimensional. It consists of a voxelised cone and cylinder, requiring less than 400 non-empty voxels stored as a linear list and passed to our renderer. Since the motion of the steam results from the motion of the train, this effect looks very natural. Adding object dynamics allows for the smoke/steam to interact with the environment.

Figure 14.7 shows steam coming from the spout of a teapot. A simple $2 \times 2 \times 20$ regular grid was used to model the steam with sixteen turbulence textures. Inter-voxel advection is used to aid in the upward motion.

14.5.3 Other Effects

By using textures from photos of people, we can produce more surreal images. Figure 14.12 shows a laser-scanned head clouded with images of those close to him. For Figure 14.12, we cropped faces from photographs and used the faces as the set of textures for our algorithm. When animated, these faces appear to flash across the head and dissipate above it. Adding a few faces to the turbulence textures used for fire gives the appearance of ghosts in the fire.

In Figure 14.5, we have a herd of cattle kicking up a cloud of dust. This technique has also been used for effects such as snow, rain, clouds and water caustics. We believe it can be extended to phenomena such as bloody tissue, running water, and blowing grass.

14.5.4 Performance

By using coarse voxel grids and textured splats, we achieve real-time speed from our method. Table 14.1 shows some performance statistics for various machines. Note that our implementation was interrupt-based causing it to only display at 60Hz on the Onyx. Our method requires fast 2D texture-mapping capabilities and the ability to change the associated texture for each splat quickly. Hence, the poor performance on the SGI Indy which does not have texture support in hardware. We have found that a 32×32 texture gives very good results and only requires 2K of texture memory for each texture used. Typically, using eight textures requires only 16K of texture memory to achieve real-time results. For machines with more memory, more complex dynamics can be achieved by using more and larger textures. Due to the low number of primitives, our method is pixel fill limited; that is, the actual number of pixels that are displayed determines the frame rate.

Table 14.1. Performance measurements of our method on various machines.

Window size	Voxels	02	Indy	Octane/MXI	Onyx2/IR
320×240	1560	12Hz	.39Hz	36Hz	60Hz
640×480	1560	12Hz	.063Hz	24Hz	60Hz
1280×960	1560	5Hz	.02Hz	8Hz	30Hz
320×240	780	20Hz	.8Hz	36Hz	60Hz
320×240	390	30Hz	1.6Hz	40Hz	60Hz
320×240	195	60Hz	3Hz	72Hz	60Hz

14.6 Conclusions

We have presented a novel extension to volume rendering of density clouds for animated gaseous or amorphous materials. The technique gives visually realistic animation, yet is efficient enough to be embedded into the next generation of video games or real-time virtual environments. Our technique has a wide variety of uses including, but not limited to: games, medical simulations, flight simulators, industrial simulations, scientific visualisation, and as a modelling aid for more realistic effects. Our method is capable of representing various gaseous phenomena at real-time rates by using hardware texture support and low-resolution volumes.

Several extensions to our method are possible[1]. One of the more promising extensions is the ability to specify colour in the detail along with the opacity. One such use would be to create moving highlights such as caustics. Our biggest thrust has been on dynamics and amorphous internal volume shape. We wish to explore methods to control the global shape using voxel opacities and dynamic voxel locations.

We do not consider illumination issues, such as for fire, in which the volume is a light source. Also, a spotlight directed at the volume should illuminate part of the volume. A possible solution to the first problem is to apply the textures to the objects that are nearby in the same manner as the fire is generated, but as an additive colour texture.

We need to combine our method with one of the physically-based methods on a low-resolution grid to create better global and object dynamics, while using our

---

[1] Please visit the authors' web site, *http://www.cis.ohio-state.edu/graphics/research/fire/*, for the latest information, images, movies, and a demo version.

method to create the local dynamics. With the ability to use splat locations, instead of a rectangular grid, particle systems could also be investigated as a control for the object dynamics.

Acknowledgements

We would like to thank the Ohio Supercomputer Center for the use of an SGI Onyx2 for timing calculations. We would like to thank the reviewers for their insightful comments. We also thank Naeem Shareef, Klaus Mueller and Matthew Lewis for their help in writing this chapter. This work was partially supported by an Ohio State University interdisciplinary seed grant and NSF CAREER award ACI-9876022.

References

1. Blinn JF. Light reflection functions for simulation of clouds and dusty surfaces. ACM/SIGGRAPH Computer Graphics, 1982; 16(3):21-29.
2. Reeves WT. Particle systems: A technique for modeling a class of fuzzy objects. Transactions on Graphics, 1983; 2(2):91-108.
3. Reeves WT, Blau R. Approximate and probabilistic algorithms for shading and rendering structured particle systems. ACM/SIGGRAPH Computer Graphics, 1985; 19(3):313-322.
4. Kajiya JT. Ray tracing volume densities. ACM/SIGGRAPH Computer Graphics, 1984; 18(3):165-174.
5. Perlin K. An image synthesizer. ACM/SIGGRAPH Computer Graphics, 1985; 19(3):287-296.
6. Perlin K, Hoffert E. Hypertexture. ACM/SIGGRAPH Computer Graphics, 1989; 27(3):57-64.
7. Gardner G. Visual simulation of clouds. ACM/SIGGRAPH Computer Graphics, 1985; 19(3):297-303.
8. Ebert DS and Parent RE. Rendering and animation of gaseous phenomena by combining fast volume and scanline a-buffer techniques. ACM/SIGGRAPH Computer Graphics, 1990; 24(4):357-366.
9. Stam J, Fiume E. Depicting fire and other gaseous phenomena using diffusion processes. In: Proc. SIGGRAPH '95, August 1995; 129-136.
10. Sakas G. Modeling and animating turbulent gaseous phenomena using spectral synthesis. The Visual Computer, 1993; 9(4):200-212.
11. Chiba N, Ohkawa S, Muraoka K, Miura M. Two-dimensional visual simulation of flames, smoke and the spread of fire. The Journal of Visualization and Computer Animation, 1994; 5(1):37-54.
12. Foster N. Metaxas D. Modeling the motion of a hot, turbulent gas. In: Proc. SIGGRAPH '97, August 1997; 181-188.
13. Levoy M. Display of surfaces from volume data. IEEE Computer Graphics and Applications, 1988; 8(5):29-37.

14. Drebin R, Carpenter L, Hanrahan P, Volume rendering. ACM/SIGGRAPH Computer Graphics, 1988; 22(3):65-74.

15. Lacroute P, Levoy M. Fast volume rendering using a shear-warp factorization of the viewing transformation. In: Proc. SIGGRAPH '94, July 1994; 451-458.

16. Malzbender T, Fourier volume rendering, ACM Transactions on Graphics. 1993; 12(3):233-250.

17. Shirley P, Tuchman A. A polygonal approximation to direct scalar volume rendering. ACM/SIGGRAPH Computer Graphics, 1990; 24(5):63-70.

18. Max N, Hanrahan P, Crawfis R. Area and volume coherence for efficient visualization of 3D scalar functions. ACM/SIGGRAPH Computer Graphics, 1990; 24(5):27-33.

19. Westover L. Interactive volume rendering. In: Proc. the Chapel Hill Workshop on Volume Visualization, Chapel Hill, NC, May, 1989.

20. Laur D, Hanrahan P, Hierarchical splatting: A progressive refinement algorithm. ACM/SIGGRAPH Computer Graphics, 1991; 25(4):285-288.

21. Crawfis R and Max N, Texture splats for 3D vector and scalar field visualization. In: Proc. IEEE Visualization '93, San Jose, CA, October 1993.

22. Crawfis R and Max N, Becker B. Vector field visualization. IEEE Computer Graphics and Applications, 1994:50-56

23. Mueller K, Möller T, Swan JE II, Crawfis R, Shareef N, Yagel R. Splatting errors and anti-aliasing. IEEE Transactions on Visualization and Computer Graphics, 1998; 4(2):178-191.

24. Mueller K, Huang J, Shareef N, Crawfis R. High-quality splatting on rectilinear grids with efficient culling of occluded voxels. IEEE Transactions on Visualization and Computer Graphics, 1999; 5(2):116-134.

15. Visible Human Animation

Zhongke Wu and Edmond C. Prakash

15.1 Introduction

In this chapter we address the problem of realistic modelling, deformation and rendering of human models. Our emphasis is to produce a non-traditional model that has physical features, physical deformation properties and has a wide range of applications. To achieve these goals we embark on a voxel-based human model, that has all the properties of a real-world human. The efforts have enabled us to build a prototype system, *Young_Man*, which incorporates motion authorship system into *Young*, the 3-dimensional, articulated visible human, which is used as a voxel and geometric figure model. We believe that our Young provides the visual realisation of avatars with real human features. The results are highlighted as a short movie sequence that demonstrates the feasibility of our new human modelling system.

Our objective is to accurately model interior information of heterogeneous volumetric objects for modelling and animation of physical behaviour. The test case we consider is to perform an operation on the visible human and to bring the visible human back to life. This application is new and different from the traditional use of medical data for training and understanding the inner organs of the body.

The animation of *Young_Man* involves the following major steps:

1. *Load visible human data* — the input data available is the visible human dataset [1] which is loaded into the system as a single *volume texture* (*voxture*).
2. *Clustering and discretisation* — clustering is used to separate regions of the body. An interactive discretisation of the clustered volume is done to obtain the blocks which represent each segment of the human body.
3. *Block deformation* — the visible human blocks are deformed using the Finite Element Method (FEM).
4. *Voxel texture mapping* — the original voxture is mapped to the deformed blocks during voxelisation.
5. *Render volume buffer* — this stage generates a realistic image of the visible human.
6. Repeat Step 3 for new frames.

The input visible human dataset [1] is loaded to the system as a single voxture.

An interactive discretisation of the model is carried out to obtain the blocks which represent different segments of the human body. Since it is logical to transform at the nodes/joints, the blocks have been modelled to facilitate physical motion. Step 3 is to deform the blocks based on node forces with appropriate constraints to restrict motion. For deformation we used a simplified version of FElt [2]. The critical part is to voxture-map the voxels of each original block to its deformed position. The algorithm has been successfully tested with the visible human dataset to perform simple deformations of the model. Several operations, such as lifting the torso, bending the knee, etc., have been performed. The visible human is voxture-mapped into the block representation of the human as shown in Figure 15.1. The initial block specification of the human was obtained interactively from the original sleeping posture of the dataset.

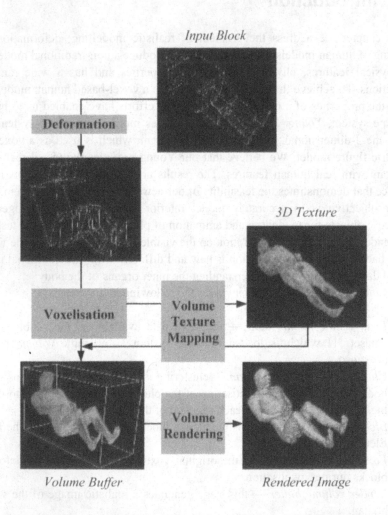

Figure 15.1. The block representation of the visible human data, and the functional modules used for generating the animation.

15.2 Volume Clustering

15.2.1 The Need and Advantages of Volume Clustering

With our visible human animation model, we faced a unique problem of separating two clusters that have overlapping voxels. This problem involves the separation of clusters that may have point, line or surface contact. In order to animate the visible human, we have to separate the hands and torso to achieve real-life movements of the hand and torso. To achieve free motion where two clusters overlap such as the hand and stomach, all the voxels that belong to the hand need to be transformed as a whole structure without disturbing the voxels that belong to the stomach. A *volume clustering* scheme is used to separate the hand from the body.

Volume clustering helps to group voxels with similar properties to enable manipulation of voxels as a single cluster. The idea is to group voxels into clusters, and to transform each cluster as a whole structure. This reduces the computation time by a considerable amount, while the interior information of the clusters is retained in voxture data. This approach has the advantages of both surface and voxel-based approaches, and it performs all the desired operations at a fraction of the original cost.

15.2.2 The Process of Volume Clustering

The first step is to analyse the voxels and to assign physical properties. Voxels are grouped together based on functional blocks. This helps to modify group of voxels with a single operation. The entire body is initially divided into several clusters.

We have used our clustering algorithm on the visible human data slices to separate the hands and torso, which are available as a single dataset. The input to this algorithm is a slice and the adjacent preceding slice; and the output is the clustered regions in a slice. As illustrated in Figure 15.2a, the input available is the pixel information. We are interested in clustering some of the pixels into the hand cluster and remaining as torso. Figure 15.2b shows the slice clustered into the torso and Figure 15.2c shows the pixels that belong to the hand cluster.

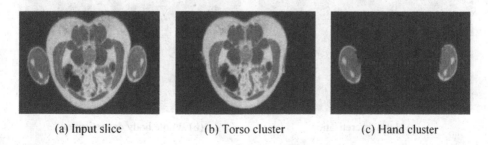

<table>
<tr><td>(a) Input slice</td><td>(b) Torso cluster</td><td>(c) Hand cluster</td></tr>
</table>

Figure 15.2. Clustering regions in a slice.

After the cluster algorithm is applied to the visible human data, we obtain a dataset with two clusters. One cluster represents all the voxels of the hands and the other all the voxels that belong to the torso. Figure 15.3a shows the stack of the original slices. Figure 15.3b shows the volume after clustering. Figure 15.3c shows the voxels that belong to the torso cluster and Figure 15.3d shows the voxels that belong to the hand cluster.

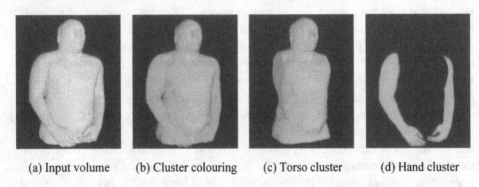

(a) Input volume   (b) Cluster colouring   (c) Torso cluster   (d) Hand cluster

Figure 15.3. Clustering regions in a volume (human hands and torso).

The next part of the process is to discretise the cluster interactively to form smaller blocks. This is now possible due to clustering. The two clusters are discretised separately to obtain a number of polyhedral blocks. These blocks are then transformed to obtain the desired motion or animation. The discretised blocks for the hand cluster is shown in Figure 15.4a and the complete human is shown in Figure 15.4b.

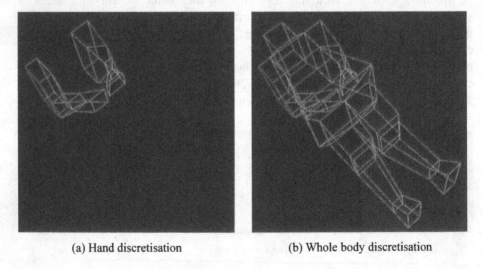

(a) Hand discretisation   (b) Whole body discretisation

Figure 15.4. Block discretisation of clustered volumes

15.3 Volume Deformation

In computer animation, the volume model of a human should be able to walk or lift his hand or grasp an object. Our goal is to develop a system that can capture deformations of very large voxel datasets, and very large inelastic as well as goal-oriented deformations. This is achieved using a goal-oriented deformation model with inverse voxture-mapping (volume texture mapping) [3].

Several interesting studies have been done and reported in literature for FEM-based elastic and inelastic deformation of 3D models for computer graphics applications [4, 5]. Recent work for deformation of voxel data has been reported in [6-10] where an attempt has been made to come up with new models for applying FEM to voxel data. However, FEM has been an established field for several decades and we decided not to reinvent the wheel.

Volume deformation starts with the identification of key voxels to specify loads and constraints. Loading is done at the block boundaries which, in turn, affects the entire block and neighbouring blocks in an FEM grid. The next step is to perform the analysis to estimate the physical deformation. Physical motion is achieved by block deformations such as folding the knee, bending the back, raising the leg for walk posture, etc. Our goal is to develop a system that can capture deformations of very large voxel datasets, with very large inelastic deformations and goal-oriented deformations.

A more detailed description of the volume deformation process has been reported in [11].

15.4 Voxture Mapping

Realistic modelling can be achieved using voxtures (volume textures). We use a voxture modelling scheme wherein we map textures onto voxels instead of pixels. This is achieved by a direct mapping from 3D voxels to a 3D texture space.

Voxture mapping is defined as the process of assigning voxtures to voxels during voxelisation. Similar to the texture look-up during rasterisation that results in a texture-mapped frame buffer, the voxture sampling during voxelisation results in a voxture-mapped volume buffer. A *footprint* is normally used to best approximate the colour of the resultant voxel.

To specify a voxture, an 8-noded polyhedron with six faces is used. In the object space, the polyhedron is represented by its vertices (x_i, y_i, z_i), $i = 1, 2, ..., 8$. The corresponding coordinates in the 3D voxture space are (u_i, v_i, w_i), $i = 1, 2, ..., 8$.

In voxture mapping, for each voxel, an inverse mapping onto the voxture space is carried out to obtain a position (u, v, w) where a voxture is sampled. The algorithm takes an input of an 8-noded block with its vertex coordinates in both object and voxture spaces. To voxelise a deformed block, for each voxel within the block, a sampling of the corresponding voxture is performed to obtain a new voxel value.

In voxture mapping, the internal information of each block is also mapped. This approach eliminates the perspective texture mapping problem. It is also view-independent. Repeating the voxture-mapping is not required for every frame for simple scaling/zoom operations, it is required only if the FEM grid or the object is deformed. Voxture mapping is performed during the modelling stage, prior to the rendering stage. The complexity of voxture mapping is dependent on the number of polyhedrons to be voxture-mapped. The main advantage is that this method results in a true 3D mapping instead of an illusory 2D mapping. It can be used in both deformation and morphing, and there is no need to perform texture look-up during rendering.

15.5 Implementation and Results

Our prototype visible human animation system, *Young_Man*, has been successfully implemented. The highlights of the system are:

- *Visible human animation.* In volume animation, the essential requirement is to specify a goal (in terms of motion and deformation) and to achieve it. For example, a sleeping visible human may be asked to wake up and walk towards a target. We use the goal-oriented deformation model to obtain key frames. An interpolation is then performed to obtain in-between frames. Parallel voxture-mapping is performed for each in-between frame. The resultant volume is subsequently sent to a parallel volume renderer for image generation.

- *Parallel volume modelling and rendering.* Two bottlenecks in visible human animation are the volume modelling and volume rendering phases. Our goal is to design a parallel algorithm for the voxture-based volume modelling and rendering of the visible human. We have developed new algorithms that exploit the full potential of SGI's shared-memory multi-processor systems. We have tested these algorithms on a multi-processor SGI Onyx. We have implemented the algorithms as shown in Figure 15.5.

- *Task distribution.* Each processor voxture-maps the cells assigned to it. The cells may vary in size. The voxture-mapping time of a cell depends on its orientation and size. A static distribution allocates the N cells to P processors. Each processor thus voxture-maps N/P cells. An image space partitioning is used so that the pixels in the final image can be distributed across processors. Each pixel can be computed independent of the other pixels in the final image. Our goal is to use this parallel algorithm to accelerate the rendering of visible human.

  Visible human walk. This has enabled us to generate animated sequences of the visible human with simple human actions. One of the movies generated shows the sleeping human waking up to a standing position. Snapshots of the movie are shown in Figure 15.6. Another makes the human walk, and it involves a coordinated hand and leg motion. Snapshots of that movie are shown in Figure 15.7.

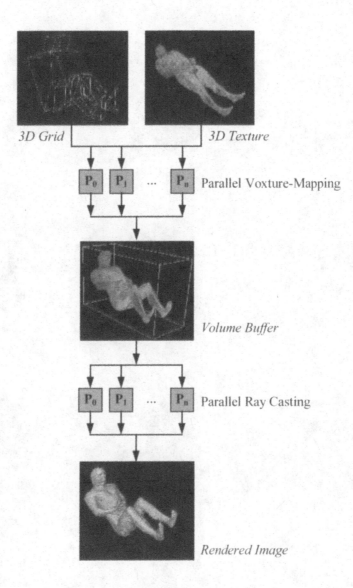

3D Grid   3D Texture

P_0 P_1 ... P_n Parallel Voxture-Mapping

Volume Buffer

P_0 P_1 ... P_n Parallel Ray Casting

Rendered Image

Figure 15.5. Parallel voxture mapping and volume ray casting.

15.6 Conclusion and Future Work

We have created a prototype human modelling system that can represent, deform and realistically animate human actors in virtual environments. This is achieved by clustering, volume deformation, parallel voxture mapping, and parallel ray casting.

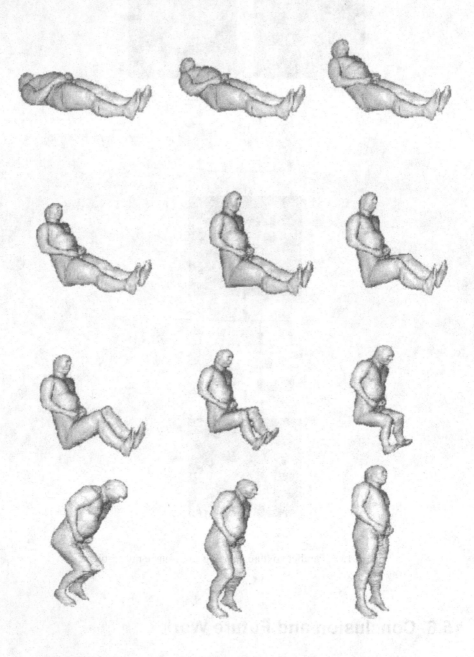

Figure 15.6. Human animation from a sleeping posture to a standing position.

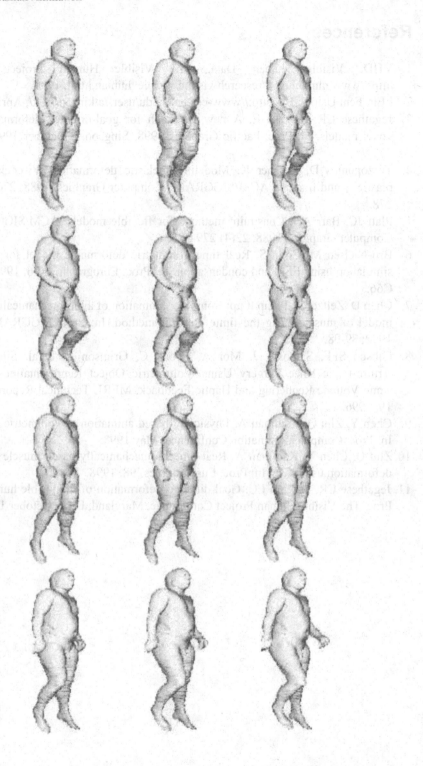

Figure 15.7. An animation sequence of a walk (with hand and leg movements).

References

1. VHD. Visible Human Data. The Visible Human Project, NIH. http://www.nlm.nih.gov/research/visible/visible_human.html, 1999.
2. FElt. Fem Using FElt. http://www-cse.ucsd.edu/users/atkinson/FElt/, April 1997.
3. Jegathese CR, Prakash E. A new approach for goal-oriented deformation of voxel models. In: Proc. Pacific Graphics 1998, Singapore, October 1998; 214-215.
4. Terzopoulos D, Fleisher K. Modeling inelastic deformation: Viscoelasticity, plasticity and fracture. ACM/SIGGRAPH Computer Graphics, 1988; 22(4):269-278.
5. Platt JC, Barr AH. Constraint methods for flexible models. ACM/SIGGRAPH Computer Graphics, 1988; 22(4):279-288.
6. Bro-Nielsen M, Cotin S. Real time volumetric deformable model for surgery simulation using FEM and condensation. In: Proc. Eurographics '96, 1996; C57-C66.
7. Chen D, Zeltzer D. Pump it up: Computer animation of a bio-mechanically based model of muscle using the finite element method. In: Proc. SIGGRAPH '92, 1992; 89-98.
8. Gibson SFF, Samosky J, Mor A, Fyock C, Grimson E, et al. Simulating Arthroscopic Knee Surgery Using Volumetric Object Representations, Real-Time Volume Rendering and Haptic Feedback. MERL Technical Report TR96-19, 1996.
9. Chen Y, Zhu Q, Kaufman A. Physically-based animation of volumetric objects. In: Proc. Computer Animation Conference, May 1998.
10. Zhu Q, Chen Y, Kaufman A. Real-time biomechanically-based muscle volume deformation using fem. In: Proc. Eurographics '98, 1998.
11. Jegathese CR, Prakash EC. Goal-directed deformation of the visible human. In: Proc. The Visible Human Project Conference, Maryland, USA, October 1998.

16. Realistic Volume Animation with Alias

Nikhil Gagvani and Deborah Silver

16.1 Introduction

Volume graphics has emerged from the field of volume visualisation. While the goal of visualisation has been to present real data (or data from simulations of real phenomena) in a visual form for better understanding, graphics has been concerned with producing real-looking images, mostly by synthetic means. Volume graphics presents a meeting point for the two in that it allows the manipulation and interaction of real data and synthetic objects. Volumetric animation offers some advantages over polygonal animation. Translucency and atmospheric effects can be achieved without special rendering considerations. Volumetric models can be broken into pieces without the need for creating new models for each piece. Computer graphics animation is the integration of several streams like modelling, manipulation and rendering and, of course, story-telling and visual art. In order to incorporate volume objects into an animation, it is essential to address all of these aspects. There has been a lot of work on volume rendering in the visualisation community, but not as much attention has been paid to modelling, manipulation and deformation.

Since volume visualisation deals with real-world data, one may argue that this same data can be used as the model for producing an animation which completely obviates the modelling step. An example would be to use the Visible Human [1] and make it walk (Chapter 15). Current volume modelling techniques include voxelisation of polygonal models as described in Chapter 7 and also in [2, 3]. Implicit modelling [4] is another way to create volumetric models.

Prior work on volume manipulation has used free-form or physically-based deformation. The computations involved spring-mass models, continuum models [5] and finite-element methods [6]. Gibson has suggested the 3D Chain Mail algorithm [7] for propagating deformations rapidly through a volume. These techniques are sophisticated since they involve the specification of material properties and setting up mathematical equations. Kurzion and Yagel [8] have proposed a method to deform the rays during the rendering phase using ray deflectors. The choice of ray deflectors for a desired target motion is not easy in their method. The runtime is proportional to the number of deflectors, which can be large for complex motions. For volume animation to become popular, manipulation techniques have to be intuitive and easily usable by animators.

In [9], we described a method to animate volumetric objects using a *Skeleton-Tree*. The method works by first thinning the volume using a parameter controlled volume thinning algorithm [10] and then connecting the thinned voxels into a skeleton-tree. The skeleton-tree is a compact shape descriptor which is easier to manipulate compared to the entire volume. The Distance Transform, which is the shortest distance from a skeletal voxel to the object boundary is stored and used to reconstruct the object. The deformed object can thus be reconstructed from the deformed skeleton-tree. In this chapter, we demonstrate the adaptability of the skeleton-tree method to commercial animation tools from Alias|Wavefront. We also describe the entire process of creating a complete animation starting from a volume model, as well as the interactions necessary between the various components in our animation pipeline.

16.2 Character Animation in Alias

Tools from Alias|Wavefront like Alias *PowerAnimator*[1] and *Maya*[1] are based on key-frame animation. Important or "key" scenes are drawn by the animator and the intervening scenes (frames) are automatically drawn by the program. Character animation is achieved via skeleton-based shape deformation tools. An animation-skeleton in Maya consists of *joints* connected by *bones*. The animation-skeleton is manipulated to cause corresponding movements of the model. Currently, the animation-skeleton has to be manually defined by the animator. The choice and placement of the animation-skeleton affects the range and accuracy of movements that can be performed. Since the skeleton is synthetically created by the animator, surface geometry needs to be bound to the joints and bones in order for it to deform as the skeleton deforms. For this purpose, surface vertices are divided into sets called *skin point* sets according to the proximity of a vertex to a joint. Movement of a skin point set is bound by default to that of the nearest joint. Depending on the pose of the geometry and skeleton during the binding process, a few skin points could join an inappropriate set which can cause the model to break during animation. Inappropriate points have to be moved to the appropriate set which is a laborious task.

In addition, special tools called *inverse kinematics* (IK) handles are added to the animation-skeleton. Inverse kinematics [11] refers to the automatic computation of joint angles based upon the movement of the lowest joint in a skeletal chain. It allows for goal-directed pose selection. An IK handle defined between the shoulder and hand automatically computes the joint angles at the shoulder and elbow when the hand is moved to a target. Constraints defined on joint rotations ensure realistic motion. Non-rigid surface deformations like muscle bulges are achieved by other special deformation tools called *flexors*. Various types of flexors can be defined for different actions such as knee bends and upper arm flexing. Flexors change the surface geometry as a function of joint movement. Setting up an animation-skeleton,

---

[1] PowerAnimator and Maya are trademarks of Alias|Wavefront.

its skin point sets and defining flexors requires a good amount of training and feel, primarily because the animation-skeleton is synthetically constructed and has no direct binding to surface geometry. Other commercial tools employ similar skeleton-based techniques for animation.

16.3 Skeleton-Tree Volume Animation

In [9], we described a method to deform a volume model using a skeleton-tree. The method consists of four steps described in the following subsections.

16.3.1 Volume Thinning

The volume is thinned using a parameter-controlled skeletonisation algorithm [12]. The algorithm takes a segmented volume as input and extracts a thinned subset called the skeleton. Note that this skeleton consists of voxels, and is different from the animation-skeleton used in Maya. A thinness parameter (TP), which is a floating-point value, is used to select voxels that belong to the skeleton; higher values of TP yield a thinner skeleton. Thinning consists of three passes over the "1" voxels (object voxels). The first two passes compute the Distance Transform of object voxels based on a weighted $<3,4,5>$ distance metric. For a voxel, we define F-neighbours (face neighbours) to be its 6-connected neighbours. E-neighbours (edge) are defined as the 18-neighbours which are not F-neighbours, and V-neighbours (vertex) are the 26-neighbours which are neither F-neighbours nor E-neighbours. The volume object is encoded in an octree [13] for space efficiency. The first pass marks object voxels which have any neighbouring voxel which is zero valued (background). A distance transform of 3, 4 or 5 is assigned for the case where the neighbouring background voxel is an F-, E- or V-neighbour respectively. These marked voxels are inserted into a boundary list. The second pass marks the neighbours of voxels in the boundary list adding 3, 4 or 5 to the distance transform for the appropriate type of neighbouring voxel. A new boundary list is created with the newly-marked voxels, and their neighbours are marked. This *boundary-peeling* process continues recursively till no voxels are left unmarked.

Once the distance transform has been computed, the final pass marks skeletal voxels. A thinness test is performed at every object voxel which measures its importance for reconstruction as compared with its neighbouring voxels. The test can be summarised in the following condition:

if $MNT_p < DT_p - TP$, add voxel p to the skeleton.

In the above inequality, DT_p is the distance transform computed at voxel p, MNT_p is the mean value of the distance transforms of its 26-neighbours and TP is the user selected thinness parameter. Typical values of TP lie between 1.0 (thicker) and 3.0 (thinner). Since the test measures the local importance of a voxel for reconstruction, thin features can be preserved if the thinness value is low. Although there is no direct control over the target number of voxels in the thinned volume, a suitable choice can be made in two to three iterations by visual inspection of the thinned output. The algorithm takes only a couple of minutes to thin a volume with about 100,000 object voxels on a single processor SGI Octane workstation.

16.3.2 The Skeleton-Tree

Volume thinning yields a set of voxels that are generally not connected. Connectivity of voxels is not necessary for reconstruction, but is useful because it lends structure to the object for easy manipulation. Since our goal is to create a volumetric approximation to the animation-skeleton, we would like to connect skeletal voxels into a tree-like hierarchical structure suitable for articulation. The voxels are first connected to form a weighted undirected graph such that every voxel is a vertex in the graph, and lines between voxels constitute edges of the graph. An edge is inserted between two voxels if they are less than a threshold distance apart and if voxels along the edge lie completely within the original volume object. Edge weights are computed as a weighted mean of the difference in distance transform values and the spatial distance between the voxels being connected. The computation of edge weights is summarised in the equation below:

$$EW_{v_1 \leftrightarrow v_2} = \alpha \cdot DIST_{v_1 \leftrightarrow v_2} + (1-\alpha) \cdot \left\| DT_{v_1} - DT_{v_2} \right\|, \quad 0 \leq \alpha \leq 1$$

where $EW_{v_1 \leftrightarrow v_2}$ is the weight of the edge between voxels v_1 and v_2, $DIST_{v_1 \leftrightarrow v_2}$ is the spatial distance between the voxels and $DT_{v_1} - DT_{v_2}$ is the difference in their distance transform values. This equation is based on the fact that voxels which are centred will have similar distance transforms and ought to be connected. The spanning tree of a graph G is a connected subgraph with no cycles which has the same set of vertices as G. The minimum spanning tree (MST) of a weighted graph is the spanning tree whose edges sum to minimum weight. Therefore, the minimum spanning tree [14] of the above graph is a connected, acyclic representation of the skeletal voxels. We call this representation the skeleton-tree.

16.3.3 Deformation of the Skeleton-Tree

Rigid body deformation of a volume object can be achieved by rotation of parts of its skeleton-tree about a pivot or by translation. Elastic and surface deformations are possible by changing the distance transform values of voxels in the skeleton-tree. Increasing the distance transform values causes the surface to bulge while decreasing the values causes it to contract. The object can also be broken by disconnecting the skeleton-tree. No special modelling is required for the broken components since the reconstruction step (described below) reconstructs the interior of the volume. The next section describes skeleton-tree deformation using Maya, a commercial animation package.

16.3.4 Reconstruction

The deformed volume object is reconstructed from the deformed skeleton-tree. Each voxel is the centre of a discrete sphere of radius equal to the distance transform at that voxel. The spheres for all voxels in the deformed skeleton-tree are filled to reconstruct the deformed object. The quality of reconstruction depends on the number of voxels in the skeleton-tree. The thinning algorithm only chooses voxels which are most important for the overall shape of the object at a given thinness value; therefore reconstruction of fine surface features like creases requires a thicker skeleton-tree. This is not a limitation because a thick skeleton-tree for accurate reconstruction has just 5% of the voxels in the original object.

Figure 16.1 shows an example of the skeleton-tree and the corresponding reconstruction for two different thinness values. A volumetric dragon is shown on the left. The data is in a 250x150x100 voxel grid and has 171041 object voxels. The skeleton-tree and its reconstruction for thinness 1.8 are shown in the top row. This skeleton tree has 1247 voxels, less than 1% of the original. The quality of reconstruction is fairly good. The bottom row shows the effect of excessive thinning using a thinness of 2.1. Note that the reconstruction quality is not as good as with a thinness of 1.8. The skeleton-tree for thinness 2.1 has only 539 voxels, which is not sufficient for good reconstruction.

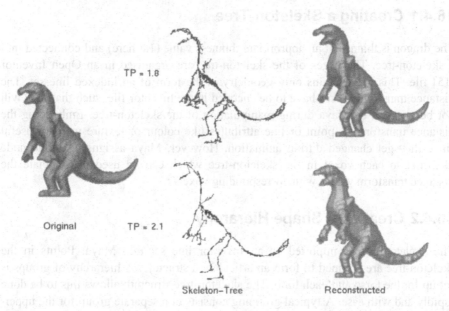

Figure 16.1. A volumetric dragon is thinned using two different thinness values, 1.8 and 2.1.The original volume rendered dragon is shown on the left. The top row shows the skeleton-tree with a thinness of 1.8 and its reconstructed volume; thinness 2.1 is shown in the bottom row. The original dragon has 171041 voxels, the 1.8 skeleton-tree has 1247 voxels and the 2.1 skeleton-tree has 539 voxels.

Using a volumetric skeleton-tree gets rid of much of the manual work required in constructing and binding a skeletal structure in an animation package. Since the voxels in the skeleton-tree are already centred within the original object, the skeleton in the animation tool can be defined along these voxels. In fact, the voxels and edges could be used directly as the animation skeleton in many cases. Errors in proximity based binding of skin point sets to joints are thus eliminated. Furthermore, bulges and creases possible with flexors in Maya can be achieved by changing the distance transform values of skeletal points.

16.4 Volumetric Skeleton Manipulation in Maya

We use Maya to animate the skeleton-tree. A skeleton-tree consists of the x, y and z coordinates along with the distance transform values of skeletal voxels. The distance transform values are critical for reconstruction, and must be preserved through all the manipulations done in Maya. Essentially, the task of volume animation has been reduced to the manipulation of points. These points are connected in a manner that approximates the shape of the original object. The volumetric dragon from Figure 16.1 is used as an example to illustrate the process.

16.4.1 Creating a Skeleton-Tree

The dragon is thinned at an appropriate thinness value (1.8 here) and connected into a skeleton-tree. The edges of the skeleton-tree are organised in an Open Inventor [15] file. This file contains only geometry in the form of an indexed line set. The distance transform values have to be encoded in the Inventor file, such that they will not be changed by Maya during manipulation of the skeleton-tree. Embedding the distance transform as point or line attributes like colour or texture was not useful since they get changed during animation. However, Maya assigns a unique node identifier to each voxel in the skeleton-tree which can be used to associate the distance transform values with corresponding voxels.

16.4.2 Creating a Shape Hierarchy

The skeleton-tree is imported as an Inventor line set into Maya. Points in the skeleton-tree are grouped to form an articulation structure. A hierarchy of groups is set up for the torso and each limb. The skeleton-tree structure allows this to be done rapidly and with ease. A typical grouping consists of a separate group for the upper-arm, lower-arm, hand, upper-jaw and lower-jaw. The points in the skeleton-tree are treated by Maya as deformable geometry. Figure 16.2 shows a snapshot of the groups in the arm and the corresponding hierarchy graph in Maya.

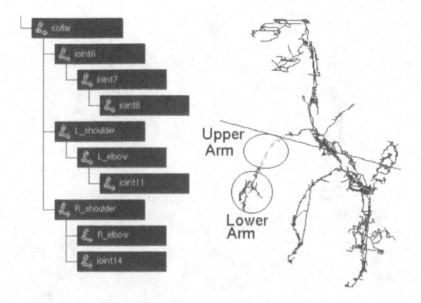

Figure 16.2. Creating a group hierarchy. Pieces of the skeleton-tree are combined into groups in a hierarchical manner. These groups correspond exactly to the animation-skeleton defined in Maya.

16.4.3 Defining an Animation-Skeleton

Maya still requires the user to define an animation-skeleton to be able to do inverse kinematics. The animation-skeleton is the internal structure that Maya uses to enforce hierarchical deformation. This is a trivial task since the animation-skeleton lies along the edges of the skeleton-tree. If the number of voxels in the skeleton-tree is small, a joint can be set up at every voxel. However, for most objects, the skeleton-tree has a few hundred voxels. Joint nodes in this case are set up to correspond to voxels at the end of limb groups defined in the previous step. Binding voxels to joints is also easy. No proximity-based binding to closest joints is required. Every limb group is bound to the joint above it and rotates rigidly about the joint. Inverse kinematics handles are attached between joints and rotational constraints are defined for the intervening joints. The complete skeleton hierarchy for the volumetric dragon is shown in Figure 16.3. Joints are shown as circles and the bones of the animation-skeleton are shown as triangles. There is a triangle for each group defined in the articulation structure. A joint is placed at the interface between two groups. IK handles between joints are indicated by diagonal lines as shown in the magnified view. When two joints are connected by an IK handle, the angles for the joints in-between are automatically computed based on constraints. Once the IK handle is set up, the tip of a limb can be moved to a target location which causes the entire limb to move. Smooth, natural motion can be achieved by appropriate choice of constraints. Key frames are specified for end deformations; Maya automatically computes the frames in-between.

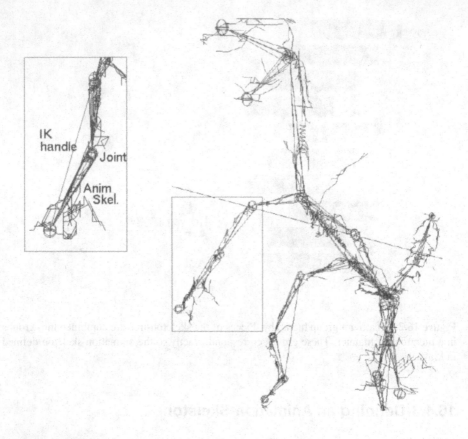

Figure 16.3. Skeleton geometry in Maya. Joints in the animation-skeleton are shown by circles; the triangles are limbs of the animation-skeleton. IK handles are shown as diagonal lines between joints.

16.4.4 Reconstruction and Rendering

The deformed skeleton-tree for each frame of the animated dragon is exported in Inventor format. Distance transform values have to be linked back to their corresponding voxels which now have different coordinates. The first frame exported from Maya has no deformations, therefore the voxels have their original coordinate values. This frame is used as a reference to construct a table of node IDs and their corresponding coordinates and distance transform values. For all successive frames, the node ID is used to recover the distance transform at every voxel. This process is illustrated in Figure 16.4. The frames with the deformed dragon can now be reconstructed by filling the spheres centred at the skeleton-tree voxels. Each reconstructed frame is then volume rendered. Playing back the volume rendered frames produces an entire, smoothly-animated sequence of the dragon moving.

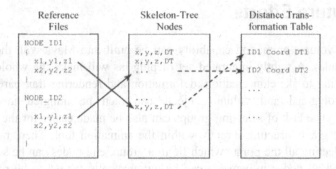

Figure 16.4. Look-up table. This is used to recover distance transform values from the deformed skeleton-tree.

16.5 Results

A complete animation was created for the dragon. A few frames of the animation are shown in Figure 16.5. The entire animation with 50 frames was completed by a student animator in less than five hours. The dragon along with a volumetric *Statue of Liberty* is animated in an MPEG movie. Notice that the statue is broken in the movie without any special modelling considerations. A similar volume animation was done with the human trachea. Figure 16.6 shows the main stem of the trachea moving.

Figure 16.5. Frames from an animation of the volumetric dragon.

Figure 16.6. Frames from an animation of the human trachea.

16.6 Future Efforts

A complete volume animation capability can be built into Maya with the help of plug-in modules. A tightly-integrated set of plug-ins will make the whole process from modelling to skeleton creation, deformation and rendering transparent to the animator. Polygonal and volume objects can then be mingled in such an environment. The task of selecting groups can also be made easier for the animator by using the graph structure directly within the animation tool. Then, rather than manually selecting all the points which lie in a group, end nodes can be selected in the graph and all nodes in-between can be automatically tagged to be part of the group. The hierarchy creation process can thus be made much easier by using the graph abstraction. The process of selecting a good skeleton can also be automated. For a selected thinness value, a reconstruction and connectivity test can be done to verify that the skeleton is not too thin.

Acknowledgement

The authors wish to thank Wesley Townsend, the Vizlab Media Assistant for creating the animations. Wesley also provided invaluable input on animation tools and techniques. The animation of the trachea was done by Sandra Cheng. The first author also acknowledges support from Sarnoff Corporation to carry out this work.

References

1. National Library of Medicine. The Visible Human Project. URL: http://www.nlm.nih.gov/research/visible/visible_human.html.
2. Huang J, Yagel R, Filippov V. Accurate method for the voxelization of planar objects. In: Proc. IEEE Symposium on Volume Visualization, October 1998.
3. Sramek M, Kaufman A. Object voxelization by filtering. In: Proc. IEEE Symposium on Volume Visualization, October 1998.
4. Bloomenthal J, Bajaj C, Blinn J, Cani-Gascuel M-P, Rockwood A, Wyvill B, et al. Introduction to Implicit Surfaces, Morgan Kaufman Publishers, 1997.
5. Gibson SF, Mirtich B. A Survey of Deformable Modeling in Computer Graphics. Technical Report TR97-19, MERL, November 1997. URL: http://www.merl.com/reports/TR97-19/TR97-19.ps.gz.
6. Chen Y, Zhu Q, Kaufman A. Physically-based Animation of Volumetric Objects. Technical Report TR-CVC-980209, SUNY Stony Brook, 1998. URL: http://www.cs.sunysb.edu/~vislab/projects/deform/Papers/animation.ps.
7. Gibson SF. 3D Chain Mail : A fast algorithm for deforming volumetric objects. In: Proc. Symposium on Interactive 3D Graphics, April 1997.
8. Kurzion Y, Yagel R. Space deformation using ray deflectors. In: Proc. 6th Eurographics Workshop on Rendering, 1995; 21-32.
9. Gagvani N, Kenchammana-Hosekote D, Silver D. Volume animation using the

skeleton tree. In: Proc. IEEE Symposium on Volume Visualization, October 1998.

10. Gagvani N, Silver D. Parameter Controlled Skeletonization of Three Dimensional Objects. Technical Report TR-216, CAIP Center, Rutgers University, Piscataway, New Jersey, June 1997. URL: http://www.caip. rutgers.edu/~gagvani/skel/visc.ps.gz.

11. Korein J, Badler N. Techniques for generating the goal directed motion of articulated structures. IEEE Computer Graphics and Applications, 1982; 2(9):71-81.

12. Gagvani N. Skeletons and Volume Thinning in Visualization. MS Thesis, Dept. of Electrical and Computer Engineering, Rutgers University, New Brunswick, New Jersey, October 1997.

13. Samet H. The Design and Analysis of Spatial Data Structures. Addison Wesley Publishing Company, Reading, Massachusetts, 1989.

14. Cormen TH, Leiserson CE, Rivest RL. Introduction to Algorithms. MIT Press and McGraw-Hill Book Company, 6th Edition, 1992.

15. Wernecke J. The Inventor Mentor. Addison Wesley Publishing Company, 1994.

PART VI

PARALLEL AND DISTRIBUTED ENVIRONMENTS

17. Multi-Resolutional Parallel Isosurface Extraction based on Tetrahedral Bisection

Thomas Gerstner and Martin Rumpf

17.1 Introduction

A variety of multi-resolution visualisation methods have been designed to serve as tools for interactive visualisation of large datasets. The local resolution of the generated visual objects, such as isosurfaces, is thereby steered by error indicators which measure the error due to a locally coarser approximation of the data. On one hand, post-processing methods can be applied to already extracted surfaces and can turn them into multi-resolutional objects, which can then be interactively inspected [1-4]. On the other hand, we can also adaptively extract the considered isosurfaces from the 3D dataset. Thereby, starting at a coarse approximation of the data, we recursively add details in areas where some error indicator points out a local error with respect to the exact data values. If the error is below a user prescribed threshold, the algorithm locally stops the successive refinement and extracts the surface on the current level. Different approaches have been presented to solve the outstanding continuity problem, i.e., to avoid cracks in the adaptive isosurfaces. In the Delaunay approach by Cignoni et al. [5] and the nested mesh method by Grosso et al. [6], the successive remeshing during the refinement guarantees the continuity. On the other hand, Shekhar et al. [7] rule out hanging nodes by inserting additional points on faces with a transition from finer to coarser elements due to an adaptive stopping criterion.

In this chapter, we will consider a method which is based on tetrahedral grids generated by bisection. These meshes are widespread and, in particular, they are commonly used in the field of adaptive numerical methods [8]. We will especially focus on the recursive bisection [9] of originally hexahedral grids. Compared to an octree approach the tetrahedral strategy has several advantages:

- Adaptive octree strategies require some elaborated matching of local isosurfaces at transition faces [7] between cubes of different resolution. Even if a continuous adaptive projection [10] is generated, the bilinearity on faces requires special care [11]. In the tetrahedral frame such difficulties are ruled out.
- A mesh generated by tetrahedral bisection consists of typically three times more grid levels than a standard octree with the same data resolution. Therefore, the granularity of adaptive grids is more flexible.

- Furthermore, the multi-level algorithm attains a compact form. The operations to be performed in each refinement step are very simple.
- Tetrahedral bisection is not restricted to structured grid data. Although we focus on this case here, an essential advantage of tetrahedral grids is their potential in complex domain approximation. By pushing refinement nodes onto the actual curved boundary, such grids may also be generated by recursive bisection, starting with a coarse initial grid.

Our approach, presented in this chapter, can be seen as a special case and a very efficient implementation of a universal concept of multi-resolutional visualisation on arbitrary nested grids [10-13]. The core of our approach is identical to the method presented by Zhou et al. [14]. It can be regarded as a 3D generalisation of the techniques presented by Livnat et al. [15] and in [16]. Besides a discussion of different types of error measurement, we will focus on improving the performance of the algorithm and its memory requirements. This invokes hash table techniques for smooth shading and the application of error indicators to evaluate data bounds on coarse grid tetrahedra which prevents us from storing min/max values. Furthermore, gauss map estimation enables us to implement a multi-level backface culling.

Finally, we will explain a load balancing concept on multi-processor graphics workstations, which leads to near optimal speed-up concerning the triangle generation rates. High resolution interactive visualisation of very large datasets thus becomes a feasible option. To give an example, the presented algorithm is able to extract adaptive isosurfaces on large grids with about 800k triangles per second on a 4 processor SGI R10000 with infinite reality graphics.

17.2 Outline of the Adaptive Algorithm

Let us consider a family of nested, conforming, tetrahedral meshes $\left\{T^l\right\}_{0 \leq l \leq l_{\max}}$.
The tetrahedra are assumed to be refined by recursive bisection. For a tetrahedron T, the midpoint of a predestined edge $e_{\mathrm{ref}}(T)$ is thereby picked up as a new node $x_{\mathrm{ref}}(T)$, and the tetrahedron is cut at the face $F_{\mathrm{ref}}(T)$ spanned by $x_{\mathrm{ref}}(T)$ and the two nodes of T opposite to $e_{\mathrm{ref}}(T)$ into two child tetrahedra $C(T) = \left\{T_C^1, T_C^2\right\}$ (Figure 17.1). In the considered applications we restrict ourselves to a specific case of such tetrahedral meshes, i.e. originally regular hexahedral grids with n^3 nodes with $n = 2^k + 1$. These regular grids are only procedurally converted to a hierarchy of tetrahedral bisection grids, the nodes of which coincide with the regular grid nodes [8, 17]. A simple alternating scheme for the refinement edge e_{ref} guarantees the conformity of the resulting grids. Straightforward index arithmetic enables us to identify data values $U(x)$ at the nodes x of the tetrahedra in a recursive grid traversal. Let U^l denote the piecewise linear function on T^l uniquely described by the data values on the corresponding nodes.

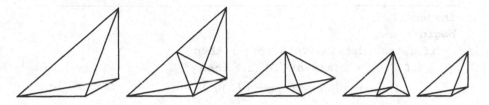

Figure 17.1. Recursive decomposition of a tetrahedron.

Multi-resolutional visualisation methods can now be implemented on the hierarchy of tetrahedral grids. Here we restrict ourselves to isosurface extraction. Other visualisation methods such as the generation of slices, or a projective volume rendering can be implemented analogously. In the latter case, in general the required back-to-front processing of tetrahedra is straightforward. The ordering of children in the recursive grid traversal solely depends on the viewing direction and the type of bisection. It can be determined in advance.

The adaptive isosurface algorithm is based on a depth-first traversal of the grid hierarchy. On every tetrahedron we check for a stopping criterion. If it is true we stop and extract the local isosurface. Otherwise, we recursively proceed onto the child set $C(T)$. If we stop on a specific tetrahedron T and refine another tetrahedron $\tilde{T}$ which shares the refinement edge with T, i.e. $e_{ref}(T) = e_{ref}(\tilde{T})$, an inconsistency occurs at the hanging node x_{ref}. This leads to cracks in the isosurface. In the case of general nested grids, we can apply adaptive projection operators to guarantee consistency. A detailed discussion on this issue can be found in [12]. Here we simply have to ensure that, whenever a tetrahedron is refined, all tetrahedra sharing its refinement edge are refined as well. This can be achieved by defining error indicators $\eta(x)$ on the grid nodes and choosing a stopping criterion $\eta(x_{ref}(T)) < \varepsilon$ for some user prescribed threshold value ε. For an arbitrary error, it still might happen that, although $\eta(x_{ref}(T)) < \varepsilon$, $\eta(x_{ref}(\hat{T})) \geq \varepsilon$ on some descendant $\hat{T}$, whose refinement point $x_{ref}(\hat{T})$ is located on the boundary of T. Therefore, the adjacent tetrahedron will possibly be refined, and an inconsistency will occur again. To avoid this we assume the following *saturation condition* on the error indicators [10]:

$$\eta(x_{ref}(T)) > \eta\left(x_{ref}\left(T_C^i\right)\right) \quad \text{for all } T \in T^l \text{ with } l < l_{max} \text{ and } T_C^i \in C(T).$$

An error indicator η is called admissible if it fulfils the saturation condition. Otherwise it can easily be adjusted in a pre-roll step. In a bottom-up traversal of the hierarchy, we construct the saturated indicator as the smallest indicator larger than the original indicator respecting the saturation condition. Let us emphasise that a depth-first traversal of the hierarchy in the adjustment procedure would not be sufficient.

Now we are able to formulate the adaptive algorithm. The depth-first traversal of the grid hierarchy can be sketched in pseudo code as follows:

```
Inspect (T)
begin
    if TetrahedronIsOfInterest (T) then
        if C(T) ≠ Ø and η(x_ref) ≥ ε then
            Inspect ( T_C^1 ); Inspect ( T_C^2 );
        else
            Extract (T);
        end if-else;
end.
```

The function `TetrahedronIsOfInterest()` checks whether the tetrahedron is a candidate for the intersection with an isosurface or not. In our case, it is checked if the current isovalue is contained in a certain data interval. An implementation of such a routine considering the already available error indicator values is described in Section 17.3.

17.3 Error Measurement

The visual impression and a sufficient resolution of the numerical data in the visualisation process is closely related to the specific type of error measurement applied in the adaptive traversal of the tree structure. In our case, error indicators will be defined on grid nodes. All nodes, except those on the coarsest level, are refinement nodes $x_{ref}(T)$ on a refinement edge $e_{ref}(T)$ with respect to a tetrahedron T. Therefore, an indicator value $\eta(x)$ measures the error on all the tetrahedra which share the corresponding edge. In what follows we will present different types of error indicators and explain some of their benefits.

Instead of considering the true data values $U(x)$ at the grid nodes, we can consider the offset values $U_\delta(x)$ corresponding to the approximation on the next coarser level. They are related to the original data values by the recursive formula:

$$U\left(x_{ref}(T)\right) = \frac{U(x_1) + U(x_2)}{2} + U_\delta\left(x_{ref}(T)\right)$$

where x_1 and x_2 are the end points of the edge $e_{ref}(T)$. For smooth data, e.g. $U(x) = u(x)$ for all nodes x with $u \in C^2$, $|U_\delta(x_{ref}(T))| = O(\mathrm{diam}(T)^2)$ which implies the saturation condition holds asymptotically on grids T^l for l sufficiently large. Let us emphasise that the handling of the U_δ values would therefore allow an economical δ-compression of the data and the original values can easily be retrieved during the recursive tree traversal. Now, we define the hierarchical error indicator $\eta_H(x) := |U_\delta(x)|$. As before, it is admissible if the saturation condition is fulfilled. The resulting isosurfaces are shown in Figures 17.2 and 17.3. Polygon and frame rates are listed in Table 17.1. Instead of isosurfaces we can analogously extract arbitrary slices and visualise data adaptively on these slices (Figure 17.4).

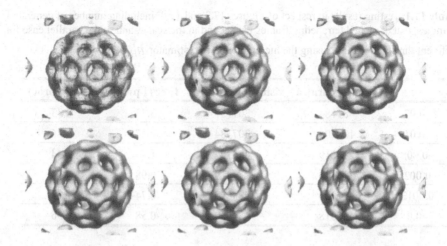

Figure 17.2. Flat (top row) and smooth (bottom row) shaded adaptive isosurfaces are extracted from a 129^3 sized Bucky Ball dataset. We consider the hierarchical error indicator for threshold values $\varepsilon = 0.02, 0.005, 0.0$, where 80K, 211K and 590K triangles are generated respectively.

Figure 17.3. Three isosurfaces are extracted from a $220 \times 220 \times 100$ (resampled to 129^3) regular CFD dataset, the velocity of a turbulent flow field above a white dwarf star (courtesy of A. Kercek, MPA Garching) for $\varepsilon = 0.01$ and isovalues 0.5, 1.5 and 2.5. The horizontal structure corresponds to the surface of the star.

Table 17.1. Testing results in respect of Figures 17.2 and 17.3, including number of generated triangles, that of visited tetrahedra, frames per second in the scalar, and in the parallel case for different threshold values ε using the hierarchical error estimator η_H^+.

ε	triangles drawn	visited tetrahedra	f/sec (1 proc)	f/sec (4 proc)
0.02	81184	201757	3.45	8.33
0.01	128709	307384	2.27	5.26
0.005	211219	487107	1.43	3.44
0.0025	315440	727419	0.98	2.43
0.00125	439230	984029	0.74	1.78
0.0	590018	1259669	0.58	1.36

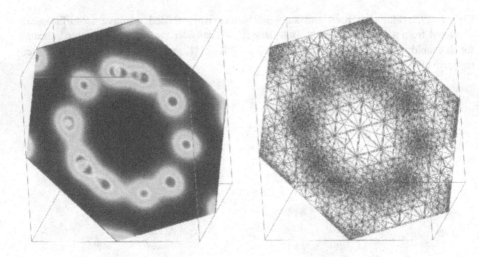

Figure 17.4. A colour shading on slices (left) and the drawing of intersection lines on faces of the corresponding adaptively extracted tetrahedra (right) is shown for the Bucky Ball dataset. For a threshold value of $\varepsilon = 0.005$ about 16 k triangles are shaded.

As an alternative to the above saturation procedure we can compute a robust upper bound for the offset values on elements by the recursive formula:

$$\eta_H^+(x) := \eta_H(x) + \max_{T_C^i \in C(T)} \left| \eta_H^+\left(x_{\mathrm{ref}}\left(T_C^i\right)\right)\right| \tag{17.1}$$

where $\eta_H^+(x) := \eta_H(x)$ for nodes appearing on the second finest grid level. These values can also be used to perform the necessary intersection test during the hierarchical extraction of an isosurface. We thereby avoid the expensive storing of min/max-values as discussed in [17].

With a focus on the geometric shape of an isosurface, we will now consider a curvature estimation. We ask for a discrete curvature quantity that locally measures the quality of the data approximation from the viewpoint of the visual appearance [11, 10]. In isosurface images consisting of linear patches we can easily recognise folds on the surface. In each tetrahedron the data gradient ∇U^l is always perpendicular to an isosurface. Therefore, at any face F, the normal component of the jump of the normalised gradient, denoted by:

$$\left[\frac{\nabla U^l}{\left|\nabla U^l\right|}\right]_F ,$$

locally measures the fold in the data function (Figure 17.5). Here, the jump operator $[\cdot]_F$ is defined as the difference of the argument on both sides of the face. This jump obviously serves as a well-founded graphical error criterion, and motivates the following definition of an error indicator for a refinement node $x_{\text{ref}}(T)$ with $T \in T'$:

$$\eta_N\left(x_{\text{ref}}(T)\right) := \left[\frac{\nabla U^l}{\left|\nabla U^l\right|}\right]_{F_{\text{ref}}(T)}$$

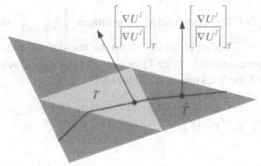

Figure 17.5. The jump of the normalised gradient is a suitable error criterion. Here the analogous 2D case is depicted.

After a possible saturation it serves as an admissible indicator related to the visual appearance. Alternatively, we can saturate this error indicator recursively by adding finer level indicator values as in the hierarchical case (Equation 17.1). Thereby, we obtain a new indicator η_N^+. Besides the representation of a visual error, this indicator allows an adaptive backface culling. Let N denote the normal of some triangle of the final isosurface triangulation on the tetrahedron $T \in T'$ and V the viewing vector from the object to the eye (we confine ourselves here to parallel projection). Then, the triangle is faced towards the viewer, if $N \cdot V \geq 0$, it will not be drawn otherwise. Now, we obtain a significant acceleration of our isosurface algorithm, if, on a much coarser grid level, we recognise tetrahedra containing only isosurface triangles which are faced away from the viewer. Then, we are already able to stop the local traversal on this level. Thereby:

$$N \bullet V + \eta_N^+(x_{\mathrm{ref}}(T)) \le 0$$

serves as an appropriate, additional stopping criterion. It can easily be seen that, on average, while arbitrarily rotating the object, we save up to one half of the computing time for an isosurface (Table 17.1).

Unfortunately, the evaluation of normals on every tetrahedron traversed in the adaptive algorithm is computationally expensive. Therefore we ask for a modification, which still ensures an adaptive backface culling. We consider an error indicator that measures non-normalised gradient jumps, that is:

$$\eta_{1,\infty}(x_{\mathrm{ref}}(T)) := \left| \nabla U^l \right|_{F_{\mathrm{ref}}(T)},$$

and analogously construct a saturated indicator $\eta_{1,\infty}^+$. Then the backface rejection criterion can be modified to:

$$\nabla U^l \bullet V + \eta_{1,\infty}(\tilde{x}_{\mathrm{ref}}(T)) \le 0.$$

The gradients $\nabla \hat{\lambda}_i$ of the barycentric coordinates $\left\{ \hat{\lambda}_i \right\}_{0 \le i \le 3}$ with respect to a reference tetrahedron $\hat{T}$ for each class of up to translation and scaling identical tetrahedra can be precomputed. If $\alpha(T)$ is the corresponding scaling factor for a specific tetrahedron T the backface test reduces to:

$$\sum_{i=1}^{3} U_i W_i \le -\alpha(T) \cdot \eta_{1,\infty}(x_{\mathrm{ref}}(T))$$

where $W_i = V \bullet \nabla \hat{\lambda}_i$ is also pre-computable. Table 17.1 shows the effect of this strategy in reducing the number of visited cells. Asymptotically, we obtain a saving of nearly ½ for fine grid resolutions.

For details on further types of error indicators we refer to [10]. Here we have focused on the above two types in order to emphasise that error indicators serve other purposes as well, such as the evaluation of data bounds or adaptive backface culling.

17.4 Reducing the Storage Requirements

Independently of the concrete type, error indicators have to be precomputed and stored on the grid nodes. A naive approach requires the same memory as the numerical dataset itself. Let us now discuss an improvement that significantly reduces storage requirements. First, we recognise that slightly increasing the indicator values does not affect the overall performance of the algorithm.

Typically, we do not need the true values but the ordering of nodes corresponding to their indicator value. We are therefore able to classify the indicator values according to the intervals:

$$(\alpha^{m+1}, \alpha^m]$$

in which they are contained for a fixed $\alpha \in (0,1)$. Then, we only have to store m which is a small integer and only needs some bits in storage instead of several bytes for a floating point number. A look-up table enables us to retrieve the α^m values efficiently.

The appearance of the extracted isosurfaces is significantly improved when smooth shading is used. Therefore, normals on vertices of the isosurface triangulation are required. For datasets of moderate size, normals can be calculated on the grid nodes of the original mesh in advance and be stored. Nevertheless, on finer grids, it is undesirable to provide three times the storage of the actual dataset to store normals derived from the data. Thus, they have to be calculated when needed at runtime. The normals are required at vertices on edges of the original grid. They can be obtained by linear interpolation of discrete gradients on the edge end points. Discrete gradients at these nodes are typically calculated by central differences in case of regular hexahedral grids, or by local averaging of cell normals. Such a normal is requested several times, once for each tetrahedron sharing the edge. We enable a retrieval of already calculated normals using a hash table for them. On a n^3 sized dataset the number of vertices on the isosurface triangulation, which equals the number of intersected edges, is, at most, $O(n^2)$ depending on the smoothness module of the discrete function U. A hash table of size $O(n^2)$ is therefore sufficient for our purpose. The pair of index vectors for the end points of the intersected edge serves as an appropriate hash key.

17.5 Parallel Implementation

In what follows we will address the question of how to run the presented algorithm efficiently in parallel on a workstation with several processors. The very first idea would be to apply a domain decomposition method with respect to the tetrahedral grid. However, this approach is not able to manage the complicated behaviour of our adaptive and hierarchical isosurface extraction algorithm. Small and large portions of the isosurface will both be located in regions of the same size. Therefore, the number of traversed tetrahedra by the algorithm in each region — which is proportional to the required computing time - will differ significantly. The problem is, therefore, how to prevent processors from getting idle.

Here, we present an efficient solution to this problem, independent of the concrete isosurface shape and straightforward to implement. Interactive visualisation in mind, we confine ourselves here to the case of a shared memory workstation where processes (threads) are assumed to have comparable access times to arbitrary local information in the complete dataset. The exchange of domain data turns out to be critical in distributed environments, although unavoidable in certain cases of very fine grids. Then, load balancing decisions have to be taken more carefully.

Initially, we set up several processes, each of which is given a subtree of the complete tetrahedral hierarchy which can be handled independently of the other processes subtrees. We denote the entry node of the current subtree of a process by its mark. In particular, we assume that the right subtree of a process has not yet been processed. If the process is going to enter his right subtree, the corresponding mark has to be shifted downwards into the right subtree.

Now, if a process has already finished its whole subtree, a new task has to be found. Therefore, the entry node of a right subtree of another process subtree is chosen as the new mark of the currently idle process. We always select the process whose mark is on the coarsest level of the grid. The mark of the process dealing with the complete subtree before, is shifted recursively downwards to the right, starting at the left child node of the former mark until it reaches a node in the right subtree which is, as yet, unvisited (Figure 17.6). This strategy ensures that a process that becomes idle is supplied with the largest unvisited subtree.

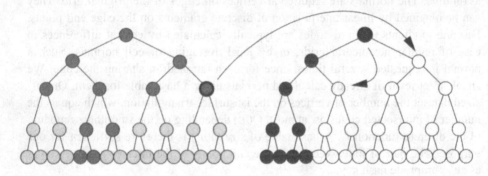

Figure 17.6. Two process subtrees are sketched. The dark grey process has already finished his job passing over all its tetrahedra of interest. The light grey nodes indicate tetrahedra which are not reached due to the adaptive stopping and the hierarchical testing. Now the dark grey process resets its mark (indicated by a thickened circle), taking over part of the originally black process subtree. The black mark is correspondingly shifted downwards.

Let us finally remark on the actual implementation in the case of 6 tetrahedra on the coarsest level of the grid hierarchy, e.g. for a cube subdivided into tetrahedra. We index them with integers 6, ..., 11. The other tetrahedra are numbered recursively. Left and right child are indexed $2i$, respectively $2i+1$ for a tetrahedron with index i. We solely have to store an array of such indices, one for each process. If a process has finished a left subtree, his mark index is set to the right subtree index until the complete tree has been processed. An idle process looks for the smallest mark index i_{min} in a list of indices for all processes, sets its mark index to $2i_{min}+1$, and modifies the other indices.

If the graphics workstation is equipped with m processors, we may start m

processes. One of them has to be reserved to push graphical patches from some buffer into the graphics hardware. The other $m-1$ processes can be occupied with actual isosurface extraction. Thereby, they collect patches to be drawn in buffers which they hand over to the first process. On a 4-processor SGI R10000 workstation with infinite reality graphics a speed-up of 2.4 and a rate of 800K triangles can thus be achieved. Detailed results are listed in Table 17.2. There we considered the hierarchical error estimator.

Table 17.2. Testing results in respect of backface culling, including the number of generated triangles and that of visited tetrahedra, with and without multi-level backface culling for different threshold values ε using the normalised gradient jump error indicator η_N^+.

ε	without backface culling		with backface culling	
	triangles drawn	visited tetrahedra	triangles drawn	visited tetrahedra
1.60	72076	181616	56918	169270
0.80	92955	227874	65485	205010
0.40	126463	301332	81081	252936
0.20	224522	521472	130262	380627
0.10	342173	781218	188072	519739
0.05	463443	1026587	256757	650741
0.00	590018	1259669	317024	772752

References

1. Certain A, Popovic J, DeRose T, Duchamp T, Salesin D, Stuetzle W. Interactive multiresolution surface viewing. In: Proc. SIGGRAPH '96 Conference, 1996; 91-98.
2. Gross MH, Staadt RG. Fast multiresolution surface meshing. In: Proc. IEEE Visualization '95; 135-142.
3. Hoppe H. Progressive meshes. In: Proc. SIGGRAPH '96 Conference,,, 1996; 99-108.
4. Schroeder WJ, Zarge JA, Lorensen WA. Decimation of triangle meshes. ACM/SIGGRAPH Computer Graphics 1992; 26(4):65-70.
5. Cignoni P, De Floriani L, Montoni C, Puppo E, Scopigno R. Multiresolution modeling and visualization of volume data based on simplicial complexes. In: Proc. Symposium on Volume Visualization 1994; 19-26.
6. Grosso R, Luerig C, Ertl T. The multilevel finite element method for adaptive mesh optimization and visualization of volume data. In: Proc. IEEE Visualization '97, Phoenix, AZ, 1997; 387-562.
7. Shekhar R, Fayyad E, Yagel R, Cornhill JF. Octree-based decimation of marching cubes surfaces. In: Proc. IEEE Visualization '96, , San Francisco, CA,

October 1996.

8. Bänsch E. Local mesh refinement in 2 and 3 dimensions. IMPACT of Computing in Science and Engineering, 1991; (3):181-191.

9. Maubach J. Local bisection refinement for n-simplicial grids generated by reflection. SIAM Journal of Scientific. Computing, 1995; (16):210-227.

10. Ohlberger M, Rumpf M. Adaptive projection methods in multiresolutional scientific visualization. IEEE Transactions on Visualization and Computer Graphics, 1998; 4(4).

11. Ohlberger M, Rumpf M. Hierarchical and adaptive visualization on nested grids. Computing, 1997; 59(4):269-285.

12. Neubauer R, Ohlberger M, Rumpf M, Schwörer R. Efficient visualization of large scale data on hierarchical meshes. In: Lefer W, Grave M (Eds), Visualization in Scientific Computing, Springer, 1997.

13. Rumpf M. Recent numerical methods — A challenge for visualization. To appear in: Future General Computer Systems.

14. Zhou Y, Chen B, Kaufman A. Multiresolution tetrahedral framework for visualizing volume data. In: Proc. IEEE Visualization '97, Phoenix, AZ, 1997; 135-142.

15. Livnat Y, Shen HW, Johnson CR. A near optimal isosurface extraction algorithm using the span space. Transactions on Visulization and Computer Graphics, 1996; 2(1):73-83.

16. Gerstner T. Adaptive hierarchical methods for landscape representation and analysis. In: Hergarten S, Neugebauer H-J (Eds), Lecture Notes in Earth Sciences 78, Springer, 1998.

17. Wilhelms JP, van Gelder A. Octrees for faster isosurface generation. ACM/SIGGRAPH Computer Graphics, 1990; 24(4):57-62.

18. A Volume Rendering Crossbar and SRAM-Based Hardware

Miron Deyssenroth, Martijn de Boer, Alexander Gröpl,
J. Hesser, R. Männer

18.1 Introduction

Volume data acquired by different imaging systems is best visualised through volume rendering [1] approaches if semi-transparency and avoidance of surface generation is imperative. Available algorithms include ray casting [2] and shadowing approaches such as the Heidelberg ray tracer [3]. Hardware architectures for real-time rendering are, among others, VIRIM [4], Cube-4 [5], and VIZZARD [6] (see also Section 1.14). The systems depend on either special-purpose chips, FPGAs or DSP processors.

FPGAs are commercial chips that can be configured as special-purpose processors by software. Internally FPGAs consist of an array of logic blocks that are small static memories. Input and output of memories can be connected by a software-configurable network so that near arbitrary combinations of small logical functions can be realised. Due to their relatively high flexibility, FPGAs have found widespread use as accelerators for computing-intensive operations like image processing and rendering.

In this chapter, we concentrate on the question of how to minimise the hardware cost of shading and compositing using a look-up table computer system. Look-up-table computer systems can be considered as an extension of FPGAs by using larger internal memory blocks for the logic functions.

18.2 The Volume Rendering Pipeline

For the following architecture, it is important to formulate the underlying volume rendering equation in detail (Figure 18.1). It is a variation of the Heidelberg ray tracer that operates on two light sources being positioned at 0° and 45° relative to the viewer. Let k be a point on the scan-line and (k, i) a sample point on the ray cast from k. $(j, j+i-k)$ is a sample point on a ray generated by the 45° incident ray. ρ_8 is the incoming voxel gray value cut to 8-bit accuracy and $|\nabla|$ the respective gradient magnitude for voxel (k, j). LUT_1 is a look-up table serving as the classification of the opacity. Then the deposited intensity of incident light at point (k, i) is:

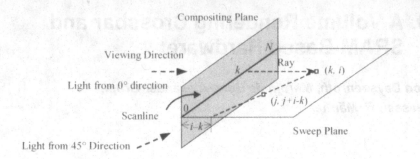

Figure 18.1. Ray processing in detail.

$$
\rho_{45} = \begin{cases}
\exp\!\left\{-\sum_{j\le i}\mathrm{LUT}_1\!\left(\rho_8(j+k-i,j),\left|\nabla(j+k-i,j)\right|\right)\right\} & i \le k \\
\exp\!\left\{-\sum_{j\le k}\mathrm{LUT}_1\!\left(\rho_8(j,j+i-k),\left|\nabla(j,j+i-k)\right|\right)\right\} & otherwise
\end{cases}
$$

for 45° rays, and:

$$
\rho_0 = \exp\!\left\{-\sum_{j\le i}\mathrm{LUT}_1\!\left(\rho_8(k,j),\left|\nabla(k,j)\right|\right)\right\}
$$

for 0° rays.

The Phong shading components are **diff0** for 0° diffuse reflection, **diff45** for 45° diffuse reflection, and **spec45** for 45° specular reflection. They are obtained by reflectance maps. Thus:

$$
S_{spec} = \mathrm{LUT}_S\!\left(\rho_{16}(k,i),\left|\nabla(k,i)\right|\right)
$$
$$
S_{red/green/blue} = \mathrm{LUT}_{red/green/blue}\!\left(\rho_{16}(k,i),\left|\nabla(k,i)\right|\right)
$$

are the classification results for the specular reflection coefficient S_{spec} and for the diffuse reflection coefficients multiplied by the voxel colour coefficients: red; green; and blue, $S_{red/green/blue}$. The ambient part of Phong shading is not considered in this architecture. The voxel colour is then given by:

$$
C_{red/green/blue} = S_{spec}\cdot \mathbf{spec45}\cdot \rho_{45}\cdot \rho_0 + S_{red/green/blue}\cdot\left(\mathbf{diff45}\cdot\rho_{45}\cdot\rho_0 + \mathbf{diff0}\cdot\rho_0^2\right)
$$

where ρ_{45} and ρ_0 represent the shadow buffers for 0° and 45° light. The colour is multiplied by the incoming intensity for 0° and 45° light (factors ρ_{45} and ρ_0) and by the factor by which the reflected light intensity is reduced before it reaches the compositing plane (second factor ρ_0).

Finally, the pixel colour is updated recursively by:

$$
C_{out} = C + C_{in}.
$$

18.3 Overall Architecture

This section discusses the rendering architecture for shading and compositing as shown in Figure 18.2. It performs the classification of a voxel RGBA according to its re-sampled gray value and gradient magnitude.

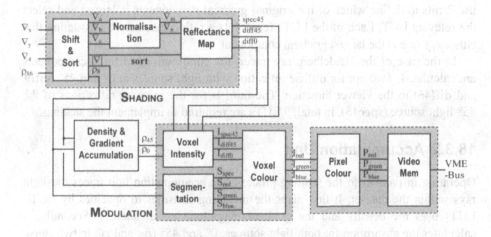

Figure 18.2. Overall architecture of the rendering system.

A geometry unit, e.g. the VIRIM geometry processor (see also Chapter 19), delivers the input data. It transfers four 16-bit values per clock cycle, namely the voxel density and three gradient components. The image is generated scan-line by scan-line. Each scan-line corresponds to a sweep plane, and each sweep plane is spanned by rays that are cast from pixels in the relevant scan-line. This sweep plane is generated using re-sampled voxels line by line, beginning with the front-most line parallel to the scan-line.

The rendering result is stored in video memory as either 24-bit RGB or 8-bit gray values. The image size is dependant only on the video memory size, whereas the minimal version contains 512×512 pixels. The supported algorithms are variations of the Heidelberg ray tracer model with two light sources, and ray casting with one light source.

In order to cope with the vast input data stream a pipelined architecture has been developed. The first problem to be solved involves the conversion of the stages shading and compositing within the volume rendering pipeline into a hardware architecture. In our design we have developed four separate units for the hardware pipeline, including the shading, accumulation, modulation, and compositing units (Figure 18.2). Their functions are described next.

18.3.1 Shading Unit

The shading unit implements Phong shading by look-up tables. This approach is similar to one suggested by Smit [7] based upon reflectance maps. The host CPU calculates a reflectance map for each possible gradient of the grid on a unit sphere. This map is stored in a small memory. For shading, it is now sufficient to solely apply the gradient as an address to this memory in order to obtain the shading value directly.

In contrast to Smit, we use three rather large 128k×9 LUTs for this purpose. The address bits are set to 8 and 9 bits for the other two re-normalised components. We use 2 bits to define which of the original gradient components is largest and select the relevant LUT. Each of the LUTs represents a reflectance map by assuming that either x, y or z is the largest gradient component.

In the case of the Heidelberg ray tracer, the contributions of three components are calculated. Two are for diffuse reflection with light sources at 0° and 45° (**diff0** and **diff45**) to the viewer direction. The third is for the specular reflections of the 45° light source (**spec45**). In total, 9 LUTs are required to implement the shading.

18.3.2 Accumulation Unit

Operating in parallel to the shading process, the accumulation unit traces the light rays within the dataset. It first maps the incoming densities to opacities by LUT_1. LUT_1 uses the density and the gradient magnitude as an address. Secondly, it calculates the absorption for both light sources, 0° and 45° (ρ_{45} and ρ_0) in two steps. It accumulates the contributions of LUT_1 (summation) and then calculates the exponential function for this result. For ray casting it is only necessary to calculate the 0° absorption. The absorption calculation is required in order to reduce the overall pipeline length. Short pipelines are advantageous as the length of the wires on the board can be kept to a minimum.

18.3.3 Modulation Unit

The modulation unit calculates the RGBA contribution of a voxel to its scan-line. Its inputs are the results from the shading unit (**diff0**, **diff45**, **spec45**), the local light intensity reaching this voxel (ρ_{45} and ρ_0), and the density (ρ_8), along with gradient magnitude ($|\nabla|$).

Internally, the modulation unit consists of the voxel intensity unit, the segmentation unit and the voxel colour unit. The voxel intensity unit multiplies the shading components by the locally incident light intensity:

$$I_{spec45} = \mathbf{spec45} \cdot \rho_{45} \cdot \rho_0$$
$$I_{diff45} = \mathbf{diff45} \cdot \rho_{45} \cdot \rho_0$$
$$I_{diff0} = \mathbf{diff0} \cdot \rho_0 \cdot \rho_0$$

The segmentation unit maps the incoming gradient magnitude and voxel density to the specular reflection coefficient S_{spec} and to the reflection coefficients (for both 0° and 45° lights). The latter depends on the colours S_{red}, S_{green} and S_{blue}.

The voxel colour unit then multiplies the reflection coefficients by the intensities and accumulates the contributions for each colour:

$$I_{red} = S_{red} \cdot (I_{diff45} + I_{diff0}) + S_{spec} \cdot I_{spec45}$$
$$I_{green} = S_{green} \cdot (I_{diff45} + I_{diff0}) + S_{spec} \cdot I_{spec45}$$
$$I_{blue} = S_{blue} \cdot (I_{diff45} + I_{diff0}) + S_{spec} \cdot I_{spec45}.$$

18.3.4 Compositing Unit

The final step is to generate a two-dimensional array of pixels from the three-dimensional set of voxels by accumulating the voxel RGB values:

$$pixel\_colour = \sum_{voxels} voxel\_colour$$

Depending on the selected mode the final picture is stored either as a set of 24-bit RGB values or as 8-bit gray values.

18.4 Implementation

The main concept behind the hardware design was the development of a purely LUT-based synchronous pipeline processor. This way, complex functions can be implemented guaranteeing a result for each calculation within one clock cycle. The disadvantage is a reduction in accuracy as SRAM LUTs of moderate size (128k×8) do not allow for a wide data path. Therefore, incoming 16-bit values have to be reduced to 8 or 9 bits by an FPGA device.

Once the data has been converted to 8- or 9-bit values the remaining processing is performed in 20ns fast 128k×9 SRAM LUTs (17 input / 9 output pins). These are generally used for performing functions of two 8-bit values but they can take any input not exceeding 17 bits.

Some units, like the density accumulation, require buffers. These are implemented as FIFOs, which generally operate as configurable delay lines and require a minimum of controller logic.

The main problem for a traditional bus-register based design is the data paths between the devices. The amount of bus drivers required would push the size and power requirements of the board beyond realisation.

A solution giving additional benefits uses ICube FPIDs [3] as central routing and switching elements. FPIDs are devices with a freely configurable network of internal data paths and are available with up to a few hundred registered I/Os. Configurations can be reprogrammed on the fly via a JTAG interface. This way the signal routing is not fixed by the PCB layout. It allows for fast interactive manipulation of LUT contents, as an FPID can easily change the connection of LUTs from the data signal paths to the host bus, in our case the VME bus.

Ideally, all SRAM and FIFO pins would be connected to the I/Os of one massive FPID, allowing for maximum flexibility and speed. Unfortunately, the required number of I/Os is not yet available on one single device and large chips cost significantly more than the requisite number of smaller chips.

A reasonable compromise has been found by using a few smaller FPIDs, each serving one of the modules discussed above. These are connected to each other as well as to the VME bus. The design can adapt to different requirements by changing the routing between LUTs through different configurations of the FPIDs. The configurations offer set-ups for loading the LUTs, testing the board and performing the rendering. In addition, an interface is provided to manipulate the LUTs from the host.

The video memory in the compositing unit does not require flexible routing. A fixed, register-based architecture has been chosen to reduce costs. Two banks make up the video memory to allow for interleaved processing. While one bank is being filled with data from the rendering system the host can read out a completed image from the other bank via the VME bus. To allow for 32-bit bus transfers, each bank is divided into four 8-bit wide sub-banks. In RGB mode, three of these banks hold the red, green and blue portions of the image while one is either left blank or used as an alpha channel. In gray mode, pixels are written successively into all four banks. This way one VME bus access can transfer either one RGB pixel or four gray value pixels.

While programmable counters limit the practical size of an image, the theoretical size depends only on the available amount of SRAM. 1MB banks provide storage for 512×512 RGB pixels or 1024×1024 gray value pixels due to the different memory architecture.

The entire processor is controlled by FPGAs. They provide counters, generate controlling signals for FIFOs and act as interfaces to the VME bus. Like the FPID devices they possess JTAG interfaces to allow on-board programming.

18.5 Simulation Results

While the general structure of the Heidelberg ray tracer algorithm has been maintained, the practical implementation of the LUT-based architecture required, and allowed for, some changes in the actual calculations. Most notably, the accuracy had to be reduced to 8 bits to match the width of the data paths.

An analysis based on a C simulation of the system [8] has shown that numerical results from the LUT architecture differ on average by 2.4% from the original algorithm implemented on VIRIM (operating at 32-bit floating-point precision) (Figure18.3). The error can be kept at a low level because of the high accuracy available during compositing.

The limiting factors in the design are the SRAM LUTs. 20ns synchronous SRAMs have been chosen which limit the performance to a maximum of 40-45 MHz in a synchronous design, while FPIDs and FPGAs would theoretically allow up to 80 MHz.

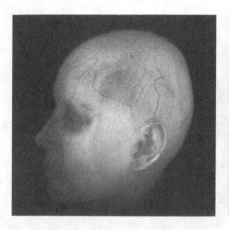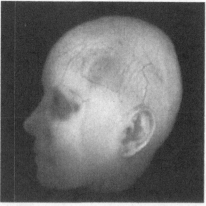

Figure 18.3. Left: rendered result of VIRIM. Right: rendered result with the proposed LUT-system.

References

1. Levoy M. Efficient ray tracing of volume data. ACM Transacton on Graphics, 1990; 9(3): 245-261.
2. Lacroute P, Levoy M. Fast volume rendering using a shear-warp factorization of the viewing transform. In: Proc. of SIGGRAPH '94, Orlando, FL, 1994; 451-457.
3. IDB 320 User's Guide, 1994, I-Cube Inc., 2328-C Walsh Avenue, Santa Clara, CA.
4. Hesser J, Männer R, Knittel G, Straßer W, Pfister H, Kaufman A. Three special-purpose architectures for real-time volume rendering. In: Eurographics '95, Maastricht, The Netherlands, September 1995; C111-C122.
5. Pfister H. Towards a scalable architecture for real-time volume rendering. In: Proc. the 10th Eurographics Workshop on Graphics Hardware, Maastricht, The Netherlands, September 1995; 123-130.
6. Knittel G, Straßer W. A compact volume rendering accelerator. In: Proc. 1994 Symposium on Volume Visualization, ACP press., NY, 1994; 67-74.
7. Van Scheltinga JT, Smit J, Bosma M. Design of an on-chip reflectance map. In: Proc. Eurographics Workshop on Graphics Hardware, Maastricht, September 1995; 51-55.
8. de Boer M. Simulation spezieller Aspekte der nächsten Generation von Spezialrechnern für die Volumenvisualisierung, diploma thesis, University of Heidelberg, 1996.

19. Algorithmically Optimised Real-Time Volume Rendering

Bernd Vettermann, Jürgen Hesser and Reinhard Männer

19.1 Background

Volume rendering is a time-consuming application. For example, real-time applications demand several billion operations per second since each voxel in an $n{\times}n{\times}n$ volume dataset is to be processed. Algorithmic optimisations can mitigate this problem by restricting the calculation of light matter interaction to only those voxels that contribute to the final image. Two of the most frequently used approaches are space-leaping and early-ray termination. These algorithmic optimisations can reduce the complexity of the volume rendering algorithm for $n{\times}n{\times}n$ volumes from $O(n^3)$ to $O(n^2)$ if the dataset has only few semi-transparent voxels.

Nevertheless, some applications demand higher speed. In this case, hardware support is necessary. Hardware-based systems achieve their speed-up compared to PC architectures by either parallel processing of tasks (e.g. the Cube-family of processors) or by pipelining (Vogue, VIRIM). The latter breaks up a complex operation into simple stages that can be processed within one clock cycle. The operations are overlapped in execution so that each new instruction starts one clock cycle later than the previous one. Often pipelining is preferred over parallel execution of tasks since it allows high speed-up with moderate hardware only.

In pipelining, virtually all data flows through one stage after the other. In this way, pipelines achieve their maximum performance. This achievable performance however is limited in practical cases. Exceptions to this data flow are called hazards. One example of such a hazard is data dependency. It occurs if a subsequent pipeline stage requires a result of another stage in the pipeline before that unit has produced the result. A typical case is e.g. "add d0, d1, d2" (adding register d0 with d1 stored in d2) followed by "mul d2, d3, d4" (multiply d2 by d3 and store result in register d4). Other typical hazards occur if the processor waits for data from memory. Each such hazard produces idle cycles in the processor until the conflict is solved.

Idle times, however, can be masked by multi-threading. In this case a program is divided into different and independent parts called threads. They have their own processor states and registers but otherwise share the address space and global variables. Multi-threading processors switch from one thread to the next (context switch) either cyclically or only if a blocking (waiting) for further processing occurs.

Processor speed is one component of high-speed rendering systems. At least as equally important is the performance of the memory system. Since datasets can be in the range of hundreds of megabytes, only cheap devices like DRAMs can be used. DRAMs are organised internally in one or several arrays. Rows play a special role and are grouped into *memory pages*. Data access first requires that a row address is asserted. All data in the corresponding page is buffered in sense amplifiers on the chip. From these sense amplifiers column addresses select the required data.

Random access cycles consume roughly 100 ns. Higher speed is achieved if subsequent data is in the same page, making row address assertion unnecessary. In this case new data can be obtained much faster. Modern DRAM interfaces like SDRAMs give a factor of 10 speed-up.

19.2 Introduction

Volume rendering is meanwhile a standard approach for visualisation of volumetric datasets [1, 2]. Its popularity in diverse visualisation applications came up with interactive software based rendering [3]. To achieve interactive rendering rates, these software approaches use algorithmic optimisation techniques. In particular, space leaping skips empty cells. Early ray termination stops ray processing if the ray intensity falls below a user-defined threshold. In addition, the sampling rate is adjusted to the underlying grid size [4].

For example, Levoy and Lacroute [3], for example, achieved more than 10 frames/s for a 256^3 dataset on a 16-processor SGI Challenge system. The algorithm depends on the precomputation of gradients and the run-length encoding of the dataset in three main viewing directions. Precomputation times of 77 seconds are mentioned. Even the fast classification approach with octrees [5] requires seconds for preprocessing.

One solution to limited software performance on conventional systems is hardware support (see 1.14). The VIRIM system [6, 4] can be considered as the first realised volume rendering hardware system that provides real-time frame rates. VIRIM's main disadvantage is the inefficient support of algorithmic improvement techniques like space leaping and early ray termination.

Another system, currently implemented at the Mitsubishi Electric Research Laboratory (MERL), is Cube-4 [7]. It is based on a skewed memory architecture and on locally communicating pipeline processors to implement the shear warp approach of volume rendering. Although it is claimed to support the visualisation of 1024^3 datasets at a 30 Hz frame rate it does not support algorithmic improvements as well.

Algorithmic improvements, if implemented efficiently in hardware, can improve the rendering speed by a factor of 10 or more depending on the dataset size and the amount of transparency [5]. DIV2A [8] has been proposed to make partial use of space leaping and early ray termination. It stops the processing of a ray if the conditions for early ray termination are fulfilled. In transparent regions it reduces only the number of computations per sample point but otherwise traverses the full volume. Thus, the complexity of $O(n^3)$ of the implemented rendering algorithm is not reduced.

A more efficient implementation has been presented with VIZZARD [9], a PCI accelerator board. By time-consuming preprocessing (several minutes for 256^3 voxels) the dataset is compressed, pre-shaded, and a distance coding is calculated. This compression is not lossless and thus the acceptance in critical applications like medicine is limited. Moreover, pre-shading degrades the image quality since the light source is fixed relative to the dataset. Finally, VIZZARD does not really solve the hazard problems in the optimised rendering algorithms. It requires several cycles for processing each sample point and then addresses the next sample point. Thus, the possible higher performance of direct hardware implementation versus software realisations is only partially used.

The problem discussed in this chapter is the efficient implementation of algorithmic optimisations into hardware. An "efficient solution" — as we define it here— should implement the volume rendering pipeline into pipelined hardware so that each sample point requires only one effective clock cycle for processing. Additionally, this solution should integrate space leaping and early ray termination in such a way that no wait cycles are needed. An architecture that, for the first time, represents such a solution is presented in the following. It will be realised in 1999 as PCI-based FPGA-board[1] running Windows NT. The PCI-board contains its complete rendering pipeline with four Lucent ORCA3 FPGA devices and its own memory bus to a separate memory board.

19.3 Rendering Pipeline

As illustrated in Figure 19., the ray processing pipeline, which was chosen for our implementation, consists of three main rendering phases. Starting from a compositing plane, rays are cast into the virtual scene. Sample points are generated by trilinear interpolation at equidistant positions on the rays. After interpolation, gradients are estimated with local difference filters[2]. Next, Phong shading[3], which calculates a reflection in direction of the observer, is applied to each non-transparent sample point. Finally, for each ray, all contributions are composited by the **over** operator [11].

For the implementation, eight processing steps are considered, which are:

1. Generation of sample point address;
2. Memory read-out and pre-classification of the dataset according to gray value and index;
3. Trilinear interpolation for re-sampling;
4. Post-classification for the assignment of opacity and voxel colour;
5. Absorption calculation;
6. Gradient estimation;

---

[1] FPGAs, Field Programmable Gate Arrays, are commercial devices that can be turned into special-purpose processors by configuration software.

[2] The current implementation uses Knittels approach of a 2×2×2 gradient [10].

[3] A reflectance map according to Smit is used [9].

7. Shading;
8. Compositing.

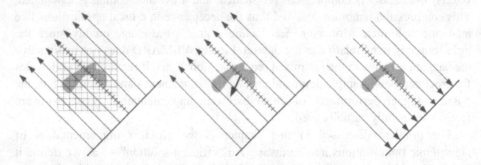

Figure 19.1. Main rendering steps: sampling, shading, and compositing. In Phase 1 rays are cast into the virtual scene, and at evenly distanced positions, sample points are generated. In Phase 2 gradients are calculated and shading is performed. Phase 3 consists of compositing operations on the reflected intensities.

The processing at Steps 3-7 is standard for volume rendering. Implementation examples of these steps in hardware can be found in other publications (e.g. Cube-4 [7], Vogue [10]). Due to our method for processing rays, only small modifications (handling a bundle of rays instead of single rays) are required for Step 8[4]. Algorithmic optimisations affect Step 1 in the rendering pipeline, the modification of which is the focus of this chapter. Adaptations of Step 2 are then necessary in order to maximise the throughput for the new processing approach, which is the second focus of this chapter.

19.4 Algorithmic Optimisations

Even with a fully pipelined hardware, processing one voxel per clock, algorithmic optimisations are necessary when the data size reaches 512^3 voxels. With a brute force approach, the time to read out 512^3 data words just once, even with fast DRAM technologies, is about a second, which makes interactive frame rates impossible. Thus, the amount of data per frame has to be reduced.

In software solutions, two algorithmic optimisations are common. The first is early ray termination. Viewing rays are cast into the volume and attenuated during their pass through material. The computation of rays is stopped if the further contribution to the overall result is negligible. This can be adjusted with a user-defined threshold.

The second optimisation technique is space leaping. It skips empty regions. To make efficient use of this technique we use distance coding [8] in a preprocessing

---

[4] In our implementation, we have to propagate the ray number along with the processed sample point. Compositing has to be applied to the pixel that corresponds to the ray of the processed sample point.

step.

For each voxel, distance coding stores its leaping distance to the next possible non-transparent voxel before rendering begins. The distance is view-independent and has only to be updated if transparent regions become non-transparent and *vice versa*. The processing with a hardware pipeline requires 8 seconds for 1024^3 and 0.125 seconds for 256^3 datasets and is implemented by a nonlinear digital filter.

Distance coding can be performed on different resolutions. For example, it can be applied on the original voxel grid and it stores one distance value for each voxel. Alternatively one distance value can be stored for each subcube of size 2^3 denoting how many subcubes can be skipped until a non-empty subcube is encountered. On the one hand, the number of such subcubes is a factor of 8 less than the number of voxels saving the corresponding amount on computation time and volume memory for distance values. On the other hand, the skipping distance is by a factor of 2 coarser than the sampling distance. Therefore it may happen that a point is unnecessarily sampled since it is one voxel distance before the non-empty region begins. The number of such additional sample points lies in the range of 10-20% which we consider as negligible. Thus, the subcube-based distance coding approach is selected in our architecture[5].

19.5 Problem Setting and Solution

To illustrate the problem of implementing algorithmic optimisations in a hardware pipeline the calculation of the next re-sample point of a ray using space leaping is explained.

In principle, the next re-sampling position of a given sample point is calculated using the distance value d of the current point which was generated by distance coding. In particular, $d \cdot \bar{\Delta}$ is added to the current sample point address where $\bar{\Delta}$ is the minimal distance vector between two re-sampling positions on a ray.

For pipeline processors, the dependence of a subsequent operation on the result of the current operation is called data hazard, which leads to performance bottlenecks. In our case, the position of the subsequent sample point address depends on the current sample point address and the current distance value d. Thus, the new address cannot be calculated before the distance value is fetched from memory. The memory read-out requires several cycles on modern DRAM (SDRAM, RDRAM) which would lead to wait-states of the pipeline.

Our solution for a hardware pipeline without these wait-states uses multi-threading [12]. In the literature, a thread is described as a process with its own

---

[5] In principle, instead of 2^3 subcubes one could have chosen larger subcubes as basis as well. The number of computations and the size of the distance memory reduce correspondingly. However, the number of additional sample points increases as well. We decided that 10-20% is an acceptable upper limit for our architecture. Additionally, our distance coding implementation can make use of the parallel subcube read-out mechanism of the hardware. Thus, empty subcubes can be detected with one memory read cycle instead of the 8 necessary without this feature.

process state and registers, but sharing its global variables and the address space. Single rays are considered as threads that are processed in a round robin order. The variables for every ray like start, final and current sample point has to be stored.

This solves the above mentioned data hazard problem. Instead of waiting for the required information to generate the next sample point, other threads (rays) are processed in the pipeline to hide waiting cycles.

Starting from this data flow approach the new volume rendering architecture is described next. The modifications of the volume rendering pipeline are mentioned and the hardware solution for the context (thread) switch is explained.

19.6 Hazard-Free Pipeline Architecture

Figure 19.2 shows the structure of the new hardware solution. The right hand-side of the figure depicts the main steps 2-8 of the above mentioned volume rendering pipeline.

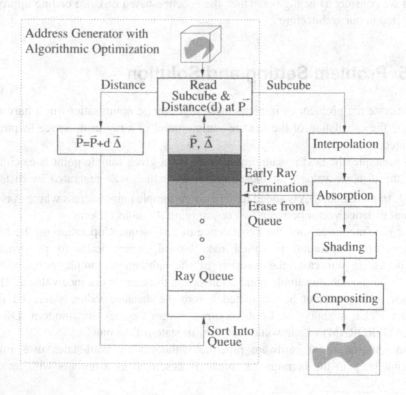

Figure 19.2. Pipeline structure.

On the left of the figure is the modified address generator (ray queue). It solves the data hazard problem by implementing the context switch hardware for multi-threading.

In the ray queue all information connected with rays stored, i.e., the current sample point position $\vec{P}$, and the minimal distance vector between two re-sampling positions, $\vec{\Delta}$. At the beginning, $\vec{\Delta}$ and the ray start point $\vec{P}$ are stored in the queue for each ray. Then, for the first ray, the first 2×2×2 subcube around $\vec{P}$ is fetched along with the corresponding distance value d from the distance dataset. While the subcube is passed to the subsequent volume rendering pipeline, the distance value is used only for generating the address of the subsequent sample point by $\vec{P} + d\vec{\Delta}$. This result is then stored in the ray queue.

To achieve parallel processing, these operations are pipelined. While the address of the subsequent sample point for the first ray is calculated, the subcube and distance information for the second ray is already fetched.

Early ray termination is realised inside the absorption unit of the pipeline. In the absorption unit, the decrease of the virtual light intensity of the rays during interaction with the material is calculated. The intensity is compared with the user-defined threshold. If the intensity is lower, the ray will be erased from the queue.

Wait states occur only if there are fewer rays in the queue than there are cycles needed to fetch the distance value and calculate the next ray position. Simulations showed that this occurs less than 1% of all cycles per frame.

19.7 Memory Architecture

The performance of a volume rendering system strongly depends on both the rendering pipeline and on a fast suited memory architecture[6]. For a high-speed volume rendering system it is especially important to make use of modern memory devices. Due to large volume datasets, low cost memories like DRAMs have to be considered. In addition, for performance reasons, modern memory interfaces like SDRAM (or RDRAM) are required.

We consider SDRAMs with four internal DRAM banks. Each of these DRAM banks is able to provide 1024-byte data of the selected DRAM page accessible in less than 10 ns. Changes between pages consume 90 ns.

The memory architecture (Figure 19.3) is specially optimised for the rendering algorithm described above:

- Resampling a point requires access to eight neighbouring voxels for interpolation. The volume memory is distributed among eight independent memory modules each with a data bus of 16 bits, so that every 2^3 subcube is accessible in parallel.
- For space leaping, the distance values are necessary in parallel to the 2^3 subcubes, for which one of the eight memory module contains additional 8 bits of the data bus.
- The memory architecture is adapted to our rendering algorithm for minimising page changes of the DRAMs. DRAM pages are organised such

---

[6] See also [6] where a similar memory architecture is presented.

that they hold full subcubes of the dataset like realised in [6]. When a ray crosses the border of the current subcube, the neighbouring one has to be loaded. However, the previous data cube may be required again for the next ray. To be direction-independent and to have a minimal number of page reloads, 8 neighbouring subcubes must be kept in parallel SDRAM banks. This means that every module needs 8 internal SDRAM banks (Figure 19.3). Note that the SDRAM chips are organised in a 4 (banks) × 2M (words) × 16 (bits) manner, so that at least two chips are required in order to have the eight banks available. Since eight neighbouring data cubes are available in parallel, a reload operation (with the high penalty of page changes) can be avoided. Page changes contribute to 3% idle time in the optimal case if all voxels are read out at once. The subsequent results show that in most cases this optimal case can be approached well.

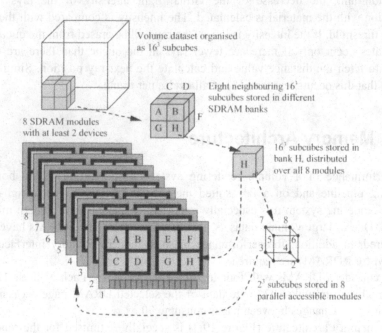

Figure 19.3. Memory structure with 8 modules containing 2 devices with 4 DRAM banks.

Each memory module is addressed individually. The detailed module addressing, as shown in Figure 19.4, uses the lower nine bits for selecting the column address in the SDRAM chips. Address bit "z4" selects one of the two devices. Address bits, "x4" and "y4", are used for selecting one of four internal banks in the SDRAM chip. The address bits "xn", "yn" and "zn" are directly mapped from the X, Y, Z-coordinates calculated by the address generator.

According to the overall architecture described above, multiple rays are considered in parallel. We have now the freedom to choose these rays for a maximum coherency, which consists of $n \times n$ bundles of rays. Simulations have shown that an 8×8 bundle is a good choice.

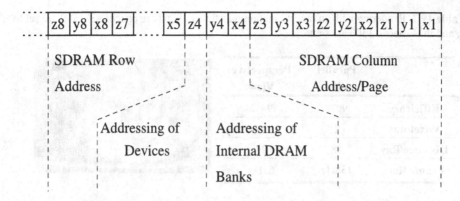

Figure 19.4. The detailed addressing scheme.

To get the maximal coherency, updated sample point positions have to be sorted into the queue, because the rays get different space leaping values. This is done in a hardware ray queue with $O(1)$ operations in a variation of insertion sort. The sorting is done with the accumulated distance values.

19.8 Overall System

The pipeline described so far is currently implemented on a PCI-board based on FPGAs. The prototype will work in a standard PC with Windows NT/LINIUX as the operating system. The front-end will be based on a graphical user interface. Later it is planned to set it up as plug-ins for commercial rendering packages.

The PCI-board supports the complete rendering of 8×8 tiles which compose the rendered image. The software has to split the complete picture into these tiles, store for one after the other the ray parameter on the board and fetch the results for display.

19.9 Results

In order to evaluate the efficiency of the proposed architecture and the memory systems we have simulated the PCI-Board in C. As basis for the simulation, a fully pipelined system is selected. Each operation consumes one clock cycle of 10 ns. Hereby, the memory access is pipelined with three cycles latency, the pipelined evaluation of the distance value amounts to two cycles latency. Finally, Steps 2-5 in the volume rendering pipeline are realised in the hardware pipeline with nine stages (included three cycles for memory read-out). As test dataset we used a CT of a human jaw (256×256×128 voxel) as shown in Tables 19.1-19.3. The results include only the time used by the PCI-board. Not included are the times to set up the parameter at the board and the time to display the results on the screen.

Table 19.1. Rendering with an opacity mapping as threshold where opacities ≤ 1300 are set to 0, and those above 1300 are set to 1.

	Parallel View	Perspective View
Efficiency	90%	94%
Voxel/Ray	2	19
Distance/Ray	18	27
Frame Rate	138Hz	63Hz

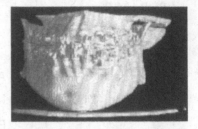

	Parallel View	Perspective View
Efficiency	88%	94%
Voxel/Ray	9	28
Distance/Ray	17	35
Frame Rate	105Hz	45Hz

	Parallel View	Perspective View
Efficiency	90%	93%
Voxel/Ray	11	16
Distance/Ray	18	23
Frame Rate	94Hz	73Hz

Critical parts of the architecture, like the ray queue sorting and the distance coding filter, are already simulated in VHDL. A synthesis of the VHDL code led to a design that achieves 100 MHz clock rate for a 0.8μ CMOS ASIC process. An implementation of the design in Lucent FPGAs (OR3T125) reaches 40MHz.

To show the data dependencies of the algorithmic optimisations, a human jaw dataset is rendered from three viewing points: from the front, from an oblique and from a lateral viewing position. Further, different classifications with various levels of transparency are applied.

The results in these three tables show that the whole system operates at nearly full speed (more than 90% efficiency on average). The number of sample points per ray considered (Voxel/Ray + Distance/Ray) lies in the range of 10-15% of all 8 million voxels for the threshold mapping and about 25-40% for semi-transparent mappings. Most important is the frame rate that reaches a peak of 138 Hz in the best case. This high rate is obtained with parallel projection. For perspective views (40° viewing angle), the coherency of the rays is reduced leading to a reduction of the frame rate by a factor of two.

Table 19.2. Rendering with a linear opacity mapping where opacities ≤ 1300 are set to 0, and those above 1300 are increasing linearly to 1.

	Parallel View	Perspective View
Efficiency	91%	95%
Voxel/Ray	9	24
Distance/Ray	21	31
Frame Rate	92Hz	53Hz

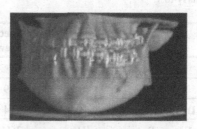

	Parallel View	Perspective View
Efficiency	90%	94%
Voxel/Ray	20	34
Distance/Ray	28	41
Frame Rate	57Hz	38Hz

	Parallel View	Perspective View
Efficiency	92%	94%
Voxel/Ray	24	27
Distance/Ray	33	36
Frame Rate	50Hz	46Hz

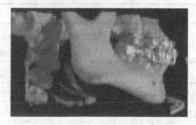

19.10 Brute Force and Half Resolution Rendering

To be able to evaluate the advantages of algorithmic optimisations we switched off space leaping and early ray termination and the same simulations were taken as before. Table 19.4 shows that with algorithmic optimisations the rendering speed quadruples by reducing the resolution by two in each coordinate direction. This is in agreement with the $O(n^2)$ complexity as assumed [3]. An extrapolation of the algorithmic optimisation approach for datasets of 1024^3 voxels gives a 4 Hz rendering rate in the optimal case.

In contrast, the brute force approach shows an $O(n^3)$ complexity. Furthermore, for the 256×256×128 dataset it is a factor of eight slower than the method with algorithmic optimisations. Interestingly, early ray termination contributes only to about 20% of the savings from algorithmic optimisations. This result underlines the relevance of space leaping information.

Table 19.3. Rendering with a half transparent opacity mapping where opacities ≤ 430 are set to 0, opacities ≤ 1170 are increasing linearly to 0.07, and those above 1170 are increasing linearly to 1.

	Parallel View	Perspective View
Efficiency	96%	97%
Voxel/Ray	40	99
Distance/Ray	13	14
Frame Rate	54Hz	26Hz

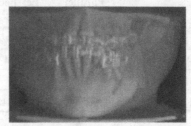

	Parallel View	Perspective View
Efficiency	95%	97%
Voxel/Ray	48	135
Distance/Ray	14	14
Frame Rate	47Hz	20Hz

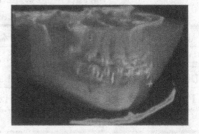

	Parallel View	Perspective View
Efficiency	95%	97%
Voxel/Ray	48	135
Distance/Ray	14	14
Frame Rate	47Hz	20Hz

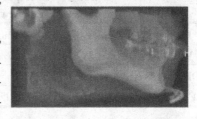

Table 19.4. Results for brute force and optimised approaches for 256×256×128 and 128×128×64 datasets.

	Brute Force, Front Parallel View		Algorithm Optimisations, Front Parallel View	
	Full Resolution	**Half Resolution**	**Full Resolution**	**Half Resolution**
Efficiency	97%	97%	91%	93%
Voxel/Ray	254	127	9	9
Distance/Ray	0	0	21	21
Frame Rate	12Hz	93Hz	92Hz	380Hz

19.11 Conclusions and Outlook

In this chapter an architecture has been presented that allows the realisation of algorithmic optimisation techniques for volume rendering in hardware in an efficient way. The architecture shown here is currently being built up. In addition, further investigation is being carried out to study whether this performance will scale up with faster DRAM interfaces (e.g. from 100 MHz to > 400 MHz) and more rendering pipelines.

References

1. Levoy M. Display of surfaces from volume data. IEEE Computer Graphics and Applications, 1988; 8(5):29-37.
2. Lichtermann J. Design of a fast voxel processor for parallel volume visualization. In: Proc. the 10th Eurographics Workshop on Graphics Hardware, Maastricht, The Netherlands, 1995; 83-92.
3. Lacroute P, Levoy M. Fast volume rendering using a shear-warp factorization of the viewing transform. In: Proc. SIGGRAPH '94, Orlando, FL, 1994; 451-457.
4. Brady M, Jung K, Nguyen HT, Nguyen T. Two-phase perspective ray casting for interactive volume navigation. In: Proc. IEEE Visualization '97, Phoenix, AZ, 1997; 183-189.
5. Knittel G. A PCI-based volume rendering accelerator. In: Proc. the 10th Eurographics Workshop on Graphics Hardware, Maastricht, The Netherlands, 1995; 73-82.
6. Günther T, Poliwoda C, Reinhart C, Hesser J, Männer R, Meinzer H-P, Baur H-J. VIRIM: A massively parallel processor for real-time volume visualization in Medicine. In: Proc. the 9th Eurographics Workshop on Graphics Hardware, Oslo, Norway, 1994; 103-108.
7. Pfister H-P. Towards a scalable architecture for real-time volume rendering. In: Proc. the 10th Eurographics Workshop on Graphics Hardware, Maastricht, The Netherlands, 1995; 123-130.
8. Zuiderveld KJ, Koning AH, Viergever MA. Acceleration of ray-casting using 3D distance transforms. In: Proc. Prlc. Visualization in Biomedical Computing, Chapel Hill, 1992; 324-335.
9. Van Scheltinga JT, Smit J, Bosma M. Design of an on-chip reflectance map. In: Proc. the 10th EuroGraphics Workshop on Graphics Hardware, Maastricht, 1995; 51-55.
10. Knittel G, Straßer W. A compact volume rendering accelerator. In: Proc. Symposium on Volume Visualization, 1994, ACP press, NY; 67-74.
11. Foley JD, van Dam A, Feiner SK, Hughes JF. Computer Graphics: Principles and Practice, 2nd Ed., Addison Wesley, Reading, MA, 1990.
12. Chaudhry G, Li X. A case for the multithread processor architecture. Computer Architecture News, 1994; 22(4):9.

20. Hardware Accelerated Voxelisation

Shiaofen Fang and Hongsheng Chen

20.1 Introduction

In volume graphics [1], 3D objects are represented as discrete, voxel-based regular volumetric models, and processed by volume rendering and manipulation techniques. Since volume graphics also supports the modelling and visualisation of objects' inner structures and 3D amorphous phenomena, it provides a uniform computer graphics framework for intermixing synthetic objects and sampled volume datasets, and it offers a viable and potentially more powerful alternative to surface-based computer graphics. One of the main obstacles for volume graphics to achieve this goal, however, is its limited support to the modelling operations of volumetric and geometric objects.

Historically, the need for direct interaction with 3D objects, such as interactive object manipulations in CAD, has been an important driving force for surface-based computer graphics. A very rich set of surface graphics techniques and algorithms have been developed to provide interactive graphics support for applications such as solid modelling and animation.

In order to achieve and even surpass the capabilities of traditional surface graphics, volume graphics needs to provide efficient rendering support for applications involving dynamic volumetric scenes and interactive manipulations and operations of volumetric and geometric objects. Although hardware and software solutions for fast volume rendering have been developed for regular volume representations, voxelisation algorithms that generate the volume representations from complex geometric and volumetric models are still too slow for interactive modelling operations. This chapter offers a hardware-assisted solution to this problem with general curve, surface and solid objects and *volumetric-CSG* models.

Conceptually, voxelisation is a set membership classification problem for all voxels in a regular volume against a given 3D model. It can also be considered as a 3D extension of the 2D scan-conversion process. In recent years, a number of curve and surface voxelisation algorithms have been proposed [2-7]. Broadly speaking, these algorithms aim to provide efficient ways to extend 2D scan-conversion methods to a volumetric domain. This requires additional sampling in the third dimension for each scanline. Although several important theoretical issues, such as *accuracy, separability* (or *tunnel-free*), and *minimality*, have been addressed in previous publications [2, 4, 8], a central issue, namely the voxelisation speed, has received very little research attention. As a result, existing voxelisation algorithms are not able to provide interactive feedback for object operations. In addition, existing algorithms are object-type specific, i.e. a different algorithm needs to be employed for a different type of object (e.g. lines, circles, polygons, quadratic surfaces, etc.), leading to implementation difficulties for general volume graphics tools.

Solid object voxelisation, on the other hand, has not been sufficiently studied. Solid objects are normally represented by their boundary surfaces, commonly defined as graphics primitives such as OpenGL polygons. Since the interior of a solid object is not explicitly represented, solid voxelisation can be difficult, and it requires, in principle, an inside test for each voxel involved. Surface voxelisation methods cannot be used since they do not generate the interior voxels that are necessary for the volumetric representation of solid objects. The only available algorithm is the one based on point classification by Lee and Requicha [9], which is too slow for interactive applications.

Another common solid representation is the Constructive Solid Geometry (CSG) method [10]. Graphics techniques for CSG models have been studied by many researchers. Most of such efforts are focused on the direct display of CSG Objects [11, 12]. With volume graphics, the CSG method can also be extended to include volume datasets as CSG primitives. Such models are called *Volumetric CSG* (or *VCSG*) models [13], and are potentially useful for combining geometric and volumetric objects in one common modelling environment. There are also a number of voxelisation and volume rendering techniques for CSG or VCSG models. They include the Beam Oriented voxelisation algorithm [14], the volume sampling approach [15], the point sampling algorithm [16], the octree-based rendering algorithm [13], and the distance volume algorithm [17]. In general, these algorithms reconstruct a volume for the entire CSG or VCSG model in some form, which is then rendered by a volume rendering algorithm. Since these volume reconstruction algorithms for CSG or VCSG models are very slow, the VCSG technique has not yet provided effective support for interactive volumetric modelling.

This chapter presents a set of new algorithms for the fast voxelisation of a wide range of 3D objects, including curve, surface and solid objects and Volumetric CSG models. The algorithms make use of existing hardware in modern graphics workstations, such as frame buffer operations and 3D texture mapping, and are able to accomplish very fast voxelisation and volume rendering for these types of 3D objects. A central idea is to generate slices of the underlying models in the frame buffer and then write each frame buffer image to either the texture memory or main memory for volume reconstruction and rendering. Based on this approach, three algorithms are developed for curves/surfaces, solid objects, and Volumetric CSG models, respectively. Frame buffer blending functions are used to carry out the necessary model evaluation computation during the process of slice generation. After the voxelisation result is written to the texture memory, the volume model can be immediately and interactively rendered by 3D texture mapping.

For the convenience of presentation, we will use OpenGL as a representative surface graphics programming interface, and the algorithms have indeed been all implemented in OpenGL. However, the approach, in principle, can also be used with other graphics APIs that can provide ways to access the required hardware features. Compared to other voxelisation methods, this approach is clearly much faster, and very easy to implement, though their performances somewhat depend on the actual implementations of the surface graphics systems. In the following, we will first present the curve/surface voxelisation algorithm in Section 20.2. The solid voxelisation algorithm will be described in Section 20.3. In Section 20.4, the Volumetric-CSG (VCSG) model and its voxelisation algorithm will be presented. Some implementation experience and results will be given in Section 20.5. Further discussions about the advantages and disadvantages of this approach compared to other approaches and alternatives are given in Section 20.6. We conclude this chapter with a few more remarks and future work in Section 20.7.

20.2 Curve and Surface Voxelisation

The curve and surface voxelisation algorithm generates a volume representation for a scene consisting of an arbitrary number of curve or surface objects that can be accepted by OpenGL [18]. These include various types of lines and polygons, quadratic curves and surfaces, NURBS curves and surfaces, etc. The algorithm is based on the fact that surface graphics displays a curve or a surface generated by a 2D scan-conversion (or rasterisation) process. When only a slice of the object is displayed, the result is essentially a slice of the volume from 3D scan-conversion. Since 2D scan-conversion is almost always implemented in hardware, 3D voxelisation can take advantage of it for better performance.

The algorithm takes a slice-by-slice approach by moving a *Z-plane* in a front-to-back order, as shown in Figure 20.1, and by rendering all the curve and surface primitives within each slice using standard OpenGL rendering and clipping functions. The resulting frame buffer image of each slice becomes one slice of the voxelisation result.

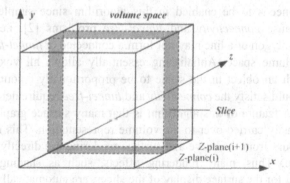

Figure 20.1. Volume slicing.

Since writing the frame buffer to the texture memory is a much faster operation than writing to the main memory, each slice of the voxelisation result in the frame buffer should be first written to a 3D texture memory for visual examination by volume rendering, and later written, as a whole volume, back to the main memory. In this algorithm, the Z-distance between adjacent Z-planes determines the Z-resolution of the volume representation. The resolutions in the X and Y directions are defined by the size of the display window. The following procedure outlines this algorithm:

```
procedure SurfaceVoxelization (int N)
begin
    Create a window of size NxN;
    Define a 3D texture object of size NxNxN;
    Define desired lighting and texturing;
    Enable polygon and line antialiasing;
                                    { Setting the slicing parameters }
    Compute the bounding box of the scene;
    zplane1 = Z value of the bounding box front face;
    zstep = bounding_box_size / N;
                                    { Slicing loop }
    for i = 1 to N do
        zplane2 = zplane1 + zstep;
        Define the thin orthogonal viewing volume;
        Clear frame buffer;
                                        { Fill all surfaces }
        Display all surfaces in FILLED mode;
                                        { Draw curves and polygon edges }
        Display all curves/surfaces in WIRE_FRAME mode;
        Write frame buffer to 3D texture memory;
        zplane1 = zplane2
    end for;

    Render the texture object by 3D texture mapping;
    Save the 3D texture object to main memory;
end
```

Antialiasing needs to be enabled in this algorithm since simple pixel centre sampling can cause *connectivity* and *tunnel-free* problems [2], i.e., the voxels generated for a polygon or a line may not form a connected or *tunnel-free* surface or curve in the volume space. Antialiasing essentially allows all voxels that have intersections with an object in the scene to be proportionally coloured, which, as shown in [4], would satisfy the *connectivity* and *tunnel-free* requirements.

An interesting feature of this algorithm is that many surface graphics rendering effects can be easily carried over to the volume representation. This is because the actual pixel colours from the curve and surface rendering are directly copied to the resulting volume. Thus, many rendering effects, such as shading and surface texturing enabled for the surface display of the slices, are automatically stored in the volume representation, and can be rendered later without extra computation.

20.3 Solid Voxelisation

In OpenGL, the boundary surface of a solid object may be defined by OpenGL surface primitives such as polygons, quadratic surfaces and NURBS surfaces [18]. In the solid voxelisation algorithm, the validity of the boundary representation is assumed, i.e., the algorithm will not work properly with invalid boundary representations [19]. Multiple solid objects may also be considered as one solid representation as long as the boundary surfaces of the different objects do not intersect.

For a given solid representation, the voxelisation algorithm aims to generate the set of voxels that are either inside or on the boundary of a solid object. The algorithm operates similarly to the surface voxelisation algorithm, i.e., it proceeds slice-by-slice in a front-to-back order, with the boundary surfaces displayed within each slice. The frame buffer pixels filled by the display of the current slice constitute the boundary voxels of the solid object within this slice. The object's interior voxels, which also need to be filled, are, however, not explicitly scanned by this process. To generate the interior voxels, the algorithm employs the frame buffer blending function feature in OpenGL with a logical **XOR** operation to carry the boundary information to the interior of the solid object. This approach is based on the fact that when shooting a ray from a pixel to the object space, the *entering* points and the *exiting* points on the ray against a solid object always appear in pairs, and the voxels between each pair of *entering* and *exiting* points are the interior voxels.

The above process requires a binary colouring system. For simplicity, we will assign 0 at all colour bits for empty pixels, and 1 at all colour bits for filled pixels. In addition, the graphics system also needs to disable all rendering features that may alter the drawing colours, such as lighting and shading, antialiasing, texturing, and alpha blending. When a slice is drawn with the **XOR** blending function enabled, all bits of a frame buffer pixel will be set to 1 when a surface is projected to the pixel for the first time. The "1" bits will stay at 1's in the subsequent slices until another surface is projected to the same pixel, which will reset all "1" bits to 0's again. Since without antialiasing only pixel centres are sampled in the 2D scan-conversion of the boundary surfaces, when the object is entirely contained in the volume space, each pixel is guaranteed to meet the solid's boundary in pairs. Thus, after all slices are drawn, all interior voxels will be properly filled with the full colour. This process is shown in Figure 20.2, viewed on the *XZ* cross section plane, for a solid sphere.

The volume generated by the above process can, however, have missing voxels in two cases:

1. *Incomplete boundary.* Without antialiasing, the surface boundary of the solid is not completely voxelised, for the same reason that causes the surface connectivity problem discussed in Section 20.2. A missing boundary may also be caused by the **XOR** operation at the *exiting* points, where the pixel colours are set to 0 before the slice is written out.
2. *Missing thin regions.* For a thin region (thinner than a slice in the *Z* direction), it could happen that the *entering* and *exiting* points for some pixels

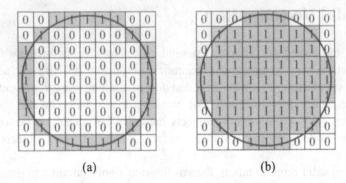

Figure 20.2. Solid voxelisation of a sphere (*XZ* cross-section): (a) the boundary pattern of the sphere surface, (b) the voxelisation result.

fall within the same slice, causing the voxels in this region to cancel each other before the slice is written out.

A simple solution to these two problems is to "superimpose" the complete set of surface voxels, constructed from a separate surface voxelisation procedure, onto the solid voxelisation result using a logical **OR** blending function. This will effectively fill all the thin regions as well as boundaries. The following procedure outlines the solid voxelisation algorithm:

```
procedure SolidVoxelization(int N)
begin
                                    { initialisation }
    Create a window of size NxN;
    Define a 3D texture object of size NxNxN;
    Compute the bounding box of the solid;
                                    { Initialise display parameters }
    Set object to full color and background to black;
    Clear frame buffer;
    Set the "XOR" blending function;
    Disable lighting, texturing, and antialiasing;
                                    { Generate the solid volume }
    for each slice do
        Define the thin orthogonal viewing volume;
        Display all surfaces in FILLED mode;
        Write frame buffer to 3D texture memory;
    end for;
                                    { Super-impose the surfaces }
    Define desired lighting and texturing;
    Enable polygon and line antialiasing;

    for each slice do
        Define the thin orthogonal viewing volume;
        Clear frame buffer;
        Display all surfaces in FILLED mode;
        Display all surfaces in WIRE_FRAME mode;
```

{ Merge with the solid volume }
```
Set the "OR" blending function;
Draw Z-plane by 3D texture mapping with solid volume;
Disable blending function;

Write frame buffer back to 3D texture memory;
end for;

Render the texture object by 3D texture mapping;
Save the 3D texture object to main memory;
end
```

20.4 Volumetric-CSG Voxelisation

20.4.1 VCSG Representation

The Constructive Solid Geometry (CSG) representation allows users to define complex 3D solid objects by hierarchically combining simple geometric primitives using Boolean operations and affine transformations [10]. It is a very popular and powerful solid modelling scheme, particularly for interactive object manipulations and design. A natural extension of the CSG method is to allow volume datasets to be used as CSG primitives, and at the same time allow the intensity values of the volume datasets to be computed during Boolean operations. Such models are called *Volumetric-CSG* models or simply *VCSG* models [13]. To have a uniform representation for all CSG primitives, all geometric primitives can be first converted into volume representations by solid voxelisation. Afterwards, the VCSG model will have only volumes as primitives at the leaf nodes. This method provides a flexible and powerful modelling scheme for the interactive manipulation and operations of volumetric and geometric objects, and can be a useful tool for many advanced applications such as medical imaging, surgical planning/simulation and amorphous phenomena modelling.

For volumetric objects, Boolean operations can be defined as *voxblt* operations [20] or fuzzy set operations [15]. However, for **union** and **intersection** operations, the intensity values of the two volumes involved also need to be blended in their overlapping regions. To do so, each Boolean operation is associated with an intensity function $v()$ that blends two intensity values into one. For binary volumes, it is a simple binary logic function. For scalar volumes, the function $v()$ defines a blending function for the composition of two 3D images. As in 2D image composition [21], different blending functions can generate very different composition results. Examples include combining CT and MRI images, and the fuzzy boundary rendering where the transfer functions of two objects need to both contribute to the rendering according to their fuzzy probabilities in the overlapping area. Some typical $v()$ functions are:

- $v(x, y) = max(x, y)$: maximum material density;
- $v(x, y) = min(x, y)$: minimum material density;

- $v(x, y) = x \otimes y$:   bit-wise logical operation;
- $v(x, y) = t_1 x + t_2 y$:   linear combination;
- $v(x, y) = t_1 x - t_2 y$:   colour subtraction.

20.4.2 Boolean Operations by Frame Buffer Blending

A frame buffer blending function is used to combine a colour value from a source (incoming pixel) and the existing colour value in the frame buffer (destination). Let C_d denote a frame buffer colour (destination colour) and C_s denote the incoming pixel colour (source colour). In OpenGL, a blending function takes the form:

$$C = (C_s \cdot F_s) <op> (C_d \cdot F_d)$$

where F_s and F_d are called source and destination factors, respectively, C is the output colour written back to the frame buffer, and *op* is the equation operation chosen from several different options, such as *addition, subtraction, MinMax* and *logical* operations. The combinations of coefficients and equations can be exploited to perform Boolean operations directly in the frame buffer for two images in the same slice drawn from separate volumes. Since OpenGL blending functions are implemented in hardware, this approach provides a very fast Boolean operation evaluation method with scalar volumes. Many different combinations can be generated to implement Boolean operations with various intensity blending effects. In our implementation, the following combinations are used for Boolean operations with simple intensity blending. The **union** operation can be implemented by *max()* as:

$$C = max(C_d, C_s),$$

or by *addition()* as:

$$C = (C_s \cdot F_s) + (C_d \cdot F_d).$$

The **intersection** operation is implemented by *min()*:

$$C = min(C_d, C_s).$$

The **difference** operation can be implemented by *subtraction()*. However, any non-zero destination colour will be turned to the full colour (i.e. [1, 1, 1] or [255, 255, 255] depending on the colour format) by a colour table to ensure a full subtraction. The function is:

$$C = max(C_s - C_d, 0).$$

20.4.3 VCSG Voxelisation

In interactive applications, the VCSG model can be modified frequently, and each modification requires a new voxelisation of the entire VCSG model for volume rendering. Thus, a fast VCSG voxelisation algorithm is essential to provide volume rendering support for interactive VCSG modelling. Since current CSG or VCSG voxelisation methods are all far too slow for interactive use [13-17], hardware acceleration appears to be the only practical solution.

The VCSG voxelisation algorithm uses frame buffer blending functions to compute the Boolean operations, and 3D texture mapping to carry out the slicing process and transformation operations. Using the solid voxelisation algorithm described in the last section, the algorithm first converts all geometric primitives, as well as volume primitives, into 3D texture objects. The algorithm will also concatenate the sequence of transformations applied to each primitive into one cumulative transformation matrix, and store its inverse with the primitive as a texture matrix. In 3D texture mapping, when a texture matrix is enabled, all texture coordinates will be transformed by the texture matrix first prior to the texture mapping process. This achieves exactly the same effect as the geometric transformation operations defined in the VCSG model.

The binary nodes (Boolean operations) in a VCSG model are evaluated one at a time, based on a depth-first traversal of the VCSG tree. Each Boolean operation generates a new 3D texture object, which replaces the subtree under the binary node. A slicing process, similar to the one used in the surface voxelisation algorithm, is employed to generate the texture volume, slice by slice, for each Boolean operation. For each slice, its central Z-plane is rendered by 3D texture mapping with the two texture volumes, respectively, and the resulting two images are blended together in the frame buffer using the appropriate blending functions, as given in the last subsection. The resulting frame buffer image is then written to the texture memory as one slice of the new texture object. This VCSG voxelisation algorithm is described in the pseudo code procedure VCSGVoxelization shown below.

This algorithm computes an intermediate texture volume for each Boolean operation, and recursively trims the VCSG tree to generate the final volume. Although a texture memory swapping may be needed to load each new texture object into the texture memory, the cost is relatively low since it is only done once (assuming the texture memory can hold at least two texture objects for each Boolean operation). There is, however, an alternative way that avoids generating any intermediate texture volume at all if all the original volume primitives (the leaf nodes) can be simultaneously loaded into the texture memory. In this case, the algorithm can compute one slice at a time through the entire VCSG tree (i.e. without trimming the tree), and store only one intermediate 2D texture in each Boolean operation node, which can later be drawn using 2D texture mapping for the next Boolean operation. In other words, the same VCSG voxelisation procedure given above is applied to one slice at a time. This will have no texture swapping at all if the texture memory can hold all volume primitives and the intermediate 2D textures at the same time. Otherwise, this alternative approach will be much slower since texture swapping will be needed for every slice.

```
procedure VCSGVoxelization(VCSG_NODE root, int N)
begin
    for each primitive do        { Preparation }
        if geometric primitive then
            convert to volume by solid voxelization;
        end if;
        Create texture object;
        Concatenate transformations;
    end for;
    Remove all transformation nodes;
                                { Start depth-first VCSG traversal. }
    Create a window of size NxN;
    tvolume = NodeVoxelization(root, N);
    Render and save tvolume;
end

TEX_OBJ procedure NodeVoxelization(VCSG_NODE node, int N)
begin
                                { Recursively evaluate and trim binary nodes }
    if node.left is NOT a leaf node then
        node.left = NodeVoxelization(node.left, N);
    end if;
    if node.right is NOT a leaf node then
        node.right = NodeVoxelization(node.right, N);
    end if;
    for each slice do
                                { Draw Z-plane with the right child volume }
        Clear frame buffer;
        Bind the texture volume of node.right;
        Set texture matrix;
        Draw Z-plane by 3D texture mapping;
                                { Draw Z-plane with the left child volume }
        Set the proper blending function;
        Bind the texture volume of node.left;
        Set texture matrix;
        Draw Z-plane by 3D texture mapping;

        Write frame buffer to 3D texture memory;
    end for;
    Return(reconstructed texture volume);
end
```

20.5 Implementation

The three algorithms described in this chapter have been implemented on an SGI
Onyx-2 workstation using a single processor Reality Engine and 64 MB texture
memory. The program is written in C and OpenGL 1.1. Hardware system
requirements include 3D texture mapping, frame buffer blending functions and a
polygon based graphics processor.

In the examples shown in Figure 20.3, each model is converted into a

128×128×128 scalar volume, and rendered by 3D texture mapping with or without shading. The shading method with 3D texture mapping proposed in [22] has been employed in this implementation. The Zucker's 3D gradient smoothing filter [23], with either a 3×3×3 or a 5×5×5 kernel, is used for gradient computation in shading.

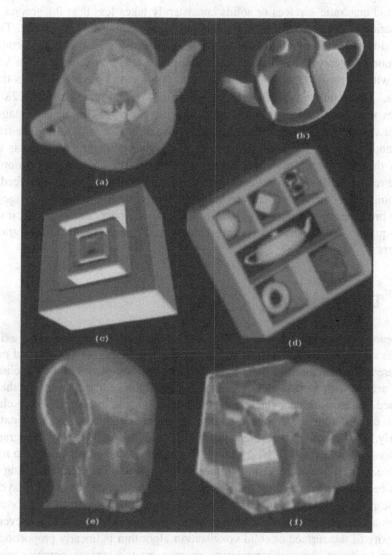

Figure 20.3. Some examples of the voxelisation algorithms.

Figure 20.3a is a surface voxelisation result rendered without shading. Figures 20.3b, 20.3c and 20.3d show VCSG models with synthetic and volumetric primitives, rendered with shading. Figure 20.3e is a VCSG model with volume datasets from CT scans. It is constructed as follows: a sphere is first intersected with the mouth area of a monkey head (CT dataset), the result is merged with a human head (also a CT dataset) by a **union** operation, and then cut (subtracted) by a cube.

The image is generated directly from 3D texture mapping without shading. Figure 20.3f shows an example of carrying the surface texture into the voxelisation result. Here the textured surface is superimposed onto a solid box, which is also part of a VCSG model. No shading is applied in generating this image.

Timings from this implementation are fairly consistent. The voxelisation of linear and quadratic surfaces or solids consistently takes less than 0.1 second. The voxelisation of a teapot with NURBS surfaces takes about 1 to 1.5 seconds. This is mainly due to the tessellation of the NURBS surfaces, which can easily generate ten times more polygons than a linear or quadratic object. The voxelisation of a VCSG model with 9 primitives of both synthetic and volumetric objects takes less than 4 seconds. The rendering by 3D texture mapping is real-time for 128×128×128 volumes with both unshaded and shaded images. However, for shaded images, a gradient volume needs to be first computed for each model, which can take from a few seconds to a few minutes, depending on whether gradient smoothing is used, and on the size of the smoothing kernel. For interactive object modification, the volume rendering time is, in general, an insignificant portion of the overall feedback time compared to the volume conversion time. Moreover, higher-quality images can also be produced by writing the volume to the main memory, and rendering it using higher-quality volume rendering algorithms and more sophisticated gradient operators.

20.6 Discussions

The approach taken here aims to provide a practical and fast solution using existing graphics systems. However, since the algorithms, to a certain extent, depend on the hardware implementations of the graphics API, certain properties of the voxelisation results are difficult to assess. For instance, antialiasing is used to ensure that the voxelised surfaces are connected and tunnel-free, but the exact result may change slightly on different systems due to the different antialiasing implementations. Similarly, the speed of the algorithms also depends mostly on the graphics subsystem rather than the CPU. Although for N slices, the algorithm needs to render the scene N times, the actual cost is far less than N times of the scene rendering cost. This is because each time only the objects that are within a slice are displayed. In fact, the main overhead costs come from the scene clipping by the thin viewing volumes and the fragmentation of the graphics primitives. In general, however, the complexity of the surface or solid voxelisation algorithm is linearly proportional to the complexity of the scene rendering process by the surface graphics system. Clearly, when the number of objects in the scene is increased, the voxelisation process will be proportionally slowed down, but not significantly more than that of the surface display process.

The basic idea of all three algorithms comes from the 3D texture mapping-based volume rendering process [24, 25]. In that approach, slices of the volume parallel to the viewing plane are generated by 3D texture mapping and composited to the frame buffer in a back-to-front order to form the final image. A similar paradigm is employed in the voxelisation algorithms. The main differences are within the slice computation step. For curves and surfaces, the slice is generated by normal surface graphics displays with a thin viewing volume. For solid objects, an **XOR** blending function is used to identify the interior voxels. For a VCSG model, more complex blending functions, along with 3D texture mapping, are needed for the computations of Boolean operations and affine transformations. Nevertheless, 3D texture mapping is an important part of these voxelisation algorithms. Although hardware 3D texture mapping is not yet supported on PCs and low-end workstations, it is indeed becoming more affordable and available in recent years. While the 3D texture mapping hardware is crucial for VCSG voxelisation, it is actually not required for curve/surface voxelisation and solid voxelisation. On machines with only 2D texture mapping, the slices can be stored in separate 2D textures, and rendered afterwards by a Shear-Warp projection process, similar to the ray casting-based shear-warp algorithm [25]. Therefore, the curve/surface voxelisation algorithm and the solid voxelisation algorithm can also be used by PCs with 2D texture mapping support.

Another related work is the OpenGL *Volumizer* by SGI. *Volumizer* provides a high level programming interface for the rendering and manipulation of volume primitives using hardware-assisted 3D texture mapping. There are two major differences between this approach and the *Volumizer* approach. First, *Volumizer* does not take a volume graphics approach, i.e., synthetic objects are not voxelised, rather directly rendered to the frame buffer and combined with volume rendering using the depth buffer. Thus, it cannot handle volumetric information. For instance, cutting through a solid object will result in an empty interior space, instead of the true solid interior as seen here. Secondly, Boolean operations and CSG modelling are not supported in *Volumizer*. This is partly due to the lack of volume representations for synthetic objects. In summary, *Volumizer* is designed for the direct graphical display of volumetric objects, while the work here is intended to provide fast voxelisation algorithms that generate the volume representations of synthetic or intermixed models.

The accuracy of a voxelisation algorithm involves both the resolution and the scalar field of the volume. Therefore, it depends on: (a) the number of slices used in the voxelisation process, (b) the size of the frame buffer window that is used to capture the images of the slices, and (c) the antialiasing methods used in the graphics system. There is clearly a trade-off between speed and resolution. However, we do not have total control over the scalar field (the actual colour/intensity values assigned to the voxels). For example, if only supersampling is used in antialiasing, there will be only a few different intensity levels for the boundary voxels. However, if more sophisticated area sampling is used in antialiasing, a true scalar volume can actually be generated for more accurate results [15]. It should also be mentioned that image quality is not always directly related to the resolution of the voxelisation. In particular, a volume from voxelisation usually does not have a continuous scalar field as a scanned dataset does. Consequently, regular volume rendering algorithms that work well for scanned datasets may not generate good images from voxelisation results. Solutions have recently been proposed using either distance volumes or volume filters to improve the accuracy of the voxelisation and the quality of the resulting images, though the cost is considerably higher [17, 26-27] (see also Chapter 4).

There is a special case in the solid voxelisation algorithm that has not been addressed in this chapter. The parity rule used in solid voxelisation may not be correct, in principle, if a vertex or some point on an edge of an OpenGL surface primitive (polygon) happens to project to the exact centre of a pixel. This is because the same pixel may be drawn several times by all polygons connected to the same edge or vertex, which, in theory, could break the parity for the intersections along this pixel. Although such a case is very rare, it certainly is a possibility. The solution to this remains an open problem, and may depend on the specific implementations of the polygon rasterisation procedures in different graphics subsystems. On the other hand, this special case can be easily corrected, when it occurs, by a small random transformation such as rotation and translation.

20.7 Conclusions

We have presented a hardware accelerated approach for fast voxelisation of curves/surfaces, solid objects, and VCSG models. The algorithms use existing surface graphics hardware, and will be able to provide volume graphics support for interactive volume modelling applications involving both geometric and volumetric objects, and inter-object operations. The main advantages of this approach are its speed, generality and easy implementation. In the future, we will further study the properties of these algorithms for more in-depth performance and accuracy analysis. We would also like to investigate 2D texture mapping based voxelisation methods for possible uses on PCs and low-end workstations. Finally, more sophisticated and efficient volume rendering methods for voxelisation results need to be developed and implemented for higher image quality.

References

1. Kaufman K, Cohen D, Yagel R. Volume graphics. IEEE Computer Graphics and Applications, 1993; 13:51-64.
2. Cohen D, Kaufman A. Scan-conversion algorithms for linear and quadratic objects. In: Kaufman A (Ed) Volume Visualization. 1991; 280-301.
3. Cohen D, Kaufman A. 3D linear voxelization and connectivity control. IEEE Computer Graphics and Applications, 1997; 17(6):80-87.
4. Huang J, Yagel R, Fillippov V, Kurzion Y. An accurate method for voxelizing polygon meshes. In: Proc. IEEE/ACM Symposium on Volume Visualization, 1998; 119-126.
5. Kaufman A. Efficient algorithms for 3D scan-conversion of parametric curves, surfaces, and volumes. ACM/SIGGRAPH Computer Graphics, 1987; 21(4):171-179.
6. Kaufman A. Efficient algorithms for scan-conversing 3D polygons. Computers and Graphics, 1988; 12(2):213-219.

7. Kaufman A, Shimony E. 3D scan-conversion algorithms for voxel-based graphics. In: Proc. Workshop on Interactive 3D Graphics, 1986; 45-75.
8. Cohen D, Kaufman A. Fundamentals of surface voxelization. Computer Vision, Graphics, and Image Processing, 1995; 56(6):453-461.
9. Lee YT, Requicha A. Algorithms for computing the volume and other integral properties of solids. Communications of the ACM, 1982; 25(9):635-650.
10. Requicha A. Representation for rigid solids: Theory, methods and systems. Computing Surveys, 1980; 12(4):437-464.
11. Rappoport A, Spitz S. Interactive Boolean operations for conceptual design of 3D solids. In: Proc. SIGGRAPH, 1997; 269-278.
12. Wiegand TF. Interactive rendering of CSG models. Computer Graphics Forum, 1996; 15(4):249-261.
13. Fang S, Srinivasan R. Volumetric-CSG: a model-based volume visualization approach. In: Proc. the 6th International Conference in Central Europe on Computer Graphics and Visualization, 1998; 88-95.
14. Shareef N, Yagel R. Rapid previewing via volume-based solid modeling. In: Proc. Solid Modeling '95; 281-292.
15. Wang S, Kaufman A. Volume-sampled 3D modeling. IEEE Computer Graphics and Applications, 1994; 14(1):26-32.
16. Breen D. Constructive cubes: CSG evaluation for display using discrete 3D scalar data sets. In: Proc. Eurographics, 1991; 127-142.
17. Breen D, Mauch S, Whitaker RT. 3D scan conversion of CSG models into distance volumes. In: Proc. IEEE/ACM Symposium on Volume Visualization, 1998; 7-14.
18. Woo M, Neider J, Davis T. OpenGL Programming Guide, 2nd Edition, Addison Wesley, 1997.
19. Hoffmann C. Geometric and Solid Modeling: An Introduction. Morgan Kaufmann Publishers, 1989.
20. Kaufman A. The voxblt engine: A voxel frame buffer processor. In: Kuijk A (Ed), Advances in Graphics Hardware III, Springer-Verlag, 1992; 85-102.
21. Porter T, Duff T. Compositing digital images. ACM/SIGGRAPH Computer Graphics, 1984; 18:253-259.
22. Westermann R, Thomas E. Efficiently using graphics hardware in volume rendering applications. In: Proc. SIGGRAPH, 1998; 169-177.
23. Zucker SW, Hummel RA. A three-dimensional edge operator. IEEE Transactions on Pattern Analysis and Machine Intelligence, 1981; 3(3):324-331.
24. Cabral B, Cam N, Foran J. Accelerated volume rendering and tomographic reconstruction using texture mapping hardware. In: Proc. IEEE Symposium on Volume Visualization, 1994; 91-98.
25. Lacroute P, Levoy M. Fast volume rendering using a shear-warp factorization of the viewing transformation. In: Proc. SIGGRAPH, 1994; 451-458.
26. Gibson SF. Using distance maps for accurate surface representation in sampled volumes. In: Proc. IEEE/ACM Symposium on Volume Visualization, 1998; 23-30.
27. Sramek M, Kaufman A. Object voxelization by filtering. In: Proc. IEEE/ACM Symposium on Volume Visualization, 1998; 111-118.

21. Volume Graphics and the Internet

Ken Brodlie and Jason Wood

21.1 Introduction

The Internet has changed the face of computing. The use of e-mail and desktop video-conferencing has made collaboration between people very easy and very natural. Application-sharing technology, such as that provided by Microsoft's NetMeeting, allows a single application to be accessed by a group of people at different locations. The Internet likewise enables collaboration between computers — the Distributed.net activity [1] harnesses spare computing power on the Internet to tackle mathematical tasks that otherwise could hardly be contemplated.

In this chapter we look at the opportunities offered by the Internet for the visualisation community, and the volume visualisation community particularly. The volume visualisation task is often computer-intensive and complex — how can the Internet help by distributing the computational load? This we shall term: *Visualisation by Linking Machines*. Again volume visualisation requires judgement and skill, particularly in the segmentation stage — how can the Internet help by distributing the human processing between a number of people? This we call *Visualisation by Linking Humans*. The field of *Distributed Co-operative Visualisation* is reviewed in detail in the Eurographics State of the Art Report [2]; our aim in this chapter is to give a more concise treatment, and to look more specifically at volume graphics applications.

We begin by looking at visualisation by linking machines. There are two main approaches. The first, which pre-dates the Web, splits the task into a number of sub-processes, and places the computationally intensive parts on a supercomputer. This is covered in Section 21.2. The second approach, described in Section 21.3, uses Web technology to distribute processing between a client front-end and a server back-end. This is an increasingly popular approach, and we shall try to compare and contrast the different styles of Web-based visualisation.

We then go on to look at visualisation by linking humans. This is much less developed. In Section 21.4, we describe some general approaches to collaborative applications, and explain why these general approaches may not be suitable for visualisation. In Section 21.5, we turn specifically to visualisation. Although the popular Modular Visualisation Environments (MVEs), such as IRIS Explorer [3], AVS [4] and IBM Data Explorer [5], were designed from the outset to support distributed processing, they were all based on a single-user model. If you want to collaborate, you cluster around the same workstation. It is only recently that we have seen extensions of these systems to collaborative operation. This has the potential to change the accepted way people undertake visualisation processing. We review the extensions of MVEs, and mention other approaches to collaborative visualisation.

21.2 Visualisation by Linking Machines: Early Days

The modern era of visualisation is often measured from the key NSF Report *Visualisation in Scientific Computing* by McCormack, de Fanti and Brown [6]. The authors saw clearly the advantages of distributed visualisation, coining the term *televisualization* to describe the application of networks to visualisation. In their model, advanced scientific computing is carried out on the supercomputer, and rendering on the workstation. In the middle is the concept of an *image computer* which "prepares visual data for humans". In a sense this anticipates the subsequent visualisation reference model of Haber and McNabb [7].

This was followed through into reality in the development of the Modular Visualisation Environments (MVEs). The first commercial system, AVS [8], was designed to allow "transparent execution of modules on remote machines ...", and this principle has been continued by later MVEs, such as IRIS Explorer and IBM Data Explorer. All allow modules to be distributed across heterogeneous platforms.

The main use in practice is to off-load computationally intensive modules onto a computer server. For example, in IRIS Explorer, the VolumeToGeom splatting module can be run on a background processor, while data reading and rendering is executed on the user's workstation. An impressive feature of these MVEs is that — having mastered the basic system — the extension to multi-processor working is extremely easy to learn. The user is completely sheltered from issues of networking.

Figure 21.1 shows a screenshot of this in action. The VolumeToGeom module is running on a server, as indicated by the bar at the bottom of the module panel with the name of the remote host.

21.3 Visualisation by Linking Machines: Web-Based Visualisation

The Web, which began as a distributed information repository, is now widely used as a distributed computing environment. The visualisation community has embraced this technology, and there is a growing field of Web-based Visualisation.

The first use of the Web for visualisation (that we are aware of) was by Ang et al. [9], presented at the IEEE Visualization '94 conference. This used the Mosaic browser as a user interface to download volume data over the Web. The data is then linked via the CCI mechanism, to volume visualisation software running on the user's workstation. This is an example of *client-side visualisation* where the

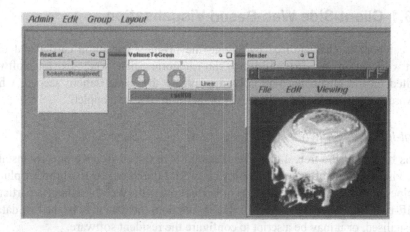

Figure 21.1. Distributed volume visualisation using IRIS Explorer.

execution is carried out on a client workstation. Since then a host of different approaches have been suggested, and quite regularly new Web-based visualisation services appear. An example is the air quality visualisation service [10] in which IRIS Explorer is used to create visualisations of air quality data on selected days. This is an instance of *server-side visualisation*, where the main execution is on a server and a visual description (in 2D or 3D) is transferred to the client for interpretation. In this particular case, it is a 3D VRML model which is returned.

The client-side versus server-side execution is the top-level classification of Web-based visualisation. However within each of these main categories there are a variety of approaches. Figure 21.2 shows a Web-based visualisation tree, which will be the basis of our description of the various methods.

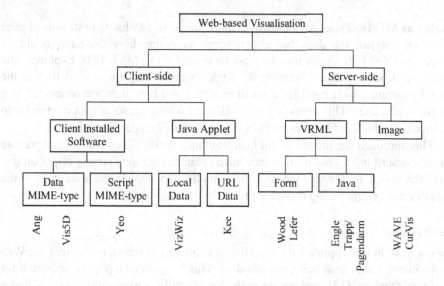

Figure 21.2. Web-based visualisation tree.

21.3.1 Client-Side Web-Based Visualisation

This category is characterised by having the primary execution carried out on a client workstation. We distinguish two sub-categories: first, where existing software installed on the client machine is used to create the visualisation; second, where software is downloaded from the server in the form of a Java applet.

Client-Installed Software

In this branch of the tree, a client workstation is assumed to have already installed some visualisation software. This software is configured either as a browser plug-in or helper application, and is fired up on arrival over the Web of data of a particular MIME-type. Even here we need a further distinction: the data may be the raw data to be visualised, or it may be a script to configure the resident software.

Data as MIME-Type. This was the original approach of Ang et al. [9] whose VIS volume visualizer was fired up on receipt of data in HDF format, identified as MIME-type *hdf/volume*. (In fact, VIS is a hybrid system, as the client which operates in this Web environment also calls on background processors to carry out the volume rendering.)

This approach has also been followed in the Web version of Vis5D [11]. Meteorological data is downloaded to a Web browser as MIME-type *application/vis5d*, whereupon Vis5D is invoked to give a weather forecast visualisation.

This approach only works for special-purpose applications where the data is of a unique type. For more general applications, such as an MVE, capable of a variety of visualisations from a variety of data types, this approach does not work: we would need to define an impossibly large set of MIME-types.

Script as MIME-Type. An alternative, more suited to MVEs, is to download over the Web not just the data, but also a script to define how the data should be processed. Yeo [12] shows how this can be done for the MVE IRIS Explorer. The user downloads a script describing the IRIS Explorer map to be used (this is the visual program which specifies a set of modules and how they are connected in a dataflow pipeline). This script has a MIME-type which causes a Java interpreter to be invoked, which in turn fires up IRIS Explorer with the specified map.

This approach has proved useful in consultancy work: the consultant can prepare a script describing a visualisation they have created; the client simply clicks on this link, the script is downloaded and the visualisation application executes — the visualisation programming is done remotely by the consultant.

Java Applet

By contrast, in this approach the visualisation software is transferred across the Web to the client, rather than being pre-installed. This has proved a popular approach for business graphics [13], and increasingly for scientific visualisation also. A major difficulty however is the security restrictions on Java applets. An applet can only read data from a file on the host from which the applet was loaded. This is a disastrous restriction because in a visualisation application the data will either reside with the client (in the case of a person visualising their own data), or be at some data repository on the Web (in the case of a person visualising some public service data, such as air quality statistics). Fortunately there are solutions, at a cost. Two approaches have been suggested:

Local Data. Here we suppose that the user has their own data to visualise. The browser "File Upload" facility can be used to upload the data to the applet host, from where it returns for processing by the applet! This was first proposed in the VizWiz applet [14], which allows isosurface and cutting plane visualisations of volume data.

Data at a URL. This is a more general approach where the data can reside at any URL — this could be a remote repository, but it could also point to a file in the user's own Web area (thus encompassing the Local Data case). The solution, used by Kee [15], is to have a Java data server application run on the applet host, to fetch data temporarily from a given URL (note Java applications are not subject to the same security restrictions as applets).

There is a nice example of medical volume visualisation which follows the client-side approach. Hendin, John and Shochet [16] describe a means of using the 2D texture mapping approach to volume rendering, in a Web-based context. A Java applet is downloaded from a server. Its role is to fetch medical data from the same server, and pass the data into a VRML world through the External Authoring Interface (EAI). The texture facilities of VRML are used to provide the volume visualisation.

21.3.2 Server-Side Web-Based Visualisation

This category is characterised by having the primary execution on a server, with the browser on a client workstation forming the user interface. This approach assumes a benevolent agency who provides both software and processing power as an Internet service (although in principle a charging mechanism could be used). Within this category, there are again two flavours, depending on the visualisation model (3D or 2D) which is returned to the user for viewing in the browser.

VRML Model

VRML is the ISO standard for the transfer of 3D worlds across the Internet. It is the existence of this standard, and the widespread availability of VRML plug-ins, which makes server-side visualisation feasible. The user specifies data to be visualised, and the visualisation technique to be used; this is transmitted to visualisation software on a server; and a VRML model is returned to the browser. We can distinguish two approaches depending on how the user specifies the request: through a form interface, or through a Java applet.

Form Interface. In this simple approach, the user enters the required information via a form, which is processed on the server by a CGI script. An early example of this approach is the air quality visualisation service, developed by Wood et al. [8], using IRIS Explorer. Figure 21.3 shows the form in which the user enters the selection of data to be visualised (location, time, pollutant), and the style of plot (block diagram or surface). The CGI script then invokes IRIS Explorer using its Skm scripting language to program a suitable map, and passes the resulting VRML back to the user.

Though this is surface rather than volume visualisation, the approach is quite general and can be applied to any visualisation. Users of the *vtk* visualisation toolkit can build their own server using instructions at the *vtk* Web site [17]. Lefer [18] describes an architecture for distributed visualisation using *vtk*, which launches a different server for each user connected to the system.

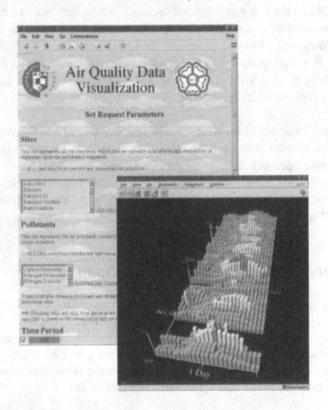

Figure 21.3. Air quality visualisation service.

Java Interface. In this approach, a Java applet replaces the form for data entry by the user. Obviously this allows greater flexibility and a more visually attractive interface.

An interesting example of this approach has been developed by Engel [19]. This implements the progressive isosurface algorithm of Ertl et al. [20] as a server-side Web application. This uses sliders on the Java applet to control the level of detail.

Another example is the Vis-a-Web system of Trapp and Pagendarm [21].

Image Approach

As an alternative to VRML, it is possible to carry out the 3D-to-2D projection on the server, and transfer the resulting image to the browser. The ability of the viewer to navigate the 3D world is obviously lost, but there may be applications where this is not a problem.

A nice example is the CurVis system of Thiesel et al. [22]. This produces visualisations of 2D fluid flow, and is targeted at mobile computing. So care is taken in the image compression in order to utilise available bandwidth as effectively as possible.

Another very interesting example is the WAVES (Web-Accessed Visualization for Engineering and Sciences) project who offer a Gnuplot service [23]. The user enters data via a form interface, and a GIF image is returned. (In fact, it is possible to have a Gnuplot command file returned as an alternative.)

21.3.3 Evaluation — Strengths and Weaknesses

The strength of the client-side approach is the close coupling between the user interface, the data and the visualisation software. For interactive applications, this is a major plus.

Of the two styles of client-side approach, the "Java applet" solutions are attractive where the processing is simple and the data is small. Because the software is downloaded, the user has no installation or maintenance issues to worry about. The "client-installed software" solutions become more attractive when the datasets are larger, and the need to download data to a server becomes a critical factor. They also score in terms of reuse: reuse of existing software in a Web environment; and re-use of the learning investment made by a user in mastering a complex piece of software.

The strength of the server-side approach is the off-load of computation from the workstation to a powerful computer server. This is the clear motivation behind the progressive isosurface application. Another advantage of this approach is that it allows simple, tailored user interfaces to be used as front-ends to more complex visualisation systems, as in the air quality service.

Of the two styles of server-side visualisation, the choice will typically depend on the nature of the data: VRML for 3D, images for 2D.

21.4 Visualisation by Linking Humans: General Approaches to Collaboration

Major scientific research is today a team effort, bringing different skills and expertise to complex problems. The analysis of their research results needs visualisation, and should be a collaborative effort, but scientists are confronted with visualisation tools designed for the single-user. This has motivated a number of efforts over the past few years to develop collaborative visualisation systems.

In this section we look at some of the approaches that have been proposed. Once again we structure the review as a tree of collaborative visualisation, as shown in Figure 21.4. The top level of the tree identifies two approaches: application sharing, a general approach which can be used for any software; and collaborative visualisation systems, which are specifically designed for visualisation.

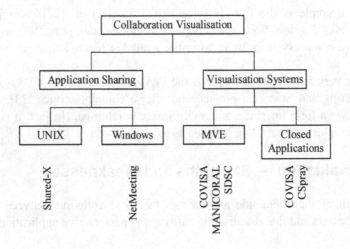

Figure 21.4. Collaborative visualisation tree.

In the *application sharing* approach, the application runs at one location, but the user interface is replicated at each participant's workstation. This is essentially an operating system extension, and so can be applied to any application. Input may be generated by any participant (perhaps with some control to allow only one person at a time to generate input); output is sent to all participants as a screen update.

Because sharing takes place at a low level, the tools are operating system dependent. Two leading products are:

- *Shared-X.* This provides application sharing for the UNIX and X Window System community;
- *Microsoft NetMeeting.* This includes a form of application sharing for the MS Windows community.

Its generality is both the strength and weakness of this approach. It is a strength because of its simplicity of operation, but it is also a weakness because it operates at a very low semantic level. It is unaware that visualisation is the application, let alone what type of visualisation system is in use. The result of this lack of intelligence is often an unusable system: the continual distribution of output screens to each participant is an impossible network load and the collaborative session can stall. In addition, all collaborators must be using the same operating system.

21.5 Visualisation by Linking Humans: Collaborative Visualisation Systems

The inflexibility of application sharing encourages a study of how to extend visualisation systems — not at the operating system level, but at the level of the application itself. This proves to be a more successful strategy, offering portability across operating systems.

Our tree again divides. We split between the MVEs which allow programming of visualisation applications, and systems which are closed applications.

21.5.1 Modular Visualisation Environments

The MVE family (IRIS Explorer, AVS, IBM Data Explorer) represent the state-of-the-art in general-purpose visualisation systems. Their design is based on a reference model, well explained by Haber and McNabb [7], in which processes are linked together in a dataflow pipeline (Figure 21.5). Data is input at one end, and passes successively through filter, mapping and rendering processes. The family is characterised by their visual programming user interface, which allows a user to construct their own pipeline. Moreover the family are open systems, in the sense that users can create their own modules and include them in the pipeline.

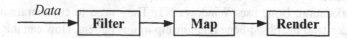

Figure 21.5. Visualisation reference model.

Wood et al. [24] in the COVISA project showed how the Haber and McNabb model can be extended to a collaborative scenario, by allowing data to flow from a pipeline on one machine, to a pipeline on another machine (Figure 21.6.

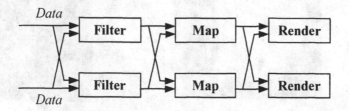

Figure 21.6. Collaborative visualisation reference model.

This has been implemented as an extension of the IRIS Explorer MVE. The system works in outline as follows. A server process manages the collaboration. When a user wishes to join a collaborative session, they launch a special *MServer* module which establishes a connection with the central server. To share, say, lattice data (the IRIS Explorer array data type), a user can connect an *MShareLat* module at an appropriate point in their existing pipeline. This automatically launches a corresponding *MShareLat* module in the visual programming area of every other collaborator. They connect this to their pipeline, and data then flows seamlessly between the pipelines.

In addition to sharing data, users can also share parameters, allowing dual control of modules. One user can also launch a module, or even a complete pipeline, in another user's visual programming area.

This is in major contrast to the application sharing mentioned above. Here the collaboration is highly aware of the visualisation application. A group of users can program the sharing of data exactly as they want.

For example, in a training situation, the instructor can launch pipelines in a learner's visual program area, and initially control all modules themselves. As the learner progresses, the umbilical chord of shared control can be progressively removed. It is not necessary for the pipelines to be the same for each collaborator. In a scenario of a scientist collaborating with a visualisation expert, the scientist could control the computational simulation process, but pass the resulting data to a visualisation expert for subsequent processing — with the end result being shared between the two people. The collaboration is programmed.

Consider a hypothetical volume visualisation scenario. Two doctors examine a patient's scan data: one doctor, whom we shall call Dr Bone, has CT data of the patient's head, showing bone and soft tissue; another doctor, Dr Blood, has SPECT data of the same patient, showing blood flow. Figure 21.7 shows the doctors, each looking at their own dataset using the IRIS Explorer Isosurface module. Blood has a UNIX workstation; Bone uses Windows NT. They need to collaborate in order to jointly understand the blood-bone relationship in this patient. How can they do this?

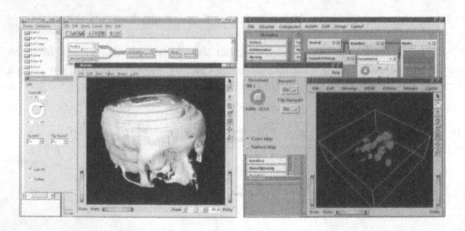

Figure 21.7. Left: Dr Bone looks at CT data; right: Dr Blood looks at SPECT data.

Figure 21.8 shows Dr Bone having joined a collaborative session with Dr Blood. Bone has launched an MShareGeom module and connected it to the input port of their Render module. At the same time, Blood in their map, connects the output port of their Isosurface module to the corresponding MShareGeom module. Geometry data then flows from Blood's Isosurface across the Internet into Bone's Render.

Bone therefore sees both blood and bone isosurfaces (having modified the transparency of bone appropriately). Note that Bone has also connected their Isosurface data to MShareGeom so that Blood likewise can see both.

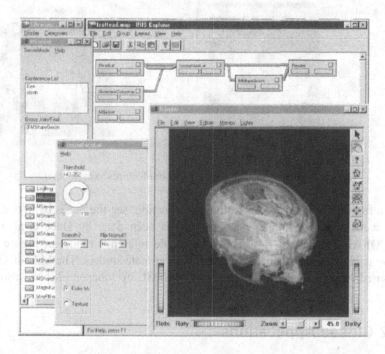

Figure 21.8. Dr Bone collaborates with Dr Blood to look at CT and SPECT data together.

However collaboration needs more than merging datasets. People need to discuss, to argue, to persuade. Desktop video conferencing and shared whiteboards are important accessories. However, in face-to-face discussion about pictures, we point to features that we wish another person to notice. Visualisation therefore needs its own collaborative tools, and we see in Figure 21.9 Bone and Blood, with separate pointers, indicating features to each other. The pointers are shared geometry between the collaborators.

This was just a hypothetical scenario but it does indicate how collaborative sessions can be programmed, just like a single-user session.

The flexibility of this approach allows us to deal as we wish with important issues in collaboration:

- *Privacy*. How private is our data? If it is private, then we can program the collaboration so that we share after it has been filtered.
- *Bandwidth*. How fast is the network connection? We can choose to exchange data at differing levels in the pipeline, according to the bandwidth available.
- *Processing power*. What is the relative power of the collaborators' workstations? Again we can program the collaboration so that heavy computation is carried out perhaps by only one team member.

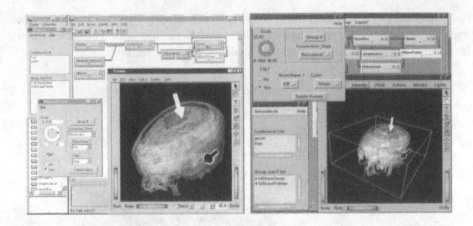

Figure 21.9. Drs Blood and Bone point out features to each other.

For a full discussion of collaborative visualisation, see the thesis by Wood [25]. Further work on collaborative visualisation has been done by Duce et al. in the MANICORAL project [26, 27]. They extend the reference model of Figure 21.6, and have gained useful practical experiences in climate studies. The MANICORAL project used AVS as the base system. Work at SDSC by Johnson [28] has also used AVS.

21.5.2 Closed Applications

The visual programming model of the MVE family is targeted at the serious visualisation user, who needs this flexibility in order to explore a dataset thoroughly. For many end-users, their learning curve is a major deterrent.

However there is another scenario, where the MVE is used as a programming language in order to create an application program for use by others. A trained MVE programmer can develop a visual program, extract the key interaction elements into a single panel, and present an easy-to-use application to a group of users. For example, we would not envisage surgeons using an MVE directly, but we would see them using a closed application developed using an MVE by a skilled visualisation programmer.

A natural extension of this is to build closed applications which include collaborative modules. Indeed this has been done with the IRIS Explorer collaborative extensions.

Finally, any article on collaborative visualisation should include mention of CSpray [29]. This is an extension of the novel Spray rendering system [30], which uses a quite different metaphor for visualisation. In Spray, a user points a "spraycan" at a set of data with the aim of extracting some particular feature such as an isosurface. In CSpray, each collaborator has a spraycan and each person can see the results of other people's visualisation. Their work includes a very careful analysis of the issues of privacy and floor control.

21.6 Conclusions

This chapter has reviewed how the Internet can help visualisation by linking computers, and by linking humans.

One small reflection: it is easier to link computers than to link humans. Collaborative visualisation requires the scientist or engineer to change the way in which they routinely work. Such a change requires a belief that the advantages are significant. The challenge for the visualisation community is to create tools that are an easy extension of the existing single-user tools, so that the transition to this new way of working is painless. That has been our aim in developing the collaborative extension of IRIS Explorer. These tools are now available as an integral part of the distributed software [31]. Our hope is that these tools will indeed change the way people work.

Acknowledgements

We should like to thank a number of colleagues and students who have worked closely with us over the last few years. Helen Wright (now at the University of Hull) played a major part in the COVISA project. Abraham Kee, Peter Stanton, Edward Teong, Alan Yeo and Alex Coyle developed various Web-based visualisation approaches. Thanks also to Stuart Lovegrove for help with both VRML and Java.

References

1. Distributed.Net web site. http://www.distributed.net/.
2. Brodlie KW, Duce DA, Gallop JR, Wood JD. Distributed cooperative visualization. In: de Sousa AA, Hopgood FRA (Eds), State of the Art Reports, Eurographics '98. Eurographics Association, 1998; 27-50.
3. Foulser D. IRIS Explorer: A framework for investigation. ACM/SIGGRAPH Computer Graphics, 1995; 29(2):13-16.
4. Lord HD. Improving the application development process with modular visualization environments. ACM/SIGGRAPH Computer Graphics, 1995; 29(2):10-1.
5. Abram G, Treinish L. An extended dataflow architecture for data analysis and visualization. ACM/SIGGRAPH Computer Graphics, 1995; 29(2):17-21.
6. McCormick B, DeFanti TA, Brown MD. Visualization in scientific computing. ACM SIGGRAPH Computer Graphics, 21(6), 1987.
7. Haber RB, McNabb DA. Visualization idioms: a conceptual model for scientific visualization systems. In: Shriver B, Nielson GM, Rosenblum LJ (Eds), Visualization in Scientific Computing, IEEE, 1990; 74-93.
8. Upson C, Faulhaber T, Kamins D, Laidlaw D, Schlegel D, Vroom J, Gurwitz R, van Dam A. The Application Visualization System: A computational environment for scientific visualization. IEEE Computer Graphics and

Applications, 1989; 9(4):30-42.

9. Ang CS, Martin DC, Doyle MD. Integrated control of distributed volume visualization through the World Wide Web. In: Bergeron RD, Kaufman AE (Eds), Proceedings of IEEE Visualization 94, 1994; 13-20.

10. Wood JD, Brodlie KW, Wright H. Visualization over the World Wide Web and its application to environmental data. In: Yagel R, Nielson GM (Eds), Proc. IEEE Visualization '96 Conference, San Francisco. ACM Press, 1996; 81-86.

11. Vis-5D web site. http://www.ssec.wisc.edu/~billh/view5d.html.

12. Yeo A. Client-based Web Visualization. MSc Thesis, University of Leeds, 1998.

13. Visual Mining web site. http://www.netcharts.com/.

14. Michaels CK, Bailey MJ. VizWiz: A Java applet for interactive 3d scientific visualization over the web. In: Proc. IEEE Visualization '97, 1997; 261–268.

15. Kee A. Visualization over WWW using Java. MSc thesis, University of Leeds, 1996.

16. Hendin O, John NW, Shochet O. Medical volume rendering over the WWW using VRML and Java. In: Westwood J et al. (Eds), Medicine Meets Virtual Reality:6. IOS Press and Ohmsha, Amsterdam, 1998; 34-40.

17. VTK web site. http://www.kitware.com/vtk.html.

18. Lefer W. A distributed architecture for a web-based visualization service. In: Proc. the Eurographics Workshop on Visualization in Scientific Computing. Eurographics Association, 1998.

19. Progressive Isosurfaces web site. http://www9.informatik.uni-erlangen.de/eng/research/vis/prolet/.

20. Grosso R, Ertl T. Progressive iso-surface extraction from hierarchical 3D meshes. Computer Graphics Forum, 1998, 17(3): 125-136.

21. Trapp J, Pagendarm H-G. A prototype for a WWW-based visualization service. In: Lefer W, Grave M (Eds), Visualization in Scientific Computing '97; Springer, Wien, 1997; 21-30.

22. CurVis web site. http://www.informatik.uni-rostock.de/Projekte/movi/proto.html #CURVIS.

23. WAVES web site. http://www.nacse.pdx.edu/Waves/Gnuplot/.

24. Wood JD, Wright H, Brodlie KW. Collaborative visualization. In: Proc. IEEE Visualization '97 Conference, Phoenix. ACM Press, 1997; 253-259.

25. Wood JD. Collaborative Visualization. PhD Thesis, School of Computer Studies, University of Leeds, UK, 1998.

26. Duce DA, Gallop JR, Johnson IJ, Robinson K, Seelig CD, Cooper CS. Distributed cooperative visualization — The MANICORAL approach. In: Eurographics UK Chapter Conference, 1998, Leeds, 1998; 69-85.

27. Duce DA, Gallop JR, Johnson IJ, Robinson K, Seelig CD, Cooper CS. Distributed cooperative visualization — Experiences and issues from MANICORAL Project. In: Proc. the Eurographics Workshop on Visualization in Scientific Computing, Eurographics Association, 1998.

28. SDSC Collaborative Visualization web site. http://www.sdsc.edu/PET/scivis/page01.html.

29. Pang AT, Wittenbrink CM. Collaborative 3D visualization with CSpray. IEEE Computer Graphics and Applications, 1997; 17(2):32-41.

30. Pang A. Spray rendering. IEEE Computer Graphics and Applications, 1994; 14(5):57-63.
31. IRIS Explorer Centre Of Excellence web site. http://www.scs.leeds.ac.uk/iecoe.

PART VII

APPLICATIONS

22. InViVo-IORT — A System for Quality Control of Intra-Operative Radiotherapy

Stefan Walter, Gerd Straßmann and Marco Schmitt

22.1 Introduction

Intra-operative radiotherapy (IORT) is a cancer treatment that is applied after the surgical removal of a tumour but still during the operation at the open situ of the patient with the objective to irradiate remains of the tumour that could not be removed surgically. Such an irradiation can be performed in a procedure where a high energy Iridium radiation source is placed over the remains of the tumour with the help of a carpet-like "flab" (Figure 22.1) that consists of a number of rubber pellets connected to each other (*Freiburger Flab* [1, 2]). Additionally a flab contains small plastic pipes, so-called "applicators", through which the radiation source is being dragged or shifted. The accurate and effective placement of the flab inside the body of the patient highly depends on the experience and knowledge of the irradiation expert. Neither an individual treatment planning can be performed, nor a documentation of the applied iso-dose in the CT scans can be made, because the position of the flab is not known in its relation to the CT dataset of the patient.

The objective of this joint project, among the Fraunhofer Institute for Computer Graphics, Städtische Kinik Offenbach and MedCom GmbH, was to develop a system that overcomes this rather inaccurate, and person- and experience-dependant technique through computer support. The digital acquisition and visualisation of the geometrical data of irradiation enables the radiotherapist to obtain an accurate documentation of iso-dose distribution, and thereby, a radiotherapy planning.

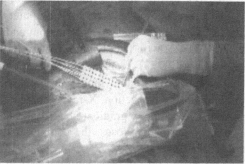

Figure 22.1. Flab with rubber pellets and flab in situ with applicator pipes.

The original working steps of the IORT procedure, as shown in Figure 22.2, are:

- *Acquisition of CT data.* A CT dataset of the tumour region of the body of the patient is acquired for surgery planning.
- *Tumour operation.* The patient is operated on, the tumour removed as long as this is surgically possible.
- *Placement of the flab.* The flab is placed at the previous tumour position over the remains of the tumour according to the experience of the surgeon.
- *Irradiation.* The radiation sources are drawn by the irradiation device through the flab pipes with stop positions and irradiation times according to the experience of the surgeon.

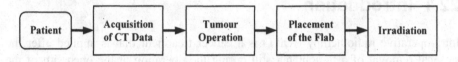

Figure 22.2. Original IORT working steps as used in clinical routine.

22.2 The InViVo-IORT System

The *InViVo-IORT* system (Figure 22.3) is based on a PC, with the Microsoft NT operating system and an additional *spatial tracking system* (6 degrees of freedom). In the current system, an electromagnetic tracking system is used (both Polhemus and Ascension systems can be used). Such a tracking system consists of a *transmitter* that builds up and controls an electromagnetic field, and a *receiver* that detects its current spatial position and orientation within the electromagnetic field. The data with the geometrical information of the receiver is transferred into the computer memory for further processing. Additionally the system is equipped with a foot pedal for controlling the recording of geometrical points with the tracking system.

The main part of the software is a system for visualisation of medical volume data, such as CT, MRI and 3D ultrasound data, that has been developed over several years in the Fraunhofer Institute for Computer Graphics [3-5]. For this application the data is acquired by a Siemens Somatom and can be read by the software directly from the CT device via the hospital network in the DICOM 3 format. The data can be displayed as 2D CT scans, oblique oriented slices in the volume data or as 3D visualisation. The available modes for 3D volume rendering include maximum/minimum intensity projection, X-ray simulation, and surface reconstruction as semi-transparent clouds or as gradient shaded surfaces [6-9]. For radiotherapy planning and visualisation of iso-doses, the commercially available Nucletron Plato system (version BPS 2.4) is used.

The procedure for the registration of patient geometry and the CT dataset of the patient assumes that the changes of the geometry of the patient caused by the

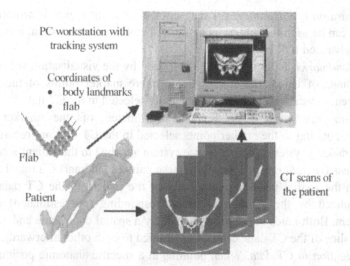

Figure 22.3. InViVo-IORT system overview: CT scans of a patient are transferred to a workstation equipped with a tracking system for acquisition of spatial coordinates of landmarks and flab geometry.

operation can be neglected. This is due to prior evaluations of the partner hospital. Although it is not generally the case, it can be assumed for the sacral region of the human body, where the massive hip bones maintain their previous geometry during and after the operation. Therefore this application focuses on intra-operative radiotherapy in the sacral region.

The registration is performed with the help of an external reference system similar to a stereotactic frame used in neuro-surgery. The external reference system consists of a plastic angle that is fixed with a screw to the hip bones of the patient (Figure 22.4).

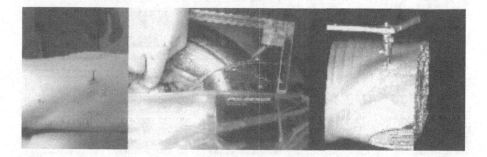

Figure 22.4. External reference system for registration: fixation with a screw at the hip bones of the patient (left), external reference system during operation at the open situ, 3D volume rendering of the tumour region of the body with embedded tumour.

As illustrated in Figure 22.5, the acquisition of the flab geometry is performed with the following working steps:

- *Acquisition of CT data.* A CT dataset of the tumour region is acquired. This data can be used for surgery planning as before and, in addition, it is used for the advanced IORT procedure.
- *CT landmarks.* After the CT data is loaded by the visualisation software, the positions of landmarks at CT slices, where marker points of the external reference system are visible, are manually selected in the CT data.
- *Patient landmarks.* The spatial coordinates of the marker points corresponding to the marker points selected in the CT data are recorded with the tracking system at the reference system attached to the patient's body
- *Patient-CT data registration.* With these pairs of landmarks, a transformation from the spatial position at the body of the patient to the CT data can be calculated by the solution of the corresponding (overestimated) equation system. Both kinds of coordinates, namely a spatial coordinate and a position in a slice of the CT data, can be transformed to each other afterwards.
- *Navigation in CT data.* When pointing at a specific anatomic position in the body of the patient with the receiver of the tracking system, the visualisation software displays the corresponding position in the CT data. With this navigation tool, a suitable position for the flab can be evaluated.
- *Placement of the flab.* The flab is placed at the previous tumour position according to the experience of the surgeon supported by the information of the navigation step.
- *Digitalisation of flab geometry.* The flab is digitised in the next step by recording several spatial positions of the pellets of the flab with the tracking system.
- *Visualisation.* After registration, the flab can be displayed embedded in the CT data, as CT scans or as a 3D volume rendering, to supervise the chosen position. With that supervision, the position of the flab inside the patient's body can be corrected if necessary.

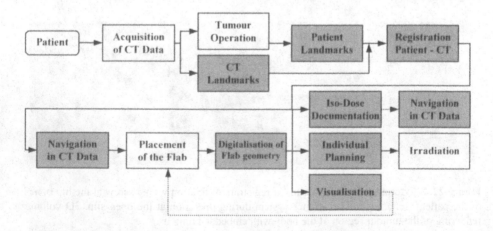

Figure 22.5. Original (white) and additional working steps for the advanced IORT (grey).

- *Documentation and radiotherapy planning.* The acquired flab geometry can be exported to the *Nucletron* radiotherapy planning system, and can be used for documentation and intra-operative radiotherapy planning by calculating optimised stop positions for the Iridium radiation source.

22.3 Accuracy of the System

A problematic issue for the accuracy of the system is the electromagnetic tracking system. The overall accuracy of the system mainly depends on the distortion free recording of spatial points (landmarks and flab pellets) with the tracking system. All available electromagnetic tracking systems have the common weakness that they can easily be disturbed by electromagnetic fields or the influence of metal in the working range. The environment in an operation room contains a lot of disturbing metals, e.g. surgery tables, clamps, scalpels, etc. Such influence can be almost completely compensated by a careful definition and evaluation of the surgical working environment (Figure 22.6).

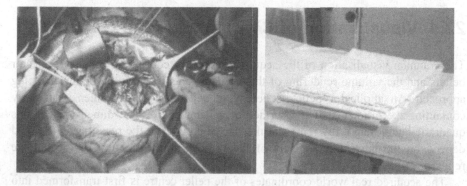

Figure 22.6. Prevention of distortion of the tracking system by metal in its working range: plastic clamp in situ and additional padding on the surgery table.

An infrared tracking system cannot be used in this application, because it needs a direct line of sight from its pointer to a detection camera which cannot be guaranteed in the IORT scenario, for example, when recording geometrical points inside the body of the patient.

The validation of the accuracy of the system has been evaluated with the help of a phantom (Figure 22.7). This phantom consists of a plastic frame with a flab mounted at a fixed position inside of the frame. The phantom contains small marker holes that are additionally filled with a contrast media for easier detection of the markers in the CT data when the CT landmarks are set. With these markers an optimal registration of the CT data with the phantom geometry can be performed. A CT data where the pellets of the flab are clear to see is acquired. The centre of each pellet is marked manually in the CT slices. After registration of the CT data with the real world coordinates and the recording of the flab pellets' geometry, these marked positions can be compared with the recorded positions and the error can be calculated. We found that our system works under clinical conditions in the surgery room with an overall accuracy of 3mm, which exceeded the accuracy of 5mm that the physicians intended to have.

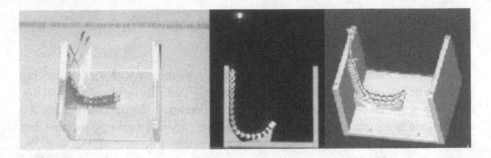

Figure 22.7. Phantom for validation of the accuracy of the system: Photo of the phantom, CT scan and surface volume rendering.

22.4 Visualisation of CT Data and Flab Geometry

The common visualisation of the acquired geometric coordinates of the applicator pellets and the volume rendering of the CT data is achieved with a bump mapping approach. An applicator pellet is hereby modelled by a two-dimensional array containing the gradients of the surface of a hemisphere. The dimensions of this quadratic bump map array represent the size of a pellet in the resulting image, and depend on the current parameters of the viewing transformation of the volume rendering system.

The acquired real world coordinates of the pellet centre is first transformed into the volume coordinate system, and then with the viewing transformation, into the resulting image. A bump map with appropriate dimensions set according to the viewing parameters is virtually placed at this position in the resulting image, and it is used to modify pixel values according to the gradient information in the bump map. The Z-position of an entry in the bump map is calculated accordingly, and compared with the depth information in a surface Z-buffer that is calculated by the volume rendering system. If the calculated Z-coordinate of a bump map entry indicates that it is nearer to the spectator than the surface calculated by the volume renderer, the new value of the corresponding pixel is calculated. By combining the original pixel value with a gradient shaded illumination, in which the gradient of the corresponding bump map entry and a virtual light source are combined, a semi-transparent sphere is placed over the surface rendering (Figure 22.8).

The system offers several modes for interactive visualisation during the intra-operative navigation. All modes support the display of the flab and the current position of the digitiser pen.

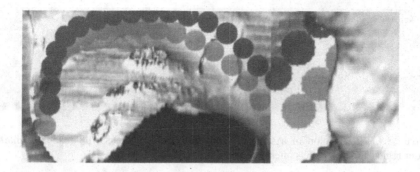

Figure 22.8. Composition of pellet geometry and volume rendering with a bump mapping technique: overlapping of surface rendering and applicator pellets can be modelled as well as semi-transparency of the pellets.

- *CT scans*. Medical users of the software are accustomed to working with 2D CT scan images and therefore the system supports a view of the original CT scans with an integrated view of the pellets of the flab intersected by this scan (Figure 22.9).
- *Orthogonal cuts*. The CT volume can be displayed as a wire frame cube with three intersecting orthogonal cuts that can be chosen freely by the user. The point of intersection of the three planes is coupled to the current position of the digitiser pen for navigation (Figure 22.10).
- *3D volume rendering.* In this mode, the 3D reconstruction of the volume with overlaid pellets can be displayed. The pellets are embedded in the volume rendered resulting image via a semi-transparent bump mapping technique regarding the depth position of the surface that has been calculated by the volume rendering system (Figure 22.11).

The tumour region can be marked manually in the CT scans and can be displayed in all visualisation modes. The images for the first two modes for visualisation mentioned above can be calculated in less than 0.1 second, and can therefore be used interactively.

The volume rendering system is based on the widespread ray casting algorithm to calculate the 3D volume views. Depending on the size of the CT dataset and the size of the resulting image which influences the number of rays of the ray casting algorithm, a 3D view of the volume can be calculated within 1 to 5 seconds. Table 22.1 shows the results obtained on a Double Pentium II, 200Mhz system with a dataset of 29Mb.

Table 22.1. Average rendering times (sec.) for different volume rendering modes and different image sizes.

3D Volume Rendering Mode	A 200x200 Image	A 400x400 Image
Surface (Gradient Shading)	1.2	3.5
Max/Min Intensity Projection	1.5	4.3

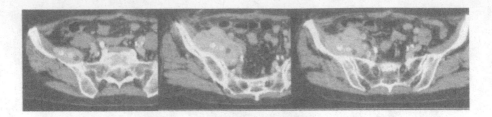

Figure 22.9. Visualisation of a sequence of transversal CT scans with manually marked tumour region and flab pellets intersected by these scans.

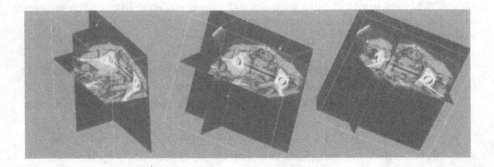

Figure 22.10. Visualisation of a three orthogonal cutting planes through the volume data with marked tumour from 3 viewing directions.

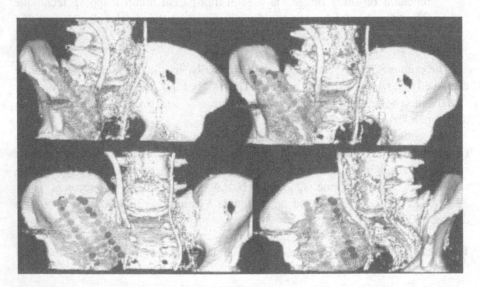

Figure 22.11. 3D volume surface rendering of a hip region with tumour and embedded flab pellets.

22.5 Clinical Experience

The first clinical trials of the system in the partner hospital have already shown the advantages of interactive navigation during the working step of the placement of the flab, and the good overview of the distribution of applicators (pellets) over the tumour region. With 3D volume rendering, it was immediately possible to see that the size of a flab chosen by the physicians was insufficient for good irradiation, which could then be corrected with an additional flab.

References

1. Kolkman J-K, Deurloo AG, Visser MH, Idzes M, Levendag PC. Reconstruction accuracy of dedicated localiser for filmless planning in intra-operative brachytherapy. Radiotherapy and Oncology, 1997; 44:73-81.
2. Vaeth J-M (Ed). Intraoperative Radiation Therapy in the Treatment of Cancer. Front Ther. Oncology, Basel, Karger, 1997; 31.
3. Sakas G, Walter S. Extracting surfaces from fuzzy 3D ultrasonic data. In: Proc. SIGGRAPH, 1995; 465-474.
4. Sakas G, Schreyer LA, Grimm M. Visualization of 3D ultrasonic data, In: Proc. IEEE Visualization '94, Washington DC, October 1994; 369-373.
5. Sakas G, Walter S, Hiltmann W, Wischnik A. Foetal visualization using 3D ultrasonic data. In: Proc. Computer Assisted Radiology '95, Berlin, June 1995; 241-247.
6. Höhne K-H, Bernstein R. Shading 3D-images from CT using gray level gradients. IEEE Transaction on Medical Imaging, 1986; MI-5(1):45-47.
7. Ohbuchi R, Chen D, Fuchs H. Incremental volume reconstruction and rendering for 3D ultrasound imaging. In: Proc. SPIE Visualization in Biomedical Computing, 1992; 312-323.
8. Pretorius D-H, Nielson T-R. Opinion: Three-dimensional ultrasound. Ultrasound Obstetric Gynecology, 1995; 5:219-221.
9. Levoy M. Display of surfaces from volume data. IEEE Computer Graphics and Applications, 1988; 8(3):29-37.

23. Volumetric Facial Reconstruction for Forensic Identification

Simon D. Michael

23.1 Introduction

The ultimate aim of any facial reconstruction technique is to produce a likeness of the face from skeletalised, burnt, badly mutilated or decomposed remains so that it bears sufficient resemblance to the individual prior to death. This reconstruction will hopefully provide a lead to enable positive identification in conjunction with other information and characteristics (dental records, radiographs, DNA and so on). Traditional sculpting methods rely on a combination of the ability, anatomical and anthropological knowledge of the artist and numerous subjective interpretations on the form of the face to produce a reconstruction of an unknown skull. Computer-aided reconstruction techniques are both quicker and more flexible but rely heavily on the size and quality of the facial database from which the reconstructions are created.

This chapter introduces a new computer-aided facial reconstruction pipeline that utilises a new approach to three-dimensional volume deformation called Hierarchical Volume Deformation (HVD). The problem of facial reconstruction is approached from a different perspective dealing with the facial soft tissues as a single unit and manipulating this volume within the anatomical confines of the sample from which it is derived. This allows for realistic transitions to be made to the soft tissues of the face in keeping with the differences in the form of the skull on which the reconstruction is based.

23.2 Facial Reconstruction

Facial reconstruction is the scientific art of visualising faces on skulls for the purpose of individual identification [1]. It is generally acknowledged that facial reconstruction may be subdivided into four approaches; (i) the restoration through replacement and repositioning of facial tissues that have been damaged or distorted but which still exist on or around the skull; (ii) superimposition techniques, the comparison of the skull with a pre-mortem photograph or portrait using photographic, video and/or computer techniques [2]; (iii) two-dimensional facial reconstruction, an artistic representation of the skull using photographic transparencies and drawings [3-5] and (iv) three-dimensional facial reconstruction, the modelling of a face over the skull using clay.

Superimposition techniques use soft tissue information (in the form of a purported likeness such as a pre-mortem photograph or portrait) and overlay the skull in an attempt to find a good fit and subsequently prove association. In contrast skeletal reconstruction techniques begin with the skull and arrange soft tissues over the bone to build up a pre-mortem likeness. All of the techniques however rely on the underlying principle of relating soft tissue to the underlying bone of the skull [6].

The science of facial reconstruction has been practised for over a century having been initially applied to the reproduction of busts from skulls purported to be those of important historical figures [7-9]. During the early 1920's the Russian palaeontologist Gerasimov began the first of many reconstructions and studies of the human facial form. He developed a technique of reconstruction where attention is focussed on the musculature of the skull and not on the soft tissue depth measurements covering the bone. In the 1940's, Krogman developed an alternative approach where strips of clay onto the skull are placed over the skull with the depth of the strips restricted by soft tissue depth markers. This general technique of using tissue depth markers and clay to recreate the facial features has been applied to the reconstruction of numerous archaeological and historical specimens [10-13] and now plays a significant role in forensic pathological and anthropological investigations to establish and/or verify the identification of skeletal or semi-skeletal human remains [12, 14, 15].

23.2.1 Traditional Techniques

The first step in reconstruction involves rebuilding the unknown skull to a sufficient level where the vertical and horizontal dimensions can be established. This important step is often necessary, as there are many occasions when the skull requiring reconstruction is incomplete or badly damaged. Next, a cast of the skull is constructed on which to build the reconstruction. This is preferred to reconstructing directly on the original skull since in many forensic cases the specimen may be required for further examination long before the work is complete. Fundamental deductions and decisions are now made regarding the age, sex, ethnic group and body constitution of the subject. This information may be obtained from the skull, complete skeleton and surviving artefacts such as clothing and other possessions found near the scene of death. Using a set of tissue depth measurements [16-18], the skull is marked with the appropriate number of anatomical points and small holes drilled at these points and filled with wooden dowels whose lengths correspond to the distance indicated by the tissue depth measurement tables. These form the outer limits of the face to be reconstructed. The angle of the nose is extrapolated from the angle of the nasal bones and the nasal spine.

The main muscles of the face are now built up with clay or similar modelling material working from the skull outwards and taking care to interpret the muscle insertions where possible. The aim is not to produce an accurate anatomical model; the exact dimensions of individual muscles are not critical to the final build of the face (the thickness of the soft tissue determines facial constitution). However, it is of fundamental importance to consider and utilise the position, direction of pull and strength of the muscles to aid the reconstruction process. The major muscle groups are built up in a strict order, following anatomical rules on points of origin and insertion. These structures are covered with a layer of clay simulating the tissues overlying the muscles. Simulation of outer layers of subcutaneous tissues and skin is achieved by laying strips of clay smoothly over the muscles, bringing the reconstruction to the level of the tissue depth markers. Finally superficial features such as the subtle shaping of the nose, lips and ears are modelled. Additional and speculative features such as creases, wrinkles and hair colour and style are not normally added to the reconstruction since such subjective touches might distract or confuse during the recognition stage.

23.2.2 Computer-Aided Techniques

In the last decade various systems have been developed that use computer software to create two- and three-dimensional reconstructions of a skull [19-28]. These systems aim to redefine the complete reconstruction process making it faster, more flexible and open to manipulation, and attempt to remove some of the perceived subjectivity introduced by inconsistencies in the application of the manual techniques and the differing knowledge and expertise of individual sculptors.

Various methods have been employed in computer-aided two-dimensional facial reconstruction. Ubelaker and O'Donnell [21] utilise electronic imaging equipment originally designed to show age progression in cases of missing children and fugitives to produce a facial reconstruction from skeletal remains. Evenhouse et al. [22] maps the generalised facial features of an average head to the size and shape of a specific skull. This average facial image is the composition of a number of frontal photographs of people of the same sex and similar age and racial affinity. Miyasaka et al. [20] describe a two-dimensional computer-aided facial reconstruction system that attempts to mimic the methodological approach associated with the two-dimensional drawing method. An image processing unit is used to establish skull morphometry to create a framework and facial contour on which to place selected photographic facial components using an image editing tool.

Although the option exists with these systems to produce various versions of a reconstruction the major concern is that by using parts or an average of photographic images a very specific set of finely defined characteristics is imposed on the reconstruction. In short, the reconstruction resembles a photograph of an individual in life. This issue was raised by Craig without resolution [29]. Ubelaker [30] advises that the features which can be reasonably predicted from the bone should be presented as accurately as possible. Apart from anomalies this tends to be very few. Craig refers to studies reporting that there is a higher identification success rate with facial images that allow the viewer to use their imagination. A more general reconstruction without specific characteristics may trigger a viewer to consider it possible that it resembles someone they know, rather than a photograph-like image of a person they do not recognise. The outcome of the reconstructions produced using these two-dimensional computer studies depends heavily on the database of features or range of photos from which it is assembled.

The first work on computer-generated three-dimensional reconstructions for forensic purposes utilised technology normally applied in cranial reconstructive surgery planning [19]. These programs allow a surgeon to manipulate a realistic three-dimensional image of the head via a computer in order to predict changes in soft tissues in response to surgical procedures on the hard tissues [31]. The first stage in reconstruction involves obtaining numerous surface coordinates using a fully automated three-dimensional laser scanner. The appropriate anatomical landmarks are manually selected around the skull and the tissue depths grown at these points to produce a smooth and featureless face mask (lacking eyes, ears, nose and mouth). Facial features are added by using scanned facial surface data from a library of previously laser-scanned living subjects. Shahrom et al. [23] applies and compares the same technique to video superimposition in two real-life case studies. Archer [28] uses a three-dimensional polygon model of the skull obtained using a digitising process such as a 3D laser scanning system. A hierarchical B-spline surface model is used onto which virtual dowels are manually placed at known anthropological landmarks. A generic facial surface is then wrapped around the model using the dowels to anchor the facial map at the appropriate tissue thickness depths. Points between the virtual dowels are smoothly and evenly interpolated using a multi-level B-spline approximation algorithm [32].

All of the studies discussed, both traditional and computer-aided, rely on a set of standard facial tissue thickness measurements as a basis for reconstruction. These inaccurate measurements are one of the major factors contributing to the inaccuracy of these techniques and facial reconstruction in general [33-35].

23.3 Soft Tissue Depth Measurements

The early practitioners of facial reconstruction provided their own tissue depth measurements through the use of puncture-based techniques that involve breaking the soft tissues at known anatomical points and recording the depth [7-9]. Much of this work was combined and it is this data [16, 17, 36] that has been used as the basis for standards used in many subsequent craniofacial identification techniques [33]. More recently it has been possible to take *in vivo* measurements using tracings of lateral craniographs [1, 37]. The use of ultrasound for the measurement of soft tissue depths of the face was initiated by Lebedinskaya et al. [38] in 1979 and has since been used to collect tissue measurements for several population groups [34, 39].

The ideal scenario would be to have simultaneous visualisation of soft tissue and the underlying bone. This was partially achieved by George [1] although the craniographs used only allowed visualisation of the mid-sagittal profile. Recent advances in the field of three-dimensional medical imaging has provided the opportunity of obtaining high quality visualisation of hard and soft tissues in a desired plane and using these to obtain accurate tissue depth measurements [40, 41].

Many of the reconstructions attempted today rely on tissue depth measurements acquired using cadavers as their source of data. Whilst it is known that the measurements were determined before embalming and within twenty four hours of death [42] it is still the case that living tissue was not used. Soft tissue distortion caused by drying and embalming can occur within hours of death and have been well documented [34, 43].

Puncture-based measurement techniques were used that involve breaking the skin of the cadaver at known points around the face. Several sources of error can potentially result from this process due to deformation of the skin as the measurement is taken. Potentially the greatest source of error in these techniques must come from the inaccurate location of corresponding landmarks on each cadaver. The task of locating bony anthropological landmarks through soft tissue requires skill and considerable training. However, with such a small margin of error luck must play a part in this process and hence more errors are introduced [44].

The standard tissue depth measurements used today contain many highly subjective landmarks that are ambiguous due to the individual interpretation of the points by the anthropologists in question. This leads to landmarks that are not readily replicable without more than a reasonable error across reconstructions. This problem also arises when one considers landmarks which are solely based on soft tissues being present. It is problematic for an anthropologist attempting a reconstruction from a skull to accurately locate the points to apply the appropriate tissue depths. Similarly, there is a high degree of guesswork involved in placing tissue depth markers at points dependent on the features one is trying to recreate.

There is also a distinct lack of data for certain facial regions. The complex contours of the face cannot be properly represented by a small set of points, particularly if the values and disposition of many of these points are equivocal [35]. Using linear measurements of soft tissues for re-modelling the face, we can only vouch for the accuracy of those areas local to the measured landmarks we use. It is not solely the use of sparsely distributed landmarks and poor measurement techniques that constitute a problem when trying to recreate the face of an unknown individual. The influence of how this soft tissue data is actually applied during the reconstruction plays a significant role in its final outcome. Without exception, it is the average values of the measurement reference tables that are used. However, average values at every landmark point may not necessarily represent a possible, realistic tissue depth combination for a single individual. Certain reconstruction methods (clay/plastic reconstruction) utilise the form of the anatomical structures to aid reconstruction. This endeavours to interpret realistically the contours between landmarks as opposed to laying the face over the landmarks and assuming that the tissue depth simply changes gradually from one landmark to the next.

Some of the problems described above have been largely overcome through the use of new medical technology such as ultrasound, lateral craniographs, Computed Tomography (CT), and Magnetic Resonance Imaging (MRI). These allow the safe collection of soft tissue measurements from large populations of living subjects. Nevertheless the practitioner must still ensure that a subject's tissue measurements are taken under normal conditions.

In a recent study, computed tomography was integrated with computer-aided reconstruction by Quatrehomme et al. [26]. This surface-based technique, similar to that proposed by Michael and Chen [24, 27] uses, the assumption that if skulls have similar forms then the corresponding faces should have main characteristics in common. Therefore a transformation is applied to a reference facial model in an attempt to approximate the face of a skull.

23.4 Volume Deformation

In recent years, the established and successful techniques of image warping [45-49] have been extrapolated to three dimensions and applied to both continuous (geometric) and discrete (volume) data. These three-dimensional techniques allow for warp independent control over lighting and viewing parameters as well as providing a marked increase in spatial configuration information [50]. Chen et al. [51] examine the theoretical implications of volume warping mainly through the extension of existing two-dimensional techniques. Several categories of warping algorithms are formally defined in the context of the overall volume morphing problem. Feature-based warping techniques utilising points, lines and disks [52] for control point specification are discussed in relation to their extrapolation from two to three dimensions in addition to extensions to two-dimensional mesh warping techniques using parametric grid and tetrahedral mesh subdivision schemes.

The feature-based warping algorithm developed by Lerios et al. [50] extends the field warping algorithm of Beier and Neely [46] into the three-dimensional domain. Control point specification is achieved through manually positioning a variety of feature elements (points, segments, rectangles and boxes) on the volume object.

A further extension to three-dimensional feature-based warping uses two sets of disk fields to specify and control the deformation of a volume [52]. The disks are introduced as an extension to the two-dimensional line segments in an attempt to overcome specification difficulties and ambiguities associated with other methods of feature specification (point, line, box). Each disk field is specified by its centre point, normal vector and radial vector. The use of disk fields allows the unambiguous encapsulation of more three-dimensional spatial information than other feature specification objects such as points and lines. Powerful global transformations such as the rotation or scaling of an object can be achieved using a single disk whilst the use of relatively few disks allows for the effective, controlled transformation of a volume.

Landmark-based volume warping using two classes of scattered data interpolation methods is discussed by Fang et al. [53]. These are Shepard-based methods and the radial basis function methods. Results obtained using the former are not always satisfactory; valleys and peaks are often observed around the control feature points in the destination volume. Conversely, the radial-basis methods produce results which are globally smoother. However, both techniques are slow, with a large dataset taking several hours to warp.

Free-Form Deformation (FFD) is a powerful, representational-independent technique for deforming an object in three-dimensional space [54-57]. Instead of deforming an object directly the user manipulates a three-dimensional parallelepiped lattice in which the object is embedded. A useful physical analogy for FFD given by Sederberg [54] is of a parallelepiped of clear, flexible plastic in which is embedded the object, or several objects to be deformed. As the plastic is deformed, the objects also deform in a smooth and consistent manner. The Extended Free-Form Deformation [55, 56] improves on the previous approach by providing an interactive and increasingly intuitive approach to modelling. It allows for the use of non-parallelepipedical three-dimensional lattices to be used in which to embed the object to be deformed. Hsu et al. [57] present a technique for directly manipulating control points. This allows points on an object modelled by free-form deformation to be moved to the specified positions by minimising the squared sum of distances between the specified and actual positions.

23.5 Hierarchical Volume Deformation

A new approach to the deformation of volumetric data has been developed that is an extension into the three-dimensional domain of work presented by Lee et al. [49, 58]. The algorithm known as Hierarchical Volume Deformation (HVD) achieves the C^2-continuous and one-to-one deformation of a volumetric dataset. The foundations of the algorithm are based on the concepts of free form deformation. In this way the object to be deformed is embedded in a three-dimensional parallelepiped lattice of control points that is manipulated to determine a deformation function that specifies a new position for each point of the object. A direct manipulation scheme based on three-dimensional B-spline approximation is used to provide localised control of the lattice from these feature points. Applying this process using a hierarchy of increasingly finer control lattices yields a smooth and continuous deformation that exactly satisfies the user-defined positional constraints.

23.5.1 Initial Configuration

A general volume V is a collection of scattered voxels each with an associated density. These voxels are commonly organised into the form of a three-dimensional regular grid with dimension ($dx \times dy \times dz$) where each voxel has an associated density value d_i lying in the range [min, max]. That is:

$$V = (x_i, y_i, z_i, d_i)$$

where ($1 \leq x_i \leq dx$), ($1 \leq y_i \leq dy$), ($1 \leq z_i \leq dz$) and ($min \leq d_i \leq max$).

To deform a source volume V_s it is first embedded within a three-dimensional control point lattice Ψ of dimension ($dx+2 \times dy+2 \times dz+2$). The initial lattice Ψ_0 has ($cx+1 \times cy+1 \times cz+1$) control points ψ_{ijk} where cx, cy and cz are the number of subdivisions required in the coarsest lattice along the x, y and z axes respectively (Figure 23.1).

The initial configuration of the lattice Ψ_0 has each control point ψ^0_{ijk} lying at the ijk^{th} position. The desired deformation of the object is achieved by displacing each of the control points from their initial positions. The trivariate cubic B-spline tensor product is used as the deformation function *w* and hence the 64 surrounding control points all contribute to the deformation.

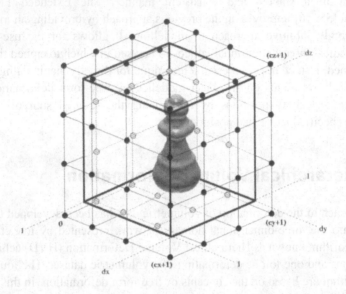

Figure 23.1. Initial configuration of the lattice Ψ surrounding the volumetric data V_s.

Given a voxel *v* in the volume V_s and (*u*, *v*, *w*) are the lattice-space coordinates of the voxel *v* at position (*x*, *y*, *z*) then the deformation function *w* is defined as:

$$w(u,v,w) = \sum_{k,l,m=1}^{3} B_k(r)B_l(s)B_m(t)\psi_{a+k,b+l,c+m} \tag{23.1}$$

where $r = u - \lfloor u \rfloor$, $s = v - \lfloor v \rfloor$, $t = w - \lfloor w \rfloor$, $a = \lfloor u \rfloor - 1$, $b = \lfloor v \rfloor - 1$, $c = \lfloor w \rfloor - 1$.
The uniform cubic B-spline basis functions are defined as:

$$B_0(t) = (-t^3 + 3t^2 - 3t + 1)/6$$
$$B_1(t) = (3t^3 - 6t^2 + 4)/6$$
$$B_2(t) = (-3t^3 + 3t^2 + 3t + 1)/6 \tag{23.2}$$
$$B_3(t) = t^3/6$$

where $(0 \le t \le 1)$.

23.5.2 Manipulation of Control Points

Controlling the movement of the lattice in order to describe a desired deformation has traditionally been achieved by manually selecting and moving each individual control point, a procedure that closely echoes the underlying mathematical model [54-56]. This can be an error-prone and slow process particularly if the user has little or no knowledge or experience with splines, where moving the control points does not deform the object in exactly the same way. Additionally the modelling and complex deformation of a complicated object can involve a substantial number of control points. This results in a high degree of clutter and difficulty in judging how the movement of a particular control point affects its neighbouring points. Despite several alternative approaches to controlling the movement of the points a suitable and convenient solution has yet to be suggested. Hsu et al. [57] proposed a technique that exactly satisfies positional constraints by calculating the pseudo-inverse of a matrix using numerical computation methods. This operation, however, becomes prohibitive as the complexity of the deformation and therefore the number of control points increase.

In order to provide an increased level of control over the deformation, two additional sets of feature points' pairings $C_s = (c_{s1}, c_{s2}, ..., c_{sn})$ and $C_d = (c_{d1}, c_{d2}, ..., c_{dn})$ are used to specify the source and destination positions of n feature points around the volume data. These points are either defined manually by the user or automatically using image processing and vision techniques and may be placed at any position internal or external to the volumetric object. This provides a means by which the user can visually identify meaningful features such as biological landmarks.

23.5.3 Mapping of Feature Points

The feature point sets C_s and C_d displace the control points of the lattice in a way that completely reflects the desired deformation. If only one feature point pairing is used to deform a volume then the displacement of the surrounding control points $(k,l,m = 0, 1, 2, 3)$ in the lattice is defined as:

$$\Delta \psi_{k,l,m} = \frac{B_k(r)B_l(s)B_m(t)\Delta c}{\sum\limits_{a=0}^{3}\sum\limits_{b=0}^{3}\sum\limits_{c=0}^{3}(B_a(r)B_b(s)B_c(t))^2} \tag{23.3}$$

where $r = u - \lfloor u \rfloor$, $s = v - \lfloor v \rfloor$, $t = w - \lfloor w \rfloor$ and $\Delta c = c_{di} - c_{si}$ represents the degree of movement of the feature point c_{si} from its original position.

Using Equation 23.3 the control points near the feature point c_{si} are displaced more than the control points further away since the function is directly related to the distance between the $(klm)^{th}$ control point and the feature point c_{si}.

When more than one feature point pairing is used to define a deformation then Equation 23.3 cannot be used. This is because the displacement calculations for one feature point in C_s can directly affect those of another point in C_s, causing it to deviate away from its intended destination, and subsequently results in the algorithm failing to satisfy the positional constraints for each point in C_s. For this reason the displacement of a control point is chosen to minimise the squared sum of differences between the movement of a point c_{sn} due to the displacement of control point ψ and the contribution of this control point towards moving c_{sn} to its required position. The displacement of a control point is therefore defined as:

$$\Delta\psi = \frac{\sum_n \left(B_k(r)B_l(s)B_m(t)\right)^2_n \Delta\psi_n}{\sum_n \left(B_k(r)B_l(s)B_m(t)\right)^2_n} \tag{23.4}$$

where $r = u - \lfloor u \rfloor$, $s = v - \lfloor v \rfloor$, $t = w - \lfloor w \rfloor$.

Using Equation 23.4 to move the control points means that the deformation function w is no longer guaranteed to be one-to-one. To retain this property the displacement of each control point is truncated along all three axes. In this way:

$$((-0.48, -0.48, -0.48) \; \Omega \; \Delta\psi \; \Omega \; (0.48, 0.48, 0.48))$$

Whilst this truncation guarantees the one-to-one property it effectively prevents a point from reaching its final destination in a single iteration of the algorithm.

23.5.4 Hierarchy of Lattices

A hierarchy of lattices $\Psi_0, \Psi_1, \ldots, \Psi_k$, where Ψ_0 is the coarsest grid and Ψ_k the finest, is used to derive a sequence of deformation functions $w_n, w_{n-1}, \ldots, w_0$. Through this repeated application of the deformation process, the movement of each point c_{sn} in C_s is accumulated until it has reached its destination position c_d. Using progressively finer lattices means that surrounding points are not influenced.

If δ_k is the spacing between control points on the initial configuration of lattice Ψ_k then the spacing between control points for the $(k+1)^{th}$ lattice is defined as $\delta_{k+1} = 0.5 \; \delta_k$. At each stage the deformation function w_i moves the feature points closer to their destination positions. The error ξ between the new deformed position of each point and its required destination is defined as:

$$\xi(w) = \max_n \left\| w(c_{sn}) - c_{dn} \right\|^2 \tag{23.5}$$

Using Ψ_k a point c_{si} in C_s can move a maximum of $(0.48\delta_k, 0.48\delta_k, 0.48\delta_k)$ if all 64 surrounding control points have maximum displacement. If each point c_{si} moves this maximum distance then the error ξ reduces by at least $(0.48\delta_k)^3$ and so the next finer lattice is used. Iteration continues using a single lattice Ψ_k until the change in error falls below $0.5(0.48\delta_k)^3$. When this occurs then the next finest lattice Ψ_{k+1} is used. This process, which is illustrated in Figure 23.2, continues until the error reduces to a level below a user-defined constant α.

Hierarchical Volume Deformation (HVD) generates the C^2-continuous and one-to-one deformation of a volumetric dataset. The use of B-spline approximation provides excellent local control over the positioning and movement of features around the object. Several existing approaches to volume deformation [50, 52, 53] are of a global nature and hence each voxel in the volume is influenced by all feature

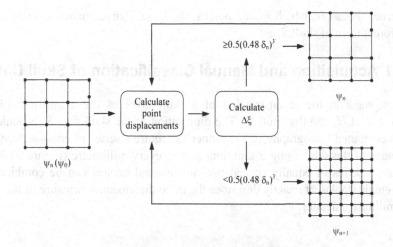

Figure 23.2. The application of successively finer lattices.

elements. This means that the time taken to warp a volume object is directly related to the number of element pairs multiplied by the number of voxels resulting in large run-times for even moderate numbers of feature points. This is not the case with HVD where an increase in the number of feature points has virtually no affect on run-time.

The use of points for feature specification provides a simple but ambiguous means of controlling deformation. Other primitives have been developed such as boxes and lines [50] and disk fields [52]. Whilst potentially more powerful than other primitives, disk fields can be difficult to specify and manipulate accurately, with unexpected movement of surrounding points a common occurrence. Existing free-form deformation techniques suffer from much the same problem [54, 55, 57]. Although commonly used for simple, global deformation of an object, higher-levels of control over a deformation can be difficult to achieve. The precise control provided by HVD enables the movement of points and their influence on surrounding areas of the volume to be easily anticipated and controlled, and this advantage, coupled with its fluidity and flexibility, makes it an ideal deformation model for use within the facial reconstruction pipeline.

23.6 Facial Reconstruction Using HVD

A new graphical pipeline for the reconstruction of facial features for forensic identification has been developed. The reconstruction of a skull is achieved through the use of the hierarchical deformation algorithm described in the previous section. Two feature point sets are used to specify the source and required destination positions of key anatomical features on the skulls.

The facial reconstruction of skull S_d can therefore be obtained by deforming a reference head H_s (consisting of skull S_s and T_s) to the shape of S_d. In this way the facial tissue T_s is deformed along with the reference skull S_s to produce a final reconstructed head H_d which should possess the facial characteristics determined by the different form of skull S_d.

23.6.1 Acquisition and Manual Classification of Skull Data

The first stage in the reconstruction of a skull involves the acquisition of the reference head H_s and the skull S_d. The digitisation of the skull data S_d is achieved using a computed tomography (CT) scanner to acquire a series of cross-sectional x-ray images of the skull using a sampling rate of every millimetre (Figure 23.3). In this way, a series of equally spaced two-dimensional images can be combined to form a single stack that exactly describes the three-dimensional structure of the skull to submillimetre detail [59].

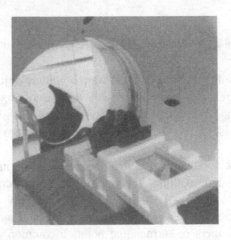

Figure 23.3. Acquisition of skull data using computed tomography.

The application of CT scanning as a data input device is, at present, limited to the scanning of deceased subjects. The very nature of CT scanning means that scanning a living subject, to the accuracy required for our purposes, would mean the use of potentially dangerous doses of radiation. Several research groups have examined the possibility of extracting the bone from datasets obtained using Magnetic Resonance Imaging (MRI) [60]. In this way, an accurate and detailed representation of the skull can be obtained without any risk to the subject and such data are equally suited to this method. However, in recent years, CT systems with reduced radiation exposure and improved image quality have become more widely available.

The reference head H_s (skull S_s and its overlying tissue T_s) that is to be used in the reconstruction process is selected from a database of heads (each head having been obtained using a CT scanner). To produce as realistic and as accurate a reconstruction as possible, the selected reference head H_s (Figure 23.4) must be the closest match in terms of sex, age and cranial form to the skull S_d. In order to facilitate the matching of the skulls, we have chosen to store the reference heads H_1, H_2, H_3, ..., H_n in the form of a tree-shaped structure. This tree has two main branches: male and female. These branches are split into several other branches each representing a different age range (young adult, mature adult and senile for example). At the root of each branch of the tree lies a subset of reference heads. These heads are similar in terms of sex and age range to the given skull and each has a feature set F_s associated with it. This is a set of feature points placed at a number of known anatomical positions around the skull. The use of a tree-structure means that selection of a reference skull that most closely resembles the given skull S_d is a matter of the investigator classifying the skull according to sex and approximate age. It would be nearly impossible to attempt to identify, never mind reconstruct, the face of an individual without this information [61]. Once these attributes have been determined [3, 6, 23, 61-63] the tree is traversed until a root node is encountered resulting in a suitable subset of reference heads.

Figure 23.4. The reference head H_s.

23.6.2 Feature Matching and Analysis of Reference Data

Given the subset of reference heads H_{r1}, H_{r2}, H_{r3}, ..., H_{rn} at the root node, the next stage of reconstruction involves feature analysis to find a single reference head that is the closest match to the given skull. Feature points are manually placed at known anatomical points around the given skull S_d (Figure 23.5). Although time-consuming, a manual approach to this task guarantees that all anatomical landmarks in one dataset are matched with the correct corresponding landmarks in the other dataset. Although several automatic approaches to the process of matching two three-dimensional datasets have been documented, the extraction and registration of anatomical landmarks remains a difficult and error-prone process hindered by the differing orientation, size and shape of individual anatomical landmarks. In addition, the method of data acquisition often introduces varying quantities of unforeseen extra noise into the data, which can result in the incorrect matching of features. This noise is usually (in the case of CT) in the form of star-burst artefacts due to the attenuation of X-rays by amalgam dental restorations.

To obtain a single reference head H_s from the set of reference heads, we compare each reference head (skull) H_{r1}, H_{r2}, H_{r3},......, H_{rn} with the skull S_d by calculating and comparing the spatial distribution of the feature sets F_{rn} and F_d . We use the closest matching skull for deformation.

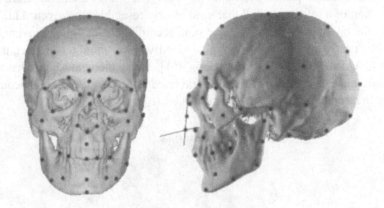

Figure 23.5. The location of the anatomical landmarks around the skull.

23.6.3 Reconstruction, Manipulation and Visualisation

The reference head H_s (with skull S_s) is deformed to the shape of the skull S_d using the feature sets F_s and F_d. The reconstruction can be adjusted simply and quickly, both during and after the initial deformation process, through manipulation of one or more control points. Facial expressions, individual features and tissue thickness variation may be incorporated into the reconstructed face through the simple manipulation of the relevant feature point(s). Visualisation of the reconstructed head is achieved through the use of an in-house volume rendering package [64]. The final reconstruction may be viewed using a variety of lighting effects, at any orientation and with varying opacity. This use of variable opacity means that we can achieve simultaneous visualisation of both the soft tissue and the underlying bone structure. A pre-mortem line up may be constructed in an attempt to increase the odds of a successful identification from the reconstruction. This could consist of several reconstructions of the same skull, each possessing varying degrees of build (emaciated, normal and obese). Animations of the reconstructed head may also be produced which may further aid the identification process.

23.7 Results

The reconstruction of an unknown skull was undertaken using the data of a male of unknown age, sex and race as the reference head H_s. The unknown skull S_d was known to be that of a 44 year old male. The anonymity of the reference head means that there is a high probability that the two skulls are of differing ages, race and even sex. These attributes are of fundamental importance to the accuracy and eventual success of a reconstruction since skull size and shape can vary greatly between population groups. The objective therefore of this preliminary reconstruction was not to produce an anatomically correct reconstruction (using the correct tissue depth model for the unknown skull) but to analyse the general shape and form of the final reconstruction. The first stage was to acquire the data for the skull S_d by computed tomography (Figure 23.3). The data for the reference head had been previously scanned. Anatomical landmarks were positioned at 50 locations around S_s and S_d denoting source and destination positions of each feature. The general shape and size of the nose was determined using the premiss that the width of the nasal aperture in the skull is approximately three-fifths of the overall width of the nose. The approximate distance at which the nose projects from the surface of the skin can be determined by taking a line at a tangent to the lower third of the nasal bone and projecting it down until it bisects a line projected outwards along the direction of the anterior nasal spine [12]. This is illustrated in Figure 23.6. Deformation of the reference head took two hours using the multi-level free form deformation. The resulting reconstruction reveals a close match with the general shape and size of the skull. The size and positioning of individual features such as the nose, eyes and mouth is extremely satisfactory. However, a pre-mortem photograph of the deceased is required before detailed analysis may be undertaken.

23.8 Discussion

All methods of facial reconstruction rely on the assumption of a relationship between the skull and the overlying soft tissue and, to a lesser extent, the characteristic features [3, 6, 33, 65-68]. Until recently, this assumption has been simplified to a set of landmark soft tissue depth data acquired through a variety of methods. It is not solely the use of sparsely distributed landmarks which constitutes a problem in trying to recreate the complex contours of the face, but also the mode of application of the soft tissue depth data. Almost without exception, it is the average values of the reference tables which are used. However, average values at every point, may not necessarily represent a possible combination of tissue depths for a single individual. Certain methods (plastic anatomical reconstruction) utilise the form of the anatomical structures to aid reconstruction. This endeavours to interpret realistically the contours between the landmarks rather than laying a face over the landmarks and assuming that the tissue depth simply changes gradually from one landmark to the next.

The new method based on volume deformation has one major advantage over surface deformation methods in that the whole of the data representing the facial soft tissues are deformed and not just the surface. The facial soft tissues change in response to the changes in the skull, thus the face is not merely a mask suspended on a restricted number of reference points. The craniometric individuality of the skull and its idiosyncrasies are maintained with this technique; asymmetry in areas of the

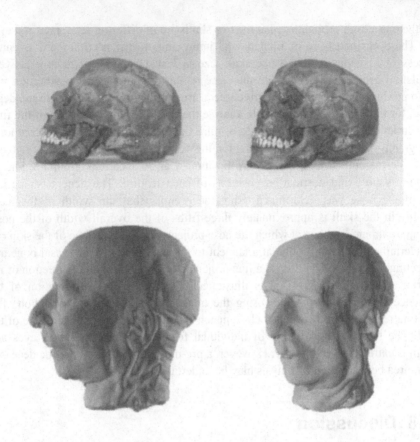

Figure 23.6. A reconstruction: (top) photographs; (bottom) final reconstruction.

skull not normally represented by landmarks will be represented. It is thus possible with this method, to abandon the use of soft tissue reference tables and rely on the more comprehensive total facial volume data integral to the system, thus eliminating the errors incurred in the use, interpretation and mode of collection of soft tissue depth data.

An additional advantage of this system is that it allows for immediate scanning of a skull in a range of states of preservation. For other methods of facial reconstruction, it has been necessary to carefully clean the skull prior to making a cast or laser scanning the skull. This method, by utilising CT scans, allows the volume data of the skull to be extracted from the surrounding soft tissue data independent of the state of those tissues (burnt, badly decomposed, mutilated and so on). A limitation intrinsic to this method is the use of a single face, since ultimately, all reconstructions will resemble that face. However, it is possible that the change in the facial proportions and contours stimulated by the differing forms of individual skulls may be sufficient to render the reconstructions individually recognisable. This is thought preferable to using an average head, since an average of cranial volume data is not an 'actual' head, it is an aggregation of a number of highly specific cranial forms. Averaging negates and contradicts the bio-mechanical and genetic specificities which contribute to the formation of a particular cranial form. When examining previous 'successful' reconstructions, many of the soft tissue features were different from those of the individual, but something triggered recognition.

A note of caution perhaps against excessive rendering of computer images or using photograph composites to make reconstructions more 'life-like'. Such methods may detract from the ambiguous form supplied by this technique and certain sculpting methods and may appear to be an exact reproduction or photograph rather than a likeness. It is perhaps more appropriate that reconstructions be kept as 'undefined' as possible to allow the form of the face to trigger the memory, rather than specific features which, in the majority of cases, are conjecture.

The facial reconstruction pipeline described has been used to reconstruct several skulls with promising results. Although close examination of the reconstruction and the unknown skull has revealed excellent correspondence between matching anatomical landmarks, there is still a need to undertake further evaluation of the technique. Both expert and public opinion are required to effectively judge the resemblance between a given reconstruction and a pre-mortem photograph of the deceased. Other areas of focus include the acquisition of data covering a wider population sample and the development of an accurate and reliable matching algorithm to establish automatic correspondence between the anatomical features of two datasets.

23.9 Conclusions

Facial reconstruction has an important role to play as a valuable tool in the initiation of the process of identification in the absence of other information. It should not however be seen as a means to verify a positive identification. Nevertheless, it is worth pursuing further research in the field and rigorously attempting to eliminate as many sources of error as possible. CT and MRI imaging techniques provide the much needed simultaneous visualisation of hard and soft cranial tissues. The use of volume deformation techniques allows the facial tissues to be dealt with as a single unit, thus freeing the procedure from the constraints and problems attached to the use of standardised soft tissue depth data tables. The reconstruction follows anatomical 'guidelines' as it is formed from a single head and the tissues deform to take up the altered shape of the skull beneath them. The method presented here is also quick and offers the flexibility of being able to view a series of reconstructions in three dimensions. With such advances, a case can be made for routinely producing facial reconstructions in the early stages of investigations instead of turning to the technique as a last resort.

Acknowledgements

The author wishes to thank Linda Nelson, the Institute of Legal Medicine Milan for providing the skull data and advice regarding forensic matters. Also to Dr. M. Chen,

University of Wales Swansea, for technical advice during this work. The author was supported by an Engineering and Physical Science Research Council (EPSRC) Research Studentship.

References

1. George RM. The lateral craniographic method of facial reconstruction. J. Forensic Sci., 1987; 32:1305-1330.
2. Aulsebrook WA, Iscan MY, Slabbert JH, Becker P. Superimposition and reconstruction in forensic facial reconstruction: A survey. Forensic Sci. Int., 1995; 75:101-120.
3. Krogman WM, Iscan MY. The Human Skeleton in Forensic Medicine, 2nd Edition, Charles C Thomas, Springfield IL, 1986.
4. Taylor KT. Techniques of facial reconstruction drawing. In: Proc. International Symposium on the Forensic Aspects of Mass Disasters and Crime Scene Reconstruction, FBI Academy, Virginia, 1990.
5. Peuch PF. Portrait of the Temple Child - A missing link in the case of Louis XVII. Int. J. Leg. Med., 1995; 107:209-212.
6. Stewart TD. Essentials of Forensic Anthropology. Charles C Thomas, Springfield IL, 1979.
7. Welcker H. Schillers sch←del und todenmaske, nebst mitteolungen uber schädel und todenmaske Kants. Fr. Vieweg und Sohn, Braunschweig, 1883.
8. His W. Anatomische forschungen ueber Johann Sebastien Bach's gebeine und antlitz nebst bemerkungen ueber dessen bolder. Abhandlungen der Mathematisch-Physikalischen Klasse der Konigl. Sachsischen Gesellschaft der Wissenschaften, 1895; 22:379-420.
9. Kollmann WM, Büchly W. Die persistenz der rassen und die reconstruction der physiognomie parehistorischer sch←del. Arch. Anthropol., 1898; 25:329-359
10. Tattersall I. Evolution comes to life. Scientific American, 1992; August: 80-87.
11. Neave RAH. Reconstruction of the skull and the soft tissues of the head and face of Lindow Man. Canadian Soc. Forensic Sci. J., 1989; 22:43-53.
12. Prag J, Neave RAH. Making Faces: Using Forensic and Archaeological Evidence. British Museum Press, London, 1997.
13. Maples WR, Gatliff BP, Ludeña H, Benfer R, Goza W. The death and mortal remains of Francisco Pizarro. J. Forensic Sci., 1989; 34:1021-1036.
14. Farrar F. From skull to visage: A forensics technique for facial restoration. The Police Chief, 1977; 44:78-80.
15. Phillips VM, Rosendorff S, Schotz HJ. Identification of a suicide victim by facial reconstruction. J. Forensic Odonto-Stomatol., 1996; 14(2).
16. Rhine JS, Campbell HR. Thickness of facial tissues in American Blacks. J. Forensic Sci., 1980; 25(4):847-858.
17. Rhine JS, Moore CE. Facial reproduction tables of facial tissue thickness of American Caucasoids in forensic anthropology. In: Maxwell Museum Technical Series 1, Albuquerque, New Mexico, 1992.

18. Helmer R, Koschorek F, Tewey B, Frauen T. Measuring the thickness of facial soft tissues using nuclear magnetic resonance tomography for the purposes of identification. Archiv fur Kriminologie, 1986; 178:139-150.

19. Vanezis P, Blowes RW, Linney AD, Tan AC, Richards R, Neave RAH. Application of 3D computer graphics for facial reconstruction and comparison with sculpting techniques. Forensic Sci. Int., 1989; 42:69-84.

20. Miyasaka S, Yoshino M, Imaizumi K, Seta S. The computer-aided facial reconstruction system. Forensic Sci. Int., 1995; 74:155-165.

21. Ubelaker D, O'Donnell G. Computer assisted facial reproduction. J. Forensic Sci., 1992; 37(1):155-162.

22. Evenhouse R, Rasmussen M, Sadler L. Computer-aided forensic facial reconstruction. J. Biocommunication, 1992; 19(2):22-28.

23. Shahrom AW, Vanezis P, Chapman RC, Gonzales A, Blenkinsop C, Rossi ML. Techniques in facial identification: Computer-aided facial reconstruction using a laser scanner and video superimposition. Int. J. Legal Med, 1996; 108:194-200.

24. Michael SD, Chen M. The 3D reconstruction of facial features using volume distortion. In: Proc. 14th Eurographics UK Conference, 1996; 297-305.

25. Tyrrell AJ, Evison MP, Chamberlain AT, Green MA. Forensic three-dimensional facial reconstruction: Historical review and contemporary developments. J. Forensic Sci., 1997; 42(4):653-661.

26. Quatrehomme G, Cotin S, Subsol G, Delingette H, Garidel Y, Grevin G, et al. A fully three-dimensional method for facial reconstruction based on deformable models. J. Forensic Sci., 1997; 42(4):649-652.

27. Nelson LA, Michael SD. The application of volume deformation to three-dimensional facial reconstruction: A comparison with previous techniques. Forensic Sci. Int., 1998; 94(3):167-181.

28. Archer KM. Craniofacial Reconstruction Using Hierarchical B-spline Interpolation, MSc. Thesis, Department of Electrical and Computer Engineering, University of British Columbia, 1997.

29. Craig EA. Facial Reconstruction. J. Forensic Sci., 1992; 37:1442.

30. Ubelaker D. Letters to the editor: Facial reconstruction. J. Forensic Sci., 1992; 37(6):1442-1444.

31. Arridge S, Moss JP, Linney AD, James DR. Three-dimensional digitisation of the face and skull. J. Max.-fac. Surg., 1985; 13:136-143.

32. Lee SY, Wolberg G, Shin SY. Scattered data interpolation with multilevel B-splines. IEEE Transactions on Visualization and Computer Graphics, 1997; 3(3)228-244.

33. Caldwell PC. New questions (and some answers) on the facial reproduction technique. In: Reichs KJ (ed) Forensic Osteology. Charles C Thomas, Springfield IL, 1986.

34. Hodson G, Lieberman LS, Wright P. In vivo measurements of facial tissue thickness in American Caucasoid children. J. Forensic Sci., 1985; 30:1110-1112.

35. Rathbun TA. Personal identification: facial reproductions. In: Rathbun TA, Buikstra JE (Eds), Forensic Anthropology. Charles C Thomas, Springfield IL, 1984.

36. Suzuki K. On the thickness of the soft tissue parts of the Japanese face. J. Anth.

Soc. Nippon, 1948; 60:7-11.

37. Dumont ER. Mid-facial depths of white children: An aid in facial reconstruction. J. Forensic Sci., 1986; 31:1463-1469.

38. Lebedinskaya GV, Stepia VS, Surnina TS, Fedosyvtkin BA, Tschebin LA. The first experience of the application of ultrasound for the thickness of soft facial tissues. Soviet Ethnogr., 1979; 4:121-131.

39. Aulsebrook WA, Becker PJ, Iscan MY. Facial soft tissue thickness in the adult male Zulu. Forensic Sci. Int., 1996; 79:83-102.

40. Phillips VM, Smuts NA. Facial reconstruction: Utilization of computerized tomography to measure facial tissue thickness in a mixed racial population. Forensic Sci. Int., 1996; 83:51-59.

41. Nelson LA. The Potential Use of Computed Tomography Scans for the Collection of Cranial Soft Tissue Depth Data. MSc Thesis (unpublished), University of Sheffield, UK, 1995.

42. Snow CC, Gatliff BP, McWilliams KR. Reconstruction of facial features from the skull: An evaluation of its usefulness in forensic anthopology. Am. J. Phys. Anthrop., 1970; 33:221-228.

43. Todd TW, Lindala A. Thicknesses of subcutaneous tissues in the living and the dead. Am. J. Anatomy, 1928; 41.

44. Schultz AH. Relation of the external nose to the bony nose and nasal cartilages in Whites and Negroes. Am. J. Phys. Anthrop., 1918; 1:329-338.

45. Wolberg G. Digital Image Warping. IEEE Computer Society, Los Alamitos, CA, 1990.

46. Beier T, Neely S. Feature-based image metamorphosis. ACM/SIGGRAPH Computer Graphics, 1992; 26(2):35-42.

47. Ruprecht D, Müller H. Image warping with scattered data interpolation. IEEE Computer Graphics and Applications 1995; 15(2):37-43.

48. Arad N, Reisfeld D, Yeshurun Y. Image warping by radial basis functions: applications to facial expressions. CVGIP: Graphical Models and Image Processing, 1994; 56(2):161-172.

49. Lee SY, Chwa KY, Shin SY, Wolberg G. Image metamorphosis using snakes and free-form deformations. In: Proc. SIGGRAPH, 1995; 439-448.

50. Lerios A, Garfinkle C, Levoy M. Feature-based volume metamorphosis. In: Proc. SIGGRAPH, 1994; 449-456.

51. Chen M, Jones MW, Townsend P. Methods for volume metamorphosis. In: European workshop on combined real and synthetic image processing for broadcast and video production, Hamburg, Germany, November 1994.

52. Chen M, Jones MW, Townsend P. Volume distortion and morphing using disk fields. Comp. And Graphics, 1996; 20(4):567-575.

53. Fang S, Raghavan R, Richtsmeier JT. Volume morphing methods for landmark based 3D image deformation. In: Proc. SPIE International Symposium on Medical Imaging 2710, Newport Beach, CA, February 1996.

54. Sederberg TW, Parry SR. Free-form deformation of solid geometric models. ACM/SIGGRAPH Computer Graphics, 1986; 20(4):151-160.

55. Coquillart S. Extended free-form deformation: a sculpturing tool for 3D geometric modelling. ACM/SIGGRAPH Computer Graphics, 1990; 24(4):187-

196.

56. Coquillart S. Animated free-form deformation: An interactive animation technique. ACM/SIGGRAPH Computer Graphics, 1991; 25(4):23-26.

57. Hsu WM, Hughes JF, Kaufman A. Direct manipulation of free-form deformations. ACM/SIGGRAPH Computer Graphics 1992; 26(2):177-184.

58. Lee SY, Wolberg G, Chwa KY, Shin SY. Image metamorphosis with scattered feature constraints. IEEE Transactions on Visualization and Computer Graphics, 1996; 2(4):337-354.

59. Rhodes ML. Computer graphics and medicine: A complex partnership. IEEE Computer Graphics and Applications, 1997; January:22-28.

60. Höhne KH, Hanson WA. Interactive 3D segmentation of MRI and CT volumes using morphological operations. J. Computer Assisted Tomography, 1992; 16(2):285-294.

61. Novotný V, Iscan MY, Loth SR. Morphological and osteometric assessment of age, sex, and race from the skull. In: Iscan MY, Helmer RP (Eds), Forensic Analysis of the Skull. Wiley-Liss, 1993; Chapter 6:71-88.

62. Leopold D, Hammer HJ, Greil H. Determination of body constitution type from the face. In: IscanMY, Helmer RP (Eds), Forensic Analysis of the Skull. Wiley-Liss, 1993; Chapter 4:47-56.

63. Ubelaker D, Scammell H. Bones: Sex, size, race, age at death. J. Forensic Sci., 1997; 47(3):332-347.

64. Jones MW. The Visualisation of Regular Three-Dimensional Data. Ph.D. Thesis, Department of Computer Science, University of Wales, Swansea, UK, 1995.

65. Lebedinskaya GV, Balvera TS, Veselovskaya EV. Principles of facial reconstruction. In: Iscan MY, Helmer RP (Eds), Forensic Analysis of the Skull. Wiley-Liss, 1993; Chapter 14:183-198.

66. Suk V. Fallacies of anthropological identifications and reconstructions. A critique based on anatomical dissection. In: Publications of the Faculty of Science, University of Masaryk, 1935; 207:1-18.

67. Saxby PJ, Freer TJ. Dentoskeletal determinants of soft tissue morphology. The Angle Orthodontist, 1985; 55:145-154.

68. George RM. Anatomical and artistic guidelines for forensic facial reconstruction. In: Iscan MY, Helmer RP (Eds), Forensic Analysis of the Skull. Wiley-Liss, 1993; Chapter 16:215-227.

24. A Morphological Approach to Volume Synthesis of Weathered Stones

Nao Ozawa and Issei Fujishiro

24.1 Background and Purpose

Lack of considering *aging* phenomena observed commonly in the real world gives rise to unreal synthesised objects. Aging effects are viewed as playing an important role in achieving seamless superposition of synthesised objects upon acquired natural scenes, for instance, in CG montages and augmented reality environments [1]. Several research groups have noticed the importance of aging effects, and recently reported promising synthesis results [2-10].

Faithful computer simulation of aging phenomena based on underlying physical principles tends to be time-consuming, and impractical for *interactive* image synthesis. This is the primary reason why *phenomenological* approaches have been exploited for visual modelling of various phenomena. In addition, *controllability* is another key issue for generating a wide variety of aged objects. Most of the above-referenced existing aging methods involve their specific texture synthesis, followed by mapping the texture onto target objects, and resulting in little controllability in representing aged texture variations depending on the object shape, and the object deformation itself.

The main focus in this chapter is placed on synthesis of *stone weathering*. Stones are a quite common building material, since ancient times, human beings have been utilising stones for creating a wide spectrum of objects; e.g. buildings, roads, bridges, belfries, and statues. They are usually exposed to wind and rain in the open for a long period, and weathered in any natural environment. Even such frequently observed phenomena need a specific phenomenological modelling method with a high degree of interactivity and controllability.

Stone objects, which are generally composed of different kinds of minerals intermixed with one another, start eroding on their surfaces interacting with the open air, leading to bumpy surfaces and rounded corners. Sometimes, fragile portions with high curvature are completely removed. It is obvious that such complex deformations cannot be achieved with traditional free-form deformation or rounding operation on solid models. Volumetric morphing and warping have already appeared in the literature [11, 12]. However, the techniques cannot be applied directly to the simulation of weathering. The primary reasons are two-fold:

- Plausible target volume, locally with high frequency components and

globally with a simpler topology, cannot be given *a priori* for a given source volume;
- Weathering is intrinsically stochastic, reflecting the physical and chemical randomness of mineral fabric with the effect of wind and rain.

Perlin and Hoffert [2, 13] present the *hypertexture* and *surflet* approaches which generate an eroded cube by taking the intersection of a cube and a fractal sphere. However, the approaches are not guaranteed to generate the same erosion effect for a given arbitrarily-shaped object. In other words, it is unclear how to determine the number, location and size of fractal spheres depending on the target object geometry. An attractive texture synthesis method related to these approaches is reported by Dischler et al. [10], where a mineral-like, macro-structured texture is synthesised by using their image- and skeleton-based approach.

Dorsey et al. [7] propose a volumetric model of near-boundary, multi-layered structure of stones, and simulate the stone weathering process by solving a specific system of finite difference equations governing the moisture-mineral interaction. As for the realistic rendering of weathered stones, they successfully take advantage of their earlier technique called *subsurface scattering*, as in [5].

This chapter attempts to simulate the effects of stone weathering in a more abstract manner than the Dorsey method [7] by *mathematical morphology* (MM)-based volumetric metamorphosis. MM [14] is expected to serve as a good abstraction of stone weathering because it is well known that practical weathering is developed by iterated dilations and erosions of stones due to water-crack interactions. Indeed, an effective MM operator, termed *weathering*, is devised herein by extending the ordinal 3D *opening* MM operator with stochastic structuring elements.

The remainder of this chapter is organised as follows. The next section clarifies the reason why the opening operator is chosen as the basis for designing the weathering operator. Section 24.3 is devoted to the detailed description of the weathering operator in the digital setting. In Section 24.4, several preliminary experiments are performed with simple-shaped stone objects to illustrate the effectiveness of the present technique. More sophisticated examples are also visualised. Section 24.5 summarises the chapter with some remarks on future research directions.

24.2 Basic Idea

MM was originally proposed by Matheron in 1975 [14]. MM provides a quite simple algebraic structure of morphological operations, which are constructed basically by *dilation* and *erosion*, plus a few other auxiliary operators. The algebraic structure of MM allows for a straightforward building block-oriented implementation of complex morphological operations. Adjustment of an argument, called a *structuring element* (SE), to the operators can lead to the ease of generating various deformation effects.

Conventionally, MM has been used as a unified framework for image (2D) and signal (1D) analysis [14]. An extension of MM to volume (3D) has also been reported [15], where the main goal is limited to volume analysis, including noise elimination. On the contrary, this chapter strives to adopt the 3D digital MM for the purpose of volume synthesis.

24.2.1 2D Opening

First, our primary attention is paid to an MM operator, called *opening*. For brevity, the effect of Euclidean opening is illustrated herein with a 2D example. The definition of opening is as follows:

$$opening(A, E) = dilation[erosion(A, E)], \, A: \text{binary image}, \, E: \text{SE}$$

As for more specific definitions of dilation and erosion in 3D, see Subsection 24.3.1. An execution example of 2D opening is shown in Figure 24.1. It is observed clearly from Figure 24.1 that the following three dominant deformation effects due to opening are akin to those due to actual weathering:

1. Corners are rounded;
2. Protruded portions are eroded; and
3. Small portions with high curvature are possibly removed.

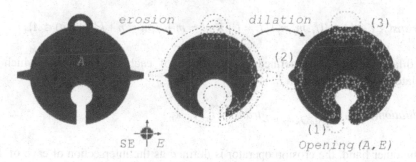

Figure 24.1. 2D opening: an example.

It should be noted here that all these effects cannot be achieved with only the erosion operator. This is the main reason why opening is adopted as the basis for devising the weathering operator. In addition, the degree of the above-described features can be controlled by the selection of the shape and size of the SE. In particular, a dynamic circular SE with perturbed radius is expected to produce a stochastic nature of real weathered stones more effectively. This is the heart of the extension of opening to weathering in the next section.

24.3 Weathering Operator

The 3D digital binary MM is employed herein to establish a practical environment for morphological deformation of volumes.

24.3.1 3D Opening

Volumetric objects are represented with a set of binary voxels whose values are 1. Let A and B denote two objects. $A \subset B$ *iff* any "1" voxel in A is also an element of B. Figure 24.2 shows a tiny volumetric object data and its set representation.

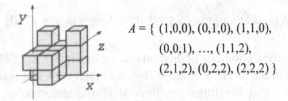

$$A = \{ \; (1,0,0), (0,1,0), (1,1,0),$$
$$(0,0,1), \ldots, (1,1,2),$$
$$(2,1,2), (0,2,2), (2,2,2) \; \}$$

Figure 24.2. Set representation of volume.

Next, the definition of 3D dilation and erosion in the digital setting are provided. Herein, *trans* denotes the *translation* operator, which is defined as follows:

$$trans(A;i,j,k) = \{(l_t, m_t, n_t) \mid l_t = l+i, m_t = m+j, n_t = n+k, (l,m,n) \in A\}$$

The dilation operator is defined as the union of each of A's voxels which is translated with an element in E:

$$dilation(A,E) = \bigcup\nolimits_{(i_n, j_n, k_n) \in E} trans(A; i_n, j_n, k_n)$$

On the other hand, the erosion operator is defined as the intersection of each of A's voxels which is translated with an element in E in the negative direction:

$$erosion(A,E) = \bigcap\nolimits_{(i_n, j_n, k_n) \in E} trans(A; -i_n, -j_n, -k_n)$$

As in 2D, 3D opening operator is defined with dilation and erosion, as follows:

$$opening(A,E) = dilation[erosion(A,E), E]$$

Figure 24.3 depicts the block diagram of opening. Figure 24.4 illustrates an opening process for A given in Figure 24.2 with an SE $E = \{(0,0,0), (1,0,0)\}$.

Figure 24.3. Block diagram of opening.

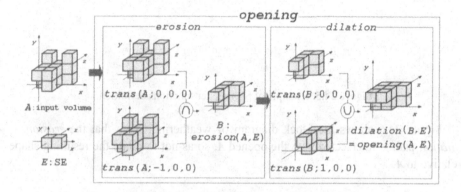

Figure 24.4. 3D opening: an example.

24.3.2 Weathering Operator

As described in the previous section, the deformation effect of the opening operator is deterministic. In order to account for the stochastic nature of real weathering phenomena, the *weathering* operator uses *erosion_p*, which differs from the original erosion in that the SE size changes, reflecting the kind of mineral corresponding to the voxel located at the centre of the SE. Specifically, another *material* volume M is introduced, whose size is the same as that of the original *shape* volume A, and when each voxel in the material volume M is referred to, predefined transfer functions are evaluated to map the kind of material to its corresponding SE size: the more fragile the mineral of a voxel, the bigger the averaged radius given to the spherical SE centred at the voxel. An example of *SE transfer functions* $W(m)$ and $s(m)$ is plotted in Figure 24.5, where each of the three kinds of minerals is identified with its interval of voxel field m, and is given its stochastic SE with radius $W(m)$ and perturbation width $s(m)$.

The actual SE radius is given within the interval $[W(m) - s(m), W(m) + s(m)]$. Consequently, *erosion_p* is defined as follows:

$$erosion_p(A, E) = \bigcap_{(i_n, j_n, k_n) \in E} trans\big(A; (W(m) + \varepsilon) \cdot (-i_n, -j_n, -k_n)\big) \qquad (24.1)$$

where we have $|\varepsilon| \leq s(m)$.

Figure 24.6 shows the block diagram of weathering. Note that the *erosion_p* – *dilation* path is intersected with the opened A, so as not to dilate the resulting shape relative to A.

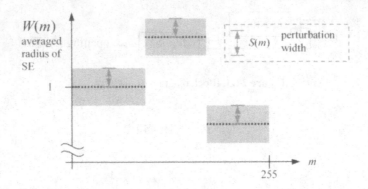

Figure 24.5. Example of SE transfer functions definition.

Figure 24.6 shows the block diagram of weathering. Note that the *erosion$_p$ – dilation* path is intersected with the opened *A*, so as not to dilate the resulting shape relative to *A*.

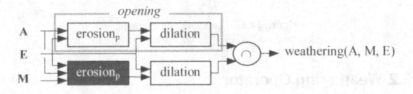

Figure 24.6. Block diagram of weathering.

24.4 Preliminary Experiments

The present MM-based volume modelling and manipulation environment was implemented, and the following experiments were performed on an SGI O2 system (CPU: R10000, Clock: 195MHz, RAM: 256MB). To simulate volumetric global illumination, a volumetric ray tracer [16] incorporated in the VolVis2.1 system[1] was employed. *VolVis* [17] is a comprehensive, diversified, and high-performance volume visualiser that has been developed at the State University of New York at Stony Brook, and is available as freeware. The visualiser makes it possible to evaluate the visual effects of the above-described operators justifiably with standard volumetric simulation of light absorption, reflection, and refraction on stone surfaces.

In the modelling of bell-shaped test volumes, the binary shape volume was created by CSG operations, and then voxelised into a 230x230x230 volume dataset (Figure 24.7a). Of course, *volumetric sculpting* [8] could be used as an alternative way to model stony objects effectively in a volumetric fashion. On the other hand,

---

[1] http://www.cs.sunysb.edu/~vislab/volvis_home.html.

the material volume was obtained simply by piling up a series of stone cross-sectional images whose pixels are randomly permuted (Figure 24.7b). The size of the material volume is the same as that of the shape volume. Then, solid texturing [19] was performed with the shape volume and the material volume. A ray-traced image of the resulting stone volume is shown in Figure 24.7c. The average rendering time was approximately 7 minutes.

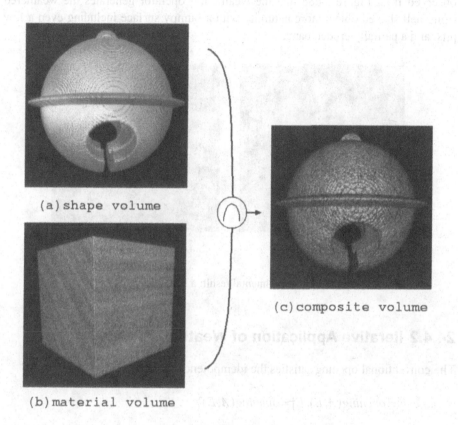

(a) shape volume

(b) material volume

(c) composite volume

Figure 24.7. Solid texturing for producing bell-shaped test volume.

24.4.1 Opening versus Weathering

Figure 24.8a is the resulting image which illustrates how the application of an opening operator transforms the bell-shaped object. It took 90 minutes to execute the opening operator, whose SE has a 6 voxel radius, on the original shape volume. The rendering time was 6 minutes, almost the same as in the case of the original volume in Figure 24.7c. This implies the well-known intrinsic advantage of volume graphics, that is, the temporal complexity is nearly independent of volumetric contents. Comparing Figure 24.8a to Figure 24.7c reveals not only that all the corners are rounded, but also that there remains only the protruded decorative horizontal band, while the top small handle is completely removed.

Figure 24.8b is the resulting image of the bell-shaped object to which the weathering operator was applied. The common material volume contains three different minerals, each of which is assigned its own interval value for the radius of SE. The average size of the used SE is the same as in the opening, but the radius of the SE has a 2 voxel-wide perturbation. The rendering time was 8 minutes. It is observed from Figure 24.8b that the weathering operator generates the weathered stone bell-shaped object more naturally with a bumpy surface including even a few pits, and a partially eroded band.

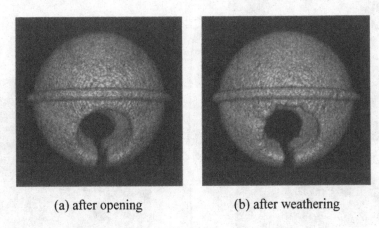

(a) after opening   (b) after weathering

Figure 24.8. Experimental result: a bell-shaped object.

24.4.2 Iterative Application of Weathering

The conventional opening satisfies the idempotence property [14]:

$$opening[opening(A, E), E] = opening(A, E)$$

From the viewpoint of volumetric metamorphosis, it implies that once a given volume is opened, the resulting volume gives a limit of transformability. Such a property does not hold for weathering, because the employed $erosion_p$ has a stochastic nature (see Equation 24.1). In general, the following relationship holds:

$$weathering(A, E) \subset opening(A, E)$$

As described in Section 24.1, practical weathering is developed by iterated dilations and erosions of stones due to water-crack interactions. The goal of the second experiment is to observe what effects are produced by iterated application of a weathering operator with a smaller SE. Figure 24.9 depicts the block diagram for the experiment.

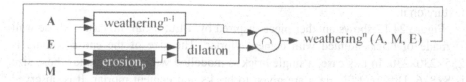

Figure 24.9. Block diagram of iterative weathering.

The same bell-shaped object volume of the previous section is used herein. Figure 24.10 shows a sequence of images where the original volume is weathered iteratively (up to 5 times) with an SE whose radius is 4. It can be observed from the sequence that iterative application of weathering can control the length of time the target object is exposed to the open air.

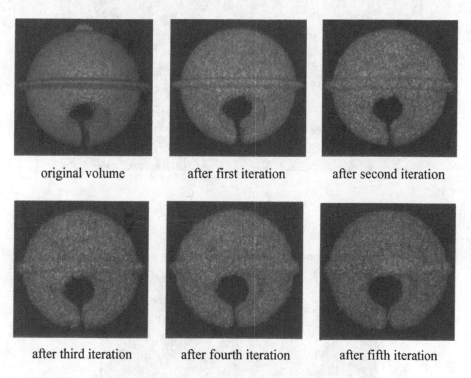

Figure 24.10. The result of iterative weathering.

24.4.3 More Sophisticated Examples

Figure 24.11 shows a natural scene image of a virtual thicket, on which an *ancient doll* synthesised with the present method is superposed. The size of the doll volume is 168x240x168. Note that a slight vestige of face features remains, which is hard to create with currently-available shape modellers. *Volumetric accessibility* proposed in [3] could be also computed to identify the hollow area and map a moss-covered texture on it.

Figure 24.12 shows another piece inspired by a European old castle whose wall is made of bricks jointed with cement mortar. The size of the entire volume is 255×230×230. In this case, a single brick is modelled with a subvolume whose size is 8×8×6. Different SE sizes are given to bricks and cement mortar. It is observed that the top of the wall and the window frames are weather-beaten.

Figure 24.11. Ancient doll.

Figure 24.12. An old castle.

24.5 Concluding Notes

This chapter has presented a 3D morphological approach to visual simulation of weathering effects on stone objects. Preliminary experiments proved that the present morphological operator can produce visual effects similar to actual weathering.

There still remain several research issues. In order to provide an interactive environment for the handling of volumes, the improvement of temporal complexity of weathering operator is crucial. The time to calculate $erosion_p$ in Equation 24.1 is strongly influenced by the cardinality of the SE. One candidate for accelerating the computation is to evaluate $erosion_p$ only with the boundary voxels in the SE. In addition, iterative calculation of $W(m) + \varepsilon$ by calling a random number generator is another time-consuming part in Equation 24.1. Accelerated calculation can be achieved by hash function-based access to a pre-calculated random number table [20].

The material volume used in this chapter is insufficient to represent the actual fabric of stones. Solid texture generation based on primitive instancing and incomplete tessellation of minerals [21] is an attractive way to generate more realistic stone material. The present weathering operator should be enhanced by using gray-scale MM [14] for making SE transfer functions more precise by reflecting the local properties of the mineral fabric structure of stones.

Further extensions to the weathering operator should account for:

- The strength and vulnerability of minerals;
- Anisotropy due to the global thermodynamical structure of stratums, such as joints;
- The flow of rain and wind on the surface of stone objects.

The addition of crack effects due to other factors such as botanical root growth is another challenging theme for synthesising more realistic stone-related aging phenomena.

Acknowledgements

The authors gratefully acknowledge Xiaoyang Mao, Mikio Iizuka, and Karen Vierow for their helpful comments and suggestions. Etsuko Aoki helped the authors in preparing the final draft of this chapter.

References

1. Fujishiro I, Ozawa N. Synthesizing weathered objects for seamless super-imposition on natural scenes (abstract). In: Conference Abstracts of International Symposium on Mixed Reality, Yokohama, March 1999.

2. Perlin,K, Hoffert EM. Hypertexture. ACM/SIGGRAPH Computer Graphics, 1989; 23(3):253-262.
3. Miller G. Efficient algorithm for local and global accessibility shading. In: Proc. SIGGRAPH, 1994, Orlando, FL; 319-326.
4. Hsu S, Wong T. Simulating dust accumulation. IEEE Computer Graphics and Applications, 1995; 15(1):18-22.
5. Dorsey J, Hanrahan P. Modeling and rendering of metallic patinas. In: Proc. SIGGRAPH, August 1999, Los Angeles, CA; 225-234.
6. Dorsey J, Pedersen HK, Hanrahan P. Flow and changes in appearance. In: Proc. SIGGRAPH, August 1996, New Orleans, LA; 411-420.
7. Dorsey J, Edelman A, Jensen HW, Legakis J, Pedersen HK. Modeling and rendering of weathered stones. In: Proc. SIGGRAPH, 1999, Los Angeles, CA.
8. Ozawa N, Fujishiro I. Rendering of metallic patinas with cleaning effect (in Japanese). In: IPSJ SIG notes, 97-CG-87, October 1997; 13-18.
9. Hirota K, Tanoue Y, Kaneko T. Generation of crack patterns with a physical model. The Visual Computer, 1998; 14(3):126-137.
10. Dischler J-M, Ghazanfarpour D. Interactive image-based modeling of macrostructured textures. IEEE Computer Graphics and Applications, 1999; 19(1):66-74.
11. He T, Wang S, Kaufman A. Wavelet-based volume morphing. In: Proc. IEEE Visualization '94, Washington, D.C., October 1994; 85-91.
12. True TJ, Hughes JF. Volume warping. In: Proc. IEEE Visualization '92, Boston, MA, October 1992; 308-315.
13. Perlin K. Surflets. In: Inakage M (Organizer) Photorealistic Volume Modeling and Rendering Techniques. ACM/SIGGRAPH Course Notes 27, Las Vegas, NV, July/August 1991; 4-1-21.
14. Giardina CR, Dougherty ER. Morphological methods in image and signal processing. Prentice Hall, Engelwoods Cliffs, 1987.
15. Sakas G, Walter S. Extracting surfaces from fuzzy 3D-ultrasound data. In: Proc. SIGGRAPH, 1995, Los Angeles, CA; 465-474.
16. Sobierajski LM, Kaufman AE. Volumetric ray tracing. In: Proc. 1994 Symposium on Volume Visualization, Washington, DC, October 1994; 11-18.
17. Avila R, He T, Hong L, Kaufman A, Pfister H, Silva C, Sobierajski L, Wang S. VolVis: A diversified volume visualization system. In: Proc. IEEE Visualization '94, Washington, D.C., October 1994; 31-38.
18. Wang SW, Kaufman AE. Volume sculpting. In: Proc. 1995 Symposium on Interactive 3D Graphics, April 1995, Monterey, CA; 151-156.
19. Perlin K. An image synthesizer. ACM/SIGGRAPH Computer Graphics, 1985; 19(4):287-296.
20. Mao X, Kikukawa M, Fujita N, Imamiya A. Line integral convolution for 3D surfaces. In: Lefer W, Grave M (Eds) Visualization in Scientific Computing '97. Springer-Verlag, Wien, 1997; 57-69.
21. Takagi S, Fujishiro I. Microscopic structural modeling of colored pencil drawings (abstract). In: Visual Proc. SIGGRAPH, 1997, Los Angeles, CA; 187.

25. Volumetric Modelling of 3D Text

Zhongke Wu and Edmond C. Prakash

25.1 Introduction

This chapter describes a new application of volume texture mapping to model 3D volumetric characters. The bit-mapped (hand-written and printed) character conveys substantial information required for 3D character generation in virtual worlds. 2D characters contain space and position signatures that can be used for modelling the shape of 3D characters. This chapter addresses the fundamental problems of 3D artistic text modelling without any additional context other than that required for 2D characters. We report on our experimental development of the 3D character modelling algorithm and its results. A generalised programming model for 3D character generation and its use is also discussed. Finally, we conclude by discussing extensions to the techniques for efficient 3D character design.

Character shape generation is a tedious process. Enormous efforts have been made to address this problem in relation to modelling 3D surface-based text. With the recent developments in volume graphics, the time is ripe to embed readable text information in volume models. The design space currently available for 2D and 3D text rendering and the pros and cons are:

- *Drawing bitmaps* — bitmaps are fast to render, but do not rotate, scale, or project well;
- *Stroke fonts* — with stroke and outline fonts, characters are rendered as connected lines, the speed tends to be slow (due to more transformation overhead) and the fonts are somewhat hard to adapt to the varying levels of detail in 3D scenes;
- *Surface fonts* — they are rendered as polygons that represent the surface of the 3D text.

Our design emphasis has been to embed 3D text into volume graphics, which leads to the following issues to be addressed:

- Method for adding 3D text into 3D volumes;
- Speed of rendering 3D text;
- Flexibility that allows 3D text to be projected, scaled, and rotated;
- Incorporation of existing hand-written text, or art work by artists.

Through our discussions, we show that the existing 2D character information can be used for modelling voxel-based 3D characters, volume texture mapping can be used for fast modelling of volumetric characters, and 3D volumetric characters can be manipulated through operations, such as stretching, rotation and scaling.

25.2 3D Text Modelling

Figure 25.1 shows the different stages in modelling 3D volumetric characters.

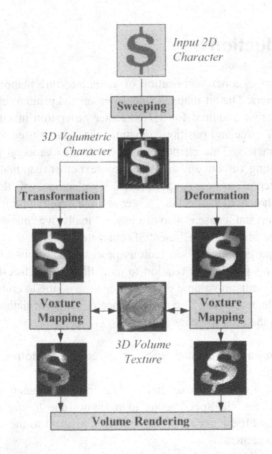

Figure 25.1. Block diagram of artistic text modelling.

From a graphics standpoint, text consists of sequences of letters (or characters or glyphs) decalled on a surface. Instead of treating every instance of text as a separate texture, one could render text from a set of characters. In 2D graphics, we are accustomed to the concept of fonts (or character sets) from which we render text. Although modern fonts are mostly defined by vector-based geometry, they can also be specified using bitmapped images, each of which corresponds to a character. Such an image may be an artist's representation of a character created using a paint program, a 2D bitmapped character from a built-in font set, or a hand-written letter. The current approach in 3D graphics treats every word or phrase written on every single surface as a distinct texture. This would let users add text to their graphics scenes, but it is expensive because of the amount of texture images that would be required if one needed to use a distinct texture for each character.

The second stage, *character sweeping*, involves the specification of the 3D sweep required. It can be a simple sweep along a vector or along a curved path. The depth of the character is set depending on the thickness required. In 3D however we still use the 2D information with the additional sweep and a corresponding texture indices associated with the character.

The input to the third stage, *character stretching*, is a 3D bounding block, which encompasses all the voxels that belong to the character after the sweeping operation. In the simplest case, the stretching is accomplished by deformation of this bounding block, and it may perform operations such as scaling, stretching, etc. There is a fine control for voxel-based deformation as requested by the user. Methods for general-purpose volume deformation have been reported in the literature [1-3]. However, none of the methods can be directly applied to volume deformation of 3D Text. For this work we have adapted the recently reported results on goal-oriented volume deformation [4, 5].

The next stage in the process, namely *volume texture mapping*, is to embed a natural 3D texture, for example, a wood texture, for the 3D character. It performs an inverse mapping from the swept volume into the 3D texture. This technique enables us to obtain a realistic carving of the final 3D character.

The final stage is to send the modelled characters to a *volume rendering* engine.

25.3 Volume Texture Mapping

25.3.1 Concept

The technique of *volume texture* (*voxture*) *mapping* is based on the coherent voxelisation approach reported in [6]. This method performs an incremental voxelisation to identify voxels in a polyhedron, and a footprint is used to obtain the voxture mapping. This method has the ability to model a volume buffer by voxture map from one or more non-rectangular texture space. The attractive feature of the algorithm is that it is length-, area-, and volume-coherent, and it can model a single volume texture from one or more 3D textures. Detailed discussions on voxelisation can also be found in Chapters 1, 7 and 20. Volumetric texture mapping is also discussed in Chapter 13.

In voxture mapping, for each voxel, an inverse mapping from the object space (i.e. volume buffer) into the texture space is computed, obtaining the coordinates $<u, v, w>$, which are used to sample the 3D texture. The main advantage of this method is that it is a true 3D mapping rather than an illusion as both the interior and exterior of the 3D character are voxture-mapped. It is view independent, and thus eliminates the problem of perspective texture mapping. There is no need to repeat voxture mapping for simple scaling/zooming operations; repeated mapping is required only when the volumetric grid is deformed. The mapping is carried out during the modelling stage, prior to the volume rendering stage, where no texture look-up is necessary.

The algorithm takes an input of an 8-noded block and corresponding texel coordinates. The texel coordinates are indices (vertices) of the original voxture. The idea is to voxelise the deformed block (obtained from the character stretching stage) and, for each voxel within the block, a voxture sampling is performed to obtain the colour information for that voxel. This process is illustrated in Figure 25.2.

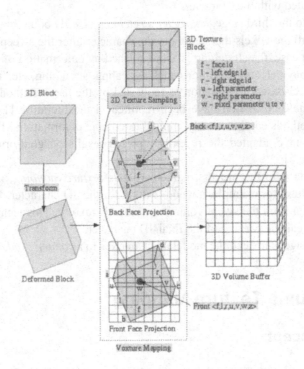

Figure 25.2. Voxture mapping of a character block.

25.3.2 Incremental Voxture Mapping

In order to describe the incremental voxture mapping, we introduce two coordinate systems. The volume buffer defines a 3D coordinate system in the object space, where the voxelisation is carried out. A voxture defines the other coordinate system, where colour information is sampled. Given a voxel $<x, y, z>$ in the object space, we need to find the corresponding $<u, v, w>$ in the voxture space. The additional input available to us is the vertex array $<P_x, P_y, P_z>$ for the polyhedron in voxel space and the corresponding array $<P_u, P_v, P_w>$ in the voxture space.

Since a voxel inside the polyhedron has a corresponding 3D texel, for non-degenerate cases, a line of voxels has a line of texels. Now we try to establish a relationship between a line of voxels to its corresponding line of texels. To get the beam of voxels along a straight line, we need to compute $Q(t)$, $0 \leq t \leq 1$ as:

$$Q = (1-t)Q_f + tQ_b$$

where:

$$Q_f = (1-t_f^w)Q_f^l + t_f^w Q_f^r$$
$$Q_f^l = (1-t_f^u)Q_f^a + t_f^u Q_f^b$$
$$Q_f^r = (1-t_f^v)Q_f^c + t_f^v Q_f^d$$

and:

$$Q_b = (1-t_b^w)Q_b^l + t_b^w Q_b^r$$
$$Q_b^l = (1-t_b^u)Q_b^a + t_f^u Q_b^b$$
$$Q_b^r = (1-t_b^v)Q_b^c + t_f^v Q_b^d$$

For each projected pixel the values that needs to be stored are: t_f^w, t_f^u, t_f^v and their corresponding identifiers e_i, e_j and f_k. Here f_k denotes the kth face of the polyhedron and i and j denote the ith and j^{th} edge of the kth face. Similarly for the back projected pixel, we need to store t_b^w, t_b^u, t_b^v and their corresponding identifiers.

These identifiers are required to index the vertex array to locate $Q_f^a, Q_f^b, Q_f^c, Q_f^d$ for the front faces and $Q_b^a, Q_b^b, Q_b^c, Q_b^d$ for the back faces. These vertex information along with the t values are used to compute $Q_f^l, Q_f^r, Q_b^l, Q_b^r$.

However, t_f^u, t_f^v can be computed incrementally by traversing the edge as $t_{i+1} = t_i + \delta t$. t_f^w can also be computed incrementally using the right and left x values. t_f^u, t_f^v are constant for all projected pixels along a scan-line.

The advantages of this scheme are:

1. All computations in 3D are reduced to one-dimensional incremental additions;
2. The vertex information need not be accessed for each voxel, instead the precomputed t values are used.

The following pseudo-code describes the process of voxture mapping in building a 3D volumetric character.

```
voxture_map_char(vert[N][3], tex_id, txyz[N][3])
begin
    for each face of bounding block do
        scan_edges(left and right buffers);
        if front face then scan_faces(front buffers);
        else if back face then scan_faces(back buffers);
        end if-else-if;
    end for;
    scan_depth(between front and back buffers);
end

scan_edges()
begin
    for each edge in the polygon do
        for each scan-line do
            if left edge then
                Incremental computation of xleft,zleft,uleft;
            else if right edge then
                Incrementaly compute xright,zright,uright;
            end if-else-if;
        end for;
    end for;
end

scan_faces()
begin
    for each scan line of the polygon do
        for each pixel between leftx and rightx do
            frame_buffer[x][y] = 1;   z_buffer[x][y] = depth;
            Increment incr_col and incr_z;
            Store face_id,left_edge_id,Right_edge_id;
            Store left_uval,right_uval for edges;
            Store middle_uval between leftx and rightx;
        end for;
    end for;
end

scan_depth()
begin
    for each projected pixel x,y of the cell do
        Lookup ff_id,ful_id,fur_id,ful_val,fur_val,front_u_val;
        Compute front texture coordinates tx,ty,tz;
        Lookup bf_id,bul_id,bur_id,bul_val,bur_val,back_u_val;
        Compute back texture coordinates tx,ty,tz;
        Incrementally store texels on 3D line in 1D buffer;
        for z = zstart to zend do
            Compute tex_u for each k;
            zcol =footprint(texture_arr[tex_index]);
            Volume[x][y][z] = zcol;
        end for;
    end for;
end
```

25.4 Implementation and Results

In our implementation we use the following data structures: an array for a 2D bitmap, an array for a 3D volumetric character obtained by sweeping and a 3D bounding block, a 3D solid texture array, an index array linking to the 3D solid texture, and a result array for a 3D voxture-mapped character.

For each character to be generated, a 2D bitmap (Figure 25.3a) is first loaded into the memory, and this is followed by a desired sweep for building a volumetric character (Figure 25.3b). The bounding block resulting from this sweep volume is then transformed and deformed, as desired. A 3D solid texture, which is also specified by the user, is then voxture-mapped onto the character block through an inverse mapping (Figures 25.3c and 25.3d).

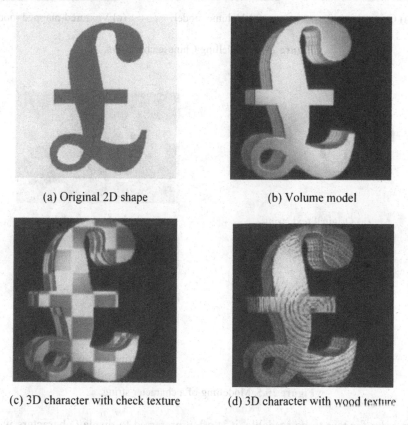

<table>
<tr><td>(a) Original 2D shape</td><td>(b) Volume model</td></tr>
<tr><td>(c) 3D character with check texture</td><td>(d) 3D character with wood texture</td></tr>
</table>

Figure 25.3. Volumetric model of a symbol character.

For hand-written characters, their bitmaps can simply be obtained from 2D scans on conventional flat bed scanners. For example, the Chinese character shown in Figure 25.4 was obtained in this manner. Figure 25.5 shows a string of characters modelled using our technique. The deformation operation is shown for a dollar symbol in Figure 25.6. All these volumes were modelled on an SGI-O2 and rendered using VolVis [7].

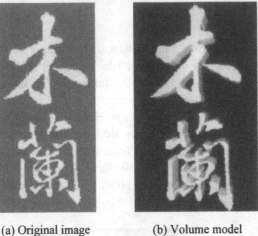

(a) Original image   (b) Volume model   (c) Voxtured-mapped model

Figure 25.4. Modelling Chinese characters.

(a) Original text string   (b) Volume model

(c) 3D string with check texture   (d) 3D string with wood texture

Figure 25.5. Modelling of a character string.

In order for text to be readable, it is often preferred to display characters with a sharp contrast against the background. This raises the *aliasing* issue in voxture sampling and filtering. The *antialiasing* can be achieved in several fronts. First, a sharp 2D character shape is a good point to start. The next step is to incorporate filtering during voxture mappings. The final step is to perform filtering at the ray sampling stage in volume rendering. The other aspect which can further reduce aliasing is to use mip-mapped 3D textures — a method which has been successfully deployed in surface texture mapping.

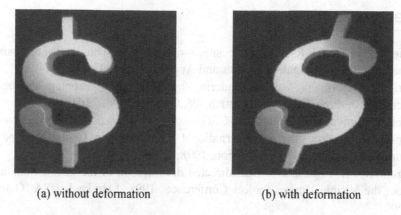

(a) without deformation   (b) with deformation

Figure 25.6. Deformation of a volumetric character.

25.6 Conclusions

We have developed a new approach for modelling 3D volumetric text. The modelling process facilitates the construction of 3D text from images of 2D symbols and hand-written characters, character transformation and deformation, and volumetric texture mapping. This technique can be embedded into various volumetric scenes (e.g. Figure 25.7), and can add a new level of realism in a wide range of volume graphics applications.

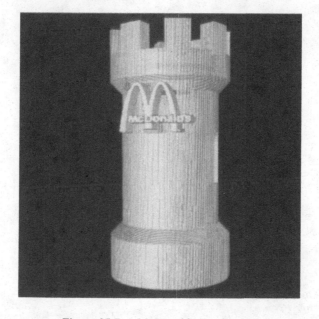

Figure 25.7. A McDonalds voxel castle.

References

1. Kurzion Y, Yagel R. Interactive space deformation with hardware assisted rendering. IEEE Computer Graphics and Applications, 1997, 17.
2. Fang S. Deformable volume rendering by 3D texture mapping and octree encoding. In: Proc. IEEE Visualization '96, October 1996; 73-80.
3. Fang S, Srinivasan R. Volumetric CSG — A model-based volume visualization approach. In: Proc. the 6th International Conference in Central Europe on Computer Graphics and Visualization, 1998; 88-95.
4. Jegathese CR, Prakash EC. Goal-directed deformation of the visible human. In Proc. the Visible Human Project Conference, 1998, Maryland, USA, October 1998.
5. Jegathese CR, Prakash EC. A new approach for goal-oriented deformation of voxel models. In: Proc. Pacific Graphics, 1998, Singapore, October 1998; 214-215.
6. Prakash EC, Manohar S. Volume rendering of unstructured grids: A voxelization approach. Computers and Graphics, 1995; 19(5):711-726.
7. Avila RS, He T, Hong L, Kaufman AE, Pfister H, Silva C, Sobierajski L, Wang S. VolVis: A diversified volume visualization system. In: Proc. IEEE Visualization '94, IEEE CS Press, October 1994; 31-38.

PART VIII

GLOSSARY
AND INDICES

Glossary

MARK W. JONES, ADRIAN LEU, RICHARD SATHERLEY AND STEVE TREAVETT

Author Index

Subject Index

Glossary

Mark W. Jones, Adrian Leu, Richard Satherley and Steve Treavett

3D aliasing — a jaggy effect at the surface of objects due to the imprecision of the discrete model of the object obtained through *voxelisation*. Also known as *object space aliasing*.

3D discrete topology — a theory that deals with the topological issues related to the discrete representation of volumetric objects.

3D raster — see *volume buffer*.

3D ultrasound — the 3D reconstruction of ultrasound images. Ultrasound is a non-invasive, non-radiative, real-time imaging modality.

absorption — a term in the light *transport equation* which describes the flux of particles travelling in a certain direction which are absorbed by the medium at some point in 3D space.

adaptive — altering the focus of the computation in order to concentrate on parts that are more important to the solution. Computation takes place in areas of rapid change, leaving parts that contribute less significantly to be computed last or not at all, for example *adaptive termination*, and *adaptive sampling*.

adaptive sampling — an acceleration technique for volumetric *ray casting* which varies the sampling step along a ray based upon the contribution from the samples.

adaptive termination — an acceleration technique for volumetric *ray casting* which stops the sampling of a dataset along a ray when the accumulated *opacity* reaches a predefined *threshold*. In this way it reduces the amount of cells that need to be processed.

adjacency relationship between cells — a connectivity relationship that determines if a cell shares a vertex and/or edge and/or a face with its neighbours. The cells are called *N*-adjacent, where the prefix *N* describes the connectivity relationship. *N* can be 6, 18 or 26. A cell has 26-adjacency if it shares a vertex, an edge or a face with its neighbours, it has 18-adjacency if it shares an edge or a face with its neighbours, and 6-adjacency if it only shares face with its neighbours. See also *N-path* and *N-connected*.

aliasing — a problem associated with the discrete nature of object representation, A binary decision occurs at each *pixel* as to whether it is inside or outside an object. This leads to a jaggy or staircase effect, which is most noticeable during animation, at the edges of the object. See also *3D aliasing* and *antialiasing*.

ambient light — the light that falls upon an object that is an amalgamation of light from all sources, for example, light sources and reflections.

antialiasing — techniques that reduce sampling artefacts, particularly jagged edges caused by abrupt changes in scene geometry, in the final image. The techniques include *supersampling,* such as *area sampling,* and *jittered sampling.*

area light source — a source of light that occupies some finite area in object space; see also *shadow rays.*

area sampling — values are evaluated at various points in space. In unweighted sampling, the sum of the samples is divided by the total number of samples. In weighted sampling, values are multiplied by constants according to their position. Typically central values are given higher weightings in order to preserve their contributions.

back-to-front (BTF) traversal — describes the direction in which the volumetric dataset is traversed in the *compositing* stage of the rendering process, that is, in a back-to-front order, the voxels are projected in the decreasing order of their distance to the image plane. See also *front-to-back (FTB) traversal.*

backward projection — the name given to a collection of *volume rendering* algorithms that work by casting rays through the image plane and into the volume data. They work in a pixel-by-pixel fashion and hence they are also called image space algorithms.

binary voxelisation — a method that produces a discrete voxel representation of a continuous solid using a binary selection of the voxels which are met (if only partially) by the object body.

binary classification — a classification method applied whenever we want to display one and only one structure inside the volumetric dataset.

bitmap — a data structure used to store an $n \times m$ image. One bit represents one pixel, which can be either on (high intensity) or off (low intensity). See also *pixel map.*

blobby model — objects created by applying some combinational operations to field data. An object is defined by an *isosurface* of a certain *threshold* of a scalar field, where each value has been calculated as the sum of the contribution of a set of primitive fields. The contribution of each primitive is calculated according to its strength and decay.

boundary representation (b-rep) — the term given to the representation of an object's surface boundary using vertices, edges and faces. See also *polygonal meshes.*

bounding volume — a simpler object, such as a sphere or box, that is used to enclose a complex object. Computation, such as visibility determination, normally takes place on the bounding volume first, and if a valid result is obtained, it is then carried out on the more complex object. See also *octree.*

BSP tree — recursively subdivides 3D space using a 2D plane of arbitrary position and orientation. Each internal node has two pointers, one for each side of the plane. Leaf nodes contain those objects that occur in their subspace.

bump mapping — surfaces shaded using shading models such as *constant shading, Gouraud shading,* and *Phong shading* are unnaturally smooth. In order to introduce a roughness into the object, the computed normals are perturbed slightly in a random or computed order. These artificial normals are used to shade the object to give a stipple, or bumpy, effect.

cell — a closed volume bounded by a number of *voxels*.

classification (of elements) — a process that classifies elements of an object (e.g. voxels) according to certain properties (e.g. position, value, and neighbouring attributes). In this way, elements can be grouped to represent part of an object. This process enables computation on each group of elements to take place collectively, or new properties to be assigned consistently to each group.

coherence — the degree to which part of an environment or its projection exhibits local similarities. Coherency can be exploited by the reuse of calculations made for one part of the environment, either without changes or with incremental changes that are more efficient to make than recalculating.

colour map — a set of transfer functions which assign colour information to the numerical values in a volumetric dataset. See also *look-up table*, *transfer function*, and *opacity map*.

colour table — an array of (usually) $RGB\alpha$ tuples, where α is *opacity*. The array is indexed using some component of the intercepted points, for example, its Cartesian coordinates.

composite volume objects — volume objects obtained through combinational operations on *convex volume objects*. See also *constructive volume geometry*.

compositing — a process of merging together all the colours and opacities that contribute to one pixel of an image. The composition can take place in a *back-to-front* or *front- to-back* manner.

compressed domain volume rendering — methods which render volumetric datasets directly in their compressed representations.

constant shading — the simplest of the shading models. This approach calculates a surface normal once per polygon, which is used in an illumination model, with the resulting intensity value used to shade the entire polygon. See also *Gouraud shading* and *Phong shading*.

constructive solid geometry (CSG) — a geometrical representation of solid objects which allows the combination of simple objects or geometric primitives through the use of a set of simple Boolean operators (i.e., union, intersect, difference, negation).

constructive volume geometry (CVG) — a constructive representation of volume objects, including both volumetric datasets and scalar fields. The combinational operations are normally defined in the real domain, and enable the construction of complex volume objects through the combination of the geometrical and physical properties of simple (solid and amorphous) volume objects.

convex volume objects — volume objects that are defined directly upon volumetric datasets.

convolution — a mathematical technique for combining two functions. In computer graphics its refers to the application of a function known as a filter function to the discrete function defining the image. Such filter functions can be defined to antialias an image, detect edges or enhance certain features.

CT scan — a set of data produced of a cross section of an object using a Computed Tomography (CT) scanner. The image describes the amount of x-ray absorbed by each of many discrete points on a slice plane taken through the object.

cuberille — a regular array of cells in which each cell has a cubic shape.

cubic frame buffer — see *volume buffer*.

data traversal — a structured way of accessing voxels values in a dataset, typically during *isosurfacing* and *volume rendering*.

deformable model — an object description that represents not only the physical appearance but also the physical characteristics of the object. Such objects are often described by particles connected by springs which allow the objects to deform under external forces, and revert to their original state using internal forces. Such deformable models are ideally suited to modelling elastic objects acted upon by physical forces such as gravity, friction, compressible force, extensible force and even heat.

density emitter model — a modelling representation for translucent solids which assumes that the medium particles (i.e. the data samples) are emitting their own light. The density of particles is modelled rather than individual particles themselves.

depth cueing — simulates the atmosphere attenuation of an object due to its distance from the viewer.

depth only shading — the distance z, is calculated from each pixel in the image to the closest object in the scene to be displayed. The intensity of the image pixel is calculated as $I = 1 - \frac{z}{Z}$, where Z is the maximum distance any object can be from any pixel.

direct surface rendering — a method used to display a surface that is inside a volumetric dataset without triangulation. The method is based on ray casting and uses trilinear interpolation to determine the surface. See also *ray casting, trilinear interpolation*, and *transverse cell*.

direct volume rendering — a collection of methods for rendering an image directly from a volumetric dataset without an intermediary step in which a surface is generated. Includes methods such as *splatting, frequency domain volume rendering, volumetric ray tracing*.

directional shading — see *gradient shading*.

directional light source — see *parallel light source*.

discrete ray path — an *N-connected* voxelised representation of the ray path along a volumetric dataset. This representation is created with a 3D line *scan-conversion* algorithm.

discrete ray casting — a method based on ray casting which uses a discretised (*voxelised*) representation of the ray path and computes the contribution of each voxel along this path to produce the final pixel value. It has the advantage of eliminating the computationally intensive interpolation for determining the value of a sample along the ray. See also *discrete ray path* and *adjacency relationship of neighbouring cells*.

distance matrix/chamfer matrix — a matrix of values used within the *distance transform* process to create a *distance volume*. Such matrices can approximate Euclidean distances with varying degrees of accuracy.

distance transform — a process of segmenting the surface of interest, and then applying a *distance matrix* in two passes. The first pass calculates distances moving away from the object towards the bottom, and the second calculates the remainder. The distances are an approximation to the true Euclidean distance.

distance volume — a volume dataset consisting of voxels whose values are the distances from the surface of interest.

dividing cubes algorithm — an algorithm similar to the marching cubes algorithm that uses a point as a 2D primitive for representing an *isosurface* inside a volumetric dataset. This collection of points is obtained through recursively dividing the cells into subcells.

emission — a term used in the light *transport equation* which describes the emission of particles inside a volume. It is expressed through the number of particles emitted per unit of time from a point in the 3D space in a certain direction. See also *absorption, scattering,* and *streaming*.

extended light source — see *area light source*.

footprint — the contribution to an image by a voxel. The footprint does not depend upon the spatial position of the voxel, and so this costly reconstruction kernel can be computed once and stored in a *lookup table*. See also *splatting*.

forward projection — the name given to a collection of volume rendering algorithms that synthesise an image by projecting the voxels onto the image plane. They work in a voxel-by-voxel fashion and hence they are also called object space algorithms. See also *back-to-front traversal* and *front-to-back traversal*.

Fourier projection-slice theorem — a theorem which states that a 2D image (obtained by taking line integrals of the volume along the rays perpendicular to the image plane) and the 2D spectrum (obtained by extracting a slice from the *Fourier transform* of the volume along a plane which includes the origin and is parallel to the image plane) are Fourier pairs. Which means that one is the inverse of the other with respect to the *Fourier transform*.

Fourier transform — a function which transforms the spatial domain into a frequency domain.

frequency domain volume rendering — a volume rendering method based on the *Fourier projection-slice theorem*. The volume is transformed in the frequency domain using a Direct Fourier Transform (DFT). Then, for each view, the discrete 3D spectrum is interpolated along an extraction plane (slice) using a filter. The interpolated spectrum is resampled to obtain a 2D spectrum which is then transformed back to the spatial domain using an Inverse Fourier Transform (IFT) to obtain the final image.

front-to-back (FTB) traversal — describes the direction in which the volumetric dataset is traversed in the compositing stage of the rendering process. In a front-to-back traversal the projection is done in increasing order of the voxels' distance to the image plane. A front-to-back traversal has the advantage of *adaptive termination*. Another advantage is the possibility of displaying intermediate images of the volume data if the axis, which is most parallel to the image plane, is taken to be the outer loop of the traversal. See also *back-to-front (BTF) traversal*.

fuzzy classification — a voxel classification method applied in order to simultaneously display more than one structure inside a volumetric dataset. See also *binary classification* and *classification*.

global illumination — the light falling upon any object in the scene is accurately calculated from the contribution of light from every other object in the scene.

Gouraud shading — a shading model based on intensity interpolation. The normals of a polygon's vertices are calculated and applied to an illumination model. The polygon is next shaded by interpolating the vertex intensities along each edge and then along each scan line. See also *constant shading* and *Phong shading*.

gradient shading — a method of using a *z-buffer* to calculate surface normals which can then be used to compute pixel intensities using a shading model. The gradient at (x, y) can be calculated as $\nabla z = \left(\frac{\partial z}{\partial x}, \frac{\partial z}{\partial y}, 1 \right)$. At pixel (x, y), $\frac{\partial z}{\partial x}$ can be approximated by the backward difference $\delta_b = z(x, y) - z(x-1, y)$, the forward difference $\delta_f = z(x+1, y) - z(x, y)$, the central difference $\delta_c = 0.5(z(x+1, y) - z(x-1, y))$, or a weighted average of all three. $\frac{\partial z}{\partial y}$ can be computed in a similar manner.

grey-level shading — a commonly used shading method which computes the normal at a point on the grid through central differences, backward or forward differences (as defined for *gradient shading*, but with 3D function $v(x, y, z)$). It is called grey-level shading because the surface orientation corresponds to the difference between the values of neighbouring voxels.

grid (data grid) — see *volume buffer*.

hierarchical data representations — spatial data representations that aim at reducing the number of cells explicitly processed during rendering. They recursively decompose the volume into uniform regions that represent the detail of the data structure.

hierarchical splatting — a volume rendering method based on splatting which approximates *footprints* with a collection of *Gouraud-shaded* polygons that can be used to build a piecewise linear approximation of a footprint function. The volume data is encoded into a hierarchical representation where each node is associated with an error, the node with the greatest error being the node that will be divided next in the refinement process. This allows the user to render a multi-resolution volume representation in a progressively refined way.

hypertexture — a method for creating textured objects with the look of fire, fur, or melting. It extends solid texturing, in that it gives a notion of whether each point is outside, inside or in a boundary around the object. The density of the object within the boundary region is altered, according to functions such as turbulence, during rendering.

image space — see *backward projection*.

intensity — pixels, light sources and discrete points have intensity associated with them. It is usually either a grey-scale value representing brightness, or a triple (I_r, I_g, I_b) representing the intensity at red, green and blue wavelengths respectively.

interpolation — a method of determining a new vector located between two existing vectors using these existing vectors and the distance between each of them and the vector to be determined. The vector can be as complex as an image, or as simple as a single real number. Interpolation can be defined by a *linear* or a higher-order function.

irregular grid — a data grid for which the cells exhibit irregular geometry (adjacent cells can differ either in size and/or shape). See also *regular grid*, *structured grid* and *unstructured grid*.

isosurface — a surface of equipotential. For a field function $f: \mathbf{R}^d \rightarrow \mathbf{R}$, the τ-isosurface, $S(\tau)$, is defined as $\{x^d: f(x^d) = \tau\}$. Every point on the surface has a function value of τ, but not any other points in the domain. τ is referred to as an isovalue. When $d = 2$, $S(\tau)$ is normally referred to as an *isoline* or a *contour*.

jittered sampling — extra samples are taken, for a pixel, at random locations, the samples are combined and averaged to give a pixel intensity. See also *area sampling*.

K-d tree — a data structure that partitions the object space, with the help of a median cut, such that either branch, at any one time, removes a similar number of voxels.

light source — a point or an object that illuminates the surrounding space. A light source is usually associated with a light intensity, a colour and sometimes some distance attenuation and angle attenuation functions.

linear interpolation — an interpolation function that determines a numerical value at a point as a linear function of the neighbouring points' values. See *interpolation*, *trilinear interpolation* and *nonlinear interpolation*.

lookup table (LUT) — a data structure that splits the domain of a function into a finite number of intervals, in each case the function output takes a constant value.

marching cubes — a popular algorithm for determining *isosurfaces* in 3D. Function values are evaluated at regular discrete points to make a 3D grid of data values (voxels). Eight neighbouring voxels (four on one slice of data, and four aligned with them in an adjacent slice) make up a cube. Since each of the eight voxels can be inside or outside of the surface, there exist 256 cube configurations. The surface can be determined using a look-up table for each of the possible cases which indicates the triangles to be added to a triangular mesh, with their vertices interpolated from known voxel positions and values.

mip-map — a texture which has been pre-filtered to a number of difference resolutions. The appropriate resolution (or an interpolation between the two closest resolutions) is chosen to texture map an object depending upon its distance from the viewer. This removes some of the artefacts that can appear when point sampling.

motion blur — the process of simulating the appearance of moving objects by blurring them in the direction of motion. This occurs in the reality of photography or cinematography where the camera shutter is open for a finite length of time, and objects have a chance to move, and create multiple images (blur) on one frame. Simulating this for computer images, both stills and animations, adds to the realism of the image.

MRI scan — a set of data produced of a cross section of an object using a Magnetic Resonance Imaging (MRI) scanner. The data describes the disturbance of the magnetic field by each of many discrete points on one slice plane taken through the object.

N-connected set of cells — a set of cells which has an *N-path* running between every pair of cells.

N-path — a sequence of cells in which all consecutive pairs of cells share an *N*-adjacent connectivity relationship; see also *adjacency relationship between cells*.

nearest neighbour interpolation — an interpolation function that assigns the nearest neighbouring point's value to a sampling point.

nonlinear interpolation — an interpolation function that determines a numerical value at a point based on a nonlinear function of the neighbouring points' values. Many nonlinear functions used in volume rendering are application-dependent, and they were defined based on the underlying simulation process that generated the datasets.

non-photorealistic rendering — an approach to image synthesis which uses various effects which do not attempt to realistically model and render the scene. While still retaining the advantages of a conventional rendering system, it can be used to produce images in a variety of traditional styles, such as oil painting or pen and ink illustrations, in entirely new artistic styles.

normal-based contextual shading — a shading method that determines the normal for a face of a cell that is on the surface of an object by examining the orientation of that face and the orientation of the four faces on the surface that are edge connected to that face.

Nyquist rate — the lowest sampling rate that can allow the proper reconstruction of a signal. If the signal has a component with frequency *f*, which is the highest frequency component, then the *Nyquist rate* is *2f*. If fewer samples are used, the reconstructed signal may not be correct, and can represent high frequency components as a lower frequency signal. This misrepresentation is known as *aliasing*. See also *antialiasing*.

object occlusion — parts of an object hidden to the viewer.

object space — see *forward projection*.

octree — a tree data structure where each node has up to eight children. It is most often used to partition 3D structures since the children of each node partition the space represented by the parent node. The process to be computed can be computed on a node. If successful the process is carried out on each of the eight children in turn. If unsuccessful, the part of the volume represented by that node can be ignored. For example, octrees are used as bounding volumes in ray tracing. If the ray being tested successfully intersects a node, it is tested against each of the children of that node, or if a leaf node, it tests for intersection with the objects within the volume bounded by the leaf. If the ray does not intersect the node, all the objects within that node are removed from the intersection computation.

opacity map — a subset of the transfer function which refers to the functions which assign opacity information to the numerical values of a volumetric dataset; see also *transfer function* and *colour map*.

opacity — usually a value between 0 and 1 which represents how dense an object is to light. If the opacity is 1 the object is opaque and obscures everything behind it, if the opacity is 0 it is completely transparent, and cannot be seen. Values between 0 and 1 represent, proportionally and linearly varying, the visibility of the object and objects behind it.

optical depth — a measure of the transparency of a ring system. When a ring is "optically thick" it is nearly opaque, whereas when it is "optically thin" it is nearly transparent.

optical model — a model which simulates the interaction between the light particles and the medium represented by the data samples. See also *transport equation* and *optical depth*.

over operator — an operator for combining images. For $C = A$ **over** B, the **over** is defined as $C = \alpha_A \cdot A + (1-\alpha_A) \cdot B$ and $\alpha_C = \alpha_A + (1-\alpha_A) \cdot \alpha_B$, where α_A, α_B and α_C are the opacities associated to the images. It is the basis for the *voxel compositing* in *volume rendering*.

parallel light source — a light source from which light falls on all objects as if from the same direction. It occurs when the light is infinitely far away from the scene.

parallel projection — the production of images wherein the projectors are all parallel to each other and are defined by a single direction vector.

particle systems — composed by a collection of particles that evolve over time. The particles have attributes associated with them such as mass, charge, or colour. The system evolves according to either random events, such as dying, introducing new particles and random motion, or by following equations for motion such as trajectories according to initial velocity and gravity and following velocity vectors in numerical simulations.

partitioning — see *spatial partitioning*.

perspective projection — the production of images using perspective. All the projectors pass through one point known as the centre of projection.

Phong shading — a shading model based on normal interpolation. The normals of a polygon's vertices are calculated, with the in-between edge normals, and thus the normals along each scan line, can be interpolated. The interpolated normals are then applied to an illumination model to give the corresponding pixel intensities. See also *constant shading* and *Gouraud shading*.

photorealistic — artificial images that closely resemble reality.

physically based modelling — creating an accurate behavioural model of an object based upon its physical properties and those of its surroundings. The motion and object shape are determined by the forces acting upon the object, and are calculated using physical mathematics.

pixel — (picture element) light intensity triples (red, green, blue) that constitute a 2D image.

pixel map — a data structure for a colour image which includes colour, resolution, dimensions, storage information, and the number of bits used to describe each pixel. When only 1 bit per pixel is used, the data structure is called a *bitmap*.

point light source — source of light in which all light rays radiate outwards from a single point. Light bulbs can be best approximated by point light sources.

polygonal meshes — a form of object representation. The object's surface is approximated by a set of planar polygons in which each edge is used by at most two polygons, and each polygon is a closed set of edges. A visualisation of the object represented by the mesh is produced using any of a number of rendering techniques.

primary rays — originate from each pixel in the image in the direction of the view plane normal for parallel projection, or from the centre of projection in the direction of the pixel in perspective projection. Each ray intersects surfaces that lie along its path, and thus spawns secondary rays to compute the contributions to the pixel's intensity due to object reflection, refraction and shadow. These contributions are combined with the object's intensity to give the intensity of the pixel.

radiosity — models the lighting in a scene by using an analogy of thermal dynamics. The light in a closed scene follows the law of conservation of energy, and all light must be accounted for. The light at any surface is the summed contribution of all the light energy falling on that surface from all light sources and object reflections. Radiosity methods calculate the interaction of light in a view independent preprocessing step, and the resulting scene description can be rendered from this model using conventional techniques. Radiosity accurately models global illumination and removes the need for the ambient lighting term.

ray casting — the process of sending a primary ray from a point in space into a scene with direction. Upon encountering an object the ray terminates, and the intensity of the point is calculated according to the shading model. See also *volume rendering*.

ray tracing — is the process of sending a primary ray from a point in space into a scene with direction. Upon intersection with an object secondary rays are spawned in order to determine all contributions to the light intensity of that point. Secondary rays determine contributions due to reflection, refraction, transparency, shadows, and light sources. See also *volume rendering*.

reconstruction filter — a filter which reconstructs the continuous signal from the values of its discrete representation.

reconstruction — the process of determining an object from a partial description of the object. For example, reconstruction of polygonal meshes from contours and reconstruction of objects from laser range data.

reflection rays — rays spawned from objects which are partial or total mirrors, in order to determine what is visible in the mirror. The rays are treated like primary rays, and may spawn other rays, including reflection rays, upon hitting an object. The origin of the ray is the intersection point with the object, and the angle of incidence is calculated using the direction of the incoming ray, and the surface normal.

registration — the geometric transformation of one *data grid* so that it matches the coordinate system of a second data grid. For example registration of CT and MRI scans. Often achieved through the use of anatomical markers.

regular grid — a data grid in which all the cells have the same size and shape. This type of grid has the advantage that it can be easily computed. See also *irregular grid*, *structured grid* and *unstructured grid*.

rendering — the process of producing an accurate impression of a scene using any of the shading models, and any of the rendering techniques such as *ray tracing* or *scan-conversion*.

rendering equation — see *transport equation*.

rendering pipeline — refers to the sequence of processes of transforming a scene description (objects, lights, etc) into a final image. It typically involves *rendering*.

scalar field — a scalar function takes one or more values, and returns a single value. A scalar field takes a coordinate and returns the value (interpolated or actual) at that coordinate.

scan-conversion — the process of calculating pixel intensities from object descriptions in an ordered pixel by pixel, line by line manner. See also *scan line*.

scan line — one horizontal line in an image, derived from the line that a cathode ray tube sweeps (scans) across during anyone pass.

scattering — a term in the light transport equation which describes the interaction between the light particles and a dataset in which the former are deflected and continue their movement. See *transport equation, emission, absorption* and *streaming*.

scientific visualisation — the collection of methods, techniques and algorithms used to extract meaningful information from multi-dimensional data.

secondary rays — produced at the point of surface intersection during ray tracing. They are created in order to find the exact colour of the intersection point due to contributions from all objects that influence the light at that point, for example, light sources, shadows created by other objects and partial transparency of the object itself and objects that lie on the path between it and a light source. These rays are determined in the same way as primary rays except that the direction is some function of the view normal and surface normal, and the resulting colours contribute partially rather than totally to the final pixel colour.

segmentation — the process of determining similar objects with respect to certain defined parameters and grouping them together. Can be semi-automatic or completely manual. See also *classification, binary classification* and *fuzzy classification*.

shadow rays — rays spawned from objects in order to determine whether or not any objects occur on a path between it and each light source, thus casting a shadow. The origin of each shadow ray is the intersection point with the object, and the directions are the directions to each light source. If the light source is an area light source, one method is to trace n rays to random points on the area, and if m rays get through, the fraction of light falling on the point from that light source is m/n.

shadows (umbra/penumbra) — created by objects obscuring light sources from other objects. In the case of area light sources the shadow will be a transition from points that can see most of the light, to points that can see no light at all. Those that are in complete shadow are said to be covered by the umbra, and those that are in partial shadow are in the penumbra.

shear-warp factorisation of the viewing plane — a volume rendering method which is based on the decomposition of the viewing transform into a *shear matrix* and a *warping matrix*. The advantage of this operation is that 3D *ray casting* is transformed into two 2D operations. A projection to form an intermediate image followed by the warping of this intermediate image to remove the distortions of the shear. The reason for the shear-warp factorisation is the alignment between the voxels in the data and the pixels in the image that it produces.

shell rendering — a rendering method based on a special data structure for the representation of semi-transparent volumes, called *shells*. A shell consists of a set of voxels, and a number of associated attributes, in the vicinity of a structure boundary. See also *fuzzy classification*.

solid textures — continuous 3D texture functions defined either mathematically of procedurally.

spatial occupancy enumeration (SOE) — a representation scheme for solid objects based on a decomposition of an object into identical cells arranged in a structured, regular grid. The scheme uses one bit to encode the presence or absence of each cell in the grid, determined by its occupancy by the object.

spatial partitioning — the process of dividing space into smaller subspaces. The reasoning behind this is the fact that processes can be carried out on fewer objects, thus reducing execution times. See *octree* and *bsp-tree* for examples of spatial partitioning techniques.

spatial subdivision — see *spatial partitioning*.

specular reflection — the highlight that can be seen on a shiny surface from particular angles. Perfect mirrors reflect light in only the direction of the reflection according to the angle of incidence, whereas any other shiny object reflects light unequally in different directions, and so the highlight is seen from different angles.

speed-up — the ratio of two program execution times that indicates the increase in speed achieved. If a program takes time S_1 to run on one processor, and time S_2 on two processors, the speed-up is S_1/S_2.

splatting — the process of projecting voxels by "throwing" them against an image plane, in order to splat their colours and opacities onto the image plane. The distribution of a voxel's energy is calculated according to its *footprint*, and the energy is added to each pixel it projects onto by compositing the colour and opacity at that point in proportion to the energy.

stereo images — images that have been created from two images produced of the same scene at slightly differing angles and view reference points, in order to approximate the position of the viewer's eyes. The images can be combined as one using one wavelength for one image, and a different wavelength for the second image (usually red and blue), and then viewing the composite through the appropriate glasses. Images can also be produced in the form of random dot stereograms, or by displaying the two images alternately, and relying upon additional hardware (glasses) to be able to synchronise the left eye with the left image, and the right eye with the right image.

streaming — a term in the light transport equation which describes the net flow of particles through a dataset. See also *transport equation, emission, absorption* and *scattering*.

structured grid — a data grid which exhibits an implicit connectivity between cells. The cells can be therefore represented implicitly and are referred to using topological (i, j, k) coordinates. Such a grid can be easily traversed and stored; see also *unstructured grid, regular grid* and *irregular grid*.

subsampling — the process of obtaining values more coarsely than is usual, and *interpolating* the in-between values. For example, instead of tracing a ray for each pixel in an image, rays are traced coarsely over the whole image with extra rays being traced in the regions of high change. Other pixels are interpolated from known pixels in the process known as adaptive rendering.

supersampling — the approach of taking more than one sample per pixel and averaging the samples to obtain a pixel intensity. See also *area sampling* and *jittered sampling*.

surface graphics — a sub-field of computer graphics that uses exclusively surface representations of the geometric objects. See also *volume graphics*.

surface normal — the vector which points, from a particular point on the surface, away from the interior such that it is perpendicular to the tangent to the surface.

surface tiling — a class of surface reconstruction methods that divide the volume into simple polyhedra (cubes or tetrahedra) and determine the intersection between each polyhedron and the *isosurface* to be displayed. The methods produce a mesh of geometric primitives (triangles, planar or non–planar polygons) which approximates the isosurface. This mesh is displayed using standard surface graphics algorithms. See also *marching cubes*.

surface tracking — a class of surface reconstruction methods that follow an isosurface through a volumetric dataset, with the prerequisite that one point on the surface is known. The surface is represented by a list of connected 2D primitives, the face of a cell, which lie on it. Cell connectivity can be established using different criteria, the most commonly used being face, edge or vertex connectivity.

template-based volume viewing — a viewing technique for parallel ray casting, in which a ray is discretised and used as a template for all the other rays cast from the image plane.

threshold — a value which represents something interesting in a particular domain. For example, in 3D isosurfacing the threshold defines the surface of interested, and is calculated such that all points on the surface have a function value equal to the threshold.

transfer function — a mathematical function which assigns different optical properties (colour, opacity, emittance, etc.) to the voxels of the volumetric dataset. See also *colour map* and *opacity map*.

transparency — the inverse of *opacity*.

transport equation — a mathematical equation which describes the transport of particles through a certain medium. In the case of volume rendering, the particles are photons (light particles) and the medium is the dataset. The aim of the equation is to describe the flux of light particles in any position, taking into account the interactions between the light particles and the dataset. This is based on the assumption that at every moment in time, the system composed of particles and dataset is at equilibrium (also known as the Boltzmann equation). See also *emission, absorption, scattering* and *streaming, rendering*.

transversed cell — a cell which has at least one of its voxels inside a surface, defined by a *threshold* τ, and one outside the surface contained in a volumetric dataset. See also *direct surface rendering*.

triangular mesh — a representation of a surface in which the only polygonal primitive is a triangle.

trilinear interpolation — an interpolation function which computes the value of a 3D point from three *linear interpolations* of the 8 neighbouring voxels.

unstructured grid — a data grid whose cells exhibit no implicit connectivity information. Therefore this information has to be represented explicitly, Such a grid has the advantage that further information may be stored in areas where abrupt changes occur. See also *regular grid, structured grid* and *irregular grid*.

viewing pipeline — refers to the process of transforming an object description (usually a mesh of vertices) to screen coordinates. It typically involves the view transformation of the object coordinates, clipping the object to the visible volume, and projecting the object. Often additional steps for mapping these coordinates to the screen coordinates are included.

Visible Human Project — a project which aims to create complete anatomically detailed, three-dimensional representations of the male and female human bodies. Datasets are available from URL: http://www.nlm.nih.gov/research/visible/visible_human.html.

volume buffer — a 3D data array which stores a volumetric dataset in the form of a collection of sampled or computed numerical data values; also called *cubic frame buffer, 3D raster* or *regular grid*.

volume data slice — a set of data points contained in a plane parallel with one of the orthogonal axes.

volume deformation (distortion) — a method used to deform one volume object into another one.

volume graphics — a sub-field of computer graphics that is concerned with graphics scenes defined in volume data types, where a model is specified by a mass of points instead of a set of surfaces. Although it is developed from *volume visualisation*, volume graphics is a far broader subject, and it is a study of the input, storage, construction, analysis, manipulation, rendering and animation of spatial objects in a true three-dimensional form. It encompasses a range of subjects, including *volume modelling, voxelisation, constructive volume geometry, volume sculpting, volume morphing, volume texture mapping, hypertextures, isosurfacing, volume rendering, direct surface rendering, splatting* and *non-photorealistic rendering*. See also *surface graphics*.

volume modelling — the synthesis, analysis, and manipulation of sampled, computed, and synthetic objects defined in volume data types.

volume morphing — a process that generates a sequence of *in-between* volumes that represent a smooth transformation from one volume object to another. See also *volume deformation*.

volume object — an object defined upon a volumetric dataset or a set of scalar fields.

volume rendering — a process for obtaining images from three-dimensional volume data by treating the data as cloudy material. Each voxel in the dataset has a colour and opacity assigned to it during a classification stage. Rays are cast for each pixel into the volume, and the colour and opacity are sampled at evenly distributed points along the ray. These samples are composited using standard techniques to produce the accumulative colour and opacity reaching the pixel. Images produced by this method usually have several differently colour semi-transparent surfaces overlaid on an opaque surface, for example, semi-transparent skin overlaid on opaque bone for an image of a CT scan. For *volumetric ray tracing* these methods employ global illumination models for shading and capture the specular interactions between the volumetric objects in a scene. See also *direct volume rendering, direct surface rendering, ray casting* and *volumetric radiosity.*

volume sculpting — free-form, interactive modelling technique based on the metaphor of sculpting a voxel-based solid material. It is used to model topological complex objects and to explore the inner structure of a dataset by gradually removing material.

volume seeds — a volume rendering technique in which the user is given interactive control of the final image. This is achieved by placing a seed somewhere in the dataset and allocating transparencies according to voxel position. The larger the distance from the seed the more transparent the voxel.

volume synthesis — the creation of a volumetric dataset, by methods including *voxelisation, volume sculpting,* and the invocation of *mathematical formulae.*

volume texture mapping — the application of a texture to the voxels in a volumetric dataset.

volume visualisation — the general term given to the process of displaying three-dimensional data. Its primary objective is to extract meaningful information from volumetric datasets, and it encompasses the methods of *isosurfacing, volume rendering* and *splatting.*

volumetric dataset — a three-dimensional collection of data values defined on a *regular* or *irregular grid.*

volumetric radiosity — a volumetric global illumination method which captures the diffuse light interactions in a scene. The basic "patch" from the classical radiosity is replaced by the voxel.

volumetric ray casting — see *volume rendering.*

volumetric ray tracing — see *volume rendering*; see also *volumetric radiosity.*

volumetric scenes — scenes in which the objects are solely defined with volumetric datasets.

volumetric textures — volume based textures used to simulate geometry. Each voxel stores a reflectance property producing local 3D illumination.

voxel — (volume element) an element of a 3D volume, holding a value, or values, representing properties of real objects.

voxel-block transfer (voxblt) — a set of operations by which a rectangular subvolume of voxels (called a *room*) can be copied within the volume buffer with arbitrary write modes and maskings. It is the 3D counterpart of bitblt.

voxelisation — the process of converting an object of one description, such as polygon meshes, into volume data. Allowing the application of volume visualisation techniques.

voxmap — a three-dimensional data array which describes a volumetric object. The term is the 3D analogue of *bitmap.*

warping — an image transformation in which pixel positions are modified according to some function. It is commonly used in image processing to correct geometric distortions caused by the image acquisition system.

wavelets — finite domain functions which are used to approximate other functions, or data. The scale at which a function is analysed plays an important role in the construction of its approximating wavelet. Used primarily for compression and analysis.

Z-buffer — an array, $z(x, y)$, of depths for each pixel in an image.

Z-buffer shadowing — a *z-buffer* calculated from the point of view of the light source. Used to render shadows; any visible points that are not visible in the shadow z-buffer are said to be in shadow.

Author Index

Author and Address	Contribution
Michael Bailey *San Diego Supercomputer Center, University of California San Diego,* *PO Box 85608, San Diego, CA 92186, USA* Email: mjb@sdsc.edu	Chapter 5
Reneta P. Barneva *Department of Mathematics, Faculty of Arts and Sciences, Eastern* *Mediterranean University, Famagusta, P.O. Box 95, TRNC, Via Mersin* *10, Turkey* Email: barneva@mozart.emu.edu.tr	Chapter 3
Dirk Bartz *WSI/GRIS, University of Tübingen, Auf der Morgenstelle 10/C9, D72076* *Tübingen, Germany* Email: bartz@gris.uni-tuebingen.de	Chapter 10
Martijn de Boer *Lehrstuhl für Informatik V, Universität Mannheim, B6, 26, D-68131* *Mannheim, Germany* Email: boer@mp-sun1.informatik.uni-mannheim.de	Chapter 18
David E. Breen *Computer Graphics Lab., California Institute of Technology, MS 350-74,* *Pasadena, CA 91125, USA* Email: david@gg.caltech.edu	Chapter 8
Valentin E. Brimkov *Department of Mathematics, Faculty of Arts and Sciences, Eastern* *Mediterranean University, Famagusta, P.O. Box 95, TRNC, Via Mersin* *10, Turkey* Email: brimkov@mozart.emu.edu.tr	Chapter 3
Ken Brodlie *School of Computer Studies, University of Leeds, Leeds LS2 9JT, UK* Email: kwb@scs.leeds.ac.uk	Chapter 21
Hongsheng Chen *Department of Computer and Information Science, Indiana University* *Purdue University Indianapolis, 723 W. Michigan Street, SL 280,* *Indianapolis, IN 46202, USA* Email: hchen@cs.iupui.edu	Chapter 20

Author and Address	Contribution

Min Chen
Department of Computer Science, University of Wales Swansea, Singleton Park, Swansea SA2 8PP, UK
Email: m.chen@swan.ac.uk

Chapter 6

Daniel Cohen-Or
Department of Computer Science, School of Mathematical Science, Tel Aviv University, Tel Aviv 69978, Israel
Email: daniel@math.tau.ac.il

Chapter 4

Roger A. Crawfis
395 Dreese Lab., 2015 Neil Avenue, Columbus, OH 43210-1277, USA
Email: crawfis@cis.ohio-state.edu

Chapter 14

Miron Deyssenroth
EMEA Network Management Development, IBM Global Services, P.O. Box 41, IBM North Harbour BIC, C2E Hants PO6 3AU, UK
Email: miron@uk.ibm.com

Chapter 18

Shiaofen Fang
Department of Computer and Information Science, Indiana University, Purdue University Indianapolis, 723 W. Michigan Street, SL 280, Indianapolis, IN 46202, USA
Email: sfang@cs.iupui.edu

Chapter 20

Issei Fujishiro
Department of Information Sciences, Faculty of Science, Ochanomizu University, 2-1-1 Otsuka, Bunkyo-Ku, Tokyo 112--8610, Japan
Email: fuji@is.ocha.ac.jp

Chapter 24

Nikhil Gagvani
Sarnoff Corporation, 201 Washington Road, CN 5300, Princeton, NJ 08540-6449, USA
Email: ngagvani@sarnoff.com

Chapter 16

Thomas Gerstner
Department for Applied Mathematics, Wegelerstr. 6, 53115 Bonn, Germany
Email: gerstner@iam.uni-bonn.de

Chapter 17

Alexander Gröpl
Lehrstuhl für Informatik V, Universität Mannheim, B6, 26, D-68131 Mannheim, Germany
Email: groepl@mp-sun1.informatik.uni-mannheim.de

Chapter 18

Jürgen Hesser
Lehrstuhl für Informatik V, Universität Mannheim, B6, 26, D-68131 Mannheim, Germany
Email: jhesser@rumms.uni-mannheim.de

Chapter 18
Chapter 19

Rami Hietala
Medical Imaging Research Group, Department of Diagnostic Radiology, Oulu University Hospital, P.O. Box 22, 90221 Oulu, Finland
Email: worm@ee.oulu.fi

Chapter 12

Mark W. Jones
Department of Computer Science, University of Wales Swansea, Singleton Park, Swansea SA2 8PP, UK
Email: m.w.jones@swan.ac.uk

Chapter 13
Glossary

Author and Address	**Contribution**

Lasse Jyrkinen   Chapter 12
Medical Imaging Research Group, Departments of Electrical Engineering
and Diagnostic Radiology, University of Oulu, P.O. Box 22, 90221 Oulu,
Finland
Email: lasse.jyrkinen@oulu.fi

Arie Kadosh   Chapter 4
Handwriting Recognition Group, ART — Advanced Recognition
Technologies Ltd., Israel
Email: arie@artcomp.com

Arie E. Kaufman   Chapter 1
Center for Visual Computing (CVC) and Department of Computer   Chapter 7
Science, State University of New York at Stony Brook, Stony Brook, NY,
USA
Email: ari@cs.sunysb.edu

Scott A. King   Chapter 14
395 Dreese Lab., 2015 Neil Avenue, Columbus, OH 43210-1277, USA
Email: sking@cis.ohio-state.edu

Adrian Leu   Chapter 6
Department of Computer Science, University of Wales Swansea, Singleton
Park, Swansea SA2 8PP, UK
Email: csadrian@swan.ac.uk

David Levin   Chapter 4
Applied Mathematics, School of Mathematical Science, Tel Aviv
University, Schreiber Building, Room 019, Tel Aviv 69978, Israel
Email: levin@math.tau.ac.il

Feng Lin   Chapter 9
Division of Computing Systems, School of Applied Science, Nanyang   Chapter 11
Technological University, Nanyang Avenue, 639798, Singapore
Email: asflin@ntu.edu.sg

Reinhard Männer   Chapter 18
Lehrstuhl für Informatik V, Universität Mannheim, B6, 26, D-68131   Chapter 19
Mannheim, Germany
Email: maenner@mp-sun1.informatik.uni-mannheim.de

Sean Mauch   Chapter 8
Computer Graphics Lab., California Institute of Technology, MS 350-74,
Pasadena, CA 91125, USA
Email: sean@gg.caltech.edu

Michael Meißner   Chapter 10
WSI/GRIS, University of Tübingen, Auf der Morgenstelle 10/C9, D72076
Tübingen, Germany
Email: meissnerg@gris.uni-tuebingen.de

Simon D. Michael   Chapter 23
Department of Computer Science, University of Wales Swansea, Singleton
Park, Swansea SA2 8PP, UK
Email: csmich@swan.ac.uk

Author and Address	Contribution

Philippe Nehlig — Chapter 3
Laboratoire IRCOM-SIC, UMR CNRS 6615, Batiment SP2MI, UFR SFA, Université de Poitiers, Bvd 3, Téléport 2, 86960 FUTUROSCOPE Cedex, France
Email: philippe.nehlig@sic.sp2mi.univ-poitiers.fr

Gregory M. Nielson — Chapter 2
Computer Science and Engineering, PO Box 85287-5406, Arizona State University, Tempe, AZ 85287-5406, USA
Email: nielson@asu.edu

Jarkko Oikarinen — Chapter 12
Medical Imaging Research Group, Departments of Diagnostic Radiology and Neurosurgery, Oulu University Hospital, P.O. Box 22, 90221 Oulu, Finland
Email: jto@iki.fi

Nao Ozawa — Chapter 24
Graduate School of Humanities and Sciences, Ochanomizu University, 2-1-1 Otsuka, Bunkyo-Ku, Tokyo 112--8610, Japan
Email: ozawa@imv.is.ocha.ac.jp

Edmond C. Prakash — Chapter 15, Chapter 25
Division of Software Systems, School of Applied Science, Nanyang Technological University, Nanyang Avenue, 639798, Singapore
Email: asprakash@ntu.edu.sg

Wayland Reid — Chapter 14
395 Dreese Lab., 2015 Neil Avenue, Columbus, OH 43210-1277, USA
Email: wreid@cis.ohio-state.edu

Martin Rumpf — Chapter 17
Department for Applied Mathematics, Wegelerstr. 6, 53115 Bonn, Germany
Email: rumpf@iam.uni-bonn.de

Richard Satherley — Chapter 13, Glossary
Department of Computer Science, University of Wales Swansea, Singleton Park, Swansea SA2 8PP, UK
Email: csrich@swan.ac.uk

Marco Schmitt — Chapter 22
Fraunhofer Institute for Computer Graphics, Rundeturmstr. 6, D-64283 Darmstadt, Germany

Hock Soon Seah — Chapter 9, Chapter 11
Center for Graphics and Image Technology, School of Applied Science, Nanyang Technological University, Nanyang Avenue, 639798, Singapore
Email: ashsseah@ntu.edu.sg

Deborah Silver — Chapter 16
Deptartment of Electrical and Computer Engineering, CoRE Building, Frelinghuysen Road, P.O. Box 909, Piscataway, NJ 08855-50909, USA
Email: silver@caip.rutgers.edu

Subject Index

3D character, *see 3D text*

3D metamorphosis, *see Morphing*

3D raster, *see Volume buffer*

3D scan-conversion, *see Voxelisation*

3D text, 379-388, 402, 406

3D texture mapping, *see Volume texture mapping*

Absorption, 176, 282, 290, 293, 372, 391, 395, 401, 403, 404

Acceleration, ii, iii, 23, 77, 130, 175, 178, 183, 185, 191, 194, 195, 197, 199, 200, 202, 203, 208, 210, 225, 248, 273, 299, 301, 309, 314, 377, 391

Adjacency, 8, 18, 20, 52, 77, 84-86, 109, 151, 190, 245, 269, 391, 394, 397, 398

Aging, 367, 377

Algorithm, ii, iii, 5, 8-10, 15, 17, 18, 20, 21, 24, 25, 27, 29, 30, 36, 38, 41-44, 48, 51-53, 55, 56, 59-62, 65, 69, 70, 72, 74, 77, 84, 87, 88, 94, 98-100, 112, 114, 116, 127, 130, 134-139, 143, 144, 146-153, 157, 158, 161, 167, 171-176, 178, 181-186, 190, 191, 193-197, 199, 200, 202-214, 216, 217, 224, 225, 230-232, 235, 236, 239, 241, 242, 244, 245, 247, 248, 253-257, 262, 263, 267-269, 273-275, 278, 279, 281, 284, 287-289, 293, 294, 298, 301-306, 309-314, 322, 341, 348, 350, 351, 353, 354, 356, 361, 377, 379, 381, 382, 392,

394, 395, 397, 401, 403

Aliasing, 7, 10, 13, 15, 16, 20, 23, 119, 137, 177, 214, 215, 387, 391, 398

Antialiasing, 3, 8, 10, 16, 17, 26, 119, 138, 151, 154-156, 231, 242, 387, 391, 392, 398

Amorphous phenomena, i, iii, iv, viii, 3, 12, 15, 18, 25, 98, 99, 114, 116, 229-233, 240, 241, 393

cloud, iii, 6, 37, 236, 239, 336

fire, iii, 12, 18, 47, 215, 218, 219, 222, 229, 230, 232-237, 239-241, 396

smoke, iii, 12, 18, 215, 218, 229, 234-236, 238, 239, 241

water, 113, 135, 213, 236, 239

Animation, i, iii, iv, viii, 17, 25, 47, 115, 158, 213, 223-225, 229-263, 301, 365, 391, 404

Architecture, iii, 20-23, 26-28, 119, 125, 134, 158, 171, 184, 279-281, 284, 285, 287-289, 291-296, 299, 300, 322, 329, 330

AVS, 317, 318, 325, 328

Basis functions, 38, 40, 41, 75, 161, 216-218, 224, 350, 352, 364

Binary dataset, 71, 74, 77

Blending function, 84, 302-305, 310, 313

Block operation, 3, 13, 15, 16, 18, 23, 26, 406

Boolean operation, 11, 13, 71, 106, 135, 141, 158, 163, 165, 166, 307-309, 313